Assassination, Politics, and Miracles

Assassination, Politics, and Miracles

France and the Royalist Reaction of 1820

DAVID SKUY

McGill-Queen's University Press
Montreal & Kingston · London · Ithaca

Legal deposit second quarter 2003
Bibliothèque nationale du Québec

Printed in Canada on acid-free paper.

This book has been published with the help of a grant from the Humanities and Social Sciences Federation of Canada, using funds provided by the Social Sciences and Humanities Research Council of Canada.

McGill-Queen's University Press acknowledges the support of the Canada Council for the Arts for our publishing program. We also acknowledge the financial support of the Government of Canada through the Book Publishing Industry Development Program (BPIDP) for our publishing activities.

National Library of Canada Cataloguing in Publication

Skuy, David, 1963–
    Assassination, politics, and miracles: France and the Royalist reaction of 1820/David Skuy.

    Includes bibliographical references and index.
    ISBN 0-7735-2457-6

    1. France – History – Restoration, 1814–1830. 2. Berry, Charles-Ferdinand de Bourbon, duc de, 1778–1820 – Assassination. I. Title.

DC256.S58 2003   944.06'1   C2002-905929-1

This book was typeset by Dynagram Inc. in 10/12 Sabon.

To Donna

Contents

Acknowledgments

I would like to express my gratitude to Professor David Higgs for his tremendous assistance, his insights, and his encouragement during my years of study and the writing of this book. I also would like to thank my publishers at McGill-Queen's University Press, in particular, D.H. Akenson, Joan McGilvray, Roger Martin, and Kyla Madden. A special thanks to Jane McWhinney for her remarkable diligence and energy in editing the text. I must also thank my other copy editors, Ambrose Holmes and Percy Skuy, for their vigilance.

Much of the research for this book was conducted in France, and a great number of people there were helpful in obtaining archival materials. I am very grateful to the staff at the departmental archives of Isère and Haute-Garonne, and the municipal archives and libraries of Grenoble and Toulouse. I was also helped by the staff at the *Archives nationales* and the *Bibliothèque nationale*.

I would like as well to express my thanks to the Humanities and Social Sciences Federation of Canada for providing funds for the publication of this book.

Assassination, Politics, and Miracles

Prologue:
The Assassination of
the Duke of Berry and
the Birth of the Miracle Child

On 22 October 1781, Marie-Antoinette and Louis XVI announced the birth of their first son. The announcement came as a great relief to the royal family, for up to that point the queen had only delivered a girl, in 1778. Not all those connected with the throne greeted the announcement with enthusiasm, however. Until then, Louis XVI's two younger brothers, the Count of Provence and the Count of Artois, had been in line for the throne. Artois was perhaps the most disappointed. He already had two sons, Louis, Duke of Angoulême, and Charles-Ferdinand, Duke of Berry,[1] whereas Provence was still childless. Upon the deaths of Artois's two older brothers, the crown would have passed to himself and then to his sons. The birth of the dauphin destroyed that dream.

Four years later the king and queen were blessed with another son. It seemed clear that the progeny of Louis XVI would fulfil their destiny to sit on the throne.[2] The Duke of Berry was three years old when the dauphin was born, and seven at the birth of his brother. At such a tender age it would be doubtful if he had given much thought to his place in line to the throne; in 1789, he stood sixth. In other words, he was not terribly important to the royal family. Over the next twenty-five years, however, in a remarkable saga that included a revolution, an empire, a restoration, an assassination, and a "miracle," the Duke of Berry became the key figure in the preservation of the Bourbon monarchy.

Two years after the start of the French Revolution, Berry's family slipped out of France under cover of darkness and set up residence in London, where the young duke remained as an *émigré* for the next two decades. Berry became a well-liked, jovial man who made friends easily, although he was considered by many to be somewhat rough-mannered, not to mention proud, petty and vain. In 1804, he met Amy Brown, the widowed daughter of a Protestant pastor. Without asking permission of his family, and ignoring the fact that Brown was not Catholic, Berry married her in a ceremony conducted by her father.[3] The couple soon had two daughters: Charlotte in 1808 and Louise in 1809.

By 1814, after twenty-three years away from France, the Duke of Berry had grown accustomed to life as an *émigré*. He enjoyed a privileged existence that, while not quite on a par with his Versailles years prior to the Revolution, was more than comfortable. He was wealthy, married, and had two healthy daughters. He enjoyed plenty of mistresses, along with the pleasures of hunting, riding, dancing, and gentlemen's clubs. He was even able to lay claim to a career as a soldier, the result of his joining Condé's counter-revolutionary army in the 1790s. History dictated, however, that his exile would come to an end. Napoleon's shocking retreat from Russia and the ensuing shattering defeats of the French army to the allied forces culminated on 6 April 1814 with the emperor's abdication. The former Count of Provence, by then Louis XVIII, was invited to return to France shortly thereafter to preside over a restored Bourbon monarchy.[4]

The Restoration had important implications for the Duke of Berry. Louis XVIII was an obese man in tenuous health, and by 1814 it was obvious he would never have children. Berry's only brother, the Duke of Angoulême, had no children, and the Duchess of Angoulême was past childbearing age. Louis XVI and Louis XVII had perished during the Revolution. Berry was therefore the last remaining male Bourbon capable of siring an heir; failing that, the crown would pass to the Orléanist line. Significantly, when Berry set sail for France soon after news of Napoleon's abdication had reached England, he was accompanied by his two daughters, but not by Amy Brown. Since Brown was not Catholic, even if Berry were to have had a son with her, that child could never have ascended to the French throne. His immediate solution to this ticklish situation was to leave her behind in London; however, their marriage remained a worrisome issue that would soon demand attention.

During this First Restoration, Berry was granted the title of *colonel général des chasseurs et lanciers*. As a high-ranking army officer, he visited barracks and military hospitals and oversaw military manoeuvres, a form of military life he enjoyed immensely. It was short-lived, however. The man royalists disparagingly referred to as the usurper soon decided that life as the emperor of France was preferable to ruling over the Kingdom of Elba. On 1 March 1815, Napoleon slipped back into France and began his march on Paris. Berry was appointed chief of the French army, a prestigious appointment to be sure, but an ephemeral one, as his army quickly disappeared in the face of the legendary emperor's approach. As thousands of soldiers and private citizens flocked back to the Imperial fold, Berry and the royal family re-enacted their earlier flight during the Revolution and left France once more. However, on 18 June 1815, just one hundred days after Napoleon had declared himself emperor for the second time, the Battle of Waterloo began, and Napoleon's presence on the world stage came to an abrupt end. On 8 July 1815, Napoleon abdicated again, and Louis XVIII returned to France, signalling the beginning of the Second Restoration.

After the Hundred Days, Berry brought his daughters back to France with him, but Amy Brown stayed in England. Whatever charms she possessed, they apparently paled in comparison to the lustre of the resurrected French monarchy, and Berry abandoned her with barely a second thought. Of course, the problem of his marriage remained. After much consternation and hand-wringing, a simple strategy was adopted; their wedding ceremony was declared invalid because royal consent had not been given. Berry was therefore free to marry without having to procure an annulment. The official position was that Brown had been his concubine, not his wife.

The Bourbon elders could now turn their attention to finding Berry a suitable wife. In 1816 they settled on Marie-Caroline, a young lady of sixteen with an impeccable pedigree. She was the daughter of Ferdinand I, the future King of Sicily, and sister of Christine, future Queen of Spain. The future Duchess of Berry had a reputation for a rather gay and lively manner, and while not considered beautiful, she had a pleasant face. As Berry was neither handsome nor bright, the pair were probably well-suited. In any event, she was chosen for her reproductive potential and not for her looks or personality. To put it crudely, she had the role of a brooding mare whose sole function in life was to produce the desperately needed Bourbon heir.

News of the wedding was greeted enthusiastically by French royalists, and Marie-Caroline's name became a rallying cry for royalists devoted to the regeneration of the Bourbon dynasty. Even a humble grenadier lauded her arrival in verse:

> She comes! Hear the cries and the cheers,
> Which follow her boat o'er the waves of Messina.
> And crossing the sea, sound out on the piers,
> The blessèd name, Carolina.[5]

The two had barely met before they were pronounced man and wife on 17 June 1816 at Notre Dame Cathedral (figs. 1 & 2).

Figure 1   Portrait of His Royal Highness the
Duke of Berry, published in honour of his
marriage. Private collection

Berry and the duchess spent the next few years primarily hosting and
attending social functions and trying to have a child. They were most
successful at the former. Their relative youth and their fondness for
most forms of recreation, particularly dancing and the theatre, made
them the only royal couple who knew how to have a good time, and
high society flocked to their many soirées. The Berry household became
a centre of the Parisian social scene. Money was of no concern; Berry
and the duchess managed to spend 1.5 million francs in the first three-
and-a-half years of their marriage. With regard to children, they had
less success. A daughter was born in 1817, but died within two days.
Perhaps to cheer the duchess up, Berry purchased the Château de
Rosny for her in Seine-et-Oise at a cost of 2.5 million francs. A year
later, the duchess delivered a long-awaited boy, but he too died, a few
hours after birth. Anxiety about the royal lineage heightened after that,
with concern that the duchess could not carry a healthy child to term.
In 1819 that worry was put to rest as she successfully delivered the future Duchess of Parma. Obviously, the sex of the child was disappoint-

Figure 2   Portrait of Her Royal Highness the
Duchess of Berry, on the occasion of her
marriage. Vinck 10139, 10 October 1816

ing, but at least the duchess had proven she could give birth to a
healthy child, and she had already shown that she could produce a boy.
The duchess was exhilarated, declaring to Berry soon after her child
was born, "Do not worry, Charles, in a year I will give you a son."[6]
Ironically, Berry might have been better off marrying his mistress, a
dancer named Virginie Oreille whom he had met during the First Restoration. He somehow found the time to carry on a lengthy liaison
with her, in addition to his military duties, his ceremonial obligations,
the aforementioned social functions, and his dynastic duty vis-à-vis the
duchess. Oreille had already given Berry a son, named Charles, on 4
March 1815.[7]

On Wednesday, 13 February 1820, Berry and his wife were together, having planned yet another evening of entertainment. That
night it was to be the Opera, where three separate pieces were being

performed: *Le Carnaval de Venise, Le Rossignol,* and *Les Noces de Gamache.* The duke and duchess arrived late, missing the first show, but that was a little consequence. The Opera was a place to be seen and to mingle with other dignitaries. The couple conversed with their friends and acquaintances, notably the Duke and Duchess of Orléans and their children.[8] The duchess complained all evening of being tired and asked to leave after the first act of *Les Noces de Gamache.*[9] At eleven o'clock, Berry agreed to escort her to their carriage so that she could go home. He decided to stay, however, and watch the final act.

Their carriage was waiting just outside the royal family's private entrance. The duchess was also escorted by the Countess of Béthizy, her lady-in-waiting, and the Count of Mesnard, her first equerry. Berry was in turn accompanied by the Count of Choiseul, his aide-de-camp, and the Count of Clermont-Lodève, his gentleman-in-waiting. Berry and Mesnard helped the duchess into the carriage first, and then the countess. After the *adieux,* the men turned back toward the Opera House. At that moment, Mesnard was on Berry's left, and Choiseul stood to his right. At the entrance were some guards and the footman, who was opposite Choiseul. To Choiseul's right was an armed guard named Desbiez, the only guard close to Berry carrying a rifle.

A single, seemingly innocuous decision can have momentous ramifications, and Berry's decision to see the rest of the show would alter the course of the French Restoration. Did he want to meet up with his mistress? Did he love opera music too much to miss the final act? Did he have plans to spend the night with friends at a party or a club? These are questions without answers. What we do know is that despite the number of people in and around the carriage, a small opening remained between the footman and Desbiez. As the men walked away from the carriage, a man holding a dagger in his right hand charged through that opening, grabbed Berry by the left shoulder, and plunged the dagger into the duke's back.[10] Berry remained standing for a moment. He then fell back into Mesnard's arms, holding the dagger with both hands, and cried out: "I'm dying! That man has killed me! I am holding the dagger."[11] Berry pulled the dagger from his body and handed it to Mesnard. He was then carried into a small guard room just inside the entrance to the Opera House, and was laid on a red velours bench. He and the duchess, now by his side and holding his hand, were soon covered in blood.

The man who had dared to assassinate the Duke of Berry was Pierre Louvel, a thirty-seven-year-old journeyman saddler who worked in the king's stables in Versailles. Not much is known about him, apart from his occupation. He had a sister, a corset-maker, and an uncle living in Paris, with whom he had dined at Versailles that very day. The only other

Figure 3   Portrait of Pierre Louvel, journeyman
saddler at Versailles, the Duke of Berry's assassin.
His only regret was not having killed the whole
royal family. Vinck, 10644

person close to Louvel was his girlfriend, a fruit vendor. As Berry lay
bleeding to death in the guard room, his assassin was attempting to elude
his pursuers. His escape was not particularly well planned; it amounted
to little more than running as fast as possible. Regardless, it might have
succeeded if not for a quick-thinking young man named Paulmier employed at a nearby café, and a *chasseur* from the Royal Guard. Together
they tackled Louvel as he was about to cross the *Arcade Colbert*.[12] Clermont and Choiseul caught up with them shortly, along with Desbiez and
three *gendarmes*, who escorted him back to the Opera House. When
Louvel was searched, another dagger was found in a case, along with the
case for the dagger that he used to attack Berry (fig. 3).

Louvel was interrogated for most of the night.[13] He answered all
questions simply and to the point, and in fact never changed his testimony.[14] He declared that he had killed Berry in order to extinguish the
Bourbon line. He had targeted the duke because he was the youngest
heir to the throne and the most likely to produce another heir. He

claimed to have acted alone, without accomplices. If he had escaped, he threatened, he would have tried to kill the Duke of Angoulême the next day. When asked if he regretted his actions, Louvel replied that his only regret was not having killed the entire royal family.

Despite the seriousness of his wound, Berry did not die in the guard room. In fact, he managed to cling to life for several hours before succumbing to his injury the following morning. Mediocre in life, Berry was nothing short of magnificent in death. As the notable historian Bertier de Sauvigny put it, "It seemed that in the face of death the blood of Saint Louis regained its virtue."[15] Berry's final hours soon took on a life of their own, and his courage became legendary. Restoration royalists pointed to his death as an example of the magnificence of the Bourbon character or, in the parlance common for that era, of the royal family's racial greatness.

Medical attention was summoned from the opera spectators. The first doctor to arrive ordered Berry moved to a larger room, and the duke's footmen carried him next door. Two more doctors arrived shortly and joined the frantic efforts to staunch the wound.[16] Still conscious, Berry asked if the assassin was foreign. When told he was not, Berry moaned that it was "cruel to die at the hand of a Frenchman." He then began to ask for a priest, and Clermont raced off to the Tuileries to summon the Bishop of Chartres.

The doctors then decided to move Berry to an administrative office upstairs, a larger and more comfortable room that could accommodate a bed that had been procured from another building and also had room for the growing number of people arriving to see Berry and assess the situation. Two feather mattresses were found for him, and a pair of drapes served as a pillow. Six chandeliers were brought in to provide light.[17] Before long, Elie Decazes entered. Decazes was the first minister in the *Conseil d'état*, a position that in essence made him the most powerful politician in France. He had been working late at the Tuileries when he was informed of the attack. Some contemporary versions have it that Artois jumped up and embraced Decazes, and asked him to return to the Tuileries and inform Louis XVIII. Others described a more hostile reception.[18] Regardless, Decazes left almost immediately for the Tuileries, and when he arrived was able to convince Louis XVIII to wait there until Berry's fate became clear.[19]

Berry's death would spell certain disaster for the Bourbon dynasty, and everyone in that crowded office knew it. Once he died, the clock would begin to tick. Louis XVIII and Artois were old men, and Angoulême was middle-aged and childless. Incredibly, without warning, Berry revealed the true reason for the duchess's fatigue that night: she was pregnant.[20] It would be difficult to exaggerate the impact of

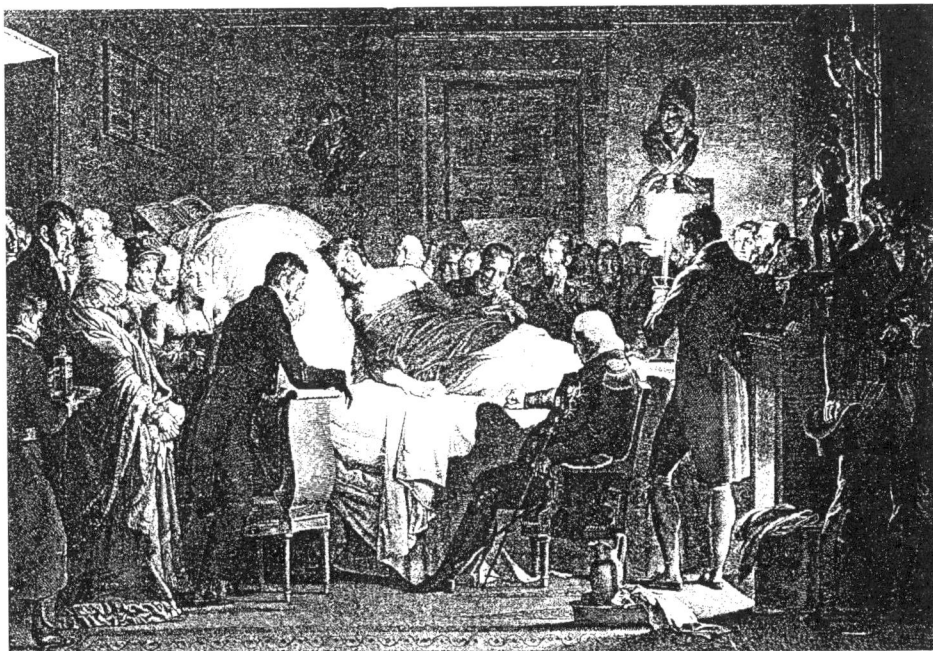

Figure 4   The last moments of the Duke of Berry. Louis XVIII sits at the foot of the bed, and the Duchess of Berry stands beside the pillow. Vinck, 10592

this news. The Duke of Berry lay bleeding to death, his life taken by an assassin; and yet, as if by miracle, the duchess was carrying a child, the final hope for the Bourbon line. Had Louvel acted two months earlier, the Bourbon dynasty would have faced a certain end.

By two in the morning, Berry was slipping in and out of consciousness, feverish and in terrible pain, complaining of a constant headache and a raging thirst.[21] Although indifferent to religious matters throughout his life, Berry became devout in his final hours. When the Bishop of Chartres finally arrived to hear his confession and give extreme unction Berry confessed with great relief, crossing himself ostentatiously.[22] It seemed, however, that he was determined to die in a manner befitting a prince of the blood. Berry implored his father and brother to bring Louis XVIII to him so that he could plead for Louvel's life. He stated several times that he did not want the blood of his assassin on his conscience when he died.[23] Forgiving his murderer was certainly Berry's finest moment, but more heroics were to follow. He also asked to see his daughters, including those he had had with Amy

Figure 5   The "miracle child," the posthumous son of the Duke of Berry. The duke and Henri IV look down from heaven. Vinck, 100705, 26 Dec. 1820

Brown, in order to say farewell and impart a final, fatherly blessing, and they were duly brought to him between four and five in the morning. The duchess was so moved that she decided to adopt Amy Brown's daughters.[24]

As Berry's condition worsened, Louis XVIII sat with Decazes at the palace waiting for news. By four o'clock, they received word that Berry had little time left. The king and Decazes left the Tuileries and headed for the Opera. Owing to his general ill health and obesity, the king had to be carried up the stairs by porters, a trip that took almost an hour. Louis XVIII went immediately to Berry's bedside and kissed his hand. Before he could say a word, Berry began to plead again for Louvel's life: "If only I can die with the hope ... that a man's blood ... was not shed for me after my death."[25] Louis XVIII paused, looked at his dying nephew and responded: "Only if it is the will of God." That reply did not satisfy Berry: "Alas, the King does not consent, and yet his forgiveness would have softened my last moments."[26] Louis XVIII seated himself in a chair at the foot of the bed, and waited patiently for the end to come (fig. 4). At six-thirty in the morning, surrounded by his family and closest friends, his hand still in his wife's, the Duke of Berry died.

Stating he had a final duty to perform, Louis XVIII gently closed his nephew's eyes.[27] At seven in the morning, the duke's now lifeless body was transported to the Louvre, where Louis XVIII visited to pour holy water on his mortal remains.

On 29 September 1820, at 2:35 a.m., seven months after the Duke of Berry was assassinated, the Duchess of Berry gave birth to Henri-Charles-Ferdinand-Marie-Dieudonné, Duke of Bordeaux.[28] The newest addition to the Bourbon royal family was promptly nicknamed the "miracle child,"[29] owing to the extraordinary set of circumstances surrounding his birth. In the eyes of the nation, this was no ordinary child; he was the product of divine intervention, a sign of God's love for the Bourbons and the French monarchy. This monarchy had suffered mightily during the previous quarter century, its property destroyed and confiscated, its representatives guillotined and exiled. The sweetness of the First Restoration had grown bitter in light of the Hundred Days. Yet, for all that, nothing could tarnish the glory of the miracle child, a boy whose very existence affirmed that the era of revolution and republicanism had ended. On the day Bordeaux was born, the dean of the diplomatic corps, the papal nuncio Msgr Macchi, voiced that perspective publicly in the following terms: "This child of sorrows, of regrets, of remembrances, is also the child of Europe; he is the prediction and guarantee of the peace and repose which must follow so many agitations" (fig. 5).[30]

Introduction:
Restoration France and
the Royalist Reaction of 1820

What is the historian to make of the Berry assassination and the miracle child? Historians generally try to find rational explanations for past events. But no hidden hand directed Louvel to act; he murdered on his own accord. Bordeaux is even more the product of luck. The assassination and the miracle child can be seen as little more than accidents of history; they just happened. Yet, these two events had a tremendously significant influence on France. The challenge for the historian is to evaluate the relevance of such accidents in light of better known and understood historical developments. That challenge is at the core of this book, as it explores how the assassination and the miracle birth merged with political, social, and philosophical developments in French history to effect radical change in the course of the French Restoration.

Restoration historians agree that France's political landscape was irrevocably altered during the nine-months following the assassination. This nine-month period is called the Royalist Reaction of 1820, an apt description for the Bourbon regime's response to Berry's death. During the Royalist Reaction, the Bourbon regime passed three laws, the so-called exceptional laws, which effectively placed all political authority solidly in the hands of the royalists and drove all forms of political opposition underground. Historians unanimously acknowledge the existence of the Royalist Reaction, but in recent years they have tended to downplay its significance, preferring to focus on what is considered a more important issue: the reasons for the July Revolution of 1830. The Royalist Reaction, and the role the assassination and the miracle child played in it, have been relegated to minor status, the consensus being that changes that occurred during and after 1820 were the product of vaster historical forces.

This trend is illustrated by two recently published books on the Restoration. In 1994 Pierre Rosanvallon published *La Monarchie Impossible*, a comparative analysis of the constitutions of the Restoration and the July Monarchy. He argued that it was fundamental flaws and contradictions in the Charter, France's constitution between 1814 and 1830, that resulted in the political impasse which pitted the governing royalists against the liberal opposition. By 1830 that impasse had become intolerable, leading the liberals to react violently against the perceived unconstitutionality of the Four Ordinances, which had been issued on 25 July 1830 to take control of the Chamber of Deputies and the press.[1] In Rosanvallon's view, the Bourbon regime in itself was irrelevant; it was the poor construction of the Charter that made political conflict inevitable and the government unworkable: either the royalists or the liberals had to go. He did not suggest that the Bourbon regime was predestined to lose this struggle – the stupidity of Charles X and his ministers accounted for that – however, he saw the Bourbon regime as an impracticable political construct from the very start. The July Revolution merely replaced the impossible monarchy with a possible one. Rosanvallon's position fits well with the generally held view, which suggests that the July Revolution was principally a political affair with relatively little impact on the general population.[2]

In 2000 Sheryl Kroen published a more comprehensive analysis of the Restoration era, entitled *Politics and Theatre: The Crisis of Legitimacy in Restoration France*. She agreed with Rosanvallon that the general population never accepted the Bourbon regime as a legitimate political authority. However, instead of focusing on the Charter, Kroen argues that the tensions that manifested themselves in 1830 arose from the regime's relentless campaign to convince the French people that it was in fact legitimate and worthy to rule. She terms the campaign "an elaborate staging," to emphasize the ephemeral character of the Bourbon regime's fruitless quest for legitimacy, and goes so far as to suggest that "negotiations over legitimate authority constituted [France's] political culture."[3] The popular response came in many forms, a veritable catalogue of anti-clerical demonstrations, political protests, seditious acts, and cultural practices, all of which Kroen interprets as evidence of the nation's rejection of the Bourbon regime.

Rosanvallon's questions about the Charter and Kroen's mountain of evidence in turn present a cogent and powerful explanation for why the regime crumbled so suddenly in July of 1830. However, Kroen's belief that the general population rejected the Bourbon regime from the beginning of the Restoration, or Rosanvallon's contention that the Charter was fundamentally an unworkable constitutional document, are simply contradicted by a close examination of the Royalist Reaction. What is readily conceded in this book is that the seeds of destruction for the Bourbon regime were planted during the Royalist Reaction, and that those seeds bore their fruit in the decade that followed.

The principal intent of this book is to redress this development in the historiography of the Restoration. The Royalist Reaction must be included in any examination of the causes of the destruction of the Restoration; it is by no means the most important, but it is vital nonetheless. What follows is a detailed analysis of the Royalist Reaction of 1820. The focus will remain throughout on the causes and the historical significance of the Royalist Reaction, and the central role the assassination and the miracle birth played in it. Naturally, this entails an examination of earlier times, and forays into the seventeenth and eighteenth century have been necessary. As well, much of what is discussed here relates directly to the July Revolution, and pointed comments are made to that effect. At the same time, in general terms, issues rooted in events that occurred after the Royalist Reaction – for argument's sake after 1821 – are not directly discussed. This book is intended to fill the historiographical gap that exists with regard to the Royalist Reaction and the assassination and miracle birth. It was felt that this narrow focus would be more useful than another broad survey of the French Restoration.

There is a second and equally important reason for a work on the Royalist Reaction. It is, quite simply, a fascinating story that occurred during a remarkable period in French history. The Berry assassination set off a dramatic chain of events that eventually led to the domination of the Bourbon regime by the ultra royalists, the extreme right wing of French politics at that time. The miracle child's impact on the Restoration was just as dramatic. Hindsight and the July Revolution have obscured how seriously the general population took the characterization of Bordeaux's birth as a miracle. In 1820 Bordeaux was deemed truly miraculous by the Catholic Church and the government, and that view facilitated the unfolding of the Royalist Reaction, just as Berry's murder initiated it.

The Royalist Reaction of 1820 developed in three distinct stages. The first was dominated by a feeling of panic; government officials scrambled to assure the public that Berry's death would not incite civil unrest or, more to the point, the overthrow of the Bourbon regime; and the media and politicians engaged in a violent polemic over the possible existence of a conspiracy to kill Berry, with royalists and liberals convinced of the others' guilt in the matter. For the most part, the government was able to moderate the panic, relying on the techniques and skills it had used for the previous six years to minimize civil unrest and political radicalism. This spirit of moderation had even survived the humiliation of the Hundred Days, evidenced by the government's crackdown on ultra-royalist excesses during the White Terror of 1815. *Union et oubli* (unity and forgiveness[4]) had been the government's rallying cry during the Restoration's moderate period (1814 to 1820), and even though with each year it had seemed that relations between royalists and liberals grew increasingly strained, a delicate balance was maintained. The result was the emergence of a dynamic and viable regime only a few years after the Napoleonic empire had crumbled. Unfortunately for Louis XVIII and his moderate royalist followers, Berry's assassination destroyed the credibility of the *union et oubli* policy. Royalists and liberals refused to tolerate each other from that moment. Moderate royalists were able to defeat the liberals in this political showdown, only to be defeated themselves the next year by the ultra royalists.

These changes began in the first three months after the assassination. Accused of conspiracy, Elie Decazes became the first casualty of the Royalist Reaction. An ultra royalist, Clausel de Coussergues, rose in the Chamber of Deputies and alleged that Decazes headed a conspiracy that was behind Berry's death. Within the week the first minister was forced to resign. To head off a crisis of confidence in the government, Louis XVIII and Artois prevailed upon Louis Armand du Plessis, Duke of Richelieu, a former first minister who had himself been chased from office a mere two years earlier, to replace Decazes.

Richelieu's principal goal upon taking office was to moderate the tone of political debate in the country. Royalist journalists, political pamphleteers, and deputies in Parliament[5] had reacted to Berry's death as if it were the first step in a Europe-wide republican conspiracy to overthrow all monarchies. Liberals responded with their own allegations of royalist conspiracies. Richelieu believed it was essential to send a clear message to the nation that Louis XVIII's government would not tolerate any further attacks on the royal family. He introduced three pieces of legislation, collectively called the exceptional laws, to the Chamber of Deputies in the days following the assassination: the liberty law, which suspended *habeas corpus* and allowed the police to arrest and detain for up to three months any person suspected of threatening the safety of the state or the well-being of the royal family; the press law, which stipulated that no newspaper, periodic journal, or illustration could be published without going through a censor; and, an amended electoral law. The liberty and press laws were introduced in

February and their passage at the end of March marked the end of the Royalist Reaction's first stage. The government's ability to push those two laws so rapidly through both parliamentary chambers illustrates the impact Berry's assassination had on France's leading politicians, an effect that was echoed throughout France's political community, in newspapers, pamphlets, illustrations, and public demonstrations. Proponents of the exceptional laws pointed to the assassination as proof positive that drastic measures were needed to prevent a civil war. In their minds, the liberty and press laws were more than simply measures to enhance the state's police and censorship powers; they represented a crucial step in fighting the revolutionary forces that had planned and executed Berry's murder.

The second stage of the Royalist Reaction began with the debate over the third of the exceptional laws, which proved to be the most controversial of the three. Under the existing electoral law, only men over thirty who paid a minimum of 300 francs a year in direct taxes were eligible to vote in deputy elections.[6] They cast their ballots in the electoral colleges of their respective arrondissements to elect 258 deputies. The amendment proposed the creation of an additional 172 deputies; however, only voters whose direct taxes put them in the top 25 percent of all voters in their department were eligible to vote for those 172 additional deputies. Elections for these 172 deputies would take place in newly created departmental colleges.[7] Significantly, however, the electors qualified to vote for the 172 deputies in the departmental colleges were also qualified to vote for the original 258 deputies in the arrondissement colleges. As a result, the amended electoral law became known as the law of the double vote. The double vote was proposed by the government in order to ensure that France's wealthiest landowners had control over the election of deputies. Direct taxes were essentially a measure of the size of one's landed property; therefore, the double-voters represented those who owned the largest estates. It was widely assumed that the *grands propriétaires* were overwhelmingly royalist supporters.[8] In this way, Richelieu hoped to create a permanent and cooperative royalist majority in the Chamber of Deputies, thereby removing the most obvious impediment to any legislation the government introduced. Strangely, one of the Four Ordinances restricted the electorate to double-voters alone. Yet, what was to foment revolution in 1830 did wonders to calm political passions in 1820. The law passed on 12 June and closed the period of civil unrest that had followed Berry's death and the introduction of the exceptional laws to Parliament.

A third stage began once the double vote became law, and it ended with a general election for the Chamber of Deputies. The Royalist

Reaction was most intense in this stage, as the government and the royalists achieved virtually all their political objectives, not the least of which was the destruction of the liberal opposition and a dramatic and widespread public acceptance of the Bourbon regime. The birth of the Duke of Bordeaux was the event that above all precipitated these developments. News of Bordeaux's birth spread across France within a couple of days and occasioned celebrations in virtually every city, town, and village. These spontaneous and enthusiastic displays of love and affection for the royal family speak to a fundamental change in public opinion over the course of the Royalist Reaction. While it would not be accurate to say the Bourbons were loved by the entire population, they were certainly accepted as the legitimate rulers of France. Bordeaux's birth brought millions of people back into the royalist fold, and the government, royalists, and the royal family basked in the glory of it all. Before the miracle child, one could still have argued that the Bourbon regime remained a political expedient, hobbled politically and symbolically by the Revolution and the Hundred Days, and largely ignored by the French people. By the end of the Royalist Reaction, the Bourbons had truly become France's royal family again, accepted as the legitimate fountainhead, be it symbolic or actual, of French political power. Granted, the incredible rise in popularity of the Bourbon regime, and of Louis XVIII in particular, did not last much beyond the first few months after the birth; yet, it has led Philip Mansel, a prominent Restoration historian, to suggest that there was in fact a Third Restoration in 1820.[9] Although short-lived, the reaction to the miracle child was filled with historical significance. A mere nine-month duration, its short lifespan is a testimony to lost opportunity rather than inconsequence, as royalists frittered away their new-found popularity by infighting and questionable political strategies. The shrewdness and unity displayed by the royalists, particularly the ultra royalists, during the debate over the exceptional laws seemed to desert them in the course of the 1820s. By 1830 the general population had again become indifferent to the Bourbon regime; the liberal opposition was united against them, and the royalists were deeply divided.

Deputy elections in November, the first held with the double vote, provided formal closure to the Royalist Reaction. The voters returned a solid royalist majority to the Chamber, and the previously influential and growing liberal opposition was reduced to rump status. The King's *Conseil*, led by Richelieu, was formed almost exclusively of moderate royalists. The liberal press had been silenced, and the ultra-royalist press forced to moderate its criticisms of the government. In short, all seemed well in France ten months after Berry was murdered. One year later, however, Richelieu was gone and the ultra royalists were in power. As is so often the case, those who begin a process of political change, in this case the moderate royalists, often lose control and are swept aside by more aggressive, radical, and better-prepared groups.

Both a thematic and a chronological approach have been adopted to assess the Royalist Reaction in its fullest historical context. Part One is thematic and each of its three chapters (law, conspiracy, and politics) highlights the key issues and themes needed to understand the Royalist Reaction's place in French history. In Part Two, a chronological approach is used to examine the Royalist Reaction in relation to events as they unfolded after Berry's death. The chapters correspond generally to the three stages of the Royalist Reaction, and every effort has been made to reference the background material from Part One to the Royalist Reaction itself.

Sources for this work were diverse and necessitate some comment. Material on the roles played by various levels of government was readily available in the *Archives nationales* in Paris and in provincial archives. The *Bibliothèque nationale* has a massive collection of material related to the Royalist Reaction – political pamphlets, speeches, eulogies for Berry, poems and songs for Bordeaux, and newspapers. The *archives parlementaires*, the official version of the parliamentary debates, were particularly useful with regard to the exceptional laws. The illustrations that form such an important part of this book were found in two comprehensive collections, the *Collection de Vinck* and Michel Henin's and George Duplessis's *Inventaire de la collection d'estampes*. Although these collections are extensive, it proved extremely difficult to obtain high-quality prints. Some of the images are not as clear as one would like. At the same time, the illustrations included in this book should be viewed as primary resource materials. They were chosen for their relevance to the Royalist Reaction and not particularly for their artistic merit or visual clarity.

The Restoration is notable for the number of memoirs published by prominent persons, and they proved to be interesting anecdotal sources of information. François-Réné Chateaubriand produced the most important literary effort related to the assassination: *Mémoires, lettres et pièces authentiques touchant la vie et la mort de S.A.R. Monseigneur Charles-Ferdinand-D'Artois, fils de France, Duc de Berry*. It was a hastily written collection of Berry's correspondence and Chateaubriand's personal commentary. In artistic terms, this was not his greatest achievement. Chateaubriand was seeking profit, not praise, and it seems he was successful in that regard. His work was read by thousands and made available in the reading rooms of most urban centres. Artistic considerations aside, Chateaubriand was a leading ultra-royalist figure throughout the Restoration, and his *Life of Berry* provides telling evidence of the nature and intensity of the royalist-liberal rivalry. It also includes a useful and concise summary of the ultra-royalist interpretation of the assassination.

These sources, while extensive, tended to reflect the politics of the capital, and therefore failed to shed any light on the popular elements of the Royalist Reaction. To investigate the Royalist Reaction in as full a perspective as possible, two local studies were conducted. Choosing appropriate locations for local studies is always difficult. France's diversity becomes problematic once a historian descends from Parisian politics to the provincial. Fortunately, the unique status, reputations, and histories of two departments made the choice relatively straightforward: Isère, and its capital, Grenoble; and Haute-Garonne, and its capital, Toulouse. In addition to providing a wider perspective on the Royalist Reaction, research in those two departments afforded a documentary record of how extensively the Royalist Reaction affected the entire French population.

In general terms, Isère and Haute-Garonne were chosen because their inhabitants symbolized liberalism and royalism, respectively. That is not to say that no royalists lived in Isère or liberals in Haute-Garonne; however, to a remarkable degree the political characters of each department were divided along these lines. To find examples of Restoration liberalism in action, one need look no farther than Isère. Examples of Haute-Garonne's royalist temperament are somewhat muted compared to Isère's; royalists had less to protest against given that France had a monarchy. Nevertheless, the manner in which events unfolded in Haute-Garonne after the assassination amounted to a Royalist Reaction in microcosm. To that end, local research in Haute-Garonne was the perfect counter-balance to research in Isère. For those unfamiliar with the particular histories of Isère and Haute-Garonne, Appendix One provides a short summary.

PART ONE

Seeds of Destruction

1 The Law:
Cracks in the Edifice

THE CHARTER:
AMBIGUITY AND COMPROMISE

On 5 June 1814, France's newest constitution, the Charter, came into force. Constitutions reflect a nation's political identity, entrenching in legal terms certain core ideals and principles around which that nation's public life is to be organized. The Charter certainly did that, despite the fact that the ideals and principles enshrined in it were in many instances contradictory. Regardless of how one characterizes the Charter, however, it was beyond doubt a remarkable example of diplomatic ingenuity. Faced with the collapse of the Empire and an imminent foreign occupation, the ubiquitous Charles Maurice de Talleyrand was able to broker a deal, encapsulated in the Charter, that resurrected the Bourbon royal dynasty. Perhaps time heals all wounds; perhaps the Bourbons represented the least offensive option; in any event, the Charter allowed France to build upon the ashes of the Empire and establish a legitimate, and for the most part viable, political state. That it did so by incorporating ideals and principles from both royalism and liberalism is a testimony to the realities of the moment. One might expect a constitution both royalist and liberal in orientation to be unworkable, dooming France to perpetual political unrest. Yet, for all its schizophrenic shortcomings, the Charter provided a workable framework within which Restoration politics could for a time operate effectively. In 1814 liberals and royalists were very comfortable with the Charter's contradictions, and by 1820, despite a number of difficult moments, most members of France's political community had accepted the Charter with all its ambiguities.

For those on the left of the political spectrum, the Charter gave voice to the type of government envisioned by Montesquieu and the Enlightenment. It established a constitutional monarchy with an executive and legislative branch. The executive consisted of the king and his ministers, who formed the *Conseil d'état*. The king had the absolute right to appoint his ministers. As a collective body, the king and the *Conseil* represented the government, and the prefects and the provincial bureaucracies reported formally to them. In addition to its day-to-day task of running the government, the executive was responsible for drafting all legislation and submitting it to parliament.[1]

A two-chambered parliament checked the executive's power. It consisted of an upper house, the Chamber of Peers, and a lower house, the Chamber of Deputies. Peers were appointed by the king, and appointments could be made hereditary. Princes of the blood were automatically members. Deputies, on the other hand, were elected. All legislation proposed by the executive required the consent of both Chambers to become law, and that is where the potential for political conflict lay. The political composition of the *Conseil* and the two Chambers at any given time determined the outcome of political issues. For example, in 1815–16 a moderate-royalist *Conseil*, led by the Duke of Richelieu, a moderate royalist himself, faced a moderate-royalist Chamber of Peers and an ultra-royalist Chamber of Deputies. By 1819 the mix had changed, and with it the character of French politics. The *Conseil*, now headed by Elie Decazes, adopted a more liberal agenda, and the Chamber of Peers became an ultra-royalist stronghold, while the Chamber of Deputies reflected a moderate royalist majority, with a significant liberal minority. The precise composition of the executive and the two Chambers prior to the Royalist Reaction will be discussed later in this chapter. It is important to appreciate at this point that the political orientation of each of these political bodies had been constantly changing prior to Berry's death.

These changes should not be viewed negatively as evidence of an unstable political system, but rather as indications of the Charter's parliamentary character. It was relatively modern in structural terms, in that it entrenched constitutional limits on the executive. More particularly, it reflected the political transformations brought about by the Revolution and by Napoleon between 1789 and 1814. A substantial percentage of France's political community rejected royal absolutism in no uncertain terms. Despite the horrors of the Revolution and the collapse of the Empire, a return to anything resembling the Old Regime was simply untenable. Not surprisingly, then, liberals were attracted by the

Charter's parliamentary features. In their minds, its overall spirit spoke directly to the issues that had driven the Revolution in the first place: equality before the law, limits on executive power, and political representation for the people. In that context, the liberals' Charter was a constitutional document that paid homage to the principles of 1789 first and foremost; to them the Bourbon regime was palatable only so long as that spirit was respected.

One might assume that royalists universally despised the Charter in principle. The very idea of a constitution could only conjure up painful memories of the Revolution. The Jacobins had ousted royal authority and replaced it with a political regime based upon a constitution passed by a parliament duly elected by representatives of *le peuple*. The Charter therefore represented a constant reminder that the Revolution and Empire were not historical accidents but very real events that had changed France indelibly. One of those changes meant that no Bourbon could sit on the French throne unless he agreed to rule in accordance with a constitution.

At first, some royalists struggled to accept the Charter. In 1814, Joseph de Villèle,[2] a deputy for Haute-Garonne at the time, offended by the notion of constitutional limits on royal authority, dismissed the Charter as an absurdity. It must be stressed, however, that royalist opposition to the Charter in 1814 was not merely reactionary, but rather a matter of conscience. Some provisions, notably article six, which protected freedom of religion, offended their religious sensibilities. The Charter challenged some of their most deeply held convictions, and the royalists' sincere attempts to come to terms with it contrasted starkly with the liberals' almost effortless acceptance of it. Significantly, in a relatively short period of time, even the most extreme ultra royalists had come to accept the Charter as a reasonable price to pay for the Restoration. "There is no real choice," wrote Chateaubriand in 1817, "but for France to live under the Charter; the alternatives are to return to the Old Regime, which is impossible, or return to the despotism of Napoleon, which is unthinkable."[3] The royalists' grudging acceptance of the Charter was made clear during Berry's wedding in 1816; a medallion displayed in the choir of the church included the image of the Charter being presented to *la France*.[4]

Royalists rationalized the Charter's objectionable provisions principally by way of interpretation and emphasis.[5] Despite its self-evident parliamentary nature, royalists tended to see the Charter first and foremost as an expression of royalism. That position was bolstered by the Charter's preamble, and also by the rhetoric of the Counter-Revolution. Two linguistic tours de force in the Charter insinuated that it was subordinate to royal authority and not the reverse. First, it situated the

Charter in the nineteenth year of Louis XVIII's reign,[6] a somewhat bizarre attempt to claim that nothing had interrupted the Bourbon monarchy since the Revolution. That statement was also interpreted to mean that the Bourbon monarchy was an immortal institution, beyond the power of human forces to destroy. Beheading Louis XVI may have ended his personal reign, but authority flowed magically to the surviving heir in a process of infinite succession. The legitimacy of the monarchy derived from God and not parliament; therefore, it was superior to the dictates of all human institutions. The preamble further reinforced this view by declaring that Louis XVIII had *octroyé*, or granted, the Charter to the French people. The use of the word *octroyé* suggested that the Charter existed only by virtue of royal authority and did not evolve from a separate source of political power. Note that royalists remained convinced throughout the Restoration that the Charter had been forced upon their king, conveniently ignoring the fact that both parliamentary chambers had accepted it.[7] Nevertheless, the Charter was acceptable to most royalists if it remained an expression of royal benevolence. It would cease to be so if it became a statement of royal subordination to a constitutional regime.

The king's right to introduce legislation to parliament and appoint *Conseil* members, his power to dissolve the Chamber of Deputies and call new elections, and his prerogative to appoint new peers and make those appointments hereditary supported the notion that the constitutional balance of power rested firmly in the king's hands. The authority of the deputies and the peers to reject proposed legislation righted that balance somewhat; however, many royalists were quick to point out that the Charter was hardly the bold expression of parliamentary democracy the liberals suggested it was.

There was also a more philosophical body of evidence to support the view that the Charter was best interpreted as an expression of royal authority. It is found principally among counter-revolutionary works. Following Louis XVI's execution, royalist ideologues were faced with the challenge of constructing a viable French royalism in exile. Religion provided the principal means of doing so, with references to God and the divine law used to refute the legitimacy of revolutionary and imperial regimes. Ultra royalists, led by Joseph de Maistre and Louis de Bonald, argued that God was the first cause of the law and that no constitution was valid unless that truth was acknowledged. Relying on examples from European history, Maistre postulated that sovereignty could not reside in the people because electorates were too small and full democracy resulted in the tyranny of the majority. Since constitutions derived their legitimacy from the people's sovereignty, neither were they a viable foundation for sovereignty. History proves, Maistre wrote, that sovereign power could only reside in the king, and not a man-made institution. In his view, the duration of a state was directly proportional to the perfection of religious principles within that state, a mysterious but visible relationship. Since the gospels had determined that only a monarchy that respected the Catholic faith was compatible with that equation, it followed that France would prosper only under a monarchical, Catholic government. Maistre believed the papacy represented the perfect example of a monarchy, although he found the Bourbon regime to be an acceptable substitute.

Somewhat less historical in approach and less interested in strengthening the Pope's power *per se*, Bonald agreed with Maistre's basic premise that a Catholic state could only flourish under a monarchy. Bonald tended to focus on relationships between groups of people rather than on the nature of institutions. His was a hierarchical and organic conception of society, with God and Jesus at the top, followed by the king, the magistrates, and then the people at the bottom, but each level below the divine was interrelated and interdependent. The natural order, according to Bonald, was an "*ensemble des rapports.*"[8] His favorite metaphor was the family; the father ruled the family, but he did so in the interests of those subordinate to his authority. Benevolence in familial relations was ordained by God, and oppressive fathers acted directly against divine will. The great father, God, and his son, Jesus, were reflected in the relationships between the king and his magistrates, the king and the people, and the magistrates and the people. Continuing the family metaphor, Bonald believed a monarchy was essential to the natural order because it treated society as a collection of families. Republics treated society as a collection of individuals, and therefore drifted into chaos because self-interest and not religion dictated the government's actions. In this context, constitutions could be useful expressions of a body of law, but that law existed by reason of natural law and must always be subordinate to royal authority, which derived its authority from God. In addition, Bonald did not believe a constitutional regime could be sustained in the long term. It needed tremendous state power to be effective, as illustrated by Napoleon's Imperial regime. Moreover, it tended towards arbitrariness because that power was not easily held in check. The advantage of the organic arrangement, with interrelated layers of familial groups, was the interdependence it cultivated under the overriding influence of divine law. In short, "the law is the will of God, and the rule for man."[9] Bonald's view suggests that the provisions of the Charter articulated principles related to the magistrate level, that is, the organization of the secular authority, but which in no way limited the higher royal authority. The Charter was therefore legitimate as long as it respected its position in the natural order; but woe to any state that attempted to elevate a constitution above a king.

When the Charter was first proclaimed law in 1814, it was its ambiguity or dual personality, the very thing that would prove so problematic in future years, that allowed France to begin to rebuild after the Empire's collapse. People were willing to accept its compromises as a reasonable price to pay for peace. Over the next few years, this pragmatic spirit gave way to political opportunism. A debate over ministerial responsibility, which had grown quite heated before 1820, provides a perfect example of the way political factions exploited the Charter's ambiguous nature. At law, ministers answered solely to the king and the *Conseil*. Some felt that ministers should be responsible to the deputies, the only representative body in parliament. The Charter was silent on this point, beyond stipulating that the king had the right to appoint his own ministers. One might have expected liberals to head the campaign for ministerial responsibility to the Chamber, but in fact, prior to the Royalist Reaction, ultra royalists were the most vocal in opposing ministerial independence. Their opposition had manifested itself immediately after the Hundred Days. The first Chamber of Deputies to follow Napoleon's defeat at Waterloo, came to be known as the *Chambre introuvable*, the impossible – or unattainable – Chamber. It was dominated by ultra royalists who refused to cooperate with the moderate *Conseil* then in power. (The general significance in political terms of the *Chambre introuvable* will be discussed below.) In regard to this issue, their position was that ministers should be required to resign if a majority of deputies rejected their legislation. Liberals opposed such a measure, and even the left-leaning Decazes ministry of 1819 staunchly refused to introduce ministerial responsibility. When the *Chambre introuvable* was dissolved in 1816 and new elections were called, the ultra royalists understandably protested the dissolution and, led by Chateaubriand, they renewed their calls for ministerial responsibility. As Chateaubriand wrote, "The minister must act in accordance with the majority; without that there is no government."[10]

The issue dropped abruptly from the ultra agenda as soon as Richelieu's second ministry fell in December, 1821, and the ultra royalists took over the *Conseil*. With equal abruptness liberals then began championing the cause of ministerial responsibility. In another about-face, in 1830, ultra royalists praised the Four Ordinances, which dissolved the current Chamber of Deputies, and called for new elections, conveniently forgetting their earlier indignation when the *Chambre introuvable* had been dismissed.[11] Liberals suffered a similar memory loss, forgetting that they had supported the 1816 dissolution with enthusiasm. Apparently, the spirit of the Charter was not offended by arbitrary government actions directed against one's political adversaries.

THE CENS COMMUNITY: MONEY AND POLITICAL ACUMEN

The political system established by the Charter was by no means democratic, but it did have democratic elements, the most prominent of which was that the Chamber of Deputies was elected. The Charter determined who was eligible to vote in those elections and who could run as a candidate. Article 40 restricted the vote to men thirty years of age or more who paid at least 300 francs a year in direct taxes. Article 38 added that deputies could be no younger than forty and must pay at least 1,000 francs a year in direct taxes. The tax qualification was called the *cens*. Those who met the *cens* formed a unique sub-community within the broader French political community. In total, they numbered around 80,000 or 0.3 percent of France's total population. The *cens* community represented France's richest men. Although politically divided, they were united by the vastness of their wealth, by virtue of which they controlled French politics. From their ranks came the members of the *Conseil*, the Chamber of Deputies, the prefecture, and most leading provincial officials. The tremendous concentration of political power in the hands of the *cens* community ensured that its members played a significant role in a political crisis like the Royalist Reaction.

Who were these men? First, they were all very wealthy. A man who met the *cens*, that is, who paid 300 francs in direct taxes, had an annual income of 3,000 to 4,000 francs. Candidates paying the 1,000 franc minimum in direct taxes boasted an annual income of at least 10,000 francs. Second, and equally as important, the *cens* itself was essentially an indication of land ownership; therefore, the *cens* community represented the wealthiest landowners in France. The reason for that relates to how the *cens* was calculated. Direct taxes consisted primarily of two separate taxes: the *contribution foncière*, based on revenue from real estate, and the *impôts des patentes*, a license required to engage in business. Of the two, the *contribution foncière* was the more considerable. Land was taxed far more heavily than other forms of wealth, and France's economy was still overwhelmingly agrarian. Virtually no elector met the *cens* without paying the *contribution foncière*. In the 1820 deputy election, only 1.2 percent of all Haute-Garonne electors did so.[13] Land ownership was even more pronounced among deputies, regardless of political orientation. Liberal deputies were three times more likely than royalist deputies to have an occupation other than "landowner" (*propriétaire*), although those numbers remained relatively small. Thirty-two percent of liberal deputies did not list land-owner as their principal occupation in 1816, as compared to 15 per-cent for royalist deputies. Moreover, between 1817 and 1819, in elections held under an electoral law that contemporaries believed favoured bourgeois (non-landowner) candidates, the percentage of non-landowner liberal deputies fell to 22 percent; that proportion fell even further to 21 percent in 1820.[14] At the same time, the *patente* was more important than contemporaries realized. The average *patente* in the 1820 election in Haute-Garonne's arrondissement colleges was 195 francs. In that election, 8 percent of all electors needed the *patente* to reach the *cens*, and the average *patente* for those voters was 184 francs. In the departmental college, 16 percent of the electors paid a *patente*, with 27 percent of those electors needing the *patente* to qualify (4 per-cent of all voters).[15] In general, however, the *patente* was a secondary, albeit often important, factor in reaching the *cens*. It was certainly far less important in reaching the thousand-franc candidates' *cens*. That remained the case even after the July Revolution, when the *cens* was lowered to 200 francs. The average *contribution foncière* for anyone paying a *patente* in the first election held during the July Monarchy was 283 francs, which meant that the average *patente* payer owned about eighty-five hectares of land.[16]

These statistics suggest that members of the *cens* had at least two things in common. They were extraordinarily rich, and their wealth was based on land. Later in the century, Marxist commentators would dismiss them as an economic group eclipsed by the new industrial wealth of the bourgeois class, a view that had a long shelf-life; how-ever, work by Thomas Beck has raised questions about this interpreta-tion. Beck has shown that the Marxists failed to take into account how the members of the *cens* community acted, particularly during the Roy-alist Reaction, and more to the point, what they thought about them-selves. Contrary to Marxist stereotypes, the members of the *cens* community hardly considered themselves to be a homogenous group. In their own minds, the 80,000 electors were a highly fractious bunch, differentiated by character and personal beliefs. Thomas Beck's rela-tively overlooked work provides the key to understanding why such an outwardly homogenous group should in fact be so divisive and hostile to each other. Beck discovered that occupation and sources of wealth were not useful indicators of political orientation. By examining indi-viduals' political experience, Beck uncovered a statistical link between those who were Restoration liberal deputies and those who held a gov-ernment office during the Revolution or a seat in the Chamber of Rep-resentatives during the Hundred Days.[17] Royalist deputies were more likely to have entered politics for the first time in August, 1815, in the first election held after Waterloo. In short, a deputy's relationship to the Revolution and/or the Hundred Days was more significant in determining his political orientation than his wealth. Significantly, that finding suggests that holding office during the Napoleonic period was not a determinant in a deputy's political orientation; both liberals and royalists worked for the Imperial regime. However, while the vast majority of royalists readily accepted Imperial posts, they refused to join Napoleon during the Hundred Days, and as noted, they did not work for the earlier republican governments.

The character of the Restoration's all-powerful *cens* community becomes truly decipherable only if one differentates between economics and politics. In economic terms, the *cens* community was relatively united – a fact that makes it clear that economics played virtually no role in the Royalist Reaction. The Royalist Reaction becomes more interesting when one considers that it divided even the wealthiest 0.3 percent of the population. Moreover, those divisions were by no means restricted to members of the *cens* community, an observation that explains why the Royalist Reaction had both an elite political and a popular dimension. By virtue of their political power, members of the *cens* community played a crucial role in the Royalist Reaction, but as will be shown in Part Two, not a definitive one.

THE HISTORY OF THE ELECTORAL LAW, 1814–20: MANIPULATION AND CREDIBILITY

The Charter had many flaws; however, the provisions relating to deputy elections, or the electoral law stood out above all others. The *cens* itself was clear enough: men at least thirty years old who paid at least 300 francs in direct taxes in an election year could vote. They could be candidates if they were forty and paid 1,000 francs. Unfortunately, clarity evaporated after that. Article 37 set out the structure for the deputy elections: electoral colleges were to be convened annually in each department for the purpose of electing deputies to a five-year term, one-fifth of the Chamber to be renewed annually. This article did not specify the number of electoral colleges per department or the overall number of deputies. Instead, according to article 35, the organization of the electoral colleges was to be "determined by law." That phase opened a Pandora's box because it did not refer to any specific body of law.

Two interpretations emerged, one procedural, the other substantive. The procedural interpretation held that any law was constitutional if it was proposed by the executive power and passed by the two

Chambers. It followed, therefore, that the rules governing voter eligibility and the organization of the electoral colleges could be determined and changed by the government. Only three provisions were mandatory in any electoral law: an age requirement, a *cens*, and electoral colleges. These three provisions were enshrined in constitutional terms by virtue of articles 37, 38, and 40, and they could be overridden only by a constitutional amendment. The corollary was that there was no constitutional impediment to the government proposing an electoral law that included all three, but that provided for more than one *cens* or established more than one type of electoral college.

According to the substantive interpretation, the phrase "determined by law" paid deference to the body of constitutional principles that must be incorporated and respected in any law, or any single provision of that law. The Charter was composed of a number of guiding principles, all arranged hierarchically one of which was the principle of equality before the law. A law that proposed more than one *cens* or type of electoral college was considered unconstitutional because it offended that principle. Equality before the law operated on a constitutionally superior level, and would be offended by the provision of one set of voting rights to those paying 300 francs in direct taxes and another for those paying a higher amount. That law would be unconstitutional even if it met the Charter's procedural requirements in the strict sense of the word.

Both interpretations had merit. But the balancing of interests required to make a constitution a workable political document also requires a jurisprudence with an agreed set of guiding legal principles. The passage of time might well have provided France with the necessary jurisprudence. But before 1820, and arguably for a long time thereafter, it simply did not exist. French parliaments had already dispensed with six constitutions between 1791 and 1804. Perhaps a constitutional court and a precedent system of some sort would have protected the Charter's electoral provisions from the capricious effects of politics. That question is also moot because France's political community was not interested in constitutional certainty. Political power was the goal, and that community preferred a constitution that was open to interpretation. It made it easier to justify any course of action. From 1814 to 1820 ministers tinkered with the electoral law in hopes of stumbling upon a magic configuration that would guarantee a docile Chamber of Deputies. Royalists and liberals supported electoral laws that made it easier for their respective candidates to win seats, and they attacked any obstacle in the most vicious of terms – Charter be damned.

The result was an acrimonious discourse on the subject of the electoral law in the years preceding the assassination. The discourse was fundamentally destructive because it had the potential to undermine the credibility of the electoral system and weakened the Charter's status. An electoral system cannot function unless its participants agree to the rules that govern elections. If personal political agendas determine those rules, then the election of a representative body becomes a farce. That is precisely what happened with the electoral system during the Restoration. The electoral law was amended repeatedly for opportunistic reasons, and government agents blatantly rigged elections. Certainly, the Charter was a young document in 1820 and had not yet attained the status of a constitutional law that existed on a level above the manipulation and exploitation of the political fray. Indifference to the symbolic importance of a stable and trustworthy electoral system, whose rules are known and accepted by the voters and the candidates, must be regarded as a defining feature of Restoration politics. Electoral results were never thought to represent the legitimate voice of the electorate. Each election spurred renewed partisan efforts to modify the law to favour certain candidates. The debate over the double vote was yet another example of just such an effort.

The government's flexible and cavalier attitude toward the electoral law had already been evident right after the Hundred Days. Deputy elections were set for August, 1815. They were to be run according to a system of indirect voting that had been in place since 1799. In this former system, the government determined the number of seats per department, and the voting took place in arrondissement and departmental colleges. The latter colleges were limited to the 600 most heavily taxed men in each department.[18] Men over thirty who met the 300-franc *cens* but were ineligible for the department college voted in the arrondissement college; they elected candidates to fill the number of seats specified for their respective department. The department college then met eight days later to choose the actual deputies for their department, half of whom had to be from the list of candidates elected by the arrondissement college.

To take advantage of the perceived groundswell of popular royalism following Waterloo, the government decided to hold new deputy elections, even though it was under no legal obligation to replace the deputies who had sat in the Chamber before the Hundred Days. They also made some strategic changes to the electoral system. They raised the number of seats in the Chamber from 258 to 402 and lowered the age qualification for candidates from forty to twenty-five, and that of voters from thirty to twenty-one. The minimum *cens* remained 300 francs, although some ultra royalists lobbied to lower it to twenty-five francs.

New deputy elections may perhaps have been needed to prove to the nation that the Hundred Days had not destroyed the political system of the Restoration. A new Chamber would represent a fresh start and confirm the legitimacy of the Bourbon regime. At the same time, the decision to hold elections so soon after Waterloo was questionable at best. The electoral law was amended because the government believed its changes would translate into a moderate royalist majority in the Chamber. However, it failed to take into account the effect of the White Terror in full swing at the time of the election. The White Terror, along with the lower age requirement, introduced an element of radical extremism to the electorate. If Louis XVIII had wanted to diffuse the tense atmosphere that followed the Hundred Days he might have been wise to keep the franchise out of the hands of wealthy young men intent on revenge after the Hundred Days.

The 1815 deputy election represented one of Louis XVIII's greatest political blunders. The lower age of eligibility, combined with ultra-royalist intimidation and violence, to which the supervising Allied troops turned a blind eye, resulted in ultra-royalist candidates' capturing 350 of the 402 seats.[19] The king had hoped to use the election as a springboard for his conciliatory *union et oubli* policy. Instead, he found himself faced with a Chamber of Deputies filled with young, inexperienced, and impulsive reactionaries[20] who had no intention of forgiving or forgetting anything. Their refusal to cooperate with the king and his ministers earned them the appellation *Chambre introuvable*. Even for Louis XVIII and his *Conseil*, too much royalism was a liability. The *Chambre* fought the government on every possible occasion, attacking the King's ministers with "irrational verbal violence."[21] *Vive le roi, quand même*, ("Long live the King, no matter what") became their battle cry: the ultras would re-establish the glory of the Bourbon throne, even if the current Bourbon king was too timid to do so. The deputies badgered Elie Decazes, then the minister of police, for not implementing with full force a series of repressive laws that collectively ushered in a legal phase of the White Terror. The thousands of republicans that were jailed or interrogated did not satisfy the extremist *Chambre*. Put every last Bonapartist and liberal in jail, the ultra deputies thundered, and drive the final nail into the coffin of the Revolution. Blonde d'Aubers, an extremist even by ultra standards, demanded the reimposition of the tithe. Another deputy called for the return of clerical control over the *état civil*, the regulation of births, deaths, and marriages. A number of deputies also proposed a scheme to compensate all *émigrés* and the Catholic Church for property confiscated during the Revolution. On 11 November 1815 a new law declared it illegal to display the tricolor cockades, carry the tricolor flag, sing revolutionary songs, or keep images of Napoleon and symbols of the Empire in public places. By order of the Ministry of Police, public officials were to destroy all physical reminders of the Revolution and Napoleon, works of art excepted. Between the fall of 1815 and the summer of 1816, piles of "emblems of liberty" – plates, chamber pots, tobacco cases, fabric, flags, prints, seals, paintings, and statues – were burned in public squares, often to the accompaniment of a mass and a sermon.[22] When the *Chambre introuvable* refused to allow the government to issue bonds backed by a million acres of national forests, royalist extremism had gone too far. The forests included confiscated Church property, and the bond issue would have conflicted with the ultras' compensation plans, whereas the government needed the funds desperately to pay down the national debt.[23] On 8 September 1816, tired of outrageous demands and lack of cooperation, Louis XVIII ordered the dissolution of the *Chambre introuvable* and called new deputy elections.

Despite the reactionary policies and general unreasonableness of the *Chambre introuvable*, the fact remains that it was a duly elected representative body that had not broken a single law or regulation. The Charter had empowered the Chamber of Deputies to withhold its consent from proposed legislation whenever it deemed fit. The grounds for the dissolution, then, were that the *Chambre introuvable* had refused to pass the legislation proposed to it, that some deputies had criticized ministers in abusive tones, and that its members had proposed certain policies deemed impolitic by the *Conseil*. In short, the *Chambre introuvable* was dissolved because the king had so declared.

Reaction to the dissolution was curious. Moderate royalists for the most part felt uncomfortable with divisions within the royalist movement but still supported the action because they were offended by the excesses of the "ultras," particularly the violence that occurred during the White Terror. At the same time, little thought was given to the precedent that had been set, and, more to the point, no attempt was made to outline the legal principles that would determine when the king was justified in dissolving a Chamber of Deputies. By failing to clarify these principles, the government lost an opportunity to enhance the Charter's status as the supreme law of the land. In practical terms, this lost opportunity resulted in the Chamber being dissolved six times during the Restoration; on the final occasion it stimulated the July Revolution. Even more curious was the reaction of the liberals, which, almost to a man, was positive. In their minds, the *Chambre introuvable* had tried to resurrect the Old Regime, complete with the *gabelle* and *lettres de cachet*. They seemed unconcerned by the constitutional and political implications of a king being able to dissolve a legally constituted legislative body of elected representatives on the grounds of what amounted to royal whimsy – the very type of arbitrary royal action that liberals claimed to despise. In 1816, however, liberals were glad to see their most hated political rivals suffer a severe blow. Yet, in 1820, during the controversy over the exceptional laws, liberals would denounce the identical type of arbitrary action; and in 1830, they were quick to support an armed insurrection when Charles X tried to dissolve the Chamber of Deputies.

Naturally, the dissolution enraged the ultra royalists, and it remained a sore point for the remainder of the Restoration, even after 1830. It became a symbol of a monarchy and a king afraid to be royal. It also became a significant piece of evidence for the ultras who were convinced that revolutionaries secretly controlled the government. Chateaubriand strongly voiced those sentiments in his memoirs: "The Chamber of Deputies has been dissolved. It does not surprise me: the revolutionaries are prospering. I foresaw that this would happen and I proclaimed it many times. People say that this ministerial measure will save the legitimate monarchy. Dissolving the only assembly since 1789 that has displayed only the purest of royalist sentiments is, to my mind, a strange way of saving the monarchy."[24]

It is important to note that Louis XVIII and his ministers did not see the dissolution as a mistake – quite the contrary. Elections to replace the *Chambre introuvable* were set for the summer of 1816 and the electoral law was amended again in the ongoing attempt to establish a permanent moderate royalist majority in the Chamber. Age requirements were raised to thirty for voters and forty for candidates. By royal ordinance dated 21 July, prefects were authorized to add twenty voters to their department colleges and ten to their arrondissement colleges. Naturally, prefects appointed men loyal to ministerial candidates.[25] In reaction to those changes and to the dissolution, ultra-royalist voters boycotted the elections. In a few instances their abstention meant that electoral colleges did not have a legal quorum, and some seats in the 1816 Chamber went vacant. Ultimately, however, the government's tactics proved effective, and while royalists continued to dominate, only 92 deputies were committed ultras, as compared to 146 moderates or ministerials. In a speech to the Chamber of Deputies, Louis XVIII stated that he would not tolerate another *Chambre introuvable*, and he instructed the deputies to "check any manifestations of exaggerated zeal."

This success perhaps served to justify the manipulation of the electoral law, at least in the minds of Louis XVIII's ministers. A more accurate assessment would be that the most important factors in the 1816 election were royalist apathy and the government's suppression of ultra-royalist intimidation. As a former member of the National Assembly, Pison du Galland of Isère, expressed it: "Extremists had lost much of their former influence ... and ministerial candidates seemed assured of victory."[26] The higher age limits may have contributed, but it is difficult to determine if young voters would have voted for ultra candidates in 1816. The White Terror had subsided by that time, and so too had the passions that had fuelled ultra excesses. From a parliamentary perspective, the 1816 election can only be viewed negatively, for, rather than fostering a trustworthy and open system, the government's amendments to the electoral law established a principle of manipulating the law to ensure a desired electoral result. That principle was reinforced by the 1816 Chamber's first order of business – yet another amendment to the electoral law. This next amendment proposed replacing the indirect system with direct voting and a single electoral college for each department. All men thirty years and older who met the 300-franc *cens* would gather in the department capital to vote in deputy elections, and as before, annual elections would renew one-fifth of the Chamber. On 5 February 1817, the amendment was proclaimed law after being quickly passed in both chambers by a comfortable margin.[27] It became known by its date, and over the next three years, royalists and liberals clashed repeatedly over the wisdom of the February 5th Law.

This time royalists and liberals agreed on one thing: the February 5th Law helped liberal candidates. (The accuracy of that assumption will be tested shortly.) First, it must be noted that in 1816 ministers and moderate royalists were concerned primarily with ultra-royalist extremism. The February 5th Law was hailed as a major step in the fight against the reactionary forces that had characterized the *Chambre introuvable*. Count Molé, a key moderate royalist figure and a powerful political advisor to Louis XVIII during the Restoration, wrote that the law brought closure to France's revolutionary past. In Molé's view, it "put an end to the Revolution by filling, at least partially, the void which its ravages left in our way of life."[28] Ultra royalists who argued against the law suggested that it smelled of democracy, Revolution-style, and therefore invited the horrors of the past once again. In 1817 such arguments were dismissed as typical reactionary rhetoric. Molé responded that even with direct elections, the *cens* ensured that the franchise was limited to a select few: "Are not the 100,000 men who pay the highest taxes still forced to choose deputies from among those who pay a thousand francs in taxes, that is, the 18,000 richest citizens of them all, out of a nation of 26 million?"[29] In the Chamber, Royer-Collard, the leading spokesperson for the moderate liberals, ridiculed the ultra royalists for even suggesting that the February 5th Law was in any way democratic. "The *cens*," he said, "made such talk absurd."[30] Three years later, moderate royalists changed their attitude, however, and joined the ultra deputies in arguing that the double vote was necessary to counteract the dangerously democratic February 5th Law.

The polemic regarding the February 5th Law was fuelled primarily by a single assumption: royalist voters were landowners, and liberal voters were bourgeois businessmen with much smaller landholdings. If that assumption was correct, and since the largest component of the *cens* was the property tax, then liberal voters would clearly never be among the most heavily taxed men in a department. Direct voting in a single college would therefore favour the liberals because it pooled the more plentiful, low-*cens* liberal voters with the less numerous, high-*cens* paying royalist voters. In contemporary terms, the *petits et moyens propriétaires* would overwhelm the *grands propriétaires*.

As soon as the February 5th Law passed, ultra royalists began to fear that the liberals would soon control the Chamber. Results from renewal elections in 1817, 1818, and 1819 suggested that they were right. Liberal candidates captured a majority of seats in each election, although the impressive liberal gains were tempered by the fact that only one-fifth, around seventy seats, were up for election in any given year. In 1819, thirty-five seats went to liberal candidates, fifteen to ministerial candidates and only ten to the ultras.[31] Liberals attributed these wins to a popular backlash against royalist excesses during the White Terror and the period of the *Chambre introuvable*. Royalists believed that their supporters, particularly the ultras, simply had not voted, alienated as they had been by the dissolution and the February 5th Law. They also complained that holding elections in department capitals had discouraged royalists from voting, as most of them presumably lived in the country.[32] Town-dwelling liberal voters therefore had an unfair advantage. By 1820 most royalists had determined that the February 5th Law needed to be amended in order to prevent a liberal-dominated Chamber of Deputies.

Thomas Beck's statistical analysis of Restoration elections suggests that royalists were correct in their assumption that their supporters were not voting. Only 30 percent of the electorate had bothered to cast ballots. Significantly, though, when turnout was high, royalist candidates won their seats; they were most often elected in colleges where over three-quarters of the electorate voted. Liberal candidates, on the other hand, were most successful when less than half the electorate voted. In addition, royalist deputies tended to win by larger margins than their liberal counterparts. Fifty-eight percent of the royalist deputies elected between 1817 and 1820 received over 56 percent of the votes in their electoral colleges, while only 29 percent of liberal deputies enjoyed similar support. In fact, in the three renewal elections prior to the assassination, a mere 8 percent of liberal candidates won 75 percent of the votes in their respective colleges. Clearly, liberal electoral successes did not represent an increase in popular support for liberal policies, but rather an apathetic or perhaps alienated royalist electorate. As will be shown in the discussion of the November, 1820 deputy election in chapter 8, Berry's assassination and Bordeaux's birth ended royalist apathy at the polls and culminated in a royalist landslide.

The argument that higher numbers of liberal voters lived in urban centres – and therefore biased elections in department capitals toward liberal candidates – may have some validity; however, more work is needed to reach a definitive evaluation. Regardless, if royalist voters had turned out in sufficient numbers, the urban/rural issue would be moot. Significantly, royalists took no responsibility for their low voting levels. Instead of encouraging voter turnout, they blamed the February 5th Law, vilifying it as the most glaring manifestation of a monarchy infiltrated and dominated by republicans.

2 Conspiracy: Who Killed the Duke of Berry?

Royalist antipathy to the February 5th Law soon took on a more personal tone. It was directed at one man, Elie Decazes, Louis XVIII's closest friend and president of the *Conseil*. As the most powerful politician in France, he seemed assured of a spectacular future. His meteoric rise to power was rarely attributed to his genius, however; his critics interpreted his success as proof of a left-wing conspiracy, of which he was the leader. In royalist circles, Decazes had acquired the reputation of liberal conspirator *par excellence*: royalist by day, pretending a deep affection for the king; revolutionary by night, organizing a network of secret societies, labouring to undermine the Bourbon regime, a pathetic caricature of his hero, Napoleon.

It is tempting to dismiss Decazes as an opportunist doomed to political extinction once his luck had run out. Certainly, his career was based upon his relationship with Louis XVIII, who referred to the younger man as his son. The king had an almost pathological need for a confidant, and Decazes enjoyed his complete confidence. At the same time, Decazes cannot be dismissed as a mere sycophant and a political nonentity. He directed a bold, albeit unsuccessful, attempt to co-opt moderate liberals into the royalist fold, a campaign that revealed him as a man with real convictions and a more than elementary understanding of the workings of French politics. He seems to have truly believed in the viability of the *union et oubli* policy. His self-interest and ambition could not be considered uncommon traits in a politician; nor is it rare for politicians to take advantage of personal connections to obtain prestigious and lucrative offices. Decazes undoubtedly suffered from comparisons to his predecessor, the Duke of Richelieu, who had an unblemished reputation for honesty and integrity. Richelieu resisted power, while Decazes hungered for it. A falling out between the two in 1817–18 contributed to the defeat of Richelieu's first ministry, opening the way for Decazes to become president of the *Conseil* in 1819. It will be argued below that Decazes should not be characterized by his weaknesses, in particular his inability to cultivate loyalty to himself among members of the *cens* community; his downfall was due, rather, to the royalists determination to characterize him as a revolutionary conspirator.

Decazes had irritated the ultra royalists almost as soon as the Restoration began. During the First Restoration, he worked closely with the notorious Joseph Fouché, the former deputy in the National Convention who voted for Louis XVI's death in 1792, and then became Napoleon's minister of police. During the White Terror that followed the Hundred Days, Decazes, as minister of police, angered members of the *Chambre introuvable* by refusing to prosecute known Bonapartists and liberals. They later laid blame for the dissolution on him, even though Richelieu and François Guizot played equally important if not more decisive roles.[1] It did not help matters when, in 1817, he threw his support behind the February 5th Law. In the following year he endorsed Saint-Cyr's recruitment law, a measure that prohibited members of the nobility from entering the officer class directly. Equally annoying to the ultras was the replacement system, which permitted individuals to purchase exemption from military duty. Ultra royalists felt that this system made it too easy for the bourgeois class, that is, liberals, to avoid military service.

Decazes's political influence increased tremendously after Richelieu resigned in December, 1818. However, he would have been wise to learn from Richelieu's mistakes. The duke had ignored the fact that, while the ultras' extremism made them difficult to deal with, they enjoyed significant popular support from the *cens* community and from France's political community in general. Richelieu was also hurt by divisions in the *Conseil*, which left him without a solid base of ministerial support. When Louis XVIII was pressured to replace his first minister, notably by the Count of Artois, Richelieu was forced to resign. Decazes duplicated Richelieu's error, making little or no effort to appease the ultra royalists, and failing to surround himself with ministers loyal to him personally.

General Dessoles initially replaced Richelieu formally as president of the *Conseil*, but Decazes took over the key post of minister of the interior and led the *Conseil* in all but name. In November, 1819, Dessoles resigned and Decazes became president. At the age of thirty-nine, Elie Decazes was France's highest-ranking politician. The Dessoles and Decazes ministries have been called the Liberal Experiment because they departed from the Richelieu ministry's practice of cultivating support from moderate royalists. Decazes hoped instead to strengthen the government's base of popular support by co-opting the moderate left. This strategy relied implicitly on the assumption that he personally could continue to count on moderate royalist support. In effect, Decazes hoped to liberalize the royalists, thereby creating a new royalism that would facilitate a political compromise between the two groups, a strategy described as an attempt to "royalize the nation and nationalize the royalists."[2] As will be seen, his strategy proved ineffective, and what ultimately unified the nation was Berry's assassination and the birth of the miracle child.

Upon taking over the *Conseil*, Decazes's most pressing challenge was to prove to the political community at large that he was trustworthy. The ultra royalists hated him. The moderate royalists remained suspicious, but were somewhat more accepting (although the speed with which they abandoned him after the assassination suggests that their acceptance really had been lukewarm at best). Even the liberals, who had the most to gain from Decazes's strategy, remained unconvinced from the start that he had their best interests at heart. They resented his status as the king's favourite, a role that reminded them of Old Regime politics. They also mistrusted his motives, even fearing a Napoleonic-style coup. Following his appointment as *Conseil* president, *La Minerve* published an article that criticized the state of French politics because it allowed individuals to become too powerful: "The time has passed when the destiny of France was tied to one man; that man has fallen and France is still standing. The favourite who wanted to be, as minister, what Bonaparte was as emperor will fall in his turn. However, the fall of the copy, or rather of the caricature, will not make as much noise as that of the original."[3]

Decazes showed a remarkable lack of foresight in replacing sixteen prefects and forty subprefects immediately upon becoming minister of the interior, thereby fuelling speculation that he was interested primarily in self-aggrandizement. He also purged the *Conseil* of all ultra ministers. A number of *émigré* officers were placed on the inactive list, and some command posts were given to former Napoleonic generals such as General Foy, who had been compromised by the Hundred Days. Decazes even authorized the return of fifty-two regicides and other Bonapartists exiled in 1815.

On 20 February 1819, Barthélemy, a leading ultra-royalist peer, submitted a resolution to the Chamber calling on Louis XVIII to introduce a law that would reorganize the electoral colleges in whatever manner "seemed necessary" in the circumstances. The resolution was clearly a call to amend the February 5th law to prevent liberals from winning more seats in the Chamber of Deputies. On 2 March, the peers passed the resolution by a wide margin, ninety-eight to fifty-five. Although the proposal died in the Chamber of Deputies, Decazes took it as a personal affront. The peers voiced their displeasure with the government's reaction to their resolution by rejecting a finance bill a few days later. The first minister decided the Chamber of Peers was beginning to resemble the *Chambre introuvable*. He was able to convince Louis XVIII that the peers represented a serious obstacle to the success of their political strategy, and, with the King's approval, he wasted little time in putting that chamber more firmly under his control. The Charter did not allow the king to dissolve the Chamber of Peers; however, he could appoint new members. On 4 March 1819, in a decision dubbed the "*Fournée*," fifty-nine new peers, mostly Decazes's friends, were appointed by royal decree. Decazes now had a comfortable majority in the upper chamber, and would no longer be bothered with agitation by the ultras from that quarter.

The *Fournée* effectively ended opposition from the Chamber of Peers by following the by now established method of dealing with an uncooperative legislative body: change the law. The government had raised and lowered the age and financial requirements for deputy elections, and similarly felt no compunction about adding new peers. In this context, the *Fournée* illustrates a mentality shared by all political groups of that period, a mentality that colours the entire political history of Restoration: a refusal to accept the existence of a viable opposition. During that period, France's political community never came to terms with the ramifications of allowing free speech, either in the press or in the political arena. In 1819 the *Conseil* legislated peer opposition out of existence. During the Royalist Reaction, this time under Richelieu's direction, the *Conseil* legislated the liberal opposition out of existence. The problem was that it was impossible to know if the liberal opposition was truly the most dangerous opponent of the government. In the case at hand, the real danger lay elsewhere. The Bourbon regime's attempt to silence political opposition prior to and during the Royalist Reaction was analogous to firefighters' efforts to douse a small brush fire in one part of the forest while ignoring a much larger fire elsewhere. The second Richelieu ministry extinguished the liberal fire with the exceptional laws, but allowed the ultra-royalist fire to burn out of control. In the end, that fire consumed the moderate royalists.

A new press law was passed by both chambers in the same month as the *Fournée*. The law, which essentially ended censorship, was championed by the Count of Serre and supported by Decazes. As with the February 5th Law, it did not attract much attention at first. Publishers no longer needed to obtain government authorization to print periodicals or newspapers; their only obligation was a small *caution* or deposit. This liberalization of the press was intended to regularize political relations, and demonstrate to the nation that Louis XVIII welcomed all reasonable expressions of public opinion. Decazes hoped the Liberal Experiment would counteract liberal charges that the Bourbon regime could not restrain its absolutist tendencies; a free press reflected the spirit of 1789 and the Declaration of the Rights of Man, and would thereby go a long way to building a relationship with the liberals.

The immediate effect of the 1819 press law was unanticipated. As Parisian and provincial newspapers proliferated, a virtual tidal wave of words swept across France. To the detriment of the Dessoles-Decazes ministries, newspapers with an extremist orientation proved the most popular. On the right appeared *Le Drapeau Blanc*, *Le Conservateur*, *La Gazette*, and the *Journal des Débats*, and on the left, *Le Constitutionnel*, *Le Moniteur*, *La Rénommée*, *La Minerve*, and *Le Censeur Européen*. Famous literary figures such as Chateaubriand, Lamennais, Fiévée, Constant, Argenson, Cousin, Bonald, and Etienne were contributors to – and often partial owners of – these newspapers. A vigorous trade in semi-periodic journals and pamphlets also developed. Generalizations are hazardous in the face of such a mass of publications, but one thing is evident: moderation was the exception, not the rule. Not only did royalists and liberals attack each other mercilessly but they both criticized Decazes's every move. Some of the most violent polemic the French public would ever read was published in the year preceding the assassination. Rather than building relationships as hoped, the 1819 press law antagonized and radicalized political relations, contributing to the explosive environment that existed when Berry was killed.

Six months after the press law was put into effect, an issue arose that allowed royalist and liberal journalists and pamphleteers free expression of their polarized views: Abbé Grégoire's candidacy for deputy of Isère in the September, 1819 deputy election. All four seats in Isère were up for renewal. Three candidates, Louis-Charles Sapey, Jacques Savoie-Rollin, and Français-de-Nantes,[4] all well-known liberals, were expected to win easily. Grégoire was a more controversial candidate – former bishop, revolutionary, member of the National Assembly, Napoleonic senator, longtime defender of the Jews, and spokesperson for the slavery abolition movement. At the heart of the controversy was the fact that Grégoire had cast a "guilty" vote at Louis XVI's trial, had accepted the Civil Constitution of the Clergy, and had held public office during the Terror. In strategic terms, his candidacy was awkward for the liberals. His past lent credibility to the perception that liberals were Jacobins masquerading under another name. However, a number of prominent liberals, including Lafayette, Berenger de la Drôme, Manuel, and General Foy, endorsed Grégoire, or at least they did not voice their disapproval publicly.

Grégoire was Decazes's worst nightmare. His candidacy – and worse yet his victory – discredited the Liberal Experiment because it associated his ministry with the radical Left.[5] The Grégoire affair also made the February 5th Law untenable in political terms. Since Decazes's strategy was having unintended consequences, with royalists and liberals at each others' throats and the government less popular than ever, the first minister decided to abandon the Liberal Experiment in favour of Richelieu's earlier strategy of ruling through the moderate royalists without recourse to either the ultra royalists or the liberals.

After a long meeting of the *Conseil* on 18 November 1819, Decazes convinced Louis XVIII to support this new direction. The first step was to amend the February 5th Law. Significantly, Decazes envisioned a new law that resembled the Barthélemy resolution, which had infuriated him earlier that year and had led to the *Fournée*. Left-wing *Conseil* members, Dessoles, the president, Saint-Cyr, and Baron Louis, resigned in protest. They were succeeded by moderate royalists, Pasquier in Foreign Affairs, Roy in finance, and the Count of Latour-Maubourg in the war department. Decazes officially became president of the *Conseil*.

Decazes trusted that these personnel changes, in conjunction with the announcement that the February 5th Law was under review, would mollify his numerous critics and win back the support of the moderate right. He was mistaken; his actions served only to further alienate liberals and royalists. The former were well aware that their collective political futures were threatened. They were particularly sensitive to any amendment of the February 5th Law, which they considered essential to maintaining a liberal presence in the Chamber of Deputies. Royalists remained silent, highly suspicious of Decazes's motives. Even the ultra royalists, who should have been pleased, expressed their displeasure. In *Le Conservateur*, Fiévée, a leading ultra journalist, articulated his faction's position in the following terms: "Under the old system the royalists were persecuted, the Jacobins were obeyed, and the monarchy was lost. Under the new system, the royalists will be persecuted, monarchist aims will be announced, but the Jacobins will be flattered while people claim they are being defied."[6]

Abandoned by both left and right, Decazes had few remaining friends when Louvel assassinated Berry. Even his relationship with Louis XVIII was not strong enough to withstand the forces that turned on him. Less than a week after the assassination, Louis XVIII accepted Decazes's resignation. To soften the blow, the king made him ambassador to England, with an annual salary of 300,000 francs. The astute Count Molé summed up the effect of the assassination on Decazes as follows: "The assassination of the Duke of Berry caused the storm that was hanging over him to break ... he was a victim of an unjust accusation and of the hatred he had aroused."[7] The editors of *La Minerve* accepted the inevitability of Decazes's resignation after Berry's death, but nevertheless denounced what they considered were slanderous attacks on the part of the ultras. Etienne wrote that Decazes's greatest error was to have thought he could collaborate with the ultra royalists after the passage of the February 5th Law. He characterized Decazes as a man too young and inexperienced to handle the burden of being first minister:

He was one who had too much self-satisfaction to gain enough experience; who often had good intentions and more often listened to bad advice; who, still too young for the difficult position he had attained, committed the very serious fault of surrounding himself with men who were even younger and less prudent ... who sometimes mistook guile for genius, lack of sincerity for profundity; who had too low an opinion of men because he judged them all according to his flatterers and his enemies at court; who knew neither how to appreciate his position nor how to understand representative government, nor how to judge the condition of France; but, if he did not do the good that he might have done, he at least prevented much evil.[8]

On 26 February, Decazes set sail for England, the first political casualty of the Royalist Reaction.

THE BERRY CONSPIRACY: "DECAZES IS THE ASSASSIN"

I intend ... to accuse the Duke of Decazes ... of aiding, by criminal neglect of his principal duties, the assassination which cost the life of His Royal Highness, the Duke of Berry, grandson of the King.

Those words, delivered by Clausel de Coussergues in the Chamber of Deputies on 15 February 1820, created the Berry Conspiracy. The principal allegation was that Louvel was not solely responsible for Berry's death; an extensive liberal conspiratorial network dedicated to destroying the Bourbon regime, a network that extended into both chambers, into the *Conseil*, and across Europe, was also to blame. In musing about the assassination some years later, Charles de Rémusat wrote that it was simply impossible to convince royalists that Louvel had acted alone, despite all the evidence to that effect.[9] The Berry Conspiracy became entrenched in the royalists' collective consciousness, and the notion that a permanent liberal conspiracy was constantly planning intricate revolutionary plots became a fixture in the general lexicon of Restoration royalism.

Rémusat recognized the immediate and profound attachment that royalists felt for the notion of a conspiracy. However, he assumed incorrectly that their allegations of conspiracy were based upon fear and paranoia. He also conveniently ignored the fact that liberals alleged a number of conspiracies of their own. Finally, many liberals also accepted the assumption that a Berry Conspiracy existed, although the liberal version suggested that the Royalist Reaction was a royalist plot to destroy them. With the advantage of hindsight, it seems clear that neither group's suspicion of the Berry Conspiracy was well founded; it was, rather, the product of a historical development that had been centuries in the making. The Berry Conspiracy was a testimony to a mentality, a state of mind that affected Restoration politics in general and had an enormous influence on the outcome of the Royalist Reaction. That mentality made conspiracy theories a legitimate means of explaining historical events. It was often the explanation of first resort not only for fringe radicals but for the political mainstream as well. It was this conspiracy mentality that made the Berry Conspiracy possible. It led royalists to believe in a conspiracy without evidence, fuelling fears that the Bourbon regime faced an imminent *coup* from revolutionaries and justifying the government's drastic actions after Berry's death. It led liberals to believe that the royalists were intent on reviving the Old Regime, a belief that in turn provided the justification for their extralegal and violent attempts to gain political power over the course of the next decade.

Coussergues withdrew his original accusation of Decazes when liberal deputies demanded firm proof; and some of his fellow ultra royalists complained that he had acted imprudently. On 12 August, however, Coussergues formally submitted his accusation against Decazes to the Chamber of Deputies. He charged Decazes, as minister of the interior and president of the *Conseil*, with failure to adequately protect Berry, claiming that his deliberate negligence represented positive evidence of his guilt. Coussergues did not limit himself to specific allegations of negligence. He also accused Decazes of leading a Europe-wide secret society that abetted the distribution of seditious works throughout France, works that warped the minds and souls of Frenchmen and incited Louvel to commit a horrible crime. Some ultra deputies were quick to support Coussergues. M. de Sailly, for example, declared unequivocally that Decazes was guilty of assassinating Berry: "I am speaking out in public: Decazes is the assassin. I denounce him to the entire French nation, as do the *Drapeau Blanc* and Monsieur de Coussergues. Yes, he is working for Napoleon's son, and his aim is to get rid of the two princes, whether by sword or poison, and when everything is ready, Louis XVIII will join his brother and his nephew."[10]

A review of memoirs written by prominent ultra royalists from the period illustrates the longevity of the royalist version of the Berry Conspiracy. It survived the July Revolution and became a key feature of the legitimist movement that followed. The Duchesse de Maillé, wife of a prominent royalist peer,[11] wrote in her memoirs that the foolishness of Coussergues's accusation aside, and despite the absence of evidence, she remained convinced that a liberal conspiracy headed by prominent government officials and deputies had planned Berry's murder. She even suggested that the officials investigating the assassination[12] were members of the same conspiracy, so it was not surprising that the true culprits were never found. Their "*grand zèle*" in her mind simply confirmed the fact.[13] Rochefoucauld, a peer and one of the most vocal ultras in that chamber, included in his memoirs a letter he had written to Artois only two days after the assassination warning Monsieur that his son's murder was merely the first step in a much broader and more violent plot to end the Bourbon Restoration. The conspirators, or the "faction" as he referred to them, would not stop with the death of the heir to the throne: "The evil faction that dreams of committing similar crimes is not yet satisfied, and the thirst for blood is not yet quenched."[14] In his memoirs, written in exile more than seventeen years after Berry's death, Baron Frénilly interpreted claims that Louvel had acted alone as further proof of a liberal cover-up. Those claims, he wrote, became the liberals' *mot d'ordre*, but in fact they merely proved their guilt. He bemoaned the fact that the true culprits were never identified, so that while "the agent who had committed the crime perished as a solitary malefactor ... the arm that had guided him remained hidden in the darkness, and apart from Decazes, everything remained in the same track. The victim's blood had been spilled in vain."[15]

Coussergues's accusation and the memoirs cited above are evidence of what many royalists had believed even before the assassination: liberalism equalled Jacobinism, and France would continue to suffer from the threat of another revolution as long as the liberal movement existed. Slanderous and incendiary attacks against government officials and royalists by liberal journalists and deputies, seditious publications encouraging violent action, the dissolution of the *Chambre introuvable*, the February 5th Law, Grégoire's election, and lastly, Berry's assassination, together proved beyond a shadow of a doubt that liberals were conspiring, en masse, to overthrow the Bourbon regime and declare the second republic.

Liberals responded by accusing the royalists of using the assassination as a pretext to cover up their own conspiratorial intentions. This was a familiar theme for liberal apologists. In 1818 an anonymous pamphleteer charged the ultras with conspiring stealthily and with precision to take over the government. He called them the "eternal tyrants of human reason" and suggested they were primarily responsible for all the political turmoil in France: "Their insane resistance insults the king, offends the nation, and is becoming a major obstacle to re-establishing social order."[16] In 1820, after the assassination, the editors of *La Minerve* echoed those charges. They claimed that royalists were exploiting the criminal actions of a lone madman to "bury all French liberties in the coffin of the French prince."[17] Editors of the *Journal Libre de l'Isère*, a liberal newspaper, repeated that accusation, fearing that the liberties enshrined in the Charter would "end up in the same tomb as the fallen prince."[18] The Count of Ste-Aulaire, a liberal deputy and Decazes's father-in-law, published a pamphlet in 1820 defending the former first minister. He claimed Decazes was a victim of an ultra-royalist conspiracy led by former aristocrats and *émigrés* motivated solely by their selfish desire to regain their old privileges. "If France is not careful," warned Ste-Aulaire, "she may once again find herself controlled by a corrupt aristocracy, and the newly born liberties enjoyed by all French citizens will be destroyed."[19] In March 1820 Paulin Madier de Montjau, a judge at the royal court of Nîmes, sent a petition to the Chamber of Deputies asserting the existence of a secret occult government made up of ultras and refractory priests, which was working to end the peace and prosperity of protestants and liberals in his region.[20]

The government's official position was that Louvel had acted alone. Count Bastard, in his extensive report to the Chamber of Peers, filed on 15 May 1820, concluded that there was no credible evidence to support the contention that Louvel had accomplices. He added that a conspiracy to kill Berry was unlikely, given how poorly the crime had been planned, luck being the primary factor in its success. Furthermore, no one had helped Louvel escape, and neither his family nor his friends had suspected anything.[21] At the same time, Bastard placed some blame for the assassination on liberal writers and journalists. In his opinion, those intellectuals had cultivated an "esprit fanatique" by criticizing government policies and accusing government agents of tyrannical and selfish actions. Bastard charged them with planting the idea of the assassination in Louvel's impressionable mind: "Harmful writings have been published, and, although they have not directly caused the murder ... it cannot be denied that hateful insinuations flowing from the pen of a careless or guilty writer may, like so many poisoned seeds, take deep root in a perverted or unbalanced mind, feed on dark obsessions, and finally bear deadly fruit."[22]

The mentality that helped create and shape the Berry Conspiracy was in turn created and shaped by two historical factors. The first related to the character of other Restoration conspiracies and the political culture that those conspiracies spawned. That culture made the Berry Conspiracy credible and explains why well-educated, intelligent, and sophisticated individuals could entertain a conspiracy theory about Berry's death. The second, which operated at a more fundamental and historical level, is rooted in the emergence of a nineteenth-century brand of conspiracy theory, a process that began in the rhetoric of the Counter-Reformation and was shaped by conspiracy theories of the French Revolution.

RESTORATION CONSPIRACY: BLUEPRINT FOR FAILURE

Political developments outside France contributed substantially to the belief that secret forces were controlling the course of human affairs. In 1817 German students met at the Wartburg Festival and burned papers inscribed with the titles of absolutist writings. They then formed an association called the *Réunion de la Wartburg*, which fourteen university professors also joined in May, 1818. On 23 March 1819 August von Kotzebue, a German dramatist and staunch royalist who had criticized the liberal movement, was assassinated at Mannheim by a student, Karl Ludwig Sand.[23] Unrest continued in 1819. The Frankfurt Diet in August passed a decree stating that only ancient assemblies were legitimate forums for political power. Riego's uprising at Cadiz had forced Ferdinand VI to accept the Cortes Constitution of 1812. South America was beset by armed conflict, as native forces fought against and eventually expelled their colonial rulers. In the spring of 1820 Spanish rebels overthrew their king, Ferdinand VII, a Bourbon himself, and liberal-inspired rebellions broke out in Naples and Sicily in June. By March, 1821, a republic had been declared in Spain, the Kingdom of Piedmont was in turmoil, and political unrest threatened the Portuguese and Greek monarchies.

The liberals, for their part, had good reason to fear the royalists. The Congress of Vienna had established a treaty system that, in theory at least, required the European nations to intervene militarily if a monarchy was threatened by a coup d'état or a revolution. That system proved effective in 1823 when French troops, led by the Duke of Angoulême, marched to Spain to end the Spanish Republic and restore Ferdinand VII to the throne. In September, 1819, at Metternich's behest, and in response to Kotzebue's murder and the student movement, the German princes issued the Karlsbad Decrees, which called for renewed press censorship and a united royalist response to the perceived growing revolutionary movement. On an even grander scale, Russia, Austria, and Prussia formed the Holy Alliance, an arrangement intended to preserve European monarchies under the guise of protecting Christianity.

Conspiracy theories and secret societies were nothing new to France. The practice of explaining historical events by pointing to hidden forces dated at least as far back as the sixteenth century. However, the Restoration era is notable for its proliferation of secret societies dedicated to overthrowing the Bourbon regime. Although conspiracies planned by such societies all failed, the existence of their plots and the publicity that surrounded the trials of alleged conspirators had significant repercussions. For one thing, the plots created an aura of instability around the Restoration. The very existence of conspiracies legitimized the conspiracy mentality, bringing it into the mainstream of Restoration politics, a development that prevented the "minimum consensus necessary for the stable existence of the [Bourbon] Monarchy."[24] Joseph Rey, a noted conspirator himself, called the years immediately before and after Berry's assassination the Age of Conspiracy. Rey expressed his surprise at the rapidity with which secret societies sprang up all over France and abroad, providing ever new recruits for the "European liberal army."[25]

Politically active men joined secret societies as a matter of course. Conspiracy was in vogue at the time, and it may be said that Restoration secret societies played as strong a social as a political role in a member's life. But Restoration conspirators had little stomach for real action. Late-night meetings at cafés and secret handshakes were their preferred activities, and when decisive and dangerous action was needed, the conspirators, notably the leaders, backed down almost every time. In hindsight it is easy to dismiss the significance of Restoration conspiracies, for few had the slightest chance of success. Even the more serious and extensive Carbonari movement of 1822–23 amounted to very little. Yet, these conspiracies were quite real to contemporaries. The police pursued all leads with a vengeance, particularly after the Berry assassination. Previously tolerated behaviour, such as singing Bonapartist songs or chanting "Long Live the Charter," was suddenly treated as a seditious act. On 22 January 1821, Claude Mounier,[26] the director general of police in Richelieu's second ministry, wrote: "Various symptoms lead us to believe that the revolutionary faction is preparing something. Perfect unity and extremely active communications exist among the liberals of Paris, Madrid, Naples, Lisbon, Turin, and London."[27]

According to one widely bruited theory, a *comité directeur*, or executive committee, made up of leading liberal figures was directing a vast revolutionary conspiracy. This belief was so pervasive that in 1822 the government set aside some 700,000 francs to determine the committee's membership. It appears now that there was no such formal body; however, at the time its existence was accepted as fact.[28] The liberal historian Achille de Vaulabelle wrote in the 1840s that a *comité directeur* had existed in 1820 made up of former members of the *Societé des amis de la liberté de la presse* who had refused to follow government orders to dissolve the society in 1819. Although Vaulabelle did not go as far as to claim that this *comité* controlled all liberal activities, he said it encouraged and provoked them. The list of names he associated with it reads like a who's-who of Restoration liberalism: Lafayette, Voyer d'Argenson, Manuel, Dupont (de l'Eure), Mérilhou, Corcelles, Beauséjour, General Tarayre, and Joseph Rey.[29] Rey, for his part, not only denied belonging to any *comité* but denied the existence of any such body.[30] Rey's penchant for exaggerating his own importance – and his willingness to confess his own conspiratorial actions in his memoirs – suggests that his denial is credible. More significant in this regard is Rey's declaration that a real *comité directeur* had been constituted by ultra royalists, the group, directly responsible for the atrocities of the White Terror.[31] Again, a pattern is discernible. Royalists allege a liberal conspiracy; liberals deny any such possibility, but in turn allege an ultra-royalist conspiracy.

It is not suggested that the conspiracy mentality was merely a product of political ill-will, paranoia, or imagination. Secret societies existed, and they did plot the overthrow of the Bourbon regime. The previous twenty-five years had left little doubt that governments could be toppled. The 18th of Brumaire was a relatively recent memory in France's political community of 1820; its members were still products of the revolutionary era, a period of political uncertainly, unpredictability, and above all, instability. The very real possibility of a successful coup contributed to a mentality that not only saw conspiracy behind every closed door but, on a more historically significant level, accepted conspiracy theories as a legitimate means of explaining current events. In short, the presence of secret societies in the Restoration period suggests that those who clung to and promoted the Berry Conspiracy were not as irrational or paranoid as they might appear to us today.

Conspiracies are always difficult to prove. For instance, can one describe as a conspiracy a group of dissenters, perhaps deadly earnest in their intentions, but who have no means of acting because they lack the most basic resources needed to carry out their plans? The police often

fabricated conspiracies to provide a pretext for arresting suspected political agitators or to illustrate to the general public that the government was in control. Certainly, most political "conspiracies" never
went beyond words exchanged in a darkened café. Yet, we do know
about a number of authentic conspiracies, and by studying them can
construct a classical model for Restoration conspiracies. This is a necessary first step to understanding the historical context of the Berry
Conspiracy. At the same time, the Berry Conspiracy diverged from this
model, reflecting a new brand of conspiracy that emerged in the
nineteenth century.

The Classic Model: The Garrison, then Paris

All conspiracies have certain common traits. A group of individuals
gather in secret to effect a given political outcome, usually the overthrow of an existing government. They are united by an ideology or
philosophy, however half-baked or unintelligible, and by a list of grievances – real or imaginary – that justify their plot. They attempt to raise
money and recruit members. Restoration conspiracies were characterized by two additional attributes: a military focus and elitism. Virtually
every plot to overthrow the Bourbon regime involved the capture of an
army garrison to be followed by a march on Paris. Once power was secured in the capital, the Bourbons would be expelled and a provisional
government declared, be it a republic, a Bonapartist regime, or a new
form of monarchy. During the Restoration, liberal conspirators attempted unsuccessfully to lead insurrections at garrisons in Grenoble,
Belfort, Saumur, Toulon, and La Rochelle. The La Rochelle insurrection deserves special mention because of the trial and execution of four
participants, known as the Four Sergeants. These men refused to reveal
the names of their leaders and were executed for their silence, becoming martyr symbols for future generations of French left-wing radicals.

Napoleon's escape from Elba nourished the belief that any coup, to
be successful, had to involve the army. At the time there was also a fear
that the *demi-soldes*, the thousands of ex-Imperial soldiers supposedly
in permanent mourning for their Emperor, were just waiting to join any
anti-Bourbon conspiracy. Jean Vidalenc's study of the *demi-soldes* has
shown this to be mere legend;[32] however, both liberals and royalists
believed it to be true. Royalists were of the opinion that the Hundred
Days had been essentially a military conspiracy and that the *demi-
soldes* represented the most serious security risk to the Second Restoration.[33] Conspiracy-minded liberals were also seduced by the *demi-
soldes* legend, and they concentrated their recruitment efforts on them
throughout the Restoration.

The assumption that no conspiracy could succeed without first taking over a military garrison points to the second attribute of Restoration conspiracies: they were elitist in character. Invariably, a small group of men planned to cure a social ill through violent action. Some popular elements existed, particularly in the Carbonari movement; however, conspiracy leaders belonged overwhelmingly to the elite class, some coming from the *cens* community itself, and the average recruit was either a student or a member of the middle class. Conspirators took it for granted that they acted in France's best interests. As a result, they gave little thought to what would happen after a garrison was taken over. They simply assumed that their heroics would signal the moment for a general insurrection. The complete absence of that reaction in every case suggests that the general population was either indifferent to or opposed to the overthrow of the Bourbon regime. In the end, conspirators' enthusiastic yet unthinking and mechanical adherence to this classical model of conspiracy doomed their efforts.

Modern scholarship has identified at least ten Restoration conspiracies between 1815 and 1823.[34] Certainly, many more were planned, some of which were real; but the majority were either imaginary or fabricated by police. Whether or not they actually existed, the political environment of suspicion made all conspiracies, no matter how far-fetched, seem real enough. One such conspiracy was called the Patriots of 1816. The prosecutor at the trial of the conspirators expressed wonder at how such a pathetic, pitiable group of men could possibly have concocted such a vast revolutionary enterprise. Significantly, the pathetic character of the conspirators led that same prosecutor to conclude that more important men must have masterminded the scheme. Royalists reached the same conclusion regarding the Berry Conspiracy, dismissing suggestions that a mere saddler could have conceived and carried out the assassination without accomplices.[35]

Not all conspiracies were so innocuous. The two most sensational, and real, Restoration conspiracies prior to 1821 were the Didier Affair of 1816 and the 20 August Plot of 1820. Although both followed the classical pattern of Restoration conspiracies, and failed in large part for that reason, they had a tremendous symbolic importance to contemporaries: they proved conspiracies existed and that conspirators were perfectly willing to use extreme violence.

On 4–5 May 1816, Jean-Paul Didier[36] led an armed band of soldiers and *officiers en demi-solde*, along with some peasants, on a march to Grenoble, planning to first overrun Grenoble's army garrison and then to continue on to Paris where they would declare Napoleon II emperor. Didier had been a lawyer in Grenoble before 1789, and had attended the 1788 Assembly of Vizille as a deputy. During the Restoration, he became a director at the Grenoble law school, but was relieved of that position for reasons of incompetence. On the eve of the rebellion, Didier issued a passionate proclamation calling on his fellow Frenchmen to rise up against the foreign occupation. "Who controls France?" Didier asked. "Lord Wellington is ruling over us! Are we his subjects?" The only solution was to fight "the infernal policies of the English" and bring Napoleon II back. History offered only one possibility: "To arms! To arms!"

Didier failed to take into account the character of Gabriel Donnadieu, the commander of the Seventh Military Division, stationed in Grenoble. Donnadieu had fought in the French army from 1792 to 1800 and had participated in the massacre of Vendean peasants. However, by 1800, Donnadieu had become an ardent royalist. He was twice arrested by Napoleon for conspiracy, but was released each time. Louis XVIII rewarded him after Waterloo by making him a division commander. In 1818 he was arrested in the so-called *bord de l'eau* conspiracy. On 30 June 1820, he was arrested again for slandering the Duke of Richelieu. (The July Revolution did not silence Donnadieu either. In 1837, he was sentenced to two years in prison and fined 5,000 francs for publishing a work deemed offensive to Louis-Philippe.)

The impulsive and ambitious Donnadieu saw the rebellion as a perfect opportunity to establish himself as a loyal defender of the throne, and ordered his troops to crush the rebels with the greatest brutality. Didier escaped to Savoie, but was soon hunted down and returned to Grenoble. A number of suspects were also rounded up. Donnadieu declared a state of siege and hastily convened a military tribunal to try Didier and his accomplices. Didier and twenty-three fellow rebels, one of whom was only sixteen-years old, were sentenced to death. A number of others, mostly well-known liberals, were arrested and exiled from Grenoble.[37] Donnadieu was granted the title of Viscount and given 100,000 francs for his defence of the crown.

The Didier Affair achieved a remarkable symbolic status with both royalists and liberals for the next fourteen years of the Restoration. Royalists equated Didier's name with liberal treachery and disloyalty, and trotted it out whenever they needed to justify a repressive measure against the liberal opposition. Liberals interpreted the willingness of army officers and government officials to summarily execute innocent French citizens as compelling evidence of the Bourbon regime's moral corruption and the tendency of monarchies to ignore the rule of law and drift toward absolutism and tyranny. In 1820 the Didier Affair was co-opted into the Royalist Reaction, as royalists and liberals used it to frame their respective interpretations of the exceptional laws and the Berry assassination. The families of those executed in 1818 tried to sue

Donnadieu for compensation, on the grounds that the general had acted improperly. Their allegations prompted a flurry of pamphlets from royalists charging that the liberals were conspiring to libel the ultra royalists through the lawsuit and shift attention away from what was a serious liberal conspiracy. Liberals naturally countered with their own pamphlets, and a national polemic ensued. In the context of the Royalist Reaction, the polemic over the Didier Affair in 1820 manifested the deep divisions between royalists and liberals that had become a permanent feature of Restoration politics, divisions that existed before Berry's assassination, but solidified and became entrenched only after his murder.

The 20 August Plot, so named for its intended start date, followed the classical pattern. A small cadre of army officers, soldiers, and other conspirators, led by General Lendru-des-Essarts, was to capture Grenoble's military garrison. Once it was secured, young militants standing at the ready in Paris would march on the garrison at Vincennes. The conspirators from Grenoble would then continue on to Paris, picking up support as they went, and join their fellow conspirators at Vincennes. A provisional government would be declared, with elections to follow. A few days before 20 August, however, government agents learned of the plot through an informer, and once the plot's leaders found their plans had been discovered, they called it off. On 20 August, Mounier published a report on the plot in the *Moniteur Universel*.

The 20 August Plot is noteworthy because of the number of powerful and famous names implicated in it, and for the importance that future liberal conspirators attributed to its failure. Joseph Rey, who along with two others was sentenced to death *in absentia* for his role in the Plot, alleged that several prominent liberals, including Lafayette and Bérenger de la Drôme, had agreed to head the provisional government. Victor Cousin was also said to have been an enthusiastic supporter; it was known that he had visited Grenoble in the summer of 1820, and a number of his students were compromised by the Plot. The high profile of the names associated with the 20 August Plot, and the uncontestable reality of the plot itself, did much to legitimize concerns about other conspiracies, notably the Berry Conspiracy that had begun to take shape a few months before, and also helped justify the exceptional laws. A perceived leniency for those arrested in connection to the plot, the three death sentences notwithstanding, led to royalist speculation that high-ranking liberal officials had conspired to allow the plot's leaders to escape entirely. Radical liberals, for their part, were pushed further underground, the Carbonari movement being the principal result. Again, we see a behaviour pattern that did not augur well for the Bourbon regime. Royalists evoked the existence of conspiracies to justify suppressing the liberal political movement at every turn, thereby naturally motivating the liberals to renew their conspiratorial efforts. Liberals seized upon the slightest sign of political persecution to justify their illegal and violent conspiracies, even if that perceived persecution was simply the government's effort to prevent the conspiracy from taking place and arrest its instigators. This vicious cycle of charges and counter-charges reflected the changed political climate in France after the Royalist Reaction. Regardless of what any group or institution did in response to a seditious act, the response was inevitably a new charge of conspiracy. The Restoration conspiracies that occurred before the Berry assassination contributed substantially to the imprinting of the conspiracy mentality across France's political landscape; and that mentality continued to exacerbate political relations for the remainder of the decade.

Elements of a Conspiracy Theory: The Enemy Beyond

We have seen how real and imaginary conspiracies to overthrow the Bourbon regime strengthened the conspiracy mentality that existed among members of France's political community. Clausel de Coussergues was not laughed out of the Chamber of Deputies. His accusation against Decazes was taken seriously because the deputies sitting in that chamber took conspiracies seriously. Newly alleged conspiracies were taken as fact with little or no direct evidence. Not that those alleging the conspiracy did not present evidence to back up their claims; proof seemed readily available. In addition to the actual conspiracies noted above, there was a proliferation of conspiracy theories. Theories lend satisfying clarity and certainty to seemingly incomprehensible historical events. In this instance, the existence of conspiracy theories legitimized new conspiracy theories, one stimulating the next.

The conspiracy theory that spawned the Berry Conspiracy had begun to take shape some two centuries before the assassination. An approach articulated by Geoffrey Cubitt offers a useful way to analyze this process.[38] Cubitt identified three elements common to all conspiracies that allow one to categorize and identify the historical roots of any particular conspiracy theory. These elements are called thematic, rhetorical, and structural. Thematic elements refer to the present circumstances or current events that give rise to a particular conspiracy theory. They speak to a conspiracy's uniqueness. The thematic elements of the Berry Conspiracy include the French Revolution, the Hundred Days, the circumstances of the crime, Louvel's background and character, and Berry's status as the last male Bourbon able to sire an heir.

The rhetorical and structural elements relate to the philosophical beliefs and historical events that shape and perpetuate a conspiracy theory. They provide the framework within which the thematic elements operate. Cubitt has identified two types of rhetorical styles: individual-centred conspiracies, which seek to identify a human network of conspirators; and plan-centred conspiracies, which identify a collective conspiratorial spirit rather than specific individuals. Neither style is mutually exclusive, and most nineteenth-century conspiracies, including the Berry Conspiracy, illustrate both. At the same time, differences exist and give rise to different forms of conspiracy.

The individual-centred style is more in line with the classic Restoration conspiracy such as the Didier Affair or the 20 August Plot. Powerful and often very public figures are accused of directing a conspiracy. Agents apprehended while carrying out the conspiracy are inevitably dismissed as minor players. The plan-centred style presents conspiracy as a sinister pattern of behaviour, without reference to specific individuals. It differentiates, for instance, between the actions of liberal figures during the Restoration and the collective effect of liberal principles. In the case of Louvel, it legitimized charges that his mind was poisoned by the publication of seditious materials, thereby dispensing with the need to find direct evidence of any accomplices. Plan-centred conspiracies are self-evidently less concrete than individual-centred ones because they relate to the conspiracy of ideas. That in turn makes them more frightening. A person can be arrested, tried, and executed, but what can be done to an evil spirit?

The third element, the structural, relates to the credibility of a conspiracy theory. It proposes parameters that define the legitimacy of any conspiracy. It explains why Masonic conspiracies were so popular in the beginning of the nineteenth century, and why anti-Semitic conspiracies became popular at the end of the century. In more recent terms, it explains allegations that the American Christian Right conspired to impeach U.S. President Clinton in 1998–99 through the Monica Lewinsky Affair. The Christian Right was extremely powerful and Clinton's declared adversary. Allegations that the Lewinsky Affair was a KGB plot would have fallen on deaf ears because the collapse of the Soviet Union had destroyed the credibility of KGB plots. A quarter-century earlier, the KGB would have presented a more credible target. Similarly, the Berry Conspiracy had a structure that made sense for its time, rooted as it was in the events of the Revolution and the nature and character of Restoration liberalism and royalism. The discussion of the relationship between Cubitt's three elements and the Berry Conspiracy will be continued in Part Two. Since the conspiracy took shape over the ten months of the Royalist Reaction, it is best considered in the context of Part Two's chronological approach.

French Conspiracy Theories: The Complex Made Simple

Additional background material will help interpret the aspects of the Berry Conspiracy that are best understood in historical terms. Unquestionably, the political circumstances surrounding the assassination in 1820 provided the specific content; however, the general character of the Berry Conspiracy was determined by certain developments that had begun hundreds of years earlier. Timothy Tackett has recently argued that before 1792 members of France's elite political community did not believe in conspiracy theories to any significant degree; if some did, their numbers were too small to consider it a tradition of any sort.[39] However, Tackett's position requires that we adopt a strict definition of conspiracy theory that includes only conspiracies with political objectives. An allegation that the Jesuits controlled Louis XV's royal court, for instance, would not fit into his analysis of French conspiracy theories. Certainly, it is readily accepted that the French Revolution, more than any previous historical event, legitimized conspiracy theories both for the elite political community and the general population. And this legitimization made the plan-centred conspiracy the principal conspiratorial style in Europe for the remainder of the nineteenth century. At the same time, it is going too far to suggest, as Tackett does, that politically motivated conspiracy theories *per se* did not exist prior to 1792, that they were not popular among France's elite political community, or that these pre-Revolution conspiracy theories had no relation to the conspiracy theories that followed the Revolution. In fact, the first stirrings of the Berry Conspiracy can be detected in the sixteenth and seventeenth century anti-Protestant discourse of the Counter-Reformation. Most of this discourse dealt with questions of heresy, but a significant number of Catholic apologists attempted to discredit the Reformation by accusing its leaders of sedition. Generally, Protestant conspiracies fell into the individual-centred style. Luther, Calvin, Zwingli, and their respective followers were demonized and charged with corrupting the souls of innocent Christians. Moreover, Protestant leaders were accused of hypocrisy, of hiding behind professions of religious faith in order to gain political power and monetary benefits. In short, the Reformation could be construed as nothing more than a petty political conspiracy.

Structural forces ensured that the Protestant Conspiracy in France focused on the royal court, for that was the most credible location for a political conspiracy. Politics was the preserve of the noble class, and a conspiracy involving lower-class individuals would have failed to attain the required threshold of credibility. Moreover, as absolutism was growing rapidly during the sixteenth and seventeenth centuries, it made sense that Catholic apologists would see conspiracy at the royal court, if anywhere. The most popular court conspiracy suggested that German intellectuals, who had gained access to the king under the guise of their literary achievements, were in reality working secretly to convert ministers and courtiers to their Protestant faith. By taking over the court, it was claimed, the Protestants would gain control of the state.

The anti-Protestant discourse provided a blueprint for the conspiracy theories that followed. The individual-centred style remained dominant; the enemy was the network of Protestant leaders. Yet, in the background lurked the suggestion that Protestant doctrine *per se* was the corrupting force. This speaks to the collective spirit of the plan-centred style. It must be kept in mind that this discourse was primarily religious, the fundamental issue was heresy, not politics. The goal of the Catholic apologists was to destroy the Protestant heresy, and political issues flowed from that goal, and not the other way around. At the same time, the existence of this collective spirit meant that a conspiracy had to be stopped on two fronts: the individual conspirators needed to be silenced along with the evil ideas that they propagated.

As the eighteenth century dawned, the focus of conspiracy theories shifted toward the political arena, although religion remained the central focus. That shift occurred within the context of the French Enlightenment, as the vocabulary of the anti-Protestant discourse was adopted by Bourbon absolutists to combat the next subversive threat: the *philosophes* and the Jansenists.[40] Absolutists did not have to look hard to find evidence of a *philosophe* conspiracy. The entire thrust of the Enlightenment was to question the rationale of the status quo, and if the men of the encyclopedia were not revolutionaries, their works were still dramatic and frightening to those whose status, fortunes, or faith depended upon the Old Regime. For the first half of the century, these apologists attacked individual *philosophes*, castigating them for being sinners and immoral persons. However, by mid-century, and increasingly as the Revolution approached, the *philosophes* were viewed as a collective entity. The absolutists had to worry not only about the great minds – the Voltaires, the Montesquieus, and the Rousseaus – but also about how the great minds were corrupting the millions of lesser, weaker, and more violent minds of their readers.

The titanic struggles between the Jansenists and the Bourbon absolutists in the eighteenth century are well documented. As became the norm in the next century, both groups accused the other of conspiracy.

Jansenists were convinced that Jesuits controlled the royal court and used their status as court confessors to direct French politics and destroy the Gallican Church. Obedient to Rome and loyal to the Pope, "the Jesuit was immorality incarnate and the unavowed accomplice of encyclopedic unbelief."[41] In 1757 the Jansenist magistrate Revol wrote that "the black cluster of [Jesuit] royal confessors" were conspiring with the devout "ministerial cabal" to persuade Louis XV that the *Parlements* were his enemies. Here we see the plan-centred conspiracy coming to the fore, as Revol added that certain elements at court "formed a systematic and studied plan to destroy the entire magistracy in France."[42]

The absolutist response was to treat Jansenism as another variety of Protestant heresy, and a case can indeed be made that Jansenism borrowed a great deal from the earlier Protestant reformers. That made it a relatively simple matter to impose the Counter-Reformation vocabulary onto the alleged Jansenist conspiracies of the eighteenth century. The Bourbon absolutists continued to persecute Jansenists right up to the Revolution, despite the fact that Jansenism as a political threat had probably reached its peak years earlier, in the 1720s and 1730s. Certainly, by 1770, Jansenism could no longer seriously challenge the monarchy. Yet, even though the threat itself had receded, the perception that it represented a serious seditious force did not fade.

We now come to the French Revolution. Timothy Tackett was correct in identifying Louis XVI's attempt to escape from France in June, 1791 – the famous flight to Varennes – as the most important catalyst to the remarkable popularity and proliferation of political conspiracy theories in France. For our purposes, it is sufficient to note that Tackett acknowledges that by the fall of 1791 the paranoid style or what he has here been called the conspiracy mentality,[43] had become widespread. Moreover, he found a difference between the styles of conspiracy suspected by deputies in the Constituent Assembly and in the Legislative Assembly. Conspiracies identified in the former tended to concern single plots or a "multiplicity of plots instigated by diffuse categories of perpetrators." Deputies in the latter, on the other hand, were increasingly preoccupied by grand conspiracy, the "monolithic master plan, directed from a single source."[44] By the time the Terror began, therefore, it would be fair to say that conspiracy theories involving religious issues had taken a back-seat to those with a political goal, and that the plan-centred style had achieved at least equal billing with the individual-centred style. Suspects were spotted everywhere, conspiring to overthrow the Republic and return the Bourbons to the throne. The alleged conspirators were not an elite group, but rather a more sinister body labelled "aristocrats." The aristocrats were not so much real people as symbols of corruption that had to be annihilated "for the good of the people," an equally vague term. The use of nebulous terms is characteristic of the conspiracy theories that became popular after the Revolution, for such language suited the plan-centred conspiracy, with its society-wide, open-ended character and its ideological underpinnings of abstract principles such as "the people," "the nation," or "democracy."

As heads rolled during the Terror, a Catholic priest in London was about to begin a work that greatly legitimized the use of conspiracy theories as a tool of historical analysis. In 1781 he had earlier alleged the existence of a permanent conspiracy to overthrow the Bourbon monarchy,[45] and the Terror naturally provided additional evidence. That priest was Augustin de Barruel, who in 1797–98 published *Mémoires pour servir à l'histoire du Jacobinisme*, a mammoth four-volume work that claimed the French Revolution had been started by a secret society. It was wildly popular and enjoyed a European audience. Barruel is rightly called the father of the modern conspiracy theory, for he was the first to put forward a body of documentary evidence to support his allegations. The presence of allegedly authentic documentary proof allowed Barruel to represent *Mémoires* as a scholarly work as opposed to a merely speculative endeavour. The most spectacular body of evidence came from documents regarding a German secret society called the Bavarian Illuminati and its founder, known as Weishaupt. Barruel also interviewed a number of alleged conspirators personally. His work was important because it managed to rationalize an extraordinarily complex event in relatively clear, simple terms, without oversimplifying so much as to strain credibility. The result was a complex conspiracy theory that made sense to his readers and had the capacity to demystify an increasingly complex world, as would later conspiracy theories that Barruel helped foster.

Barruel argued that the French Revolution had been planned and initiated by three separate groups: the philosophes, who encouraged anticlerical and anti-royalist sentiments; the Masons, who conspired against French Catholicism and the Bourbons; and anarchists, who conspired against all Christendom, all kings, and all royalist governments.[46] He condemned all three groups equally: "That coalition of the followers of impiety, rebellion, and anarchy made up the Jacobin Club; under this name, now common to the tripartite sect, the followers continued to weave their triple conspiracy against altar, throne and society."[47]

The Revolution provided the basis for the conspiracy theories that followed, but it did so in the tradition established in the Protestant and Philosophe conspiracies. For those on the right, again harking back to the anti-Protestant discourse, conspirators were characterized in moral terms – as evil entities who corrupted the innocent by exposing them to their satanic views. The labels changed over the years – Masons, Jacobins, Bonapartists, Liberals, Socialists, Communists, Jews, Dreyfusards. Structural factors determined the choice of label. During the Restoration, liberal agitation was seen as a sin against God and divine law. Liberals were stigmatized by the sins of the Revolution and categorized as inheritors of the conspiratorial torch passed from the reformers, to the philosophes, to the Jacobins, and finally to them. The royalist tendency to depict society in organic terms (as discussed in chapter 1) has relevance here also. The conspirators were analogous to germs that infected France's body politic, not only politically but religiously and psychologically as well. To stop the cycle of revolution that haunted France, the state had to eradicate the infection, just as Catholic apologists had advised their kings in the sixteenth and seventeenth centuries to rid their populace of the Protestant infection. The family metaphor, has play here as well.[48] Restoration conspiracies and seditious acts were interpreted both on a political and personal level. The overthrow of the Bourbon regime would be a political act, but it was potentially a violent action directed against the nation's father, the king, and the nation's parents and family, collectively the royal family. Liberal conspirators threatened that family, and the nation was obliged to react, at least in principle, as if their own families were under attack.

There was a fundamental difference between royalist and liberal conspiracy theories. The liberal version of the Berry Conspiracy insinuated that the ultra royalists were plotting to repeal the Charter, place Artois on the throne in lieu of Louis XVIII, by force if necessary, and reinstitute an absolutist regime, complete with aristocracy, the *dîme*, the *gabelle*, and *lettres de cachet*. The liberals dismissed the political controversy that followed Berry's murder as the ultras' attempt to cover their tracks. Note that while the alleged liberal conspirators who assassinated Berry were charged with moral crimes, the alleged ultra-royalist conspirators who conspired to take advantage of the assassination were accused of political crimes. The goal of the ultra royalists was power and money. They were not men of evil spirit who infected Christians with their heretical views; they were reactionaries who hoped to regain lost privileges. The liberals' inability to cast their conspiracy theory in similar religious and philosophical terms undoubtedly hurt the credibility of their Berry Conspiracy.

The royalist version of the Berry Conspiracy spoke to more profound fears, to the forces of Satan and God; it therefore resonated more intensely with France's political community and the general population. The royalists were also better able to tap into the trend toward the collective conspiracy. The classic court conspiracy made some sense in relation to the ultra royalists, but the time had passed for the individual-centred style. As the vast, hidden conspiracy of the collective-centred style was in vogue by 1820, royalist allegations that liberals were planning yet another revolution were, in structural terms, more suitable to the current trend in mainstream conspiracy theories. The Jesuit conspiracy theory that emerged during Charles X's reign fit that pattern. Charles X was seen as a member of that notorious order, an assumption that was interpreted as evidence that the Jesuits were the true power behind the *Conseil*. That in turn fuelled the anti-clerical backlash that Sheryl Kroen has identified as such an important contributing factor to the July Revolution.[49] It appears that people preferred democratic conspiracies over the aristocratic, which meant that the royalists' portrayal of the Berry Conspiracy achieved national prominence and wide-spread acceptance, while the liberals' version was generally ignored.

3 Politics

While it is true that to the victors go the spoils, the Allies realized, in 1814, that most French citizens would reject a restored monarchy along absolutist, Old-Regime lines because it would ignore the fundamental political, social, and religious changes wrought by the revolutionary years. Rather than insisting on the impossible, the Allies accepted the reality of post-revolutionary and Napoleonic France: the Charter was a reasonable price to pay for the restoration of the Bourbon monarchy. The spirit of compromise that facilitated that process had its legal aspects. Here we examine that same spirit of compromise from a political and philosophical perspective.

Article 11 of the Charter stated: "All investigations of opinions and votes prior to the Restoration are forbidden." That article granted amnesty to those who had held public office during the Republic or the Empire. More significant, it was a symbolic means of ending the hatred and intransigence that complicated political relations in France. That amnesty was encapsulated in the slogan *union et oubli*, translated literally as "unite and forget." The call for unity was straightforward enough; however, the word *oubli* was more problematic. Did it mean to forget the past, to obliterate the memory of the Revolution and the Empire from the hearts and minds of French citizens?[1] Or was it a conciliatory call for everyone to set aside their differences and selfish goals for the good of France, to move on, so to speak? From 1814 to 1821, the answer was decidedly the latter, in the sense of "forgive and forget." The Charter represented the legal expression of that forgiveness; people could accept it, swallow the past, as distasteful as that might be, and work together, unified under the Bourbon banner. *Union et oubli*, although perhaps naïve, was the Bourbon regime's guiding principle, its official policy, which had allowed it to survive the challenge of the Hundred Days – until it was undone by Berry's assassination and the Royalist Reaction.

The legal shortcomings of the Restoration's constitutional framework and the conspiracy mentality only partly explain why the *union et oubli* policy did not survive Berry's assassination. The final piece of the puzzle can be found in examining Restoration royalism and liberalism in the years between the First Restoration and the Royalist Reaction of 1820, and studying the way those political philosophies changed thereafter. We shall see that the policy of *union et oubli* was viable and remarkably successful prior to the Royalist Reaction, and had it not been for the events that followed Berry's death, it offered every chance of continuing to work in the foreseeable future. In other words, the failure of the *union et oubli* policy to effect a workable synthesis of royalism and liberalism in post-Napoleonic France does not demonstrate that the Royalist Reaction was in some way preordained or inevitable.[2] That synthesis was possible, and it did occur to some degree. However, certain aspects of Restoration royalism and liberalism, amplified by the Royalist Reaction, precipitated the extremism that eventually destroyed *union et oubli*.

Four groups dominated France's political community during the Restoration. On the right were the moderate royalists, also known as constitutionalists, ministerials, or simply moderates. To the far right were the ultra royalists or the ultras. The left also had two factions: moderate liberals – the doctrinaires – and a more radical faction, the independents. For the sake of both clarity and historical accuracy, it is useful to examine royalism and liberalism prior to the Royalist Reaction within the context of those four groups. Admittedly, this type of categorization can oversimplify matters. Yet, contemporaries used the same labels to refer to themselves and to their political rivals. Government officials routinely categorized voters according to those four groups, as they tried to predict the outcomes of deputy elections.[3] In addition, the Chamber of Deputies followed the custom established in the National Assembly of like-minded representatives sitting together. Each of these groups tended to vote *en bloc*, often meeting together outside the Chamber to discuss strategy. Despite such tactics, the royalists and liberals were not modern political parties with party discipline and formal memberships. During that period, differences between groups were more a matter of nuance than clear-cut divergences of opinion and ideology. To appreciate the political landscape in the years leading up to the Royalist Reaction, we must turn our attention to emotional and often quite personal questions. Although such subjective material is by definition difficult to substantiate, it is fair to say that a person's political orientation prior to the Royalist Reaction was based upon the answers to two questions: "What moral and historical lessons were to be learned from the Revolution?" and "What were the benefits and drawbacks of modernity, as defined by such developments as parliamentary democracy, constitutional monarchy, urbanization, and industrialization?"

ROYALISM: FORGIVENESS OR VENGEANCE?

Soul-searching was not the royalists' strong point. Restoration royalists were defined principally by an absolute confidence in the righteousness of their beliefs. They ignored the Revolution and Napoleon or dismissed them as historical accidents. They acknowledged that the Old Regime had not been perfect, but at no time did royalists deviate from the position that France was destined by the natural order and by God to be governed by the Bourbon royal family; nor did they find it at all unexpected that Louis XVIII should once again sit on the French throne. During the First Restoration, royalists were relatively united, content at the sudden turn of events that enabled Louis XVIII to return, and they focused on the practical matters of governing. For the most part, they accepted the principle of *union et oubli* – until the Hundred Days, that is, after which there developed an increasingly rigid dividing line between moderates and ultras.

Moderate royalists treated the Hundred Days as they treated the Revolution and the Empire: accidents of history to be ignored. *Union et oubli* remained their political mantra. Their willingness to cooperate with the political opposition, namely the liberals, did not indicate any diminished belief in the righteousness of the royalist cause. In fact, it was their unshaken faith in the legitimacy of the Bourbon regime that convinced the moderates that *union et oubli* was a viable strategy. The ultra royalists were more skeptical, interpreting the Hundred Days as evidence that the Bourbon regime needed more decisive action if it was to succeed. In their minds, the liberal opposition, be it Jacobin, Bonapartist, revolutionary, or liberal, had to be punished and destroyed. Only then could French society develop naturally and righteously. The ultras may have shared the moderates' basic vision for France, but differences in temperament led to hostility and mistrust.

The Moderates: Union et Oubli

The moderates, more than the other three groups, reflected the ambiguous or dual character of Restoration politics. As noted earlier, the Charter incorporated both royalist and liberal principles; it was at the same time monarchical and parliamentary, aristocratic and democratic. Compromise defined the Restoration. How else to explain such a conflicted constitution? Indeed, how else to explain Talleyrand and Fouché in the 1815 *Conseil*, or Lafayette and General Foy in the 1819 Chamber of Deputies?

Louis XVIII was the man most responsible for choosing *union et oubli* as the keystone of the Bourbon regime's political strategy. Significantly, until recently he was generally dismissed as a non-entity, not surprising given that he was obese to the point of immobility, without any special intellectual gifts, and had a tendency to fall under the sway of favourites. He also compared badly to his brother, Artois, a flamboyant figure, handsome, self-assured, and energetic, albeit lacking in intelligence and common sense. However, as Philip Mansel has demonstrated in his admirable biography, Louis XVIII was no fool.[4] He had returned to the throne without illusions of grandeur. It was his sense of political realism that made the Charter possible, for he was one of the few members of the royal contingent who appreciated that there could be no restoration without some type of constitution. The ultra royalists anguished over article 11, the amnesty provision, and article 6, which guaranteed freedom of religion, but Louis XVIII accepted that compromise was necessary. Too many years and too many changes made sure of that.

At the same time, Louis XVIII realized also that for royalism to flourish, France needed a real king, not a figurehead. He rejected the Charter's first draft principally because it did not proclaim the legitimacy of the Bourbon monarchy and suggested that it was the French people and not God who had called Louis XVIII to the throne. His subsequent Declaration of Saint-Ouen demanded that the Charter be *octroyée* (granted) and not imposed. The actual Charter respected Louis XVIII's wishes, but at the same time included a variety of what at the time were considered liberal-inspired provisions. In political terms, the Charter required Louis XVIII to establish, as a matter of law and custom, precisely when the king had the authority and the obligation to impose his will on the government, Parliament, and the French people, and correspondingly, when he was prohibited from doing so – a rather difficult balancing act. The king's "good pleasure" *à la* Louis XIV would not suffice, but neither could the royal will be subordinated to any other political institution. His solution was to seek a consensus of political support from all moderates, royalist and liberal. Together the moderates would work out the parameters of royal and parliamentary authority, all the while creating a political environment that marginalized extremism. Louis XVIII and his *union et oubli* policy had to accomplish all that and still deliver peace and stability to a nation weary of war and civil unrest.

Periodically, certain events – the Hundred Days, the White Terror, the *Chambre introuvable*, and liberal electoral successes – would test the moderates' attachment to *union et oubli*. Yet, up until Berry's assassination, moderation and *union et oubli* prevailed. The Hundred Days and the White Terror that followed it put the policy to the greatest test. In the summer of 1815 a few thousand Bonapartists were jailed and perhaps 200–300 men were assassinated. Over the next few months, the *Chambre introuvable* was able to force the *Conseil* to introduce repressive legislation aimed at destroying the political opposition. In response, Louis XVIII's ministers and local government officials worked assiduously to minimize the impact of that legislation. Notable in that regard was Joseph de Villèle, who as mayor of Toulouse managed to keep a lid on radical royalist groups intent on exacting revenge for the Revolution and the Hundred Days.[5] All told, during the White Terror, some 10,000 arrests were made, leading to approximately 6,000 prison sentences – a number that, without downplaying the historical significance of the Hundred Days, pales in comparison with the Red Terror of 1793–94. However, perhaps the most important psychological difference between the moderates and the ultra royalists was that the moderates were able to put it behind them rather quickly.

It should be noted that the Hundred Days strengthened *union et oubli* in two ways. First, the general population had little appetite for further conflict, and, apart from small pockets of support in the South, greeted acts of violence on the part of the ultras with a decided lack of enthusiasm. Their desire for peace translated into a widespread, albeit lukewarm, measure of support for the more moderate position adopted by the government at the dawning of the Second Restoration. The White Terror also unified moderate members of the political community against the ultras. They believed that violence on the part of the ultras would lead to a disastrous civil war that could destroy the Bourbon regime. By contrast, Louis XVIII represented peace and prosperity. So while Louis XVIII and the Bourbon regime undoubtedly lost a great deal of prestige owing to the ease with which Napoleon had swept aside the Restoration, that prestige was somewhat restituted by the fact that ultra extremism made the moderates once again the most palatable political option after Napoleon. As in 1814, the mantle of leadership fell to Louis XVIII by default.

The second effect of the Hundred Days was to provide the moderates with a pretext for purging the administration of individuals suspected of disloyalty to the Bourbon regime. Those positions were given to royalists; and in the South where the White Terror was the most severe ultra royalists took the plum spots. These appointments went a long way toward mollifying outraged feelings. Royalists who might otherwise have continued to agitate for continued violence were pacified by their new jobs. Co-opting the ultra leadership into the government fold by offering lucrative government positions reduced the ultras' demands for vengeance and allowed the *union et oubli* policy to gather momentum. The administrative purge perhaps affected some truly suspicious individuals, but its real value lay in buying loyalty, or, at the very least, acquiescence. The effectiveness of the purge raises interesting questions about the seriousness of ultra agitation during the White Terror. Clearly, it favours the viewpoint stressed above that most people looked to the Bourbon regime to put an end to conflict, as seems to have been the case in 1815. Moreover, it illustrates the change in perspective that occurred over the next five years leading up to the Royalist Reaction, as members of the political community became increasingly willing to risk unleashing the forces of civil unrest. By 1820, then, the offer of government positions – or any other placative measures – would not be enough to satisfy those who called for firm action against seditious elements in France in the wake of Berry's murder.

The dissolution of the *Chambre introuvable* illustrated the government's intolerance for extremism. The passage of the February 5th Law in 1817 and Decazes's Liberal Experiment in 1819 emerged also from the spirit of compromise that became the moderates' raison d'être. Both measures were calculated risks taken to expand the moderates' power base by combining its constituency with that of the moderate liberals. Louis XVIII articulated this strategy in a speech opening the two chambers in 1819, when he advised the deputies and the peers to avoid at all costs "the violence and ecstasy of passions" that threatened to upset the political balance upon which the Restoration rested. Even after Berry's assassination, when political forces propelled the extremists to the forefront, Louis XVIII's ministers continued to offer the remedy of *union et oubli*. During the debates on the exceptional laws in the Chamber of Deputies, ministers like Pasquier, Serre, and Siméon[6] took the podium repeatedly to denounce the spirit of extremism that fomented political and civil unrest. They asserted that responsibility for the civil disturbances that followed the assassination rested squarely upon the shoulders of those who rejected *union et oubli*, and warned that this rejection could unleash escalating factionalism and violence that could bring a return to the dark days of the Revolution. On

18 May, Pasquier declared to the deputies that, while political discussion was the hallmark of representative government, and therefore a healthy exercise for the most part, France at that moment had a greater need for calm and reconciliation than for spirited political debate.[7] This speech, published and circulated throughout France, captured the moderates' desire for peace and the cessation of political controversy that lay at the heart of the *union et oubli* policy.

The definition of Restoration royalism has confounded historians, complicated as it was by the Revolution and the Empire. The base line for any discussion of European royalism as a political construct remains Ernst Kantorowicz's definitive study of medieval royalism, *The King's Two Bodies*.[8] Starting from the twelfth and thirteenth centuries, Kantorowicz traced the gradual evolution of the idea that the royal dynasty never died. That idea had extraordinary relevance during the Restoration because royalists had to justify the return of the Bourbon monarchy after the execution of Louis XVI and the absence of any French monarchy for over two decades. The theory of the king's two bodies involves a number of interrelated, ambiguous, and sometimes conflicting factors that developed over nearly seven centuries; what follows is necessarily an oversimplification of extremely complex and nuanced historical events. A summary of the theory provides a historical context to the manner in which Restoration royalists, and moderates in particular, met the challenge of justifying the Bourbons' return in political terms.

Kantorowicz's general thesis was that English and French jurists transferred the idea of the Catholic Church as a mystical body (*corpus mysticum*) to the secular realm and the king, suggesting that the king was head of an eternal body politic just as Christ was head of the eternal Church.[9] By the fifteenth century, that analogy evolved into the concept of the king's two bodies: one a natural body that died like others, and the other a mystical body that never died.[10] The mystical body justified absolutism, for the king personified the eternal Bourbon dynasty that lived forever. The concept of the mystical body developed and grew stronger over the centuries, until it manifested itself in France as Bourbon Absolutism, derived from a variety of principles with roots in diverse legal, political, and religious sources. According to Kantorowicz, three elements of Bourbon Absolutism can be traced back to these sources: the perpetuity of the royal dynasty; the corporate character of the Crown; and the immortality of the royal dignity. These tenets in turn related to the uninterrupted line of royal bodies (that is, physical bodies), the permanence of the body politic represented by the head (the king) together with its members (royal subjects), and the immortality of the royal office, that is, of the king alone. The certainty of the existence of the magical body as a corporate and perpetual entity explains why Bourbon kings instantly embodied the crown's sovereign rights upon the death of the previous king, and also why the body politic, defined as a corporate and perpetual body, was represented by the head of that body. The phrase "The king is dead, long live the king," which became current around the sixteenth century, neatly illustrates that aspect of the theory.

Kantorowicz's 1957 work has resonated throughout the historiography of modern French history. It led historians particularly to examine changes in attitude toward the medieval theory of the king's two bodies in the years leading up to the Revolution. The execution of Louis XVI obviously represented a rejection of that theory.[11] In the leading work on the subject, Jeffrey Merrick argues convincingly that the French monarchy, starting with Louis XIV's reign, but principally during those of Louis XV and Louis XVI, lost its status as a divine and perpetual institution by allowing itself to become involved in political and religious conflicts – a process he calls the desacralization of the French monarchy. In relation to Kantorowicz's thinking, it meant that the king's mystical body was no longer accepted by the society at large. Prior to 1789, therefore, without the protective benefit of his mystical body, the king was little more than a secular, political figure, for whom, it could be argued, the general population had a deep affection, but correspondingly, against whom a growing number of well-educated people were turning. The *philosophes'* criticisms of the Old Regime, and their anti-clericalism, their demands for rational government, combined with character attacks against members of the royal family, which crescendoed in the decade before the Revolution, particularly in the pornographic literature concerning Marie-Antoinette and her alleged sexual appetites, left the Bourbon monarchy too weak to resist the challenges posed by the Revolution.

Gender historians were next to incorporate the theory of the kings' two bodies into the history of French royalism, applying it to the French Revolution. Lynn Hunt, arguably the pioneer in the field, maintained in *The Family Romance of the French Revolution* that when the Legislative Assembly voted to execute Louis XVI, they really intended to murder the king's mystical body. This was the symbolic gesture needed to replace the Old Regime's patriarchal society with a new, fraternal society, that is, the fraternity of citizens. The nature of the state did not change; it remained a perpetual, corporate, and abstract entity vested with all sovereign rights. However, the king was no longer the representative of the body politic; that honour went to the fraternity of citizens. In essence, the people, as a body politic, represented itself, and the rights that had been vested in the Bourbon kings were vested equally in the body politic. Interestingly, the family played a vital institutional role in this new body politic. The family was consecrated as the cornerstone of the Republic, with new roles and responsibilities ascribed to men and women in keeping with the changes in social life demanded by a Republic of Virtue.

The substitution of a fraternal society for the paternal society of the Old Regime proved to be unstable, as shown by the extreme violence of the Terror and the paranoid allegations of conspiracy that impelled the guillotining of suspects. However, it made one thing clear. The desacralization of the Bourbon monarchy in the eighteenth century and the establishment of the Republic as a fraternal brotherhood were historical and philosophical legacies that Restoration royalists could not possibly overcome in 1814. How could they frame the Bourbon monarchy as France's legitimate political authority when it was only the Allied troops' military might that ensured its very existence? The answer is again to be found in Kantorowicz's work despite his almost off-handed differentiation between the execution of Charles Stuart and that of Louis XVI. He stated that the former did not seriously affect or do irreparable harm to the king's body politic or his mystical body, while the latter ended the Bourbon monarchy and along with it the mystical body of the French king."[12] In certain respects, Kantorowicz was correct. Restoration royalists did not attempt to resurrect the totality of the theory of the king's two bodies. They chose one element from that theory to justify the return of the Bourbons: the perpetuity of the dynasty. That selection explains why royalists went to such great lengths to compare members of the royal family to previous Bourbon historical figures, of which Henri IV was the most prominent. Louis XVI's death killed his physical body, and it may well have killed his mystical body, but it left untouched the essential qualities of the office, personified by the king, and the office's most visible symbols, represented by the Crown. In essence, then, Louis XVIII returned to France in 1814 to assume an office that had been vacant for years, but had never been eliminated. The declaration in the Charter's preamble that it was the nineteenth year of Louis XVIII's reign integrated this view as a matter of law. In addition, royalists also grafted the family metaphor onto the concept of the perpetuity of the dynasty. Perpetuity of the dynasty meant that the Bourbon monarchy had never died, despite Louis XVI's execution, while the family metaphor provided a philosophical construct upon which French society could be based, along with the place of the Bourbon monarchy in that society. Admittedly, this is a generalization. Ultra royalists at times demanded a resurrected Old Regime; however, that was by far the exception, not the rule, and it was certainly not the case during Louis XVIII's reign, as the analysis of the

Royalist Reaction in Part Two will make abundantly clear. The truth of this contention is also supported by the manner in which the government applied the *union et oubli* policy between 1814 and 1820, the years that this study of moderate Restoration royalism examines.

The re-establishment of the Bourbon royal court provides an instructive example of the way the family metaphor interacted with the policy of *union et oubli*. Unlike the Imperial court, which was dominated by the genius of one man, the Bourbons created a family court structure whereby all members of the royal family lived together. This structure was reinforced by the fact that all the family members had genealogical importance; since Louis XVIII and Angoulême were childless, and Berry had not yet fathered a male offspring, they were all potential heirs presumptive.[13] That potential translated into high status for the entire Bourbon royal family, both at court and in the public eye. Their status was also enhanced by the size of the royal households. Louis XVIII realized that a king had to live and act in a style suitable for a monarch. Accordingly, his royal court was full of pomp and ceremony that distinguished it from any other political institution.

Some liberals, notably Guizot, Constant, and Pradt, attacked the royal court as an aristocratic anachronism, a reactionary manifestation of the Old Regime. Such criticisms usually came, however, from the former Imperial nobility and the wealthy bourgeoisie who resented being excluded from the court. Those feelings were assuaged during the First Restoration by Louis XVIII's choice to maintain the Napoleonic Imperial court structure. Significantly, personnel from the Imperial court were kept on. In fact, almost all of the outer structure of court life, social life, and the palaces remained Imperial, along with most of the court officials, especially in the technical departments. Any lingering resentment against the royal court was put to rest by reforms in 1820. Louis XVIII's tremendous national popularity following the birth of Bordeaux provided his ministers with enough prestige and influence to push though a number of reforms that earlier would have been cause for hysterical cries from the ultra royalists.

Launched by royal proclamation in November, the 1820 reforms democratized the royal household by opening the court to all social successes. The proclamation abolished anachronistic, obsolete, and simply absurd jobs. Each department was given a regular hierarchy. The most important reform was the creation of new positions, including thirty salaried Gentlemen of the Privy Chamber, twelve *écuyers cavalcadours* (up from five), thirty-two pages, and an indefinite number of unsalaried Honorary Gentlemen of the Privy Chamber.[14] The number of applications for these and other court positions increased rapidly over the next decade. The reforms effectively co-opted the previously disenchanted Imperial nobility and wealthy bourgeoisie into the royalist fold, at least until the ultra royalists alienated them again in the final years of the Restoration. The July Revolution suggests that the reform efforts were ultimately ineffective, and perhaps they were. Regardless, the attempt itself demonstrates the moderate royalists' commitment to *union et oubli*.

The grandeur of the royal court also signified, unmistakably, that royalism had returned to France. Here again Louis XVIII proved his political astuteness. He often insisted upon the strictest adherence to court ceremony and protocol. He knew that the Restoration would flounder if the monarchy did not regain its status as the political and cultural cornerstone of France. It need not enjoy the same powers as its Old-Regime predecessor, but a similar level of prestige and status was essential.

While court reforms played an important symbolic role in popularizing the king, the royal family, and the Bourbon regime, the court's fundamentally elitist character limited its mass appeal. Yet, it is essential to understand that moderate royalists worked diligently to promote the royal family to the nation at large. The most dramatic example of this effort was government-sponsored *fêtes*, celebrations that took place simultaneously across France, to commemorate a person or an event.

The *fêtes* can be distinguished from other public demonstrations by their distinct self-serving purpose: publicize the Bourbon royal family to the entire nation. Neither "frivolous nor simple," the *fêtes* promoted the Bourbons as a monarchical power with good taste and originality,[15] qualities that suggested what a royal family should be. To that end, the subject-matter for a *fête* was chosen with great care, and government officials attended very closely to all details, even down to the text to be read at a given church service and the prescribed tone of voice. The *fêtes* had to be royal celebrations, not French, a distinction that accounts for the preference for themes related to martyred Bourbons rather than military victories after 1789. *Fêtes* for political events, such as the proclamation of the Charter, would likewise have drawn attention to the liberals, whereas royal marriages, deaths, and coronations were strictly Bourbon affairs. One of the First Restoration's earliest *fêtes* was a religious ceremony in memory of victims of the Revolution, which was held on 5 May, the anniversary of Louis XVII's and Henri IV's death. Other acceptable themes for *fêtes* included Louis XVIII's entry into Paris in 1814, Berry's marriage in 1816, the anniversaries of the executions of Louis XVI and Marie-Antoinette,[16] Louis XVIII's death, and Charles X's coronation. The most popular and politically effective *fêtes*, however, were those related to the Royalist Reaction: the Berry memorial services in March, 1820, and the Bordeaux birth in October, 1820 and the baptismal celebrations in May, 1821.

These three *fêtes* played a strategic role in spreading the government's official interpretation of the assassination and the miracle birth to the general population. This official interpretation, discussed in greater detail in Part Two, was intended to popularize the Bourbon regime by claiming a providential relationship between God and the royal family. The family metaphor guided this process, ensuring that government officials emphasized the familial bonds that, according to royalist doctrine, characterized French society. The merging of the family metaphor and the *union et oubli* policy into the official interpretation of the assassination, the miracle child, and the Restoration *fêtes*, speaks also to an old-style of politics that coloured much of the Royalist Reaction, a personal style rooted in the Old Regime and absolutism. The symbolism and techniques used by the government and its supporters during the Royalist Reaction to promote their political agenda were reminiscent of some that dated back at the least to the eighteenth century. The government's and the moderates' reliance on dynastic and familial references to enhance the *union et oubli* policy should be seen from that perspective. Not that they wanted the Old Regime back; they wanted the return of the Old Regime's political sensibility. Disagreements were to be handled like family disputes. Children could argue with their parents, but even though they might be uncomfortable with parental authority, that authority was to be respected and ultimately submitted to; and under no circumstances were children to use violence. Likewise, parents were to respect their children and listen to their objections when appropriate. Louis XVIII and the moderates wanted nothing more than that Restoration politics function in the same manner.

References to the Counter-Revolution made in *fêtes* prior to Berry's assassination suggest that while the Republic had cruelly broken the chain of Bourbon rule, the break was merely temporary, a blip in their otherwise centuries-old rule.[17] The iconography of Restoration *fêtes* illustrates that point.[18] *Fête* organizers used pre-Revolutionary names and titles, revived Old Regime offices, such as the stewardships of Silverware, of the King's Privy Chamber, and the Wardrobe, and of the King's Bedchamber, and brought back Old Regime personnel into service.[19] A number of Old Regime *fêtes* also returned, such as the *Voeux de Louis XIII* and the *Processions de la Fête-Dieu*.[20] Pictures and statues used at Restoration *fêtes* served to affirm the legitimacy of Bourbon rule in dynastic terms, all the while stressing the family metaphor. Bélanger, the organizer of a *fête* for Louis XVIII's return to Paris in May, 1814, emphasized the dynastic and familial themes in a report on that *fête*: "This is not the celebration of a conqueror, entering on a warrior's chariot, surrounded with piles of arms and with laurel branches; it is that of a beloved monarch, removed from his country by political troubles, whom Providence has restored to the love of his people; it is the festival of a father returning to the bosom of his family after a long absence."[21] Figures of former Bourbon kings were commonly displayed to magnify the splendour of the Bourbon dynastic history, a monarchy founded by Clovis, whose worth was illustrated by the saintliness of Louis XI, the piety of Louis XII, and the magnificent characters of Charles V, Charles VII, Henri IV, and Louis XIV. For Bordeaux's baptism, the statues of Clovis, Charlemagne, Saint Louis, and Henry IV[22] were displayed for the same reason.[23] Military symbolism abounded as well, along with images of the king as a patron of the arts, surrounded by books, manuscripts, maps, and musical instruments.

The central government did not immediately recognize the usefulness of the *fêtes* in its campaign to promote royalism. During the First Restoration, and in the first few months of the Second, local government and Church officials had relative freedom to organize *fêtes* in their respective departments and dioceses, and these officials often took liberties with the *fêtes*, allowing their political views to colour the ceremonies. For example, in July, 1815, the Bishop of Toulouse ordered a *Te Deum* to honour Louis XVIII and "to atone for the insults towards God during the Revolution."[24] These sentiments contravened the principles of *union et oubli*, and steps were taken to prevent similar occurrences in future *fêtes*. As of 1816, Parisian officials began to take over. That decision was also bolstered by the realization that national *fêtes* offered an effective and inexpensive means of spreading the royalist vision. By the end of that year, local autonomy over *fêtes* had ended. Even archbishops needed approval from Paris to hold a non-religious *fête*. Government *circulaires* were regularly sent to prefects and Church officials ordering not only the date, but the precise form and content for all national *fêtes*.

This centralization took place within the context of *union et oubli*, as a review of national *fêtes* in the departments of Isère and Haute-Garonne will illustrate. In 1814 four official *fêtes* were organized in Grenoble: to celebrate Louis XVIII's return to the throne (May), to honour the peace treaty signed between France and the Allies (June/July), to mourn Louis XVI and other victims of the Revolution (28 June), and finally, to commemorate a royal visit from Berry and Artois (13 October).[25] A great deal of time and money went into the 1814 *fêtes*, particularly the royal visit. Hundreds of letters flowed from the prefect's office to the sub-prefects and the mayors, as preparations were hastily made for Artois's and Berry's arrival. An *arc de triomphe* was built in Grenoble to welcome the father and son, and a large banquet was held in their honour. The prefect attended personally to the smallest detail, and issues such as seating arrangements produced volumes of official correspondence. All told, the event cost thousands of francs.[26] The memorial for Louis XVI and other victims of the Revolution was also a splashy affair. Grenoble's leading public figures led a large procession through the city to the cathedral, where the prefect had spent some 5,000 francs for refurbishing and painting, organizing the music, and buying books and flowers.[27]

In 1815, as the anniversary of Louis XVI's execution approached, Louis XVIII decreed that the anniversaries of the deaths of Louis XVI and Marie-Antoinette, 21 January and 16 October, respectively, were to be national days of mourning. The royal ordinance simply provided a date for the *fête*; the details were left to the local authorities. With complete freedom to organize the event as they saw fit, officials in Grenoble and Toulouse both tended towards the reactionary, denouncing in no uncertain terms virtually everything associated with the Revolution. In Grenoble, in a *circulaire* announcing the memorial service to his fellow clergymen, Bishop Simon characterized the Revolution as an act of "murder, ruin, and regicide that destroyed France and Europe."[28] He eulogized Louis XVI in the grandest possible terms as a Christ figure who had "consecrated his entire life to the happiness of his people; it was for these same people that he shed the last drop of his blood."[29] Simon ended the *mandement* with a plea to remember the other royal martyrs, Marie-Antoinette, Madame Elisabeth, and Louis XVII.[30] Another example of the central government's delegation of responsibility for *fêtes* was the destruction of the physical reminders of the Revolution and the Empire ordered by the Ministry of Police in November, 1815. The order gave public officials the right to confiscate and then destroy these items. Once they had possession of these objects, many public officials decided to hold ostentatious public ceremonies to burn them. The sermons that followed invariably extolled the virtues of the Counter-Revolution. The Revolution was declared a horrible nightmare, and a direct link drawn between Napoleon, the Hundred Days, and the Terror. The *drapeau blanc*, *fleurs-de-lis*, and portraits of Louis XVIII were prominently displayed, along with Christian symbols such as a cross or a statue of Christ.[31] Public officials made the decision to hold these ceremonies on their own; in fact, they were under no obligation to burn the items at all.[32]

These displays of exuberance would all but disappear by the fall of 1816, as the *Chambre introuvable* was dissolved and the central government decided to exercise tight control over future national *fêtes*. After the Marie-Antoinette memorial ceremonies in October, Vaublanc, the minister of the interior, prescribed in detail precisely how the two martyred Bourbons were to be remembered. In the future, no sermon was to be given. Instead, the Testament of Louis XVI, written just before his execution, and Marie-Antoinette's letter to Madame Elisabeth written the morning of her execution, were to be read to the congregation.[33] In preparation for Marie-Antoinette's memorial in 1816, Louis XVIII sent a letter to all archbishops and bishops expressing his desire that the letter be read without a sermon.[34] And from 1816 to 1824, ministers of the interior continued to send reminder letters to prefects, archbishops, and bishops regarding the testament and the letter. After 1824, when Marie-Antoinette's memorial was combined with that of Louis XVI, the restrictions were relaxed and some preaching was permitted. However, the reading of the testament and the letter was obligatory, and the minister of the interior still felt the need to urge restraint: "It should remind the French people how the most sublime virtue can be ignored and sacrificed in those dreadful crises called revolutions, but it should also be holy, as was the noble victim to whom we offer this tribute of public grief."[35]

Bishop Simon in Grenoble took those instructions to heart. On 17 January 1816, in contrast to the reactionary and bellicose tone of his 1815 *circulaire* announcing Louis XVI's memorial service, he sent a *circulaire* to his curés ordering that no sermon was to be given: "We will refrain from making a long speech that will rekindle your sense of anguish for such a tragic event."[36] The prefect of Haute-Garonne did not immediately take note. In announcing Louis XVI's memorial service, he reiterated the reactionary note Bishop Simon had sounded a year before: "We expect the Nation formally to disavow a crime committed by the same factions that overturned the altar and throne, oppressed the people, and kindled the disastrous conflagration which has ravaged ... Europe. In the meantime, the authorities cannot too strongly support the pious intentions of the French people, who offer their prayers and tears to the Eternal Being in expiation of a most horrible crime."[37] The mayor of Toulouse expressed his grief in even more exaggerated tones. He called the Revolution "the most sorrowful and dreadful time ... twenty-five years of calamities" and the worst catastrophe in history. He pledged that the French would never rest until all traces of the Revolution had been crushed: "We will not retrace the unspeakable struggle, the innocence, virtue, heroism of the victim, the cowardice, baseness and rage of the executioners." Finally, he claimed that the Restoration had strengthened, or tightened, "the gentle ties" that united forever "the nation to the glorious family of its kings."[38] Significantly, the mayor's bellicose tone was absent from all future memorial *fêtes* in Toulouse. When announcing the 1817 memorial for Louis XVI, the mayor of Toulouse explained the reason for the *fête* in simple terms: "The anniversary of the death of Louis XVI is a time of mourning and expiation for the whole of France, and particularly for the loyal people of Toulouse."[39] Subsequent memorials for Louis XVI and Marie-Antoinette were announced in similar fashion.[40]

Ministerial instructions were generally followed to the letter, with some notable exceptions. For example, in 1818, at St Jean de Bournay (Isère), during Marie-Antoinette's memorial service, the *curé* leading the service became somewhat excited when he read Marie-Antoinette's letter and decided to add a gloss of his own, the focus of which was a rant against the evils of the Revolution and the excesses of the Jacobins. However, he saved his harshest words for the treacherous constitutional priests, "those who had forsaken their duties."[41] His comments were swiftly reported back to the prefect. Bishop Simon became personally involved and sent a letter to the prefect stating that he had spoken to the *curé* and guaranteed a similar incident would not happen again.[42] The incident illustrates the government's desire to avoid antagonizing liberal sentiments and shows how diligently officials worked to make the *union et oubli* policy effective.

The central government's control over the *fêtes* had a positive and a negative effect on its own intentions. On the plus side, it assured that the desired message was delivered to the general public in an appropriate manner. Reactionary priests and overly emotional prefects were silenced in the interests of uniting the nation under the Bourbon banner. On the other hand, this centralization made the *fêtes* rather banal affairs. Once Parisian officials took command, the *fêtes* in Grenoble never matched the extravagance or level of enthusiasm that had marked the 1814 *fêtes*, at least prior to the assassination.[43] Officials carried out the instructions they received from the capital in a perfunctory manner, and national *fêtes* soon took on a homogeneous nature. The focus of a typical *fête* was a church service. The *fête* was announced at sundown the night before by church bells. In large centres, government officials, members of the municipal council, military officers, and Church officials would lead a street procession to the cathedral. Sometimes the service was followed by a procession to the *hôtel de ville* where another function was held. Large crowds watched, and as many people as possible were allowed into the church. Theatres, cafés, billiard halls, and other public meeting places were closed and all public works suspended. National *fêtes* in smaller towns and villages followed the same basic routine on a more modest basis.[44]

While the central government's use of the *fêtes* as a political expedient began in earnest only in the fall of 1816, the Church played a pivotal role from the start and continued to do so until the end of the Restoration. Whenever possible, an archbishop, bishop, or *curé* would lead the service to honour the occasion, and religious allegories and symbols decorated the church interior. At Berry's wedding, a blue banner was hung in the choir, decorated with figures of saints whose names had been given to Bourbon princes and princesses. During the ceremony, the protection of those saints was invoked. At Bordeaux's baptism, large medallions were placed throughout Notre Dame, surrounded by roses and representations of French saints. In 1825, at Charles X's coronation at Reims, images of *prélats* who had honoured the Gallican Church by their piety, science, and virtue formed a long frieze accompanied by numerous religious statues and icons.[45]

The involvement of local parishes with the Restoration *fêtes* also raises questions regarding the complex relationship between the Church and the Bourbon regime. This subject did not emerge as an important issue during the Royalist Reaction, and so it will not be discussed in great depth here. However, since it does shed some light on Restoration royalism, a few comments may be useful. The Restoration was an obvious godsend for the Catholic Church. The counter-revolutionaries of the 1790s made the defence of the Church's interests one of their core principles. Moreover, it appears that a number of *émigrés* became quite devout in exile (although it is difficult to measure the sincerity of that faith). Artois is a good example of that change. He had gained a well-deserved reputation for sexual exploits and general carousing prior to the Revolution. In exile, he came to realize the evil of his ways and was henceforth a strict Catholic. Artois's religious awakening was replicated throughout the *émigré* community, particularly among women. Louis XVIII refused to accept the Charter until it acknowledged Catholicism as France's official state religion, although he compromised by accepting article 6, which guaranteed freedom of religion. The Church took advantage of that official status by launching a series of missions from 1815–20 designed to stimulate attendance at mass and rejuvenate the faith among the populace. It also worked vigorously to build up the clergy. Both efforts were relatively successful. Over the course of the century, the Church enjoyed a spectacular revival, with tremendous increases in the number of male and female religious orders, seminaries, and recruits to the clergy.[46]

Little need be said about the impact of the Revolution on the fortunes of the Gallican Church. It lost its land, its sources of revenue, and its official status. The Concordat of 1801 allowed the Church to return officially to French soil, but it did so firmly under Napoleon's control. The Restoration gave it official status once again; however, the people were in no mood to pay the *tithe*, and owners of the *biens nationaux* were hostile to any suggestion of compensation. As well, the government was intent on keeping the Church under state control. It was quick to make use of the Church when convenient,[47] particularly when it came to the *fêtes* – but only on its own terms. The fact that the Bourbon regime had dominated the Church before the Royalist Reaction suggests that moderate royalists had come to implicitly accept the separation of church and state. They disagreed with the liberals on precisely where the line should be; however, it was clear the moderates felt that while the Church was free to administer to the nation's spiritual needs, its political presence was permissible under government supervision alone.

The moderates conceived of a just society as a Catholic society, but not exclusively so. That perspective remained after the Royalist Reaction. In 1821 secondary education was placed under the supervision of the bishops. Mgr Frayssinous, an ecclesiastic, was appointed Grand Master of the University. In 1822, the course given by doctrinaire thinker François Guizot at the Sorbonne was cancelled. In 1824 the episcopate was given the right to appoint primary teachers. Laws were also passed to insulate the Church and Catholicism from criticism. In 1822, for example, two new press offences were created: "criticism of the divine right of kings" and "outrage to religion." In 1825 the infamous Sacrilege Law was passed, making it an offence punishable by life imprisonment to profane sacred vessels; profanation of the consecrated host was punishable by death. The passage of this law, which incidentally was never applied, played into the hands of anti-clerical liberals, who claimed that it represented precisely the type of legislation one could expect from a government controlled by Jesuits and the Church. At the same time, even during Charles X's reign, the Church was prohibited from exercising any real political power, the only exception perhaps being in the education field. The Church's influence there remained controversial for the remainder of the century, until 1905, when Émile Combes passed the Law of Separation, officially proclaiming the separation of church and state in France.

What should we make of moderate royalism in historical terms? Was the ultras' ascent to power inevitable, and must we therefore consider the moderate era as transitional? Those questions are complicated by the personalities of the two second Restoration kings. Louis XVIII's poor health ensured that eventually his ultra-leaning brother would become king. The king's prerogative to appoint his own ministers, the other political powers enjoyed by the executive branch of the government – not the least of which was the sole right to introduce legislation to Parliament – and Charles X's political proclivities together suggest that *union et oubli* may have had a tenuous lifespan at best. In Part Two, however, when the Royalist Reaction is examined more closely, it will be argued that Charles X aside, *union et oubli* was a viable policy that was undone principally by the ramifications of Berry's assassination and the miracle child, two events that were obviously beyond the moderates' control. Without the Royalist Reaction, it is doubtful whether Charles X could have appointed an ultra *Conseil*, and the opposition in the Chamber of Deputies, which manifested itself in any event, would have been that much stronger. The Decazes ministry would not have fallen in February, 1820, and the Liberal Experiment might have had some chance at success. In fact, a rapprochement between moderate royalist and liberal deputies had seemed in the works. Before Berry's death, liberals were ready to agree to a modification of the electoral law, and even a few ultras, including Villèle, supported it. Equally significant, the radical left appeared ready to cooperate with Decazes. It was for that very reason that Lafayette and most of his fellow independent deputies did not attend a banquet in Paris on 5 February 1820 to celebrate the anniversary of the passage of the February 5th Law.[48] Granted that much of this thinking is speculative, and one might conjecture that the Age of the Ultras would have arrived regardless. Yet, the historiography to date has tended to dismiss the viability of the *union et oubli* policy and has ignored why and how the Royalist Reaction brought it to an end. Ironically, the reasons for the ultimate demise of that policy illustrate why it was viable in the first place. Within moderate royalism itself lay the seeds for the destruction of the moderate era: perhaps the years following the collapse of the Empire required more decisive leadership; the timing of the Liberal Experiment may have been premature; the willingness to compromise to extremists was undoubtedly misguided. Yet, the seeds of success were there, too. Unfortunately for the moderates, the assassination and the miracle child nourished the former, so that Charles X was able to ascend to the throne unfettered by a strong opposition that could have neutralized the effects of his ultra royalist bias.

The Ultras: Vive le Roi Quand-Même

The Duke of Richelieu was perhaps the quintessential moderate royalist. A practical man, he worked to achieve his goals by building as broad a consensus as possible. He rejected extremism from all quarters, finding the far left and far right equally offensive. He rejected liberal extremists out-of-hand as revolutionaries and Bonapartists; reconciliation with them was pointless. However, Richelieu feared opposition from that quarter less than he feared the ultra royalists. He felt that the left were isolated, few in number, and without popular appeal. On the other hand, ultra royalism gave voice to the grievances felt by a significant number of members of France's political community and by the general population still angered by the Revolution and by Napoleon.

Richelieu's assessment was accurate, the ultras were extremists, but by no means a fringe group. Their popularity was evidenced by the *Chambre introuvable* and despite some setbacks in the years preceding the Royalist Reaction, they remained a potent force on the political scene. It is to these most royalist of men that we now turn our attention.

The ultra royalists are difficult to pin down. Reactionaries and political dinosaurs they were to some degree – not to mention uncompromising, intransigent, stubborn, self-righteous, judgmental, and selfish. Yet, so too were they shrewd, loyal, dedicated, and principled. Of the four political groups that dominated the Restoration, the ultras were the most consistent in their views and the most likely to base their political actions upon philosophical and religious beliefs.[49] Yet, a fundamental paradox complicates any attempt to define ultra royalism during the moderate era. Loyalty to the king was the essence of being an ultra; however, most ultras detested Louis XVIII's *union et oubli* policy, and many of them who had joined Louis XVIII in exile did not like their king. In response to *union et oubli*, the ultras replied, *vive le roi, quand-même*; that is, in this instance, "save the king from himself."[50]

Historians have generally dismissed the ultras as mere reactionaries and political blunderers.[51] The ultras' rejection of many aspects of modernity, particularly philosophical principles such as parliamentary democracy and individual rights and freedoms, has contributed to that characterization. Certainly, the fact that the ultras dominated French politics for less than a decade – and the ignominious reality of the July Revolution – contributed substantially as well. The ultras ultimately lost the political battle against the liberals, and so have suffered a corresponding loss in historiographical terms. Finally, on a more subjective level, it may be that the modern mind rebels against ultra royalism, rooted as it was in an organic conception of society in which the group takes precedence over the individual, God and Providence determine the course of events, and a nation is unified by a single religion and a powerful monarch. It is too old-fashioned, too "Old Regime." Interestingly, the ultras' pathetic actions prior to the July Revolution, and their equally pathetic actions during it, stand in stark contrast to their actions during the Royalist Reaction of 1820. Ten years before their political extinction, the ultra royalists were the most decisive and effective of all the political players; and that decisiveness and effectiveness was largely the result of a doctrinal purity unique to them. The ultras' rigid attachment to the principles of ultra royalism served them well in the months following Berry's assassination, just as it proved to be their undoing in 1830.

As noted earlier, ultra royalism as a political force was born during the Hundred Days. The First Restoration was a honeymoon period in which the future ultras were generally content with the revival of French royalism and the end of the Empire. Overjoyed with what must have been unimaginable only a year earlier, the ultras cooperated with their moderate royalist confrères. The Hundred Days ended this period of cooperation. After Waterloo, the moderates remained committed to *union et oubli*, whereas the ultra royalists demanded retribution. Their reasons were primarily psychological. Divisions among royalists, republicans, and Bonapartists had become blurred during the nearly fifteen years of Napoleonic rule. Royalists had come to terms with the Empire; they had accepted official positions and Imperial titles, and rejoiced with the nation as Napoleon's army marched from victory to victory. Many royalists had spent their entire adult lives under Imperial rule, and they fully expected that rule to continue. Napoleon's escape from Elba and the clashes that followed re-established clear dividing lines between royalists on the one side, and Bonapartists, republicans, and liberals on the other. Old feelings were rekindled, as memories of the Revolution, memories of betrayal, rejection, and terror surfaced. These psychological wounds, experienced in person or second hand through the older generation, created ultra royalism. The ease with which Napoleon had marched back to Paris, and the pathetic resistance to him, made it quite clear that a substantial percentage of the population was hostile to the Bourbons. As a result, the ultras did not see the Second Restoration as a continuation of the First. The honeymoon was over, and more importantly, the rose-coloured glasses were off. A Bourbon sat once again on the throne, but the monarchy was still under constant threat. To protect it and truly re-establish royalism in France, the ultras believed it was necessary to continue the Counter-Revolution until the revolutionaries and all manifestations of the revolutionary spirit were stamped out forever. They saw the dawning of the Second Restoration as an opportunity for this cleansing. The White Terror represented that decision in action, while the end of the White Terror and the dissolution of the *Chambre introuvable* marked the final break between moderate and ultra royalists.

In his book on Berry, Chateaubriand presented France with two choices: revolution or royalism. The first, he wrote, reflected the spirit of the Terror of 1793 and the tyranny of Bonaparte; the second reflected the spirit of Christianity. He defined royalism in unequivocal terms: "legitimacy accompanied with all its memories, surrounded by the majesty of the ages; the representative monarchy supported by the great landowners, defended by a vigorous aristocracy, strengthened by all moral and religious powers. Anyone who cannot see this truth can see nothing, and is doomed to destruction; apart from this truth everything else is theory, chimera, illusion."[52] The vehemence of these words, expressed by the most eloquent of the ultras, forcefully captures the ultra spirit. Their political actions were determined by a rigid mindset that perceived the world in black and white. Nevertheless, these beliefs were not simplistic or primitive. They had taken shape in response to extremely complex historical events – the Revolution and the Hundred Days. The ultras believed that France was on the edge of the abyss and it was their sacred duty to save her. To avoid repetition of the mistakes of 1789, it was vital that government policy be ultra royalist. Yet, Louis XVIII's *union et oubli* expressly contradicted that attitude. The ultra royalists were in an awkward position. As Joseph de Villèle wrote to his wife a week after Berry's death: "The royalists are lost without the King; the King is lost without the royalists." How were the ultra royalists to rule when their King opposed them? The answer, continued Villèle, was straightforward: "We must join the *Conseil*."[53] In other words, the ultras should take over the government.

By 1816, with the dissolution of the *Chambre introuvable*, it had become clear that real political power resided with the *Conseil* and not the Chamber of Deputies. The ultras had to change their political objectives to reflect this reality. The 1819 press law, which removed censorship, helped considerably. Ultra royalist newspapers sprang up overnight, and their success attests to the popular appeal of the ultra message. Many of the leading literary figures of the day, including such writers as Chateaubriand, Lamennais, Bonald and Maistre, were ultra royalists, and were either part owners or regular contributors. They rarely missed an opportunity to direct a vituperative remark at the government and Louis XVIII's ministers. Berry's assassination put the *Conseil* within reach of the ultras; indeed, soon after it, two ultra royalists, Villèle and Corbière, were appointed as ministers without portfolio.

Ultra royalism changed with its attainment of political power. Once the *Conseil* was theirs, and particularly after Charles X became king, the qualities that had made them such a potent political force before and during the Royalist Reaction became quite dangerous to the long-term viability of the Restoration. The determination and single-mindedness that had carried the day for them in 1820 gave way to shortsightedness and inflexibility. The ultras were unable to compromise in the face of political realities or to accommodate to the demands of power.[54] As is often the case, extremism is effective in opposition only. At the same time, the ultras were extreme by definition; their extremism reflected a devotion to certain core religious principles that took precedence over political expediency. Those principles held that the Revolution was a perversion of the natural order, a historical development that threatened the nation's moral purity, an evil and satanic corruption. As Bonald articulated this perspective: "National rulers ceased to protect Christianity; it was weakened and fell prey to those terrible revolutions in Europe. The nations were carried along into those revolutions, and their leaders perished at the hands of people corrupted by irreligion."[55] A few years earlier, in 1797, Maistre had provided a recipe for revolution that prefigured Bonald's assessment of more recent French history and also justified the options offered by Chateaubriand to the French people. Maistre asked, "How does one make a revolution?" His answer was simple: "Religion must be overthrown, morals flouted, all forms of property destroyed, and innumerable crimes committed; for this devilish work, so many vicious men were needed that perhaps never before had so many vices combined for such an evil end." Here we have a concise list of exactly what the Revolution gave France: it corrupted religion, perverted morality, and destroyed property. Fortunately, continued Maistre, an antidote to revolution existed: "To re-establish order, the king will call on all the virtues; he would wish to do so, no doubt, but by the very nature of things, he will be forced to; his most pressing concern will be to unite justice with mercy; worthy men will appear to fill the positions where they may be useful; and Religion, lending its sceptre to Politics, will give it the strength which it can obtain nowhere else."[56] Again a concise listing is provided. This time we are told the benefits that ultra royalism would bring to France: true religion, virtue, and justice.

The ultras' historical perspective has been termed "traditionalism" for its seemingly obsessive attachment to the Old Regime. Their interpretation of history was subjective in the extreme. But the liberals did the same; they refused to accept any connection between their politics and the excesses of the Terror or the Napoleonic era. While the ultras looked to the past to justify their concept of natural order, they did so with the intention of ridding France of an evil influence. Ultra traditionalism was therefore less an attempt to justify the re-establishment of an aristocracy in the style of the Old Regime than an illustration of the ultra royalist desire to restore the natural order of a just, Christian society, an order cruelly overthrown by the Jacobins and the Bonapartists.

In many ways, the ultras conceived of the natural order in the same way as the moderates. Both groups viewed society in organic terms; familial relationships created a hierarchy of interconnected groups, with God at the top, followed by the king, the royal family, the nobility, the magistrates, and finally, the people. This is the classical family metaphor. However, ultras differed in that they recognized no ambiguity in the configuration. For them, the natural order demanded absolute obedience for it derived from nothing less than divine law. Years before the Restoration, Maistre had written that the Counter-Revolution was not

reactionary because its purpose was to restore the natural order ordained by God: "The return to a state of order cannot be painful because it will be in accordance with nature, and because it will be aided
by a secret force, whose action is entirely creative. We will see the exact
contrary of all that we have seen before."[57] Providence featured prominently in the ultras' natural order. They interpreted the Restoration itself
as the product of Providence, a righting of a wrong, so to speak. In *Considérations sur la France*, Maistre noted gleefully that Providence began
to punish the regicides almost immediately after Louis XVI's execution.
More than sixty regicides were already dead, he claimed, many having
met a violent end.[58] Faith in a mystical connection between Providence
and the Bourbon regime was confirmed by Bordeaux's birth; Providence
had intervened directly in human affairs to preserve the Bourbon lineage. Again, while most royalists accepted the role of Providence in human affairs, this mystical connection fit more neatly into the ultras'
belief system and justified their rejection of the *union et oubli* policy. In
Législation primitive, Bonald affirmed that it was not civilization that
added to man's understanding of the truth, but rather that the understanding of the truth created and improved civilization.[59] For ultra royalists, "truth" meant a strong monarchy supported by a loyal nobility. It
did not mean cooperating with liberals and Bonapartists.

The double-vote law of 1820 proposed the creation of a second electoral college reserved for the top 25 percent of voters in each department, who paid the highest amount in direct taxes. Ultras endorsed the
double vote to a man. In 1817, 1818, and 1819 liberal candidates had
dominated the three successive renewal elections held under the single
college system. Although modern research suggests that those liberal
victories had resulted primarily from royalist apathy, the ultras attributed them to the presence of electors from the lower levels of the *cens*,
that is, the bourgeoisie. Ironically, modern research has shown that the
ultras enjoyed strong support from the entire electorate, and they would
have benefited greatly from a lowering of the *cens*. Yet, after the assassination, the ultras focused their efforts exclusively on raising it.[60] In that
context, the decision to support the double vote is significant because it
gave the balance of power in the Chamber of Deputies to the *grands
propriétaires*, a small minority of the *cens* community. Clearly, ultra
support for the double vote suggests they assumed the *grands propriétaires* would vote for ultra deputies, an assumption that in turn is in-
dicative of an elitist or aristocratic view of politics. Note, however, that
the *cens* represented an aristocracy not of birth but of landed property.
That distinction is instructive, for it identifies an important element in
the ultras' traditionalism: soil mysticism. Soil mysticism refers to the belief that a man's moral qualities related proportionally to the size of his

land holdings: the greater one's property, the finer one's character. Soil mysticism therefore inferred that double-voters – being of higher moral character – would vote for the candidates that would best serve French interests; presumably, those with smaller holdings had inferior characters that prevented such altruistic voting.

It must be kept in mind that not only had the Old Regime nobility survived the Revolution relatively intact but they had positively thrived during the Empire. Napoleon allowed most of the *émigrés* to return, and they very quickly resumed their positions at the upper-echelons of French society.[61] However, an important change had occurred in the theoretical justification for their elevated stations in life. Although the Imperial nobility had much in common with their pre-1789 counterparts, the titles they received were intended to honour their service to the state. Imperial titles may have indicated a higher status, but that status was accorded by virtue of a personal deed and not parentage. The rejection of aristocracy during the Revolution and the Napoleonic ideal of a meritocracy made it impossible for all but the most obtuse of royalists to justify their titles and their political and economic power on traditional and hereditary grounds. Yet, a justification was needed, and the ultra royalists ultimately chose land ownership, or soil mysticism. As the term implies, soil mysticism represented more than the titular right to land. It signified a loftiness of character and the ability to withstand the corrupting influences of bourgeois forms of wealth. This exaltation of stewardship of the land was accompanied by a rejection of urban values, even though ultra royalists commonly resided in large cities, at least part of the year. The corruption of Paris and the moral ugliness of city living, central themes in ultra diatribes against liberals, were contrasted with an idealized vision of rural life, typified by the *grands propriétaires*. This anti-urban/bourgeois bias also indicates an anti-modern perspective. While royalist and liberal moderates looked optimistically to the future, eagerly greeting news of recent industrial advances both in France and abroad, the ultras resisted rapid change in European society. They did not want to stop progress *per se*, but wanted France to move forward according to traditional values, as articulated by the Bourbon regime, the Catholic Church, and landowners.

The Royalist Reaction of 1820 marked the final occasion during the Restoration when moderate and ultra royalists set aside their differences and worked together. The short-term political result of this cooperation was the exceptional laws. On a grander scale, it also led to a Third Restoration. Louis XVIII and the royal family would never again be as popular as they were during the Royalist Reaction. But that spirit of cooperation was short-lived. Ultra deputies and journalists remained dissatisfied with the few ultra royalists in the *Conseil*, and considered the government's handling of events after Berry's death, especially the way Richelieu dealt with the participants of the 20 August Plot, to be weak-kneed. The ultras had rarely kept silent in the interests of national unity, and they did not start after the Royalist Reaction. As a result, relations between the ultras and the moderates rapidly deteriorated. Even ultra unity disintegrated. Two factions developed: a minority group called *la faction impatiente* or *la pointe*, led by Chateaubriand and Bourdonnay, who refused to cooperate with the Richelieu ministry at all; and a majority group called *la faction circonspecte*, led by Villèle and Corbière, who, although cautious at first, seemed willing to compromise. Their willingness to cooperate explains why Villèle and Corbière were the first ultras invited to join the *Conseil*. However, even the cautious ultras' desire to cooperate was rather limited; by the summer of 1821, *la faction circonspecte* was openly calling for Richelieu's dismissal, which occurred six months later.

LIBERALISM: DENY AND ACCUSE

Restoration royalists had a distinct advantage over their political rivals. The monarchy and the Catholic Church were powerful institutions around which royalists could rally. Liberals had no equivalent unifying symbol or icon, and as a result, liberalism is more difficult to define. Under the liberal banner fell a variety of political groups: republicans, Bonapartists, constitutionalists, parliamentary democrats, and even revolutionaries. Liberals were unanimous in one respect, however. They believed that the French Revolution had not been about the Terror, but about the Declaration of the Rights of Man; it was not the Law of Suspects, but *liberté, égalité, fraternité*. By extension, the Empire was not about Napoleonic tyranny. It exemplified through its military glory the greatness of the French nation. Restoration liberalism prior to the Royalist Reaction must be analyzed from this defensive perspective; it could not help being saddled with the burden of the Revolution's excesses and Napoleon's colossal defeats. Liberals were often identified by default; they were simply people who were uncomfortable with calling themselves royalists, even if they agreed with much of what the Restoration stood for and what the Bourbon regime was doing. It was a question of degree, rather than of starkly differentiated opinion.

For the first few years of the Restoration, this revolutionary legacy hung like an albatross around the liberals' collective neck; France's political community continued to equate the Revolution with the Terror. Moreover, the Hundred Days and the fall of the Empire were difficult times for the nation as a whole. The economy was in disarray and

France was occupied by the Allies. As the Second Restoration began, the liberals faced a generally hostile population, and they struggled to avoid being associated with the Jacobins. Interestingly, against all odds, the liberals never seemed to doubt that one day they would rule France. They interpreted the Revolution and the Empire not as deviations from France's expected historical development, but rather as healthy and desirable steps in that development. They hit upon a single, defining strategy to achieve their political objectives: demonize the royalists as reactionaries dedicated to reestablishing the Old Regime. This strategy floundered as long as the moderate royalists practised *union et oubli*. But the ascent of the ultras to power gave the liberals a credible target to demonize. So while the liberals interpreted the Royalist Reaction in apocalyptic terms, it was in fact the beginning of their political renaissance. With the ultras in power, liberalism took on a more defined, coherent, and robust character. Napoleon's death on 5 May 1821 also helped in that regard. As noted by the Duke of Broglie, "the name of Bonaparte had imposed itself, willy-nilly, on their [the liberals'] plans; the name they dared neither accept nor reject weighed on them and embarrassed them."[62] With his passing, the liberals were able to chart their own direction. However, we are getting ahead of ourselves. Before the Royalist Reaction, the liberals languished in opposition, unable to discredit the *union et oubli* policy. Liberal disunity was partly to blame, but their inability to create viable symbols or icons was a greater problem. Moderate liberals adopted the Charter as their idol. Extreme liberals idolized the Revolution. However, until the Royalist Reaction set in motion the chain of events that brought the ultras to power, those symbols or icons paled against the brilliance of the Bourbon regime and the Catholic Church. For that reason, there is relatively little to say about Restoration liberalism prior to the Royalist Reaction.

The Doctrinaires: The March of Progress

Beyond the single conviction that France's future prosperity depended upon a strict adherence to the Charter, it is hard to know precisely what the doctrinaires believed in. It has been said that their defining principle was to recognize no principles.[63] As a result, no school of thought developed, nor was a leader proclaimed. Historians study the more famous names – Pierre-Paul Royer-Collard, François Guizot, Count Molé, Camille Jordan, Charles de Rémusat. Yet, these men pretended not to lead anyone, nor belong to any group; if anything, they led by example. At the same time, the doctrinaires' political views were not without a philosophical basis, and to understand that, it is best to look to the writings and actions of Pierre-Paul Royer-Collard, the doc-trinaires' semi-official spokesperson during the Royalist Reaction. Royer-Collard proposed the following formula: true liberty was possi-ble only to the extent that an equilibrium existed between State power and individual rights. Put another way, a just society must first estab-lish a public authority and then create public liberties to balance that authority against the needs of individual liberty. This was the role of the Charter. As a constitutional document, and despite its obvious shortcomings, the Charter provided an acceptable form of executive power and an equally acceptable form of legislative power. To the doc-trinaires, the actual structure of these powers was not important, as long as the result was a workable balance. In this sense, the doctri-naires were quite similar to the moderate royalists. Both groups searched for the *juste milieu*, believing that political considerations out-weighed any single doctrinal or philosophical issue. However, they parted company with moderate royalists over the question of the mon-archy. According to the doctrinaires, the monarchy was tolerable only as a practical form of executive power for France at that time; it was a convenience, or, as Royer-Collard put it, "a tradition, but a national one." The Bourbon monarchy was a useful institution to facilitate the establishment of a post-Napoleonic government, but it was in no way divine or essential.

The doctrinaires' doctrinal flexibility is shown by Royer-Collard's voting pattern prior to 1820. In 1815 he voted to re-establish the *cours prévôtales*, courts that played a central role in the White Terror. In 1816 he voted in favour of a law similar to the 1820 liberty law. In 1817 he agreed to the censorship of the periodic press. In 1818 he voted for a bill that would have forced journals and newspapers to pay a *caution* or de-posit. Yet, he also voted for the 1819 press law and against the excep-tional laws. Until the Royalist Reaction hardened and clarified political divisions, Royer-Collard and his fellow doctrinaires rarely felt the need to vote or act one way or another. They tended to vote as they saw fit in the circumstances, just as long as the balance of power enshrined in the Charter was respected.

The philosophical basis of doctrinaire thought extended beyond Royer-Collard's political concepts as well. This philosophy, perhaps better described as a liberal worldview, spoke with a modern spirit that ordered society in scientific, economic, and political terms. Rather than idealizing rural land-ownership, the doctrinaires idealized abstract principles, seeking to improve society by defining rights and freedoms. Radical French thinkers would adopt this practice, although in more dramatic fashion, from Saint-Simon and Fourier, on to Proudhon. That is not to say these radicals recognized any connection with the doctrinaires; however, during the Restoration the doctrinaires were the political group that did the most to promote abstract principles as the vehicle to social improvement. The 1848 Revolution and the hatred directed at the July Monarchy in the years leading to it have obscured this connection. Certainly, by 1840 no serious radical would have chosen to associate himself with the doctrinaires. Yet, as odd as it may seem, those future radicals owed a philosophical debt of sorts to these moderate liberals of the Restoration.

While it is important to acknowledge the doctrinaires' contribution to French political thought, prior to the Royalist Reaction they comprised a small minority of France's political community, with an equally small, but influential, presence in the Chamber of Deputies. Time was perhaps the most serious impediment to enlarging their political audience. The abstract principles that informed their political ideas and actions, principles associated with the Enlightenment and the Revolution, lacked the weight that only maturity can provide. As well, the Revolution itself still cast a shadow over such ideas as constitutionalism and parliamentary democracy. One of the doctrinaires' most impressive achievements was to lift those abstractions out from under that shadow. Works published during the 1820s by Thierry, Guizot, Cousin, and Thiers, to name but a few, persuaded the French political community that liberalism did not equal Jacobinism, but rather modernism; liberalism represented the future and was not a recasting of past horrors. If anything, in their view, it would be more appropriate to level those charges at royalists, whose traditionalism harkened back to the horrors of Bourbon absolutism.

Since doctrinaire views on modernity are central to understanding these thinkers, they deserve additional comment. Royalists often expressed themselves in dramatic religious terms, with an emphasis on sin and retribution. In the eighteenth century, the Church projected an image of a God to be dreaded, using fear of damnation as the stick to ensure religious observance. That would change in the next century when a God of damnation gave way to a God of love and mercy.[64] However, before 1830 the Church still interpreted the effects of Revolution and the Empire as God's punishment for the sins of the nation. The doctrinaires, on the other hand, thought in abstraction, with no concept of sin and retribution. Their words and actions bore witness to a faith, but not a religious one. They believed the human condition was destined to improve, albeit with the occasional unavoidable accidents that were worth the price in the long run. In 1817 Charles de Rémusat, for example, expressed this faith in the future betterment of humanity in a letter to his wife: "I envision a process of improvement, slow perhaps, but never interrupted. Far from imagining a perfect state created suddenly, out of nothing, I see in the imperceptible but steady movement of human ideas a progress in which I can trust for a better future, setting apart accidents such as the flood in Noah's time and the invasion of the Goths in the Middle Ages, which for a long time postponed success and even the first attempts at civilization."[65]

Rémusat's great hope for the future, despite the uncertainly of the present, encapsulates the modern spirit that characterized nineteenth-century European liberalism. The doctrinaires typified this spirit, particularly during the Royalist Reaction. They avoided the radical measures adopted by extremist liberals, holding firm in their belief that things would improve. In their minds the goal was to achieve a balance of interests, the *juste milieu*; and their patience was eventually rewarded, for when the dust settled after the July Revolution, political power fell to them.

The Independents: Fire and Glory

For most of the Restoration, particularly in the first ten years, the doctrinaires were in reality neither as extreme or as revolutionary as they claimed to be; they were overshadowed by their more radical liberal cousins, the independents. The independents proved to be as radical as wealthy men could be.[66] As well, more so than the doctrinaires, the independents lacked a concrete or unifying philosophy; they really had no meaning without reference to the ultra royalists. In short, their principal ideology was to oppose.[67] Significantly, their opposition was not rooted in Restoration politics, but in the Revolution/Counter-Revolution discourse. If the Revolution cast a shadow over the doctrinaires, for the independents, the legacy of the Revolution was a coat of armour to be worn proudly. They were self-proclaimed defenders of the Declaration of the Rights of Man and caretakers of the principles inherent in its rallying cry, *liberté, égalité, fraternité*. By extension, their self-appointed duty was to fight against reactionaries who wanted to revive the Old Regime. The independents spoke with the theatrical vocabulary of the Revolution, and they were really only comfortable when their words and actions were returned with the equally dramatic vocabulary of the Counter-Revolution. The ultras cooperated in full, matching insult for insult.

Personality accounted for the independents' popularity. Some of the most celebrated men in Restoration politics were in their ranks – Destutt de Tracy, Benjamin Constant, Marie-Joseph Lafayette, Paul-Louis Courrier, Jacques Lafitte, Casimir Perier, Jacques-Antoine Manuel, General Foy, General Lamarque, and General Sébastiani. It would be a disservice to the intellectual abilities of these men to suggest that their politics lacked real substance. Yet, the lives of Lafayette and Constant suggest that they were highly principled men who seemed to have no principles. One thing is clear: both men, along with their fellow independents, were concerned with how best to protect individual citizens from arbitrary state action. Benjamin Constant summarized this principle as "the jurisdiction of the sovereign ending at the point where individual independence and existence began."[68] The independents' acute sense of individuality also explains their attachment to the Revolution; in their minds, it symbolized the battle between individual rights and oppressive state tyranny in the clearest historical terms.

The mere existence of a restored Bourbon monarchy made it a simple matter for the independents to project their enmity toward the Old Regime onto the Bourbon regime. At the same time, this projection entailed some stretching of the truth. Louis XVIII's regime had little in common with that of Louis XIV; nor did Restoration governments come close to exercising the oppressive police powers employed during the Imperial era. No matter, the independents loved to denounce tyranny, whether it existed or not. Their point was to promote themselves as defenders of the French people, and their *raison d'être* was to criticize a royalist government. Such self-justification was the independents' defining trait. They convinced themselves, often on the flimsiest of pretexts, that the Bourbon regime was the Old Regime incarnate, and that extra-legal actions, including outright conspiracy, were therefore warranted. Independents loved to refer to the passing of the exceptional laws as the final straw, which freed them to organize a *coup* to overthrow the Bourbons and institute a government more in line with their sensibilities.[69] Such rationalizations naturally raise questions about the independents' commitment to the Charter and the Bourbon regime. Their willingness to play with the facts, their tendency to attack the government vituperatively on virtually every issue, and their participation in seditious activities all strongly suggest that these "principled men" paid little more than lip service to the legalities inherent in the constitutional they claimed to hold so dear.

The independents' ambivalence toward the use of violence and conspiracy to achieve political ends follows a tendency in the historical development of the left to accept violence as the option of first resort in effecting change. This legacy of violence began with the Revolution, and is seen most clearly in the extreme socialist and anarchist ideologies of the nineteenth century. The Left's worship of the Revolution often brought tragic results, as generations of revolutionaries led senseless and empty protests, building barricades easily toppled by the army – protests that in turn gave the government of the day the excuse it needed to stamp out the political opposition.[70] Writing in *Revue des*

Deux Mondes in 1857, Rémusat criticized the independents' propensity for self-justification and violence in the strongest terms: "The rule of liberty, noisy, restless, giving voice to opinions and feeding passions, becomes intolerable and impossible if violence occurs ... Passionate language, exaggerated grievances, unjust accusations are inevitable in the debates of a free country ... men attack what they wish to reform as if they intend to destroy it."[71]

Over the course of the 1820s, the independents' political influence diminished; they were little more than distinguished relics[72] when the July Revolution began. More meteoric than their moderate confrères, the brilliance of their personalities had by then simply burned out. However, that would take some years. During the Royalist Reaction, the independents articulated their views with a distinctive style. They led the battle against the exceptional laws, both in the Chamber of Deputies and in the press. They more than the doctrinaires must therefore assume primary responsibility for losing that battle. Moreover, their lack of doctrinal purity and coherence – and even sincerity – also contributed to the liberals' inability to mount an effective campaign against the exceptional laws. The royalists were able to inform their defense of the laws with a clear and precise philosophy. The liberals, particularly the independents, had no such philosophy and they would suffer as a result.

In 1815 Talleyrand and Fouché were invited to join the *Conseil*. Chateaubriand's description of the event is laced with irony: "I sat down in a corner and waited. All at once a door opened; silently there entered Vice leaning on the arm of Crime; Monsieur Talleyrand supported by Monsieur Fouché. The infernal vision passed slowly before me, went into the King's study and disappeared. Fouché was coming to swear his loyalty and pay homage to his sovereign; the regicide vassal, on his knees, put the hands which had brought down Louis XVI between the hands of the martyred king's own brother; the apostate bishop stood surety for the oath."[73] Did the Bourbon regime face an impossible challenge, as it tried to moderate political tensions after the collapse of the Empire? One might ask if it was even reasonable, under the circumstances, to suggest that royalism and liberalism could coexist. Was the Restoration doomed to failure from the start, as historians such as Rosanvallon and Kroen have argued? The desire for peace and stability provided the initial impetus for moderation during the Restoration; however, that desire could not sustain the regime forever. As has been argued, there was nothing inherent in Restoration royalism and liberalism prior to the Royalist Reaction to prevent the Bourbon regime from continuing for any number of years, and most certainly beyond 1830. It was the Royalist Reaction, and not royalism and liberalism, that set in motion the series of events that culminated in the July Revolution. It resulted in the abandonment of the *union et oubli* policy and its replacement by an increasingly ultra royalist agenda. Clearly, the seeds of its decline were sown at this time. It is therefore ironic that the Royalist Reaction also represents the Bourbon regime's greatest moment of triumph. The assassination of the Duke of Berry and the birth of the miracle child gave rise to a royalist revival that swept the nation. This revival held the promise of a glorious future in which Bourbon kings would rule France forever. Of course, that future was not to be. To understand why, we must turn to the Royalist Reaction itself.

PART TWO

The Royalist Reaction of 1820

4 February:
The Royalist Reaction
Commences

On Thursday, 14 February 1820, at approximately 6:30 a.m., seven excruciating hours after being stabbed by Louvel, the Duke of Berry died. Louis XVIII then took leave of his nephew, accompanied by Elie Decazes. Historians have long quoted a conversation reported to have taken place between the two as they rode back to the Tuileries. As the story goes, Louis XVIII said that Decazes would be blamed for the assassination and would be asked to resign from the *Conseil*. "They will try to take political advantage," the King said, "but I will demand that you remain my first minister. They will never separate us."[1] This conversation, real or invented, illustrates how quickly the assassination was politicized. Scarcely had Berry taken his last breath when these two men were plotting their political strategies. The last two weeks of February would prove Louis XVIII prophetic; for once the king and his minister had stepped outside the Opera House, the Royalist Reaction of 1820 had begun.

DECAZES FALLS FROM GRACE

Decazes had good reason to be worried. His close association with the dissolution of the *Chambre introuvable*, the February 5th Law, the *Fournée*, and Grégoire's election made him the ultras' favourite whipping boy. His decision to moderate the Liberal Experiment by the fall of 1819 and to introduce an amended electoral law had lost him the trust of the liberals. His only hope of surviving on the *Conseil* was to re-establish ties with the moderate royalists. The amended electoral law was the first step in that strategy, and Decazes had been working on it the night of the assassination. This new law was to reintroduce a second electoral college reserved for the highest paying *cens* voters in each department. Decazes was confident his amendment would bring the moderate royalists back on side. In fact, he had even managed to convince some influential ultra deputies, Villèle among them, to support the amendment, which he planned to introduce later that month. Moreover, a number of prominent liberals, specifically those who believed Grégoire's election was an embarrassment to their cause, had suggested amendments to the February 5th Law similar to Decazes's proposal.[2] This anticipated support gave him some hope that the doctrinaires could be convinced to support his ministry as well.

The Chamber of Deputies met a few hours after Berry died. Decazes had decided he could not afford to wait until the end of the month to act. Instead, he entered the Chamber armed not only with the amended electoral law but also with two other pieces of legislation. Collectively, the bills were intended to show that he recognized the seriousness of the crime, that he was taking immediate and appropriate action to bring those responsible to justice, and that he would do whatever was necessary to maintain the public peace. The amended electoral law differed slightly from the one Decazes had been working on. It proposed a two-tiered voting system. Those paying less than 400 francs in direct taxes would vote in one college, and those paying more would vote in a separate college. The principal difference in Decazes's new scheme was that those voting in the second college would also vote in the first. This was the first time the double vote concept had been formally introduced to the Chamber. It reflected the widely held assumption that there was a direct relationship between land ownership and royalism. Decazes believed the 400-franc *cens* voters to be loyal royalists, whose antipathy towards the February 5th Law and to him personally would be assuaged by additional electoral clout. The other two laws were of the law-and-order variety. The first was a press law that re-imposed strict censorship. Penalties for contravention included a temporary or permanent suspension of publication, the loss of the *caution* (deposit), fines ranging from 200 to 1,200 francs, and possible imprisonment for any editor or owner. The other law gave the police the power to arrest and detain without trial for up to three months anyone suspected of threatening state security or the safety of the royal family.

These three pieces of legislation were essentially echoed by Richelieu's later exceptional laws, and the eventual passage of those laws suggests that Decazes's strategy was fundamentally sound. But the minister had underestimated his own lack of popularity. The first order of business for the Chamber on the fourteenth was straightforward enough. The Chamber of Peers was granted the right to try Louvel for treason. The next order of business did not unfold as smoothly. Some deputies proposed that the Chamber send an official "Address" to Louis XVIII expressing their collective horror at the crime and offering their profoundest condolences. A violent debate erupted between ultra and liberal deputies over its wording. Led by Bourdonnaye, the ultras demanded that along with condolences there should be a statement that the Chamber would endorse any measure needed to "control the pernicious doctrines that attacked all civilization and threatened the existence of France's political body." General Foy, an independent deputy, responded that condolences were sufficient. The matter went to a vote, with the ultras carrying the day. The final address included the declaration that the deputies were "ready to assist with equal energy and devotion, according to our constitutional duties, in the measures which Your Majesty's wisdom judges necessary in such grave circumstances." The Peers' address mirrored this declaration, stating they would support "all the measures which the gravity of the situation may require."

Those addresses were published in newspapers throughout France, with particular notice given to Foy's rather impolitic objection. Certainly, the controversy did not augur well for Decazes. Regardless, he remained determined to promote his laws in the Chamber the next day. He declared to the deputies that the laws represented nothing less than "the stability of their institutions, the triumph of the monarchy, its independence and the guarantee of its liberties."[3] Clausel de Coussergues took the podium next. He accused Decazes of being an accomplice in Berry's assassination, either by directing Louvel personally, by failing to provide adequate protection, or by refusing to prosecute those whose revolutionary rhetoric poisoned the minds of people like Louvel; and he promised to submit a written accusation shortly. Some ultra deputies thought Coussergues had acted too rashly, fearing that his accusation would encourage liberals and moderate royalists to rally behind Decazes and his laws. They were wrong. The accusation turned Decazes into a political and social pariah overnight. Later that day at the Château de Saint-Cloud, Decazes and his wife were very publicly snubbed by the royal family. A rumour began to circulate that on the night of the assassination when Decazes had entered the room to see Berry, the duchess had jumped into the arms of Artois, her father-in-law, and shouted, "Papa, Papa! Take that man away! I cannot bear the sight of him; he terrifies me. O heavens! He is going to poison my child!"[4]

Coussergues's accusation was patently absurd. Not a shred of evidence ever connected Decazes to Louvel. Yet, most royalists assumed his culpability not because he had told Louvel what to do but rather because his politics encouraged Louvel. This assumption speaks to the power of the conspiracy mentality. It lent credibility to Coussergues's accusation, and led to Decazes's demise. Even such staunch liberals as the editors of the *Journal Libre de l'Isère* accused Decazes bitterly of having "wounded our institutions, and yet having escaped from the terrible responsibility which will be borne by those whom French liberty will blame as it descends into the grave!"[5] Abandoned by his fellow ministers, rejected by liberal and royalist moderates, and accused of complicity in Berry's murder, Decazes played his final card on 16 February by offering Louis XVIII his resignation. He expected his protector to refuse it, and for a time the king seemed inclined to tough it out, even as Artois and the Duchess of Angoulême harassed him to accept it.[6] However, after four days it became too much, and on 20 February Louis XVIII accepted his first minister's resignation.

While the king agonized over Decazes, others schemed to replace him. Rumours abounded. The most intriguing was that a group led by Talleyrand, Vitrolles, and Fiévée would take control of the *Conseil*, pass Decazes's three laws, and call an immediate deputy election. Villèle was convinced that Talleyrand was actively involved in a conspiracy to overthrow the government.[7] In the end, however, Artois proved to be the most active schemer. He knew his brother would not accept an ultraroyalist first minister, so he promoted a man not compromised by an attachment to any single faction. That man was Louis Armand du Plessis, Duke of Richelieu. Ironically, Artois had played a leading role in the fall of Richelieu's first ministry in 1818. Richelieu was offered the first minister's post the following year, a post ultimately given to Decazes, but he declined, believing that the royal family, notably Artois, did not support him. However, by appealing to Richelieu's strong sense of civic duty, and warning of civil unrest if he refused – and by pledging his undying support on bended knee – Artois managed to convince Richelieu to return to political life. On 26 February Richelieu was named president of the *Conseil* for the second time. That same day, Decazes set sail for London.

Decazes's resignation and Richelieu's appointment were greeted with almost universal approval. Moderate royalists worried about Artois's growing influence, but on the whole they were relieved that a man with Richelieu's reputation for honesty and loyalty to the Bourbon regime was heading the government. Ultra royalists were, naturally enough, ecstatic at Decazes's fall from grace. In his memoirs, Jules de Polignac recalled that occasion: "I believe I heard my parents and their friends, dyed-in-the-wool ultras, talking of Monsieur Decazes as if he were a Jacobin, applauding his fall as if it would save the monarchy."[8] The Marquis de la Maisonfort wrote in his memoirs that while Coussergues' allegations were unfounded, Decazes nonetheless deserved his fate, not for treason, but for supporting "an absurd system." In his view, "Decazes fell because he was a victim, not because he was guilty."[9] In a less charitable frame of mind, Royer-Collard dismissed Decazes as a "cadaver that can no longer walk,"[10] and saw in Richelieu the best defense against the ultra royalists. The independents were also glad to see Decazes go; his decision to abandon the Liberal Experiment had alienated them already. At the same time, Richelieu was no great friend of theirs, and they awaited the returning first minister's actions with some trepidation.

PANIC IN THE PROVINCES

On the national stage Coussergues's accusation was the first and most public manifestation of the conspiracy mentality. That mentality also manifested itself at the local level. In the two weeks following the assassination, Charles Weiss, a librarian in the city of Besançon whose politics reflected a doctrinaire perspective, noted in his journal that there was a tremendous increase in police activity, with streets patrolled by military personnel and guards posted at strategic sites. Everyone waited for something to happen, believing the assassination would certainly be followed by an act of greater violence. On 21 February Weiss wrote, "We are on the eve of great events."[11]

Local government officials also expected these great events, and as soon as news of the assassination had filtered out from Paris they prepared feverishly to confront them. A comparison between the conduct of officials from Isère and Haute-Garonne is instructive in this regard. We now know that radical liberals in Isère did pose a security risk: a secret society called *l'Union* flourished; Grégoire had recently been elected there; the *Journal Libre de l'Isère*, a popular liberal newspaper, attacked the government in virtually every issue; and throughout the Royalist Reaction a number of serious anti-Bourbon demonstrations were held. Regardless, in the weeks following Berry's death, local officials took few added precautions and generally reported that all was calm. On the other hand, while Haute-Garonne offered virtually no risk to the Bourbon regime, officials there readied themselves for what they feared would be the next revolution.

Clearly, local politics influenced official reaction to the assassination. In the case of Isère, the liberal presence necessitated a pragmatic approach: punish those caught in the act, but take care not to alienate moderate liberals who would be offended by overly aggressive police action. Grenoblois liberals had been complaining of an excessive police presence for years,[12] so it is not surprising that Isère's newly appointed prefect, Baron Haussez,[13] decided to act with caution. The preponderance of ultra royalists in Haute-Garonnne, by contrast, led its prefect, St-Chamans,[14] a man already obsessed with conspiracy, to organize a department-wide search for revolutionaries.

On 18 February Haussez sent a letter to all sub-prefects, mayors, and police commissioners in Isère informing them of the assassination and instructing them to be on the lookout for signs of trouble; public peace had to be maintained at all costs.[15] Only the Vienne police commissioner bothered to reply, reporting that all was calm.[16] Two days after sending that report, however, Vienne's police commissioner arrested six men for singing seditious songs at a tavern.[17] And in Grenoble, an individual named Urbain Petiet was overheard making derogatory remarks about the royal family. He was arrested but soon released.[18] Not everyone got off quite so lightly; in the Commune of Chatte, a M Rosset, formerly convicted of vagabondage and theft, was arrested for uttering seditious and injurious statements about the royal family and received a two-year sentence.[19]

St-Chamans sent a similar letter to his subordinates in Haute-Garonne, but with a substantially different effect. His office was flooded with reports on the department's well-being, and the tone and content of the reports speaks to an expectation of violence and seditious activity, despite the fact that little of the sort occurred. Urging the utmost effort, the sub-prefect of Villefranche told the mayors in his arrondissement to "pay the greatest attention to all the gossip that may arise concerning this appalling event … and to find out where it originates." They were to pay special attention to any travellers spreading false news or causing "alarming rumours," watch them closely, and arrest them if necessary. He was to be informed of any arrests immediately. He then instructed his subordinates to search for any texts or *affiches* that appeared to support "seditious and anarchical principles," to seize and destroy the offending material, and arrest the author.[20] The sub-prefect of St Gaudens reported that he had instructed his *gendarmes* to watch closely for signs of unrest, "with the strictest surveillance possible." His arrondissement was calm and tranquil; however, he suspected "there were pockets of resistance and anarchy."[21] A few days later, the sub-prefect reported to St-Chamans that if a conspiracy to kill Berry existed, his agents had found no evidence of it.[22]

The penchant of police officials to create mountains of sedition out of molehills of suspicion was illustrated by Toulouse's police commissioner in his first report to St-Chamans after the assassination. After a tour of the streets and cafés, he noted with great vehemence that during his inspection several people had grimaced as he walked by, an act he considered to be "a sign of disapproval."[23] Following up on those grimaces, the police commissioner put two people under surveillance: an officer *en demi-solde* said to be a known Bonapartist who had actively supported Napoleon during the Hundred Days and who in 1819 had been questioned for shouting, "Long Live the Emperor"; and a women who claimed she had known about the assassination two days before it was announced publicly, and was at that time residing with an individual known to be hostile to the Bourbons. Neither person was ever arrested. St-Chamans considered the following two incidents serious enough to warrant a report to the minister of the interior. The first involved a statement made in a café implying that the assassination was caused by plans to change the electoral law. When questioned, however, the suspect was found to have merely been repeating what he had read in the newspapers and had no firsthand knowledge of Berry's murder.[24] The second incident involved a women who stated that the entire royal family had been killed. Again, nothing came of the incident. Muret's sub-prefect asked the prefect for advice about the report of a man with liberal connections in Toulouse, who stated that in the next two weeks there would be "other events." St-Chamans advised him to try to identify the man and question him as soon as possible, but the man was never found. The sub-prefect noted a few days later that all the mayors in his arrondissement had been instructed to keep a close watch on suspicious persons, but that so far nothing worth investigating had turned up.[25] The mayor of Blagnac reported to the Prefect that a *procès-verbal* had been issued against two people: an individual who had made disparaging comments about the royal family, and a German man who had made derogatory comments about Berry. Again, neither matter went to trial.[26] Baron Gary, the *procureur général*, investigated a report that two men travelling on horseback were suspected of making "a very worrying statement" about the assassination, but the men were never found, nor were the statements confirmed.[27]

One incident deserves special attention, for it encapsulates the exaggerated fear of sedition that existed among government officials, the police, and the judiciary in the two weeks following the assassination. On 19 and 20 February, a man named Etienne Jouvenet, who had falsified his name and occupation, allegedly made seditious statements to an innkeeper in the town of Noé.[28] He had apparently made derogatory comments about Berry in another town as well. Upon Jouvenet's arrest, the sub-prefect of Muret went so far as to suggest that the mayor of Noé, the official who had sworn the *procès-verbal* against the accused, should be arrested for negligence for failing to investigate the incident with sufficient speed. St-Chamans reported the incident to the minister of the interior in some detail. Finally, at Jouvenet's sentencing some time later, Baron Gary took the opportunity to launch a blistering attack on revolutionaries, Bonapartists, and liberals.

Clearly, these officials did not consider Jouvenet's comments to an innkeeper in a tiny town in Haute-Garonne to be an insolated case. Without any evidence to suggest that Jouvenet belonged to a secret society or was actively planning a conspiracy against the government, they immediately linked his comments to Berry's assassination and to a supposed liberal conspiracy that threatened the Bourbon regime. Their response to Jouvenet was less a legal action against a dangerous individual than a confirmation of their suspicion that the assassination signalled the beginning of the next revolution. That the response was triggered by innocuous comments made by an obscure man to an innkeeper was beside the point.

THE MEDIA

In his journal entry for 17 February, Charles Weiss wrote that after the prefect had announced Berry's death, he had waited impatiently for *Le Courier* to arrive to learn the details of the crime. Parisian newspapers and extracts from them began to appear in the provinces by the nineteenth; within five days of the event, France's literate community had access to information on the assassination, along with updates on the royal family, Berry's funeral arrangements, and Louvel. The speed with which information on the assassination was disseminated throughout France testifies to the emergence of a modern communications network, in which the press played a leading role. Other parts of the network were the semaphore, forerunner to the telegraph, and the visual media, an industry that published inexpensive pictures or illustrations for the general public.

Media coverage of the assassination in the two weeks after Berry's death is more than a testimony to the effectiveness of France's communications network; it also provides evidence of a curious aspect of the Royalist Reaction. To a remarkable degree the newspaper articles and illustrations published in February regarding the assassination expressed the most significant themes and issues that characterized and drove the Royalist Reaction over the next ten months. This was a measure of the media's market savvy – they clearly knew a good story when they saw one. It also speaks to the rapidity with which the assassination became a politicized event of national importance.

The Press

Circulation numbers belie the central role newspapers played in the dissemination of political information during the Restoration. The total monthly circulation for all French newspapers by 1830 barely reached 50,000. The *Journal Libre de l'Isère*, one of the most popular and influential provincial newspapers, had only 400–500 official subscribers. However, far more people had access to newspapers than those figures suggest. Reading rooms – *cercles* and *cabinets littéraires* that provided full access to leading Parisian and local newspapers – existed in every major town in France. In 1820 thirteen different newspapers were carried by the *cercles* and *cabinets littéraires* in Villefranche, an arrondissement near Toulouse, and Toulouse itself had eleven separate reading rooms where one could find virtually every important newspaper, along with a wide selection of political pamphlets and literary works.[29]

Interestingly, it was exactly the same article – referred to here as the "assassination article" – that broke the story in both Isère and Haute-Garonne. The article was published in Isère by the *Journal de Grenoble* and the *Journal Libre de l'Isère*, and in Haute-Garonne by the *Journal de Toulouse*.[30] The assassination article, likely a reprint from a Parisian newspaper, presents clear evidence of the rapid politicization of the assassination, and for that reason is described in some detail below. It also shows how a newspaper's political orientation determined its readers' general impression of the assassination.

Rather than describe the assassination in chronological fashion, the assassination article offered information on particular moments during the night. As a result, the reader is drawn to certain themes rather than mere facts. First, the attack was described briefly. Louvel was said to have seized Berry from behind, stabbed him with a dagger, and then left him to fall to the ground bathed in blood. Berry was then taken into the guard room, followed by the duchess. Next, we are told how the king closed his nephew's eyes after his death: "the King went right up to the bed, and bathed the face of his dying son with tears; His Majesty closed the Prince's eyelids himself, kissed him and bade him a last farewell." Berry's bravery was then commended. According to the article, Berry knew that he was mortally wounded. Accepting his death with grace, he told his doctors, "I am greatly touched by your care, but it will not prolong my life, for my wound is mortal." The article stressed that throughout the night, despite his tremendous pain, Berry continually pleaded that Louvel's life be spared. The *Journal de Toulouse* noted: "Many times in the middle of his sufferings, he was heard to ask the King to pardon that man, which was the only term he used for his murderer, out of generosity, and, as he lay dying, repeated continually that he pardoned him."[31] The description of the crime ended by revealing that the duchess was pregnant. Readers were told how Berry suddenly begged his wife, who had held him in her arms for some time, to take care of their unborn child. "At the sight of the duchess's despair the prince begged her to think of the child she was carrying in her womb." It was added that the unborn child was some consolation for Berry's loss. A thumbnail sketch of Louvel was then provided. He was thirty-six, without wife or child, and had worked as a saddler in the king's stables. Louvel denied there were any accomplices. He had planned the assassination, by himself, for five years. Motivated by his hatred towards the Bourbons, he chose his victim for one reason only: "to put a complete end to the royal family." Louvel was, the article concluded, "the most revolting example of blind and dreadful fanaticism."

Beyond these statements, the assassination article gave voice to an interpretation of Berry's death that would prove authoritative, not only among the news-reading public in Isère and Haute-Garonne, but among all members of France's political community. The groundwork was laid for the transformation of Berry's public persona: the brave duke was struck down from behind by a cowardly assassin; he then acted heroically throughout the night, even asking that his assassin's life be spared, a merciful act worthy of a Christian martyr; as a soldier he knew he was going to die that night, and so acted accordingly, with honour. The revelation that the duchess was pregnant must have both shocked and fascinated readers. Given the due date, the duchess was just over two months pregnant at the time of the assassination; if Louvel had acted sooner, the Bourbon line would have come to an end. Even a modern reader might be tempted to attribute the coincidence to a higher power; in 1820 it was the hand of providence that was seen to have the principal role in the miracle of the Duchess' pregnancy.[32] The description of Louvel set the stage for an interesting comparison between the criminal and the royal family. Louvel came across as a revolutionary fanatic, a man without family, a man without conscience, a regicidal descendant of a regicidal Convention that had sentenced Louis XVI and Marie-Antoinette to death. Conversely, Berry was a descendant of a long line of Bourbon martyrs and a martyr to the counter-revolutionary cause, the reincarnation of Henry IV, and a symbol of Bourbon greatness. He was a family man, virile, Christian, and brave. The duchess was loyal to the end, remaining by Berry's side the entire night. She was now mother to all of France, for she carried in her womb the key to France's future – the future king of France. Finally, Louis XVIII acted admirably and with dignity; and it was only fitting that he should have been the one to close Berry's eyes,[33] for he was a man accustomed to death.

The two Grenoblois newspapers added little editorial comment to the edition in which the assassination article appeared. Not so for the *Journal de Toulouse*. Four entire pages plus a supplement were dedicated to the event. A few editorial notes preceded the article. The editors suggested that Louis XVIII was an even more tragic figure than Berry, for he had suffered so long and so terribly. In fact, the assassination was simply unfair; one man should not have to endure that much, particularly considering what he had done for France: "That noble monarch, restored to his people after twenty-five years of troubles, which affected both him and his people, who has brought back to us peace, independence, and legal freedoms, and who heard the last sighs of his adopted son, the next hope of the throne, and of France."[34] The editors boldly pronounced that Louis XVIII's strength of character would prevent the act of one lone assassin from destroying his efforts to restore peace in France: *union et oubli* would not die with Berry, but would in fact be strengthened by it.

The ultra-royalist press in Paris resolutely pointed the finger of blame at Decazes and the revolutionary doctrines that his policies encouraged. Charles Nodier wrote in *Le Drapeau Blanc* that the knife that killed Berry was "neither a dagger, a sword, or a knife, but a liberal idea," adding that the real assassin was a clause in the February 5th law.[35] In an editorial in the *Journal de Toulouse*, readers were told that the real assassins were the revolutionary ideas that inspired Louvel: "This is indeed a strong accusation against those deadly counsels of insurrection and revolutionary daring which we have so often opposed. For when they come from the pens of certain sophists they are only signs of dishonesty or crazy dreaming; they take on a deadly aspect when they reach men with violent but limited minds, beginning in delirium and ending in crime."[36]

That belief was echoed in an extract published in the *Journal de Toulouse* from the deliberations of the *Cour royale de Toulouse*. Mathieu-Louis Hocquart, the *premier président*, blamed the "horrible assassination" on the "the most evil effects of these doctrines which continually poison the spirit of the people."[37] Baron Gary wondered why society allowed the propagation of revolutionary doctrines that created men like Louvel: "This, Gentlemen, is the dreadful fruit of these impious and anarchic doctrines that we have frequently mentioned here, these doctrines which are subversive of religion, morals and legitimacy, which are spreading from one end of Europe to the other."[38]

Liberals responded promptly to suggestions that liberals and liberalism in general had played a role in Berry's death. In *La Minerve*, editors

charged that royalists were simply using the assassination as an excuse
to attack their political opponents and boost their own popularity:
"The ministers and ultras want to bury all French liberties in the coffin
of a French prince, hoping to hide their evil intentions behind the royal
tomb."[39] Only a week after Berry's death, the editors of the *Journal
Libre de l'Isère* stated that liberals, whom they called the "friends of
liberty," were always the royalists' first target: "The grief of those who
defend liberty is great indeed, for these are the men who, for twenty
years, have been asking for laws, not blood, and who have always been
the first victims of political intrigue. They have not been seen in public
shedding crocodile tears and making a show of their grief, nor have
they been seen with that devilish smile which, for several days, has been
on the lips of those who call themselves ultra royalist."[40] In the next issue, the editors responded to Richelieu's introduction of the exceptional laws by charging that royalists were using Berry's death as a
pretext to destroy the liberties enshrined in the Charter: "The nation is
accused of a dreadful complicity, and the act of one man must be attributed to all; our liberties and the prince who swore to defend them
are going to be buried together."[41]

The assassination article introduced Louvel to the French public.
And although the introduction was rather brief, the article refered explicitly to the conspiracy question and the influence of revolutionary
doctrines on Louvel's mind. In terms of the attack itself, the article simply noted that Louvel had struck from behind. What followed was
more significant: beyond a few biographical details, the readers were
told that Louvel was interrogated immediately and denied having any
accomplices; he had been planning to kill a member of the royal family
for almost five years; his motivation was clear – extinguish the Bourbon line. In summary, the assassination article depicted Louvel as a fanatic, a characterization that was probably accurate. The *Journal de
Toulouse* published extracts of Louvel's interrogation by Decazes at
length. Louvel denied any connection with the liberals, stating that he
was motivated solely by hate: "I had no accomplices ... I was moved to
this act, which I had been contemplating for five years, by my hatred
for the Bourbons, who are the enemies of my country. I know I will be
executed, but I have no reason to regret my life."[42] He had targeted
Berry, he said, because he was the youngest heir to the throne.[43] The
newspaper also reported that Louvel expressed no regrets or exhibited
any emotion when taken to view Berry's body a few days later.[44] The
Journal Libre de l'Isère noted that during Decazes's interrogation Louvel was told that Berry had requested that his life be spared. Knowing
that, he was asked, would he still have committed the crime? "Yes, indeed," Louvel replied coldly, "I would do it again."[45]

Of the three newspapers, the *Journal Libre de l'Isère* showed the most interest in Louvel. Its editors seemed heavily invested in proving that liberals were not involved in the assassination. In the 22 February edition, it reported that Louvel had testified to the *juge d'instruction*, M. Grandet, that he did not have accomplices, and that he "planned and carried out the execution on his own."[46] On 29 February the *Journal* complained that *Le Drapeau Blanc* was slandering Grenoble's reputation by publishing ridiculous rumours about Louvel. It accused the ultra paper of mistakenly reporting that Louvel had gone to Elba before killing Berry and had had a correspondence with someone from Grenoble.[47] In fact, Louvel did go to Elba in September 1814, although during his two-month visit he did not meet with Napoleon or his officers. Moreover, he passed through Grenoble on his return, and accompanied Napoleon to Paris during the Hundred Days. There were rumours that Louvel had certain documents on his person in Grenoble that spoke of Napoleon's return to France in the coming spring; however, those documents were never found, nor was there any evidence that Louvel corresponded in Grenoble with a member of a secret society.[48] Another short article in the *Journal Libre de l'Isère* contradicted a report in *Le Drapeau Blanc* that on 19 February, only five days after Berry's death, anti-monarchical demonstrations, complete with the hanging of the *tricolore*, had broken out in Grenoble and throughout Isère. According to the editors of the *Journal Libre de l'Isère* the report was nothing but a lie, but ironically the same newspaper that criticized liberals for causing unrest was also calling royalists to arms in the face of liberal provocation.[49] A few days later, the editors ridiculed a magistrate and an unnamed ultra newspaper that suggested Louvel was part of a larger conspiracy. Two days earlier, the article added, the same newspaper had erroneously reported that Louvel had escaped from prison with the help of his accomplices. It concluded sarcastically by thanking the ultra royalists for spreading rumours and charged that they must take responsibility for the damage their lies caused.[50]

On 26 February, the *Journal Libre de l'Isère* published a lengthy article claiming to provide for the first time the authentic details of Louvel's life. Little was said of his physical features, other than that he had grey eyes, and that his face was not particularly expressive or animated. He was described as "morose, unsociable, restless, and silent," a private man who rarely spoke to anyone. Louvel, it claimed, stated he had planned to kill a member of the royal family since the beginning of the First Restoration. In 1814, he travelled to Calais hoping to kill Louis XVIII, but arrived three days after the King left. He then changed his sights to one of the three princes, eventually

settling on Berry, and from that moment on dedicated his life to eliminating the royal family at any cost.

The newspaper also added that many journals had reported falsely
that Rousseau's *Social Contract* was found at Louvel's apartment. The
only significant political work was a copy of the Charter, without
notes. Finally, in a separate article, the *Journal Libre de l'Isère* cited a
report from the journal *Aristarque Français* stating that Louvel was being bled by doctors in order to soften him up. Such a practice, they
charged, would be atrocious, inhuman, and unacceptable, even when
dealing with an assassin. That accusation was denied in an official report to the Chamber of Peers by the Count of Bastard, who stated that
Louvel received in prison all the care that justice and humanity necessitated, "in spite of the horror his crime inspired."[51]

The print media by and large ignored the duchess. Immediately
after the assassination, local newspapers reported on her for a few
weeks, providing details of where she went, how she felt, and what
she wore. During that period, the duchess was always portrayed as a
grieving widow, *une épouse inconsolable*. Her courageous behavior at
the Opera was praised by everyone. Newspapers noted that she followed Berry into the guard room after the attack, and never left his
side after that, holding him for most of the night, despite the blood
and the overall horror of the situation.[52] Her pregnancy was reported
with interest. The editors of the *Journal de Toulouse* wrote that the
impending birth mitigated the sting of Berry's assassination – at least
somewhat: "Perhaps the prince whom we mourn is not entirely gone;
when he was on his deathbed he turned his last thoughts and those of
France to the hope he bequeathed to us. But if we accept that hope, if
we refuse to believe that that crime could disinherit us from a part of
our political future, then the sight of that royal grief must be painful
to the hearts of Frenchmen … it exists in the womb of the grieving
wife who saw him fall into her arms. Precious fruit of so short a
union!"[53] However, after this initial period of interest, and apart
from a few similar references, the press did not often comment on the
duchess's condition until just before Bordeaux's birth. Perhaps super-
stition accounts for the silence, or maybe the press simply did not
consider her to be particularly interesting. Certainly, gender plays
some role. The duchess would be used by the government and the
royalists for political purposes, but she would not be allowed to participate directly in political matters during the Royalist Reaction.
They preferred her as a symbol, and they would invoke her name to
reinforce the government's official interpretations of the assassination
and the miracle birth.

The Visual Media

Newspapers did not include pictures until the last third of the nineteenth century; visual images of historical events and important people were furnished by a separate industry, the visual media. The assassination and the miracle birth were a godsend for the visual media. Other events of the period offered occasions for numerous illustrations – such as the Bourbons' return in 1814, Grégoire's election in 1819, the Spanish Campaign of 1823, Louis XVIII's death in 1824, and Charles X's coronation in 1825. However, those illustrations paled in comparison to the number, the variety and the commercial longevity of the assassination illustrations. By April 1820 a consumer could choose from approximately 100 different illustrations. The rate of publication fell to between fifteen and twenty in 1821, and then down to two or three every year thereafter. However, new assassination illustrations even appeared after the July Revolution, the last one, a portrait of Louvel, being published in 1836.[54]

The assassination illustrations did not arrive on the market haphazardly. A well-organized, established, and growing industry was ready to take advantage of any commercial opportunity. Politically oriented illustrations had become very popular since the Revolution. *Les Imageries* reached their peak in popularity only after the Restoration, in the form of *canards*, large, printed posters with writing underneath, but much of what made those later illustrations popular was developed during the preceding decade. Jean Adhémar, the leading authority on printed material in France, attributes the success of the *canards* to their ability to "provoke in the strongest manner, feelings of surprise, joy, astonishment, and most often, horror."[55] That assessment applies equally to the assassination illustrations, as editors and engravers[56] published some of the most interesting, provocative, and compelling visual images the French public of the time would ever see.

Relatively new printing technologies also powered the growth of the visual media. Production times shrank from months and years to mere days. In 1785 an artist named Bervic began an illustration of Louis XVI using traditional methods; he finished in 1790. Compare that with the fact that illustrations of the fall of the Bastille were for sale by 28 July. Illustrations of Charlotte Corday's assassination of Marat were also available within weeks.[57] The first assassination illustration on record was published on 23 February, less than two weeks after Berry's death. Distribution had become equally sophisticated. In addition to the numerous Parisian print shops, illustrations were produced in Lille, Nancy, Lyon, Avignon, Nantes, Rouen, and Chartres, and internationally, in England,

Germany, and Holland. On 25 February, a picture of Louvel stabbing Berry was published in England.[58] This distribution network ensured that popular illustrations were available across Europe.

Precise sales figures are virtually impossible to find. Adhémar reported that four thousand copies were made of an illustration called "The Last Moments of the Duke of Berry"; however, he did not know how many were sold.[59] Nevertheless, the available evidence suggests that assassination illustrations were a tremendous commercial success. At least half of them were available for sale by the end of April,[60] with perhaps another 20 percent published in the three months after Bordeaux's birth. Evidently, sales were sufficient to persuade editors to publish them by the dozen. Judging by the publication dates, the assassination remained extremely marketable until the end of April. During that time, editors published mainly scenes of the crime and death. Once interest in those began to wane, they turned to other aspects of the assassination to drive sales until the end of 1820, when the market no longer supported more than a few new assassination illustrations a year.

The extensive use of lithography is another strong indicator of commercial success. Significantly, almost 40 percent of all assassination illustrations were published as lithographs. Lithography permitted the publication of virtually unlimited quantities, very quickly, at a relatively low cost, while other techniques had limited runs and therefore were more expensive when printing large numbers.[61] W. McAllister Johnson described lithographs as "a tool of social information" that "afforded the opportunity of recording, perhaps for the first time, anything one could wish to depict."[62] In 1824 Adolphe Thiers wrote that lithography was nothing short of a revolution in the way information was made available to the general public: "Now an artist can pick up his pencil and note down his ideas directly, as they come to him, then deliver these rapid sketches to the press, which prints them even more rapidly. This allows the artist to seize every impression that strikes him, to note all the images that cross his mind, to capture all the transient aspects of nature."[63] In the same article, Thiers spoke of crowds gathering around the print shops that offered lithographs for sale: "The public gathers in front of the print shops, inspecting the many lithographs that decorate them, taking pleasure at seeing prints that were true likenesses, gay and titillating, and easy to understand." The extensive use of lithography among the assassination illustrations meant that editors intended to print them in quantity, and as quickly as possible, to meet a strong public demand. That conclusion is supported by other factors connected with lithography. At the time it was the newest and the most advanced printing technique.[64] It permitted artists to create

more detailed and precise works than ever before, and therefore generally only suited the more skillful artists. These factors meant lithography was somewhat more expensive, at least in terms of the initial
investment, than other printing techniques. That editors chose lithography in 40 percent of the cases despite the expense, when lithography
was by no means the most popular technique, identifies the assassination and the miracle birth as an extremely marketable and lucrative historical event for the visual media.

The assassination illustrations must be analyzed in the context of the
dynastic implications of Berry's death. As will be shown, personal elements were downplayed or simply ignored. That distinction was important to the government and the royalists for it allowed them to
make the following declarations: the royal family may have lost a relative, but the entire nation had lost their future father; the duchess was a
widow, but she was joined in mourning by all French women;
Bordeaux was a new member of the royal family, but at the same time
every French citizen had gained a son; and finally, Louvel not only
murdered Berry but he had committed a revolutionary act. These declarations encapsulated the government's official interpretation of the assassination and the miracle birth. The assassination illustrations
promoted these declarations more directly – and self-evidently more
graphically – then any other medium; and they were second perhaps
only to the Restoration *fêtes* in their ability to transmit the official interpretations to the general population.

The illustrations differed from the *fêtes* in that the visual media were
not controlled by the government. Certainly, censorship prohibited the
publication and sale of illustrations critical of the Bourbon regime;
however, the government could not force the industry to publish assassination and miracle birth illustrations. That the visual media did so
in substantial numbers, and with such apparent commercial success,
speaks to a unique marriage between an official political strategy and
commercial opportunity. There was clearly no market for illustrations
that attacked Berry or any other person who supported the official interpretations.

The government's official interpretation of the assassination manifested itself in the illustrations primarily through personalities. There
were five categories of assassination illustrations: the crime scene, the
death scene, pictures mourning Berry's death, images of Louvel, and
pictures of Bordeaux. Each of these categories promoted the public personas of four featured individuals: Berry, the duchess, Louvel, and Bordeaux. In the course of the Royalist Reaction, new public personas
would develop for each of them. The fact that over 250 illustrations fit
so neatly into this configuration testifies to the remarkable dominance

of the official version of events across the spectrum of public opinion. Equally remarkable is the observation that the illustrations published in February introduced nearly all of the principal themes that would be featured in all the assassination illustrations – except, of course, the un-born Bordeaux's persona. Having said that, creative editors did not wait for his birth to publish miracle child pictures; some began to ap-pear as early as May.

Turning to the illustrations published in February, we see evidence of the public personas of Berry, the duchess, and Louvel as they would emerge during the Royalist Reaction. Each of their personas will be en-larged upon in chapter five, as most of the assassination illustrations were published later, in March and April; however, the illustrations published in the two weeks after Berry's death require separate treat-ment in order to show how quickly and consistently the public perso-nas were manifested.

Two illustrators named Bulla and Charon released a seven-part series of images depicting moments from the night Berry was killed. The first in the series, "Assassination of the Duke of Berry,"[65] was the prototype of the crime scenes that later poured onto the market in March and April. Naturally enough, Berry, Louvel, and the duchess dominated. Berry had just helped the duchess into her carriage, and Louvel was about to stab him from behind. A sense of motion and the suddenness of the attack was conveyed by the unsuccessful attempt by the duchess, a guard, and two members of the royal entourage to warn Berry. Other crime scenes would place the actors in different positions, add or sub-tract people, change the sequence of events, or alter the location and appearance of the Opera House and the carriage; yet the essential ele-ments remained the same.[66] Berry, the prince, robust, virile, and ele-gant; the duchess, the tragic wife, pretty, helpless, and terror-stricken; and Louvel, a sinister, dark, and shadowy character, shown in stark contrast to the splendour of the royal victim and his wife (fig. 6).

The next illustration in the Bulla-Charon series, published 26 Febru-ary, was a death scene (see page 12).[67] As with the crime scene, this pic-ture contained the basic elements of all future death scene illustrations, which, as a collective body of visual materials, determined how Berry's final hours were viewed – literally – by the general public. The promi-nence of a rather svelte looking Louis XVIII, shown at the foot of the bed, is noteworthy. His appearance in a number of death scenes con-veyed the impression that he had attended to Berry for most of the night, when in fact he arrived barely an hour before Berry died. From a marketing perspective, however, the King's presence made any death scene much more dramatic and interesting. The image of the Duchess on her knees and in tears, as seen in this illustration, was typical for

Figure 6   "Assassination of the Duke of Berry." Dozens of similar illustrations were published in the first few months after Berry's death. Vinck, 10547

most death scenes as well. This pose reinforced her image as a tragic figure and laid the groundwork for her public persona as the Good Wife. Finally, in its fullest context, we see an illustration glorifying the Bourbon royal family, thereby emphasizing the dynastic elements of the assassination. This dynastic emphasis comes through more clearly in another illustration titled "The Thirteenth of February, 1820." The duke and duchess are together at his bedside. The duchess has her arm around Berry, and in the other hand she holds a handkerchief, presumably to wipe away her tears. The *Cordon du St Esprit* lies across the bed. This is a mourning illustration, a picture of a couple that will never be together again. Yet, one must ask, for whom is the duchess mourning? Note Berry's robust figure, a barrel-chested, powerful looking man, sitting upright in what was his death bed. This is clearly a symbolic portrait of the couple. We know Berry was in agony the entire night, drifting in and out of consciousness, and some illustrations of the death scene show him that way. Yet, here we see the Duke of Berry as a prince of the blood, a future king. Note also the duchess's demeanour. She is visibly upset, but she appears strong and supportive. In most images of the death scene, the duchess is overcome with grief, crying

Figure 7   "The Thirteenth of February, 1820." Berry died a hero's death, begging forgiveness for his assassin. "Thus a Bourbon seeks revenge and thus he dies." Vinck, 10583, 25 Feb. 1820

uncontrollably. Here she presents a princess-like image, controlling her emotions as a woman worthy of being a queen. The caption below the picture refers to Berry's forgiveness of Louvel, an act that was said to illustrate his "generous heart." It ends with the line "thus a Bourbon seeks revenge and thus he dies." In other words, this is how royalty behaves in the face of death. We see here a pictorial image of Bourbon greatness (fig. 7).[68]

Most illustrations had a caption and some sort of explanatory text below the picture, usually a reference to the last words of the dying Berry. The text also usually complemented the official interpretation of the assassination depicted in the illustrations. The three most famous phrases, the first two of which appeared in February illustrations, were as follows: "Pardon! Pardon for the man who stabbed me!"; "How cruel it is to die by the hand of a Frenchman"; and, "O ma Patrie! Malheureuse France!"[69] That these phrases often constituted the sole caption, with no accompanying explanation, is an indication of just how well they were known. The repeated mention of Berry's gesture of forgiveness not only in illustrations but in newspapers, pamphlets, *mandements*, and parliamentary speeches, illustrates a key element to Berry's new public persona: he became a magnificent man, pious and magnanimous, his character deeply rooted in Christianity – how else to understand a man who forgave his assassin as he lay dying? Enthusiastic bishops would compare this act to that of Jesus forgiving his murderers from the cross. With his new persona Berry was promoted to the status of a heroic figure, whose name justifiably belonged with other great Bourbon figures from the past. It is somewhat ironic that while so much of Berry's public persona derived its legitimacy from his forgiveness of Louvel, in the end his pleas were ignored and Louvel was executed. Clearly, the government interpreted his forgiveness solely in symbolic terms, and in no way took it as a reason for sparing Louvel's life. Likewise, the general public seemed far more intrigued with the idea of a dying man forgiving his murder than with Louvel's actual pardon.

The two other captions were Berry's supposed responses to being told his assassin was French. The *cruel* phrase speaks to the frustration royalists had felt since 1789 toward a nation that constantly rejected them. Louvel's nationality should have surprised no one; prior to the Royalist Reaction only the most naïve person could have believed the Bourbons were popular. Perhaps the phrase is best thought of from the royal family's perspective; it gives voice to their dedication to France. Berry's pain derived from his learning that a citizen of the nation he loved so dearly had rejected him so violently. The phrase *O ma Patrie* relates to this idea of rejection and is the most loaded with meaning. The word *patrie* translates literally as country, but as with the German word *Volk*, it refers to all that makes France a great nation. It is a spiritual word, not geographic. Revolutionaries used it after 1789 when speaking of the "new France," the light unto other nations, and revolutionaries and counter-revolutionaries continued to use it thereafter to signal their respective idealized notions of France. *Malheureuse* became a mainstay in counter-revolutionary writings. In this context, it means "unfortunate" in a divine or providential sense, expressing a magnificent, enormous distress that transcends politics and history to touch the realm of good and evil. Taken as a whole, the phrase taps into the royalist belief that the French nation, betrayed first by the Revolution and then by Napoleon, had been betrayed once more by Louvel. Berry's death was therefore a spiritual loss for all Frenchmen, and an act contrary to Christian and Gallican values. This sentiment contributed substantially to Berry's posthumous redefinition as a counter-revolutionary figure of the first order, and reinforced the thinking of those who saw the assassination as a revolutionary act. In subsequent months, several illustrations depicted Berry rising to heaven, to be greeted by other Bourbon martyrs, notably Louis XVI and Marie-Antoinette. This fervour suggests that the battle against the Jacobins was not over, that the revolutionaries had not disappeared, and that diligence was needed to protect the royal family from additional attacks. The possibility of more violence against the royal family, combined with the threat of renewed civil unrest, provided a useful pretext for the government's political strategies, particularly as Richelieu's ministers attempted to steer the exceptional laws through the Chamber of Deputies.

A final February illustration deserves notice. It is a simple, rather crude portrait of Louvel, published by an editor named Engleman. Louvel portraits were published over the next sixteen years, so it is difficult to determine when interest in them was highest. Few were ever deposited with the *Bureau de l'imprimerie et de la librairie*. Common sense suggests most were published at the time of his execution. Regardless, the general public would naturally want to see Louvel's picture, which explains why this illustration was rushed to market. When comparing the Louvel illustrations, one is struck by the fact that he virtually never has the same face. No attempt was made to portray Louvel's features accurately. It was market forces that determined what he looked like. Editors published a Louvel portrait they thought would sell. At the same time, it is possible to categorize the faces of Louvel into two groups: non-descript and fanatical. The February portrait fell into the first category. We are greeted by an innocuous, frail-looking man. It appears Engleman just wanted to offer a face for sale (fig. 8).[70]

Editors who opted for the fanatical Louvel were similarly motivated, but they hoped to appeal to those caught up in the Berry Conspiracy. Again, as the months passed, the public would have an opportunity to buy just such a picture. Louvel's public persona as a fanatical revolutionary perfectly complemented Berry's public persona as a counter-revolutionary martyr. What is interesting in that regard is that the government was never able to prove any connection between Louvel and the revolutionaries, or for that matter, any dissenting political group. Louvel was a Bonapartist, but his love for Napoleon was ignored. Louvel as a Jacobin evoked more fear, which in turn translated into renewed support for the Bourbon regime. Royalists simply ignored the lack of hard evidence, preferring fiction to fact, most likely motivated by the attractiveness of the Berry Conspiracy, both in psychological

Figure 8   An early "portrait" of Pierre Louvel,
rushed to market. Publishers needed a face to sell.
Vinck, 10643, 25 Feb. 1820

and political terms. The conspiracy mentality so prevalent among members of France's political community facilitated the blind acceptance of Louvel's revolutionary persona. In short, it was too good a persona to pass up. He was also too useful politically, as cannon fodder against the liberals. Louvel's fanatical revolutionary face appeared regularly in illustrations throughout the remainder of the Restoration, and even after the July Revolution, proving its long-term commercial attractiveness to the conspiracy-minded royalist population.

THE BERRY ADDRESSES

Following the assassination, Louis XVIII received thousands of "addresses" from across France offering condolences for Berry's passing. This fact did not in itself mean the general population mourned Berry. Sending an address to the king after an important event was a long-established French tradition. For instance, addresses poured into Paris in 1815 after Louis XVIII's triumphal return, and after the duke and duchess's first son died in 1818. Self-interest complicates their import, as addresses were usually sent to the king through official government channels, generally via a prefect's office. They were also published in newspapers, a convenient way to proclaim one's royalism and loyalty to the government. To that end, self-interest must account to some extent for the remarkable number of Berry addresses, and also for the predominance of public functionaries among the signators. Prefects, mayors, and members of municipal councils led the way, followed by sub-prefects, police commissioners, and lesser government officials. Clearly, those who held government posts were expected to sign. Self-interest was illustrated further by the great pains prominent royalists took to ensure that their particular address was published in local newspapers, and that they were given proper credit. The mayor of Toulouse sent an angry letter to St-Chamans because Toulouse was not included in a list published in *Le Moniteur* of cities that had sent the most Berry addresses. Baron de Montbel, a wealthy and influential ultra royalist from Haute-Garonne, joined the mayor of Caraman, in expressing their joint indignation to St-Chamans at the failure of the *Journal de Toulouse* to print that city's address accurately. And Mathieu-Louis Hocquart sent a letter to the *Journal de Toulouse* because the *Journal des Débats* had printed an address from the *Cour royale* without noting that he was responsible for sending it. The omission was duly noted in a subsequent edition.[71]

While the king and his ministers were not foolish enough to accept the addresses at face value, they were more than willing to refer to them as evidence of a popular royalist revival. On Louis XVIII's behalf, Claude Mounier, the director general of police, sent a letter to all the prefects expressing the king's sincere thanks for such an outpouring of affection. The addresses illustrated, Mounier wrote, in a letter that was subsequently published, "the unanimity of sentiments ... expressed by citizens of every class, and the devotion and loyalty of public officials."[72]

Addresses were certainly motivated by self-interest, but only partially. Government officials may have signed a Berry address out of prudence; however, they may also have sincerely wanted to send their condolences. If self-interest was present, then so too was sincerity, and it is the expression of sincerity that we find evidence of a real and popular Royalist Reaction. First, public officials were not the only signatories. Quite often addresses were signed by the residents of the city, commune, or canton. One address from the citizens of Grenoble had 626 individual signatures, and another included some 500 names. In Toulouse, the mayor set up a register at Place Capitole for the general public to sign. The actual wording of the addresses also suggests their sincerity. Even if the decision to send an address was based wholly or partly on a desire to demonstrate publicly one's loyalty to the Bourbon regime, their authors had complete freedom over how to word their condolences. And as the following analysis will reveal, the words chosen expressed an intense, emotional response to Berry's death that transcended political or selfish motivations.

The addresses emphasized three sentiments: horror at the crime, loyalty to the royal family, and a desire for vengeance against the perpetrators of the assassination. The first two sentiments were to be expected in the circumstances. In most addresses they were linked. The assassination itself was referred to as the atrocious crime, the frightful crime, this horrible assassination, or the execrable assassination, and the assassin was inevitably the scoundrel Louvel. The address of the Chamber of Peers referred to their "profound grief," and the "feelings shared by the whole of France." The deputies expressed their horror in even stronger terms: "Dismay has already spread to all classes of people here in the capital, followed by public indignation ... The whole of France wishes to strengthen the links that bind the French people to your noble house; for neither liberty nor public order can exist without it." Addresses from Isère and Haute-Garonne contained similar expressions of grief and loyalty. The following address from the mayor, the municipal council, and the principal inhabitants of the village of Caraman, which is near the château of Joseph de Villèle, was typical: "The inhabitants of the town of Caraman ... stricken with horror, indignation and sadness at the news of the horrible assassination ... are compelled to express their regret, hope and loyalty to the throne ... to France, which is one with the Bourbon family ... we hope for the long existence of that beloved line on which our hope and our happiness are based."[73] The municipal council of Pamier described its collective grief as follows: "The dreadful blow that has just struck down the youngest descendant of Saint Louis has been felt even here in our mountains; bitter tears flowed from our eyes, and the profound grief which we feel can only be compared to the silence of death." The members of the Royal Agricultural Society of Haute-Garonne adopted a historical approach to proclaim their "profound grief": "Our hearts are rent by the knowledge of the devilish plots laid against your noble family which has, for eight hundred years, been the object of love and reverence to the people of France." Note in the following address from Grenoble's municipal council the intensity of the sense of loss, particularly as it related to the Bourbon dynasty:[74]

At the moment when all French hearts are in mourning for that most heinous crime, Your Majesty need not urge his faithful subjects to express their sentiments. A horrible parricide took from us one of the illustrious pillars of your throne and, it seems, wished to extinguish the ancient line of our kings. We feel more deeply than ever, if that is possible, the need to strengthen the ties that unite us to the august family of the Bourbons. At the moment when a long succession of princes seemed assured and when all those who are happy to have lived under your rule could leave to their posterity the prospect of being governed by the descendants of good King Henry, must that hope be destroyed in an instant? The regrets of the inhabitants of this province, which in former times gave its name to the heir to the throne, must be even stronger.[75]

The appearance of the third sentiment, the desire for vengeance, is perhaps the most significant for it was not really necessary, either by reason of etiquette or self-interest. In a *circulaire* to the prefects after the passage of the press and liberty laws, Richelieu commented on the enormous number of addresses sent to Louis XVIII after Berry's death. He stated that the sentiments expressed in them did not stop at the offering of condolences, but included a demand for vengeance: "Public horror reaches beyond the crime itself to the doctrines which prompted it ... it rejects these doctrines of irreligion and revolt which have so long been harmful."[76] In Besançon, Charles Weiss noted in his journal that the municipal council in his city was split into moderate and extremists camps, with the latter "full of exaggeration and of a desire for vengeance."[77] Louvel's declaration that he had acted alone was widely publicized and would have been known to most signatories, or at the very least to the government officials. Yet, the repeated calls for vengeance in the addresses suggest that most signatories chose to ignore Louvel's testimony; they also offer further evidence of how quickly suspicions of the Berry Conspiracy gained public acceptance. Note that regional politics have relevance here. In liberal areas such as Isère, calls for vengeance were conspicuously absent, in Haute-Garonne, they were rampant. They blamed liberal rhetoric directly for cultivating the spirit of revolution that propelled Louvel to carry out his plan. The municipal council of the Commune of Pin implored the king to "stop the progress of this revolution which still thirsts as savagely ... for the blood of the Bourbons as it did thirty years ago ... Sire, crush the head of this hydra without a second's delay."[78] Re-establish the religion of your fathers, the Council wrote, and you will lay the groundwork for a golden age for future generations and Louis XVIII's name will live forever. It added that only the king could destroy "the revolutionary faction ... the Jacobins" from spreading anti-religious and subversive doctrines in society. Toulouse's *Cour royale* sent a very long and ardent address to Louis XVIII advising him to "rid the country" of all "the doctrines of revolt and death that are conspiring to bring back a second era of terror and barbarism." The true perpetrators of the assassination were identified in terms that would not be out of place in the most extreme counter-revolutionary propaganda: "This grievous assassination ... is the very natural result of the corruption bred by crime in the lower classes of society, the unleashing of anarchy, the permanent conspiracy which openly attacks the foundations of social order, the evident return to intrigues which recall the worst periods of the Revolution. These all predict an imminent ruin for our unhappy country and your Majesty can only protect his people by using the forces given him by Providence for that purpose." The address ended with an ominous promise that upon the king's order Frenchmen throughout the country would rise together and "close the revolutionary abyss." Similar expressions of vengeance came out of Pamier: "We beseech you, stop the flood of pernicious doctrines, which alone caused the blood of your noble family to be shed, and which, every day, is destroying society; restore the state religion to its lustre and influence ... the anti-social principles of modern philosophy produce only bitter fruit."[79]

The assassination energized France's political community. A crisis was proclaimed and calls for action were sounded. Drafting and signing a strongly worded address to Louis XVIII calling for retribution against the liberal accomplices to Berry's murder, or one pleading for calm and reconciliation, enabled virtually anyone – from prominent politicians and writers to ordinary citizens – to participate. The addresses provided perhaps the only opportunity for thousands of individuals to express publicly their views on the assassination. The fact that so many chose to do so must have been extremely gratifying to all royalists, regardless of what motivated the signatories. The government and the royalist press accepted the addresses as a powerful demonstration of the nation's love for the Bourbon regime and Louis XVIII, and also as a declaration of support for whatever measures the government deemed necessary in the circumstances. Certainly, the calls for vengeance were prevalent enough to substantiate such an interpretation, but it is equally certain that the influence of self-interest makes such declarations suspect.

What, then, to make of the addresses? They should best be considered as evidence of a powerful and immediate reaction by royalists, and even by somewhat passive supporters of the Bourbon regime, against the perceived enemies of France who were assumed responsible for Berry's assassination. That reaction in turn lit the fuse for the ensuing fireworks over the exceptional laws and the violent words exchanged between royalists and liberals during the Royalist Reaction.

BERRY'S FUNERAL

From 17 to 22 February, Berry's body was displayed in the Tuileries. The who's-who of France's political community came to pay their respects, along with thousands of other well-wishers. On 22 February Berry's remains were transferred to Saint-Denis on a chariot covered with flowers and garlands for his funeral. He would remain there in state for three more weeks, the coffin placed on a large platform, covered by a richly embroidered cape, illuminated by two tall candle-sticks.[80] The government seized on the funeral as an opportunity to propagate the royalist creed and to glorify the Bourbon dynasty. Some 365,000 francs were spent planning the funeral and decorating the church. In aesthetic terms, however, the funeral was actually a banal affair, lacking originality or a personal touch. The usual visual symbols were trotted out – obelisks or oriental granite and pictures of Berry held by angels – but much was copied from earlier *fêtes* and unrelated to Berry's own life, apart from two silver obelisks representing his dead children. Lack of preparation time was principally to blame. Organizers had to move quickly, and artistic flair had to give way to practical considerations.[81] Nevertheless, no one dared criticize the funeral for those reasons. The press noted the décor only briefly, and not at all negatively, but gave great attention to the guests. And the notables came out in force. Arriving at 10:00 a.m. were the members of the *Conseil, les maréchaux de France*, members of the chambers of peers and deputies, representatives of the diplomatic corps, the Church, the *Cours de cassation et des comptes*, the *Cour royale*, the *tribunaux civils et de commerce*, the *grands cordons et chevaliers des ordres de Saint-Louis et de la Légion-d'Honneur*, the *officiers-généraux et supérieurs*, and other civil and military functionaries. At 11:00 a.m. Angoulême, the Duke of Orléans, the Duke of Bourbon, and other royal family members arrived. Last to arrive, of course, were the Duchess of Berry, the Duchess of Orléans, and the Duke of Chartres, followed by Louis XVIII.

Berry's funeral was not about the death of a man but about the assassination of a Bourbon. It was a counter-revolutionary *fête*, and the attendance of the royal family and France's leading dignitaries proved that royalists were ready to fight for their *patrie*. The funeral also illustrates the personal approach to politics that typified the government's official interpretation of the assassination throughout the Royalist Reaction. Most significantly, Berry's death was portrayed as a loss not merely to the royal family but to all French citizens. The government officials, politicians, military officers, and clergymen attended as representatives of the nation. The funeral reinforced the organic vision of society vital to

Restoration royalism, in which the royal family members, headed by the king, were symbolic parents to the communities that collectively comprised the nation. This profoundly familial form of political imagery would gain prominence as the Royalist Reaction continued. Berry's funeral was part of the process whereby the assassination took on the proportions of a national tragedy, a process furthered by the Berry memorial services in March, the Berry Subscription established in April, the Bordeaux fêtes, and the Chambord Subscription.

The departure of Decazes had been a terrible personal blow for Louis XVIII. Within two weeks, he had lost his nephew and been forced to dismiss his closest friend, a man he considered to be his son. France's political community thought Decazes's dismissal signalled the approach of a serious political crisis that threatened to topple the Bourbon regime. Richelieu believed, therefore, that his principal task on taking office was to give assurance that he and his fellow ministers were in control of the situation. Curiously, he decided that the best way to do so was to reintroduce Decazes's three laws to parliament: the liberty, the press, and the double-vote laws. These laws were immediately dubbed the "exceptional laws," a collective name by which they are still known. Over the next two months, political debate in France was focused entirely on the first two, putting the already tumultuous relations between royalists and liberals into complete turmoil. French politics was radicalized more than ever: moderates were marginalized, as extremists from both sides of the spectrum took centre stage. Outstanding scores needed to be settled, and the liberty and press law debates afforded an opportunity to do so. In March and April, the Royalist Reaction began in earnest.

5 March–April: The Royalist Reaction in Earnest

In March and April, the political and the popular elements of the Royalist Reaction tended to develop along separate but parallel lines; similar issues were discussed, but from different perspectives. The political element focused its debate on the liberty and press laws, in a controversy that really concerned France's political community alone. It laid the foundation for the even more controversial debate on the double vote, and forced the participants to declare their views openly: one could be royalist or liberal, but nothing in between. The popular element, on the other hand, transcended the confines of politics. Memorial services, newspapers, illustrations, the Berry Subscription, and the publication of Chateaubriand's book on Berry ensured that millions of citizens were touched by, or at least informed of, the Duke of Berry's death and the duchess's pregnancy. The resulting groundswell of national support for the Bourbon regime culminated in the November deputy elections and the discrediting of the liberal movement. The popular element had a secondary effect as well: the establishment of new public personas for the three central characters of the assassination: Berry, the Duchess of Berry, and Louvel. The development of their personas occurred in conjunction with the government's official interpretation of the assassination, and helped to increase national support for the Bourbon regime. This was a period of intense drama: the battle had commenced.

THE GRÉGOIRE CONTROVERSY OF 1819

Certain aspects of the polemic over the liberty and press laws were unique to the circumstances of the assassination and the Royalist Reaction. At the same time, that polemic seemed to follow the pattern of the polemic over Abbé Grégoire's candidacy and election as a deputy for Isère a year earlier. Similar strategies and arguments were employed by virtually the same groups. In many ways, the Grégoire controversy provided the blueprint for the liberty and press law debates that followed. To study that relationship, we must back up a bit and turn our attention to the deputy election of September, 1819.

Grégoire announced his candidacy in August igniting a highly emotional national debate over the nature of the French political system. The controversy was rooted in the fact that, as a member of the National Assembly, Grégoire had cast a "guilty" vote at Louis XVI's trial. Moreover, he had accepted the Civil Constitution of the Clergy, had held public office during the Terror, and had sat in Napoleon's Senate. Grégoire's reputation as a Jacobin was reinforced by the decision of many prominent liberals to endorse his candidacy enthusiastically, thereby confirming royalist suspicions that prominent liberals were conspiring against the Bourbons.[1] Spurred on by recent electoral gains,[2] the more radical liberals clearly believed the time was ripe to flex their muscles. A Grégoire victory would open the door for other prominent independents to run in subsequent elections and send a clear message to the government that it should continue and even accelerate the introduction of liberal policies.

The anti-Grégoire forces, on the other hand, were very clear about why voters should reject Grégoire. Pamphlets published before the election hammered away at Grégoire's revolutionary past. One pamphlet noted that in 1792 he had written an article that recommended abolishing the monarchy and trying Louis XVI for treason. It added that Grégoire had sat with the *montagnards* during the Terror, most notably when the Girondists were persecuted.[3] The pamphleteer asked rhetorically: Do voters want to elect a person whose return would symbolize "revolutionary anarchy?"[4] Grégoire's supporters may have believed he had repented his past, "but there are crimes and even faults that must be punished and marked with a seal of disapproval to prevent the return of such infamous acts."[5] Another pamphlet mocked his reputation as a defender of liberty. Grégoire was deemed "one of the men who approved the assassination of Louis XVI" and a "fierce republican." Under Bonaparte, it charged, he was a "member of that compliant Senate which, each year, in accord with the tyrant's wishes, harvested the youth of France and voted for his taxes." Furthermore, his cooperation was well rewarded – with a pension of some 36,000 francs per year.[6]

Grégoire's supporters responded in dramatic fashion; they dismissed his critics as reactionaries, and categorized ministerial candidates as puppets of the *Conseil*. Liberal pamphleteers urged voters to unite against the corrupt forces that threatened to destroy France's constitutional monarchy and abrogate the Charter. A lawyer from Grenoble named Duchesne published a pamphlet that typified the way liberals rationalized Grégoire's revolutionary past.[7] First, he noted, since article 11 of the Charter forbade "all investigations" into opinions expressed and votes cast prior to the Restoration, those who attacked Grégoire for his past were breaching the Charter.[8] Second, Grégoire had never sentenced Louis XVI to death; he had merely stated that he was guilty.[9] Third, Grégoire was never a *montagnard*, but as president of the Convention had been obliged to sit with them. Likewise, he was not a Jacobin, but had to correspond with *la société des jacobins* following a decree of the Convention. Finally, during his tenure in the *Conseil des Cinq-Cents* and the senate, and in numerous writings, Grégoire had constantly called for unity and an end to fractious debates. Grégoire's candidacy, Duchesne concluded, provided loyal Frenchmen with the opportunity to put an end to the Counter-Revolution by electing "a zealous defender of your liberties ... a declared enemy of privilege, of exceptional measures, of financial depredations, and of political corruption."[10]

Grégoire's supporters implored electors not to be misled by the "slanders of the ultras and the ministerial party."[11] Of course they were not averse to casting aspersions of their own. An anonymous pamphlet, for example, demeans Grégoire's opponents as being "little to be feared ... like invalids with chronic heart disease."[12] Grégoire's detractors were dismissed as "The Men of 1815,"[13] intent on destroying the precious freedoms won after so much hardship, while ministerial candidates were nothing more than self-serving bureaucrats enriching themselves at the public's expense. The hypocrisy of those "supporters of the Old Regime," wrote M. Duchand, a former soldier, was exemplified by their so-called declarations of loyalty to the Charter, even as they supported unconstitutional laws.[14] Those who supported Grégoire were "motivated by passion for the public good"; his opponents were consumed by "the petty interests of family, society, or locality."[15]

The pro-Grégoire forces also stressed the need for a united front. The election was hailed as a test of character, the outcome of which would determine France's very future. Duchand argued that France's constitutional regime was "not settled on solid foundations; only honorable and trustworthy institutions can consolidate it; unhappy experience has taught us that a country that lacks such institutions cannot hope for liberty, happiness, or lasting peace."[16] It was indispensable, therefore, that only those loyal to the Charter, namely, the liberal candidates, sit in the Chamber of Deputies.[17] An anonymous pamphleteer thundered that liberals must unite and form "an indestructible mass," opposing the efforts of "the enemies of our liberties, the evil inspirations of the ultras, and, the secret intrigues of the ministerial party."[18]

While Grégoire was successful in the election,[19] his supporters never saw him sit in the Chamber. Ultra and moderate royalists were both outraged. Few royalist deputies accepted Grégoire's claim that he had never voted for Louis XVI's death. A full-blown debate broke out in the Chamber over what to do. Interestingly, the issue was not whether Grégoire should be allowed to take his seat; there was virtual unanimity, even among the independents deputies, that his presence would be intolerable.[20] The debate focused instead on finding the appropriate grounds to excluding a deputy who had been duly elected. The government and the royalists did not trifle with constitutional niceties. In their view, the presence of a regicide in the Chamber of Deputies was an affront to the memory of Louis XVI, to the institution of the monarchy, and to Louis XVIII. *Indignité* provided the needed pretext for annulling Grégoire's election. Lainé, a member of the *Conseil*, stated this position forcefully: "The presence in this assembly of the man whose name is associated with such dreadful notoriety is incompatible with liberty, with royal legitimacy … it is … a … motive for annulment which, to me, is unanswerable, that is, the unfitness of the elected member."[21] Bourdonnaye, an ultra deputy, argued that failure to annul Grégoire's election would subject the king "to public contempt … imprinting upon [the deputies] the seal of infamy," and further, that such a failure would admit a tacit acceptance of Louis XVI's execution, thereby justifying his murder.[22] He reiterated Lainé's position that "*l'indignité*" was sufficient grounds for keeping Grégoire out of the Chamber: "I am not going to dispute the forms of the contested election; the sole objection is the unfitness of the man elected." Comte de Salaberry concurred: "I vote for the expulsion of the fourth deputy of Isère, by reason of unfitness, for the expulsion of one of the murderers of Louis XVI, for the expulsion of the enemy of kings."[23]

The liberal deputies, led by Benjamin Constant and Jacques-Antoine Manuel, claimed that the position of the government and the royalists was unconstitutional because the Charter barred any inquiry into past votes and opinions. By using Grégoire's past against him, the government was giving in to reactionary forces, Manuel admonished, when he took to the podium: "This is not only a usurpation of power, an instrument of tyranny, which is being proposed; it is really an attack on the Charter, nothing less than a counter-revolution."[24] Few men sitting in the Chamber, he added, were unsullied by past events: "After thirty years of Revolution, who is there who has not taken some part in the disorders we have witnessed? Who has not been both an actor and a victim? Who has not often changed roles?"[25] He and Constant proposed a different tactic: declare Grégoire's election illegal because he was not domiciled in Isère.[26] Article 42 of the Charter required that half the deputies elected from each department have a political domicile in that department.

Three of the Isère deputies did not meet that requirement, and since Grégoire came fourth in the election, his seat should be vacated. Why did the liberal deputies insist on the Charter argument? Three reasons stand out. First, Grégoire had run as an independent candidate, and the liberal community in Isère had rallied to his candidacy. And that same community later rallied to defend his election. Therefore, attacks on Grégoire represented attacks on liberals generally. The domicile argument provided a simple and technical means of ending the controversy that many independent deputies felt would only hurt their chances of re-election. Second, a number of liberal deputies felt threatened by the possibility that they could be expelled because of their past.[27] Third, liberal deputies prided themselves on their adherence to the Charter, and many felt that annulling the election on the ground of *indignité* was unconstitutional. The use of legal means would validate the Charter, rather than the king's injured sensibilities.

The domicile argument was fundamentally sound, and there was no clause in the Charter that allowed a duly elected deputy to be expelled because of his political career prior to the Restoration. Yet, the majority of deputies accepted only one argument: Grégoire's election had to be annulled because he had cast a guilty vote at Louis XVI's trial. Emotion, not the Charter, carried the day. As will be seen, emotions were also to hold sway in the exceptional law debates. Perhaps learning from the Grégoire controversy, the government promoted the laws by focusing on emotionally oriented issues rather than constitutional arguments. So while liberal deputies charged that the exceptional laws breached the Charter, ministers and royalists responded that their passage was necessary to the maintenance of order. Fears rooted in the Revolution and the Hundred Days provided the government with a playing card that the laws' opponents could not trump. As a result, Louis XVIII's ministers were able to push all three exceptional laws through both Chambers in less than four months.

In April, 1820, an election was held to fill Grégoire's seat. In a somewhat surprising result, a moderate liberal candidate, Camille Teisseire, won the seat in a victory that testifies to the power of Isère liberals. Still, Baron Haussez was satisfied with the result. In a report to Mounier, the prefect of Isère wrote that the failure of the ultra and independent candidates represented the true victory, for it signified a return to moderation in the area.[28]

DEBATES ON THE LIBERTY LAW AND THE PRESS LAW

The Liberty Law allowed for a set period of incarceration for individuals assumed to be dangerous, without their being charged with any crime.[29] The Press Law had an equally specific purpose: censorship. Richelieu recommended censorship in order to avoid further scandalous and outrageous attacks against the government; attacks that were fuelling the revolutionary fervour that was sweeping across France. He accused the liberal and ultra-royalist press of antagonizing France's political factions, and he singled out the liberal press for playing to its revolutionary audience. It was his hope that the press law would, "while silencing the forces of unrest, prepare the way for the passage of a law establishing freedom of the press on a just basis, and ... add whatever measures are necessary to make that law effective."[30]

In strategic terms, the liberty and press laws played an important role in relation to the double vote. Richelieu expected the electoral law to be the more problematic of the three, so he introduced it only after the liberty and press laws were passed. Even in the earlier *Chambre introuvable*, recalcitrant deputies had been a continuous and serious impediment to the *Conseil*'s ability to pass legislation. Moreover, as a body, the Chamber of Deputies had become increasingly hostile to the government; extremists frequently took advantage of the podium to voice their views to the nation at large. Richelieu felt that a less vocal chamber would help to moderate the tone of French politics. In addition, since the electoral law affected every deputy directly, it was reasonable to expect the deputies to take a more active interest in amendments to the electoral system than in the legislation related to *habeas corpus* or censorship. Introducing the liberty and press laws first would allow him more accurately to determine the deputies' state of mind. If those laws and his ministry overcame this "baptism by fire,"[31] then he would be able to move confidently to the more difficult task of passing the double vote.

In debating Grégoire's eligibility to sit in the Chamber of Deputies, ministers and royalists latched onto the *indignité* argument, a self-evidently emotional, extra-legal strategy. In the liberty and press law debates, the forces supporting the laws adopted a similarly emotional approach. The laws were promoted as the deputies' best chance to fend off the revolutionaries and protect the Restoration. They went as far as to propose a constitutional principle that the Charter could be suspended at the government's discretion whenever the monarchy was threatened, as long as the suspension was temporary, a serious crisis existed, and the greater good of the nation was served. Siméon reduced this principle to a single formula: "Authority must recognize necessity."[32] This unprecedented constitutional principle of course entailed the risk of abuse of power, but Richelieu allayed such concerns by assurances that the laws would terminate at the end of the Chamber's next session. Throughout the debates, ministers reiterated that the laws would have a limited lifespan.[33] Ironically, Decazes also tried to sell his liberty and press laws as temporary acts. Perhaps too many deputies at first considered Decazes to be a principal cause of the crisis, for once he resigned, the laws' temporary status suddenly made them palatable, and the constitutional issues they raised were ignored.

Precedent was also on the pro-law side. A bill similar to the liberty law had been passed in 1817.[34] Article 4 of the Charter guaranteed the liberty of all persons; however, that guarantee could be limited if prescribed by law. Also, although an accused was granted the constitutional right to a fair trial, that right was not defined. Those provisions were interpreted by most participants in the debate to mean that any guarantee of liberty could be curtailed as long as such limits were duly passed by legislation in both parliamentary chambers. Press censorship had an even longer history; it had been the rule rather than the exception ever since the Revolution – and continued until the Third Republic.[35] As a result, deputies were not offended by the suggestion of censorship. Article 8 of the Charter had established the right to publish and print freely.[36] During the Hundred Days, Napoleon had granted that right, limited only by "la responsabilité légale."[37] However, soon after Louis XVIII's return to Paris, strict censorship was imposed.[38] In March,1819, under Serre's guidance and with Decazes's support, a new press law was passed practically eliminating censorship. Authorization to publish was no longer needed, and publishers simply paid a small *caution*.[39] The immediate result of that liberating law was a tidal wave of new publications. Parisian and provincial newspapers proliferated, especially those with an extremist orientation.[40] The 1819 press law also stimulated some of the most violent polemic the French press would ever produce. In fact, it was the belligerent behaviour of the press in 1819 that convinced Louis XVIII, his ministers, and many moderate deputies that the re-imposition of censorship was indeed appropriate in the circumstances. That reaction, combined with promises that it was a temporary measure, made the press law acceptable to a majority of the deputies.

Richelieu and his ministers were adamant about the purpose of the two laws; they were needed to "maintain the public order." The first minister evoked Berry's name to substantiate this position: "The assassination of 13 February is the regrettable proof for the necessity of passing the laws. They provide a bulwark against such dangers, against the attacks and plots directed against our Princes, the Throne, and the security of the state; and only by such measures can the government guarantee safeguards to both society at large and to itself."[41] He stated unequivocally that nothing less than the survival of the monarchy was at stake: "In order to preserve these benefits, to enjoy them in peace together with the mildness of our laws and the character of the nation, all

Frenchmen must gather around the Throne and repel those who, with evil counsels and false hopes, would still like to engage on the dangerous and bloody path of revolution." Besides, Richelieu concluded, the laws would not affect "les bons citoyens."

His ministers and the ultra royalists echoed those sentiments. Siméon lectured the deputies on the principal lesson of the Revolution: governments must move quickly and decisively when their authority is challenged.[42] Pasquier added that France needed to remember the previous thirty years: "We have seen liberty perish first by the power of unbridled license, then by that of unlimited despotism."[43] Villèle charged that those opposed to the laws were relying on the same techniques and subversive doctrines as used by the leaders of the Terror.[44] Rochefoucauld, an ultra peer, stated categorically that the only people opposed to the laws were those who profited from the destruction of public order, namely, conspirators and revolutionaries.[45] Courvoisier, an ultra deputy, argued even more strongly that the liberty law was necessary to protect France's religious institutions and political freedoms from a second revolution: "The assassination has terrified us; the need to prevent it happening again, the need to put a halt to this perverted kind of progress which threatens to overturn religion and morals, monarchy and liberty, the unrest which has greatly increased in the last two years, these are the reasons for this bill."[46]

Some ultra deputies went a step further, maintaining that the term "exceptional" was a misnomer, and that arguments regarding the temporary status of the laws and the existence of a political crisis were irrelevant. Headed by Bonald, this group proposed that the laws were indeed constitutional and should be passed because they flowed naturally and directly from the government's duty to protect society from disorder. They were needed to punish the guilty, and therefore represented a legitimate legislative action.[47] This line of reasoning was founded on the ultra-royalists' organic vision of society, whereby collective needs took precedence over individual rights. Bonald endorsed both laws as necessary, righteous, and moral: "The proposed measure is a natural consequence, and at this time a necessary one, of the supreme law, the law for the preservation of society against human passions."[48] The present government, he added, should be commended for its actions, rather than censored because the liberty and press laws transgressed certain liberal principles.[49] Josse-Beauvoir provided a more graphic metaphor for this organic vision, as he explained why press censorship was necessary: "[The press] circulates poison through all parts of the body of society with the speed of an electric spark, and by this flood of ideas, which delivers public opinion over to political tricksters, they are again endangering the throne of Saint Louis."[50]

Speaking on behalf of the *Conseil*, Pasquier accepted the ultras' overall position regarding that duty, but only so far as to justify the laws as temporary and extraordinary measures. He rejected soundly any suggestion that the Charter was inherently subordinate to monarchical authority and the duty to maintain order.

Liberal deputies in turn responded with the strongest possible rhetoric. Benjamin Constant questioned how laws relating to press censorship and arbitrary arrest would prevent a deranged assassin from killing another member of the royal family: "The minister has not mentioned any act other than the assassination of the Duke of Berry; however, this bill would in no way have prevented such a crime. Thus it is clearly shown that this law is useless."[51] Most liberal deputies accused the government of adopting a Terror mentality in proposing laws inspired by the memory of Robespierre and the Committee of Public Safety.[52] During a heated debate over the press law, Laisné de Villevesque accused the government of substituting the Terror for the Charter: "Have you forgotten that it was [the Charter] which broke the bonds, soaked in blood and tears, with which the Convention had strangled France? That it broke the sword of Terror? Would you now destroy the very thing that saved us?"[53] The Charter, he continued, was the only true defence against another Terror, a significant fact considering the government wanted to legislate the Charter out of existence. Lafayette countered that the laws would destroy the Charter and thereby circumvent the people's right to liberty.[54] He equated the Liberty Law to the Law of Suspects. Timid men, said Lafayette, failed to block the passage of that horrible law, and today the same timidity would result in its return.

Led by Bejamin Constant, a few deputies adopted Laisné de Villevesque's approach, suggesting that the two laws illustrated a concerted attempt to resurrect not the Terror but the Old Regime, or as Constant put it, a *Régime Nouveau*, complete with *lettres de cachet*, a *censure*, *élections oligarchiques*, and a new aristocracy of double voters.[55] The liberty and press laws, he claimed, were despotic acts in the style of France's former absolute monarchs; laws that proved France's *Régime Nouveau* respected the unscrupulous and suspected the innocent.[56] The ministers, stated Constant, may have assured the French people that their newly acquired powers of arrest and censorship would not be abused, but those assurances were based on little more than self-serving testimonials on ministerial loyalty, honesty, and purity.[57]

The liberal press in Grenoble joined their like-minded deputies in rejecting ministerial assurances that the laws would be temporary and in the public's best interests. For the few weeks after Berry's assassination, the *Journal Libre de l'Isère* ran a number of articles accusing the ultra royalists and the government of using the assassination as a pretext to pass oppressive laws aimed at crushing the liberals' political influence.[58] A principal theme in those articles was the denial of any liberal involvement in the assassination. In an article describing how the inhabitants of Grenoble reacted to Berry's murder, the *Journal Libre de l'Isère* decried the fact that liberals, "the friends of law and liberty," were "always the first victims of political intrigue," even though "these men ... for thirty years have been asking for laws, not blood." The article concluded that royalist crocodile tears did not fool anyone; their hypocritical smiles were clearly visible beneath their public expressions of mourning.[59] On 24 February, in an article condemning the proposed press law, the same editors charged that Richelieu "wished to use the current state of unrest as an excuse to pass these new exceptional laws."[60] And in another editorial, they argued that the proposed laws in no way maintained public order, because the current state of unrest was in fact caused by the royalists' false accusations and not by the liberals: "The assassination, the crime which put the nation into mourning and which, in so many ways, afflicted the friends of liberty, seemed to be the signal for disorder. The expressions of grief of the eternal enemies of our rights, our tranquillity and our liberty, were cries of rage; their condolences were howls of hatred and vengeance; the funeral torches became brands of division, ready to set everything alight ... cruel men took a ferocious delight in taking advantage of the crime of one individual to treat all Frenchmen as criminals."[61] The editorial concluded by accusing royalists of trying to reinstitute a tyrannical regime. It exhorted the government to study history and see that tyrants were always defeated in the end: "Read our history, read the history of all peoples, consider the events which are taking place in Spain, look back to 1794 and 1815, and then, be tyrants if you dare."

As late as 21 March, as the debate over the press law was drawing to a close, the *Journal Libre de l'Isère* continued to attack the government's position. It published a letter from a man living in the mountains of Chartreuse stating that, while people were horrified at Berry's murder, they were equally horrified at those who were taking advantage of the assassination for personal gain. The exceptional laws represented a slander against the French people for they suggested that the government mistrusted all twenty-eight million Frenchmen. Such calumny could only lead to tyranny and dictatorship. The writer concluded by predicting that not only would the exceptional laws prove ineffectual, but they were very likely to stimulate the very revolution they were intended to prevent: "The indignation of [the inhabitants of the Alps] reached its peak when they saw cold, calculating men, hungry for power and gambling on the affliction of the prince and the horror of the French people, grasping hold of this lucky opportunity to ensure the success of those plans so fatal to freedom with which they have long menaced us."[62]

Adopting a remarkably threatening tone, the newspaper followed that letter with an article about the Journée des Tuiles, the riot in Grenoble on 7 June 1788. In still another article the editors added that Isère took its revolutionary reputation seriously: "The people of the Dauphiné still venerate its memory."[63] It seemed almost as if the liberals accepted that the liberty and press laws were going to pass, and were intent on taking a few final pot shots at the government before the inevitable happened. At the same time, this rhetoric seemed to justify the passage of the very laws the liberals argued were not necessary.

As the debate raged on, the conspiracy mentality continued to make its presence felt. Paulin Madier de Montjau, a judge at the royal court of Nîmes, sent a petition to the Chamber of Deputies asserting that a secret occult government made up of ultras and refractory priests existed in Paris. The Chamber even discussed this petition a month later on 25 April. The Parisian liberal press, notably *La Rénommée*, *Le Constitutionnel*, and *Le Censeur Européen* covered the story closely. In an open letter to the *Journal de Toulouse* after Berry's death, Baron de Puymaurin, a deputy for Haute-Garonne expressed his views on the assassination. The government in 1820, he stated, was in exactly the same situation as it was in 1790, and Louis XVIII was in the same position as Louis XVI had been: plots threatened to overthrow the Bourbons, and revolutionary doctrines were spreading the anti-Bourbon infection. Puymaurin argued: "The fatal day of 13 February 1820 exposed the regicide faction who want to destroy the monarchy and the noble house of Bourbon. A monster, by assassinating the Duke of Berry, has destroyed the hope of France; he has massacred the whole dynasty ... There is thus a plot against the security of the State. Can the State be separate from the King? Will you allow some conspirators to destroy the finest kingdom in Europe, on the pretext that they are not conspiring against the person of the King? The King and the Nation are inseparable; would you separate them in order to see these sacred objects of your love and veneration destroyed, one after the other?"[64]

Provincial officials did not let their guard down either. Puymaurin's charges were seemingly confirmed when the *tricolore* was hung from a bridge in Toulouse on 28 March. The police conducted an extensive search for the culprits, but without success. On the same day, in Besançon, a *marchand* accused a young traveller of reading seditious verses in public. The accused could not pay the *caution*, and so had to remain in prison until the next session of the *cour d'assises*.[65] A few days earlier, a soldier from the Besançon garrison had been arrested for uttering Bonaparte's name.

Public unrest spread to Grenoble, particularly its law school. That faculty had been a bastion of liberalism and republicanism since its founding in 1801.[66] Professors and students at the school had flocked to Napoleon during the Hundred Days, and even after Waterloo continued to agitate against the Bourbon regime. Understandably, this intransigence led a number of local and Parisian officials to call for the closure of the school. The Grenoble law school had been somewhat compromised by the Didier Affair. Didier had been a professor at the school, and although no students or professors were implicated, the government continued to suspect that members of the school had played some role in the attempted coup. After the Didier Affair, Achard de Germane, Isère's *procureur général*, and Montivaut, the prefect, advised the minister of the interior to suspend the school: "There can be no further delay in taking effective measures to rid our town center of this hotbed of anarchy ... we demand that the Law Faculty be shut down."[67] In 1817, General Donnadieu, as commander of the Seventh Military Division in Grenoble, sent a letter to the minister of war denouncing the school's professors and students: "It is outrageous that the King should pay professors to educate young men in everything that is most opposed to his government and the laws of the Nation."[68] A month later, Bertier, the prefect at the time, acknowledged the liberal tendencies of Grenoble law students: "I cannot conceal that these young men are not generally thought to have the right spirit. Republican principles, which are common in this region, predominate with them. I have learnt, in individual conversations and contacts, that their discussions and activities are not always in the interests of the legitimate government."[69]

While Royer-Collard remained president of the *Commission de l'instruction publique*, the law faculty was safe. He even complained in writing to the minister of the interior about what he termed ultraroyalist intriguing against the law school, stating that extremists were trying to "take advantage of the faults of a few students to suggest that all the students were conspiring against the government; whenever there is any agitation in a department vague accusations are made against these young men ... The authorities denounce the faculties to the ministers without bringing up anything against them or their members."[70] In 1819 he was replaced by Baron Cuvier, and the school lost its Parisian protector. In an *arrêté* dated 30 November 1819, the Academic Councils throughout France were given the power to fine or even suspend students who spoke irresponsibly within the confines of a university. A year later, as the Royalist Reaction was heating up, Cuvier extended the *arrêté* to include statements made off university grounds as well, pointing to the Grenoble law school to justify his decision. His letter to the rector of the school made it clear that the students had better behave: "They must prove, by virtue of their behaviour in the outside world, that the principles that their professors have been at pains to inculcate have influenced their hearts and guided their actions. All scandals, all political quarrels, all acts of disrespect to legitimate authority cannot be tolerated."[71] On 24 April Cuvier sent a letter to be read to all the law students in Grenoble: they were henceforth forbidden to express publicly any opinion regarding political affairs, adding that they would have time for that when they were forty, that is, when they qualified to stand as a candidate for deputy. These actions, along with the passage of the liberty and press laws, had the opposite effect intended. Grenoble law students continued to agitate against the government, but with an increased vigour, initiating and leading a number of public disturbances. By 1821 exasperated Parisian officials finally suspended the law school.

On 15 March the liberty law passed through the Chamber of Deputies by a wide margin, 134 to 115. On March 30 the press law passed even more easily, 136 to 109. Both laws came into force on the thirty-first. The final tallies indicate a sincerity on the part of the royalist deputies. They truly believed that Berry's assassination represented a serious threat to the Bourbon regime, the proverbial tip of the iceberg. The fact that these deputies accepted the temporary status of the laws to be a sufficient safeguard against any abuse of power attests to how little they were concerned with abuse of power in the first place. Clearly, the assassination had put the deputies into a revolutionary frame of mind. Convinced it was their responsibility to stop the approaching apocalypse, and inflamed by the effects of the conspiracy mentality, a majority of them accepted the ministers' assurances at face value. In this sense, the liberty and press laws were not seen only in terms of an increase in police powers and censorship; they were also viewed as decisive and admirable steps in the royalist battle against their perpetual enemy, the revolutionaries.

The press law was in retrospect the more important of the two. Few people were ever arrested under the liberty law. In fact, most of the publicity surrounding that law came from a national subscription set up by prominent liberals to pay legal costs for those arrested under it. On 4 April, editors from a number of Parisian newspapers were charged under the press law for announcing the subscription. Prosecutors characterized the subscription as having "provoked citizens to disobey the law which suspends the guarantee of individual liberty and of having misunderstood the constitutional authority of the King and the two chambers." The following month, Lyon's *cour royale* issued a *mise en accusation* against several prominent liberals. A M Gros, a lawyer from Grenoble, was also arrested and charged with being an accomplice for distributing the subscription prospectus. Beyond this, however, the liberty law affected few people directly.

The press law was a different matter. Soon after it was passed, Mounier issued a *direction générale* to the prefects, advising them to apply it in its widest sense, according to the spirit of the law. They were to censor any article deemed contrary to the "morality and religion, or that contained matter critical of the King, members of the royal family, or that included attacks on public officials or prefects" – even articles that vaguely affected the spirit in a factious manner or adversely affected public safety.[72] In other words, the government could censor whatever it wanted.

Censorship applied to all newspapers regardless of political orientation. Ultra-royalist publishers were outraged. As loyal citizens, they wondered why a law intended to silence revolutionaries applied to them. Their fury resulted in one of the strangest political alliances of the nineteenth century, as liberal and ultra publishers both called for the repeal of the press law. Alphonse Martainville, owner of *Le Drapeau Blanc*, wrote a few months after its enactment that the press law illustrated the Richelieu ministry's corrupt nature and cowardice: "The Royalists are most certainly correct to say that under a JUST government existing laws would have been adequate to repel attacks on society, without the need for exceptional laws; however, for men without courage and dignity, arbitrary power is easier and more agreeable to exercise than justice."[73] Ultra protests against the press law foreshadowed the permanent division between moderate and ultra royalists that followed the Royalist Reaction of 1820. For the moment, though, the two groups put aside their differences to push the liberty and press laws forward.

On 1 April the *Commission de censure* was established in Paris, and within six weeks similar commissions existed in every department. Despite what ultra-royalist publishers claimed, liberal newspapers suffered the most. By the end of April, 127 articles had been cut from *La Renommée*, and by October, 40,000 lines had been removed from *Le Constitutionnel*. *La Renommée* was suspended for most of May and the first two weeks of June, and financial pressures eventually forced it to close. In a final act of defiance, *La Renommée* printed Madier de Montjau's petition in full. Pressure from the commission also forced *L'Indépendant* to merge with *Le Censeur Européen*, which in turn merged with *Le Courrier Français*. Unable to print what their readers wanted, liberal newspapers had to combine forces or shut down, thereby limiting the ability of liberal journalists and writers to reach a national audience.

The press law had an even more devastating impact on provincial newspapers. Liberal publications, such as *L'Écho de l'Ouest* from Rennes and the *Journal Libre de l'Isère*, and even the ultra-royalist *La Ruche d'Aquitaine*, were hounded by the censors, all but ending the rapid growth of the provincial press that had begun in 1819 when censorship was lifted. The censors were so strict at first that a frustrated editor of the *Journal Libre de l'Isère* printed the following list of "truths" that the commission permitted: the current temperature, that crops suffered in the winter, and the time Grenoble's city gates closed. Newspapers were even prohibited from leaving blanks to indicate censorship. A Rennes law student complained bitterly in a pamphlet he published himself that the press law made it virtually impossible to follow politics, which in turn allowed the government to act arbitrarily, without fear of public protest: "Censorship keeps us in the most complete ignorance of everything that is happening at any distance from us; our newspaper, not wanting to be servile, has become almost worthless; our only political barometer is the faces of the monarchists."[74]

Censorship remained in place for the remainder of the Restoration. A loophole in the press law allowed pamphlets and non-periodicals to escape censorship for a few months. From April to June, 1820, an avalanche of pamphlets regarding the exceptional laws descended upon France. On 26 July 1821 that loophole was closed, and censorship was complete. Again relaxed by the law of 29 September 1824, it reappeared in full vigour with the law of 18 July 1828. The 1828 law was noteworthy because it marked the last time – until 1944 – that newspaper owners were held personally liable at law for the content of their papers. Liberals declamed against the censorship provision in Charles X's Four Ordinances, but once in power they saw little advantage in allowing a free press. Article seven of the Charter of 1830 may have guaranteed freedom of the press, but by 16 February 1834, all newspapers were subjected to municipal authority. The French press remained muzzled from that time on, with only the occasional lifting of government control, until the advent of the Third Republic.

THE BERRY MEMORIAL SERVICES

So firm was the central government's control over all national fêtes that after the assassination local officials waited to receive permission from Paris before they could organize any public memorial for Berry. Instructions arrived on 13 March, signed by Louis XVIII and Siméon, ordering a memorial service for 24 March. The highest-ranking church official in each diocese and all prefects received the order, and they in turn ordered their subordinates to make the necessary arrangements. On 24 March, therefore, in an amazing display of organization and central authority, virtually every church in France held a Berry memorial service.[75]

The initial order from Paris showed again the familial approach to politics that had characterized Berry's funeral. "The whole of France has shared in our grief," the order read; "Each family has, no less than if they had been injured themselves, felt the blow which struck our royal family." In essence, the memorial services were not ordered because the royal family had lost a relative but because the nation had lost a son. Church officials participated eagerly, most bishops and archbishops considering the occasion important enough to issue a *mandement*, in poster form, to be hung throughout the diocese. In the *mandements*, these priests took the opportunity to voice their views on the assassination from a religious perspective. In Grenoble, Bishop Simon described Berry's death as a catastrophe of Sodom-and-Gomorrah proportions: "A terrible monster has been exposed to the French people, a monster with a human face who is ignorant of God and who blasphemes against Jesus Christ." Near the end of the *mandement*, Simon reiterated the reference to Christ, noting that the Bourbons seemed destined to be martyred for France. However, they were not simple martyrs, wrote the Bishop, but martyrs distinguished by "*des sentiments surhumains*," whose deaths illustrated the glory and power of Christ and the magnificence of Christianity:

It is impossible that there exists a single French citizen who does not consider the Bourbons to be cruelly and unjustly calumniated; that family which is so good, so charitable and so virtuous; that family which has suffered so many misfortunes, been showered with so many tears; that family which is so admirable, so astonishing, so worthy of our pity, of our respect, of our love, of all the affection in our heart. Can there be a single Christian who does not see in the death of the Duke of Berry, heroic religion, superhuman sentiments, marvels of every kind, calm, serenity, a truly heavenly end, the certain sign of immortality and happiness. The blood of the Bourbons is the blood of martyrs; let us then unite it with the blood of Jesus Christ.[76]

The Berry *mandements* also provided an opportunity for the Church to chastise the flock for their lack of devotion. The assassination was interpreted as God's retribution against a nation that had turned its back on the Lord. In their Berry *mandement*, the *vicaires-généraux* of Toulouse, for example, called on their fellow Christians to repent and return to Jesus Christ. They identified revolutionary doctrines as the root cause of the assassination, "the wicked doctrines which stifle re-morse in the hearts of villains, and sharpen the daggers they hold in their regicidal hands." Berry's death was held up as definitive proof of the "profound malice"of men who "devise evil plots" and carry out "the most dreadful of crimes." Bishop Simon also blamed the assassi-nation on the *esprit du siècle*. All French people, he proclaimed, were partly responsible for Berry's death, because of "that spirit of indepen-dence and pride, of irreligion and immorality, the root cause of all our misfortunes and all our crimes."

The control exercised by the central government and the Church over the memorial services resulted in a certain degree of homogeneity. The typical service was quite simple. A mass, attended by local digni-taries, was held in Berry's memory. A eulogy was given by a priest, fol-lowed by a *Te Deum* at the end of the service. A procession sometimes preceded and/or followed the service.[77] Regional political orientation did play a role, as the following comparison between the memorial services held in Grenoble and Toulouse illustrates. In Grenoble, Bouchard, the *vicaire-général*, ended his sermon with a call for unity, and stressed the fact that Berry forgave Louvel before he died: "There, like Him, you will pardon your executioner, you will triumph over your nature, you will repeat the words of our divine master; Father, forgive them." Put aside your hate, he pleaded, and end the factional-ism that is destroying France.[78] The sermon in Toulouse carried no such message. Rather than hearing a message of forgiveness, the con-gregation was warned that the Revolution and the evil doctrines it propagated were solely responsible for the horrendous attack. Money and greed are not always to blame for crimes like these, the preacher proclaimed. In this case, listen and look for "secret whisperings, impi-ous doctrines, and licentious rantings which can inflame angry men, those men consumed with a smoldering rage, those professional fanat-ics who are so dangerous."[79]

The Berry memorial services symbolized a France united behind its king and the Bourbon regime. They also show how popular custom, in this case national *fêtes*, combined with historical circumstance to pro-duce a political result. Certainly, the services provided an opportune occasion for the government and the Church to speak to the entire na-tion at once, as much as that was possible in 1820. The Berry *mande-ments* and the eulogies articulated the three central components of the official interpretation of the assassination: Berry's public persona was redefined in heroic and dynastic terms, and as a counter-revolutionary martyr; second, liberals were associated with revolution and to be blamed for Berry's death; and, third, the revolutionary era was de-clared over and France proclaimed a royalist nation. All that remained to put the finishing touch on this interpretation was Bordeaux's birth, after which the royalists could claim that Providence had ordained the Bourbon rule over France. The government's ability to so quickly and successfully seize the opportunity presented by Berry's death to disseminate the core messages of its campaign to popularize the monarchy and the royal family also demonstrates the effectiveness of France's communications network and the relative modernity of its political system. The government was able to launch a national publicity campaign, all the while maintaining strict control over what was said, how it was said, and when it was said. This was more than a mere demonstration of centralization, of which historians since Toqueville have made so much. The memorial services evidence a cohesive and unified public policy articulated by a national government, with all branches of the bureaucracy working together. There were hints of the Old Regime to be sure – the prominence of the Church and the use of the pulpit most particularly – not to mention the use of the national *fête* for political purposes. At the same time, the entire project suggests that a well oiled political machine was at work, one that did not rely on Old Regime political forms, but on pre-existing and clearly defined public institutions standing at the ready.

As noted in the previous chapter, the modernity of France's political system was also evidenced by the reaction of the French media to Berry's death, and it is with regard to that issue that we continue our investigation of the Royalist Reaction's popular elements.

THE MEDIA AND PUBLIC PERSONAS

The most concentrated media coverage of the aftermath of the assassination occurred in March and April. Although equally intense from one medium or another later on – newspapers, pamphlets, books, or in illustrations, – coverage was never as comprehensive as in these two months. In print and in pictures, the nation was flooded with information and images about the Berry story. That information related mostly to the politics of the Royalist Reaction, specifically the liberty and press law debates, the subjects that occupied the attention of most journalists and political pamphleteers. However, within the context of that media coverage, and some other published materials, we see something quite new arising: the full development of new public personas for Berry, the duchess, and Louvel. Previous media coverage of these main characters, as touched on briefly in the previous chapter, had been primarily factual. After February, the press and the visual media responded to the symbolic ramifications of the assassination, a shift that dovetailed neatly into the government's official interpretation. That is not to say

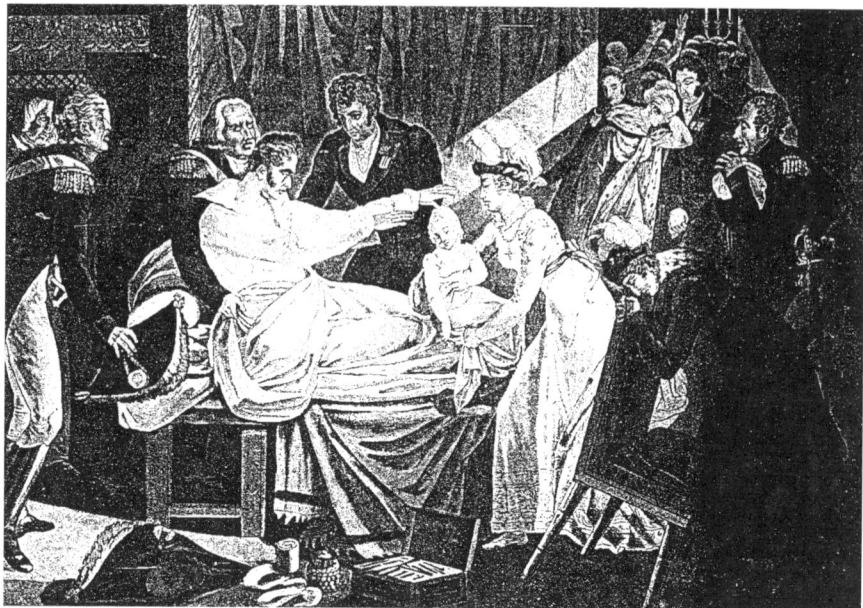

Figure 9   Berry blessing his daughter, a common theme among images depicting moments from the assassination night. One of a series of six illustrations. Vinck, 10571, 3 April 1820

the assassination itself was ignored; the visual media still published a number of crime and death scenes. The Bulla-Charon series continued with a picture of Berry after Louvel had run off. He was shown slumped in the arms of Choiseul and Mesnard, with the duchess embracing him.[80] Two others from that series focused on what proved to be a popular image: Berry blessing his daughter (fig. 9).[81] The duchess had left Berry to fetch their daughter during the night. Interestingly, his two daughters from his liaison with Amy Brown came as well, but no editor published a picture including them. It is also revealing that Louis XVIII appeared in several blessing illustrations, even though he had not arrived at the Opera when Berry blessed his daughter. A similar series of illustrations, this one published by F. Delpech of Vigneron, also attempted to pictorialize the most significant moments of the assassination: Berry sitting in the guard room just after the attack, his being moved to the *salon d'administration*, his being given the last rites, and finally, a blessing scene.[82]

Berry was obviously the centrepiece of the official interpretation of the assassination. Members of the media literally fell over themselves rushing to praise the fallen prince. Dozens of eulogies were published. Perhaps the most grandiose eulogy of all was delivered at the Abbey Church of Saint-Denis, in Paris, on 14 March, by Hyacinthe-Louis de

Quelen, the Archbishop of Trajanople and Coadjutor of Paris. His words sounded a mournful cry at the grievous loss France had suffered:

He received a warrior's education; he saw those with no religion as children gone astray; his heart, impregnable to vengeance, was always open to the cries of the unfortunate. He was lively almost to the point of brusqueness; he made up for the wrongs of his life up to that point with such grace and charm that their absence would almost have been regretted. He was full of nobility and frankness, and could not imagine treason or baseness. If he was sometimes led astray by the strength of his passions, there were two passions which should win him pardon for the others, his love of country and love of glory. This good prince was murdered; France will never be consoled. The nation will erect monuments to him, and his memory will always be held dear.

The press was particularly fond of anecdotes extolling Berry's most admirable character traits. One article told how Berry's staff had advised him to fire his footman because of certain unpaid debts. Instead, Berry decided to speak to him, and found out the man was supporting seven children. The prince met all the children and stated that the four oldest were now his responsibility, so the debts could be paid off.[83] Another anecdote recounted the story of an officer who had lost his commission because of false accusations made to Berry. When Berry found out the truth, he immediately gave the officer back his commission and made up for any lost salary. Another told of a noble woman who had asked Berry to help a poor family. The prince gave generously, stating, "This is not much; but next month I shall have plenty of money and then I shall be able to do more to help the poor." Yet another anecdote presented Berry as the caring father. When Berry was visiting at Bayeux, it recounted, a large crowd gathered around him. He heard a child cry, "I've lost my sabot." Berry ordered the crowd to look for it: "Gentlemen, let us look for this poor child's shoe; no one must suffer because I have come to Bayeux."[84] The *Journal des Débats* printed a summary of a sermon by Abbé de Maccarthy, a well-known ultra-royalist priest from Toulouse, noting that it was the third time since the assassination that the abbé had preached on the subject of charity. Maccarthy cited Berry as a perfect example of a charitable man. He then recounted an incident in which Berry had given away all the money he had in his purse to a beggar the day before he was killed.[85]

Editors also used Berry anecdotes as subject-matter for illustrations. The best example was a booklet of twelve illustrations called *The Duke of Berry, or the Virtues and Good Deeds of a Bourbon*, published by Édouard Hocquart.[86] Each illustration depicted a heroic moment from Berry's life. In "Act of Humanity," Berry and the duchess were driving past the *Pont de Neuilly*, when they came across a soldier who had

Figure 10   The Duke of Berry shown directing firemen and
offering solace to the injured. One of a series of fourteen illustrations publicizing his heroic actions. Vinck, 10626 (13)

fallen off his horse and broken his leg. The compassionate Berry insisted on stopping to help. He made sure that the soldier received medical assistance and even accompanied him on foot for a time. "Act of
Generosity" depicted the story of Berry seeing a small boy carrying a
large basket of bread. Feeling such a load was too heavy, Berry offered
to deliver the bread himself. Berry then took the boy home and gave
the boy's father money to buy a donkey so that the boy would not have
to carry such heavy loads in the future.[87] A second "Act of Humanity"
portrayed Berry's "zeal for the public good." Berry was shown dressed
in his finest clothes complete with top hat, standing in front of a burn-
ing building, directing the firemen "in the midst of the flames" and
helping to care for and console the wounded (fig. 10).[88]

Berry did not really have a career. But if asked, he would probably have responded that he was a soldier. That was not untrue; he was a *colonel général des chasseurs et lanciers* and had fought with Condé. However, in reality, Berry was more a prince than a soldier, enjoying the uniform and prestige of office more than active military service. But his credentials as a soldier were not important; after his death, it was expedient to focus on Berry's military career. Certainly, the myth of Berry's military prowess was related to the royalists' desire to compare him to Henri IV and Louis XIV, as the Archbishop of Trajanople's eulogy illustrated. The archbishop went so far as to suggest that the names Berry and Henri IV were interchangeable because there was so little difference between their lives: "Now I ask you," he said, pointing to Berry's portrait, "could this not be a portrait of either Henri IV or the Duke of Berry?"

By the king's order, all French soldiers wore a *crêpe* mourning band on their arms and shoulders.[89] A group of men calling themselves royal volunteers, *emigrés* from the town of Armentières in Nord, sent an open letter to the *Journal Libre de l'Isère* bemoaning the assassination and vowing revenge: "Our colonel is no more!!! ... the blood of Berry is still flowing; clouds hide the light from our eyes, and plunge France into the darkness of the tomb. We are armed, Sire, to avenge the death of our brave colonel! Speak, and we will call a truce to our grief, but never accord one to the enemies of your noble house."[90] The *Journal de Toulouse* published an address to Louis XVIII from the *officiers en non-activité* of the town of Saint-Gaudens, who wrote that they were as eager to risk their lives to defend the Bourbons as were their counterparts in Nord: "We offer all our best wishes to the descendants of the brave and good King Henri ... our swords are always ready to serve against his enemies."[91]

In his book on Berry, Chateaubriand characterized Berry by his military stature – not in terms of physical size, but by virtue of his vigorous nature, energy, and bearing.[92] We are even told that Berry had the same build as Louis XIV.[93] Chateaubriand suggested that this military nature was the reason for his womanizing, noting that a soldier without a war, exiled from his country, with nothing to do could hardly be chastised for certain infidelities. Despite being wrong "in the eyes of religion," such behaviour arose from a love of glory, and could hardly be condemned in a soldier. Besides, womanizing was a healthy weakness for royalty. It showed spirit: "When the people of France condemn their rulers too severely for their weakness in pursuing love and glory, they should be afraid of condemning themselves."[94] The *Journal de Toulouse* described Berry in martial terms as well: "A Prince, a friend of soldiers who were drawn to him by the irresistible attraction of his knightly form and martial behaviour."[95]

Figure 11   "Act of Courage." "A son of France does not
wait for glory, he rides forth to meet it." Vinck, 10626 (12)

Berry's heroic persona, rooted in his military background, dominated the crime and death scene illustrations. He was pictured as a
strong and vigorous man, alert and conscious until the very end,
bravely facing his death, even though an eye witness wrote that after
midnight Berry had barely moved and drifted in and out of consciousness.[96] Moreover, he was in horrible agony, suffering from a rising fe-
ver, and weakened by loss of blood. Yet, a number of illustrations
showed a still-powerful Berry sitting upright to greet Louis XVIII
only an hour before he died.[97] The glorification of Berry's military exploits was also emphasized by the clothes he wore in the illustrations.
He was always dressed in uniform. Hocquart's booklet celebrated
Berry the commander, courageously leading Condé's army into battle,
magnanimously pardoning two soldiers who had deserted, or gra-
ciously preventing his troops from massacring a much smaller rebel

force.[98] "Act of Courage" depicted a conversation between Berry and a foreign general as the duke led some of Condé's troops into battle. Obviously unaware of the fearless character he was dealing with, the foreign general suggested that Berry drop to the back of the troops, rather than risk death by riding at the front. Berry is said to have responded: "A son of France does not wait for glory, he rides forth to meet it" (fig. 11).[99]

Hardly a religious man when he was alive, Berry was represented after his death as a deeply pious man. Chateaubriand wrote that his infidelities, "which religion deplores, but human frailty excuses," never interfered with his devotion to Christianity. He cited the example of Henri IV, who shared Berry's love of women, but also never lost sight of his place before God: "He was often weak, but always faithful, and his passions were never known to have undermined his religion."[100] He added that Berry knew God as more than just a word, and he trembled as he waited for the *tribunal suprême*: "Martyrdom opened the gates of heaven to him, and he did not think he was pure enough to rejoin the holy king and the martyred king."[101] Louvel, Chateaubriand declared, was produced by revolution, but Berry by religion.[102] A report on the assassination, filed with the Chamber of Peers in May, also noted Louvel's secular nature, suggesting that a lack of religious training was the original cause of his becoming an assassin: "His instruction in the Christian faith seems to have been neglected, and there is no doubt, Gentlemen, that it is in this ignorance of religion, in this impious freedom from divine precepts, that we will find the first cause of this deplorable crime."[103] Berry's religious character was also emphasized in a marble sculpture by J. Pradier. The martyred Berry, hand on heart, is supported by the female figure of Religion, who is holding a cross (fig. 12).[104]

The visual media did not focus particularly on Berry's image as a counter-revolutionary figure; that image came through more strongly in the print media, in the *fêtes*, and in the exceptional law debates. Illustrations generally emphasized Berry's dynastic greatness. However, a few editors published illustrations that provided a graphic expression of Berry's martyrdom. In "The Apotheosis of the Duke of Berry" (fig. 13), Berry's body is seen transported by angels up to heaven, where a floating St Louis and Henri IV, and a genuflecting Louis XVI wait to greet him. Below, a woman personifying France reclines in front of a view of Paris, mourning Berry's death, her arm upraised.[105] The presence of Louis XVI is a self-evident reference to the Revolution, with Henri IV symbolizing Bourbon martyrdom. Interestingly, that illustration was published in 1822, that is, two years after the Royalist Reaction, when concern over the revolutionaries had died away

Figure 12   The Duke of Berry depicted dying a martyr's
death in the arms of Religion. Pradier finished the sculpture in
1825. Vinck, 10617, 12 Feb. 1823

somewhat. Another illustration with the same title, this one published
in 1820, shows Berry greeted in heaven by Henri IV, St Louis, and
the principal royal victims of the Revolution: Louis XVI, Marie-
Antoinette, Madame-Elisabeth, and Louis XVII. Note that here we
have dynastic and counter-revolutionary symbolism blended together,
with the former perhaps slightly more prominent than the latter. Berry
is met by Henri IV, the largest figure in the picture; St Louis is the next-
closest figure to Berry. In contrast, Louis XVI stands in the background, while his family sits off to the side. The Prince of Condé, who
led the counter-revolutionary army in the 1790s stands in the background as well. Below is a much smaller picture of *Espérance* holding
an anchor, the symbol of hope. She is gazing into a crib, with shields

Figure 13   "The Apotheosis of the Duke of Berry." This
lithograph, by N. Monsiau, was presented to Louis XVIII.
Vinck, 10609, 26 Sept. 1822

with the coat of arms of France and the Two Sicilies resting against it.
The Counter-Revolution is obviously an important image in the illustration, but it is muted somewhat by the prominence of Henri IV and
the *espérance* imagery (fig. 14).[106]

By the end of April, Berry's new public persona had become permanent and authoritative in the royalist media. It survived the July Revolution and inspired the Legitimist movement. Before 14 February 1820,
Berry had the reputation of being a fun-loving, womanizing man
whose character edged towards the vulgar. A day later, he was on his
way to becoming a dynastic and heroic figure, a martyr to the royalist
cause. Exemplifying that change is an illustration published in March
showing Berry lying in state on a catafalque.[107] The descriptive text referred to Berry as "a prince through whom, by virtue of his birth,
coursed the blood of thirty kings." He was "the protector of the arts,

Figure 14   The Duke of Berry welcomed into heaven by his
royal ancestors. Vinck, 10610

the friend of the warrior, the supporter of the poor, the consoler of the
sick, and the hope of all Frenchmen." Included as well were Abbé
Edgeworth's words to Louis XVI at his execution, which ended by proclaiming God's paternal love for "the descendants of Saint Louis."

Which person appeared in more assassination and miracle child illustrations than any other? The answer may surprise: it was the Duchess
of Berry. In the crime scenes, she was invariably pictured in the carriage, and in death scenes she was usually seated next to Berry. In Bordeaux illustrations, the duchess was usually shown holding her son, or
pointing to him for some reason, whether to direct the gaze of some
mythological figure or to show a Duke of Berry floating in the heavens
where his child lay. The duchess became the darling of the visual media
during the Royalist Reaction; and the result was a transformation in
her public persona that was every bit as dramatic as that of her husband. It carried her to the heights of national fame, and made her one
of the most popular royal figures of the era.

The reasons for this transformation are more complex because of her sex. (The issue of gender will be dealt with at length in chapter 8, where the miracle child's influence on the duchess's public persona will be discussed.) As Bordeaux's birth played a major role in the development of her public persona, a full discussion of gender issues as they related to the duchess must wait until we focus on his birth. It is noted here to make the reader aware that the Duchess's sex needs to be taken into account when analyzing the public personas of the Royalist Reactions' principal characters. The politics of the Royalist Reaction and the official interpretation of the assassination and the miracle child influenced the public personas of all four characters, but only the duchess's image was altered directly by gender issues.

By way of introduction, the term "gender" is used here in the context of the historical process that excluded women from participating in political society, often called the public sphere, and forced them to remain in the domestic, or private sphere. This process emerged during the second half of the eighteenth century and strengthened during the revolutionary era, as increasingly high barriers were placed in front of publicly minded women. Naturally, this is a generalization, as certain women did participate in public life despite the barriers. At the same time, the historiography on the subject remains firm, that by 1820 the public/private sphere split was an indelible part of France's social fabric, and politics was a male monopoly. Gender politics is relevant to the Duchess's public persona because it forced strictly domestic characteristics onto her. Any political significance that her persona may have contained related solely to her status as a member of the royal family, that is, to her membership in the Bourbon dynasty, rather than to her as a person. This is not to suggest that her public persona was preordained by gender politics; yet, the sexual stereotypes that led to the determination that women were unsuitable for public life also prevented the duchess's public persona from developing along the political lines seen with Berry, Bordeaux, and Louvel. Another factor is that the duchess's public persona developed in reaction to two different events, Berry's murder and Bordeaux's birth, and each event contributed a unique, albeit interrelated, component to her overall public persona. Finally, while Berry's public persona developed in the context of the Royalist Reaction, the duchess's developed in relation to both the Royalist Reaction and to Berry's transformed public persona. Her new persona had to fit his; she had to be worthy of the duke's greatness – not an easy task, given that she was still alive.

Defining the duchess's public persona is made easier by the fact that she did not really have one prior to the assassination. Berry and the duchess had toured the country after their marriage, so she was not unknown outside of Paris; but her popularity was restricted to that circle of French elites who saw her at the functions she and Berry so loved to host and attend. Given her age and Berry's propensities, it seems likely that this lifestyle would have continued for the foreseeable future, and had it not been for the assassination, the duchess's public persona may well have continued to rest upon her social abilities. That is not to slight those abilities; they served an important political function, which explains why the royal treasury allowed the couple to spend 1.5 million francs on household expenses in three and a half years.[108] The royal family desperately wanted to re-establish itself as the centre of French culture. Louis XVIII put considerable revenues into reviving the French royal court,[109] and this couple's talent for hosting social functions was an integral part of this strategy. Destiny, however, determined that the duchess's public persona would acquire loftier and more profound attributes. Those attributes coalesced into two symbolic representations: the Good Wife persona and the Good Mother persona. In the first role, the duchess is portrayed as the grieving widow forever mourning the passing of the great duke. Of course, the Good Wife persona made little sense unless the object of the duchess's yearnings was truly worthy of such profound sorrow. To that end, her Good Wife persona reinforced Berry's heroic and dynastic persona: he was a man worth grieving for. The Good Mother persona had to wait for Bordeaux's birth, and so will be discussed in chapters 7 and 8. That image supported the official interpretations of the assassination and the miracle birth by promoting Bordeaux as a true miracle proving the divine and providential favour enjoyed by the Bourbon regime.

As we find again and again when dealing with the government's actions during the Royalist Reaction, dynastic symbolism is the best starting point for analyzing the duchess's personas. Rooted in the national tragedy that was the assassination, the Good Wife persona promoted the notion that her grief was shared by millions of French citizens. The duchess became the nation's widow, as her widowhood became a powerful and politically useful symbol for the Bourbon regime. To illustrate this element of her public persona, we will begin by answering a single question: Why did she grieve? Did she grieve because her husband and the father of her child had died, or because the Bourbon dynasty was threatened with extinction? Certainly her Good Wife persona expressed both a personal and a dynastic element; however, the latter generally dominated. During the Royalist Reaction, France was presented with a duchess overwhelmed by the great loss the entire nation had suffered. Her own personal grief was devalued, at least in comparison to the dynastic implications of Berry's death.

The early press coverage initiated this process. She was referred to constantly as Berry's inconsolable wife. She was said to have become a

Figure 15   The Duchess of Berry in mourning.
A fragment of a larger painting by official court
painter François-Joseph Kinson, which was displayed in the Salon of 1822

virtual recluse, and it was reported that she did not take her first walk
in public – a two-hour stroll in the Jardin des Tuileries – until 27 March.
It was also reported that the duchess's apartment was shrouded in
black cloth and that she only appeared in public thereafter in a funeral
crêpe. Significantly, the press often added that her intense personal loss
was diminished somewhat by the approaching pregnancy: "The child
breathes in the womb of the grieving wife who saw him fall into her
arms, the precious fruit of such a brief union." This statement suggests
that if she gave birth to a boy, the pain of her husband's assassination
would be easier to bear (fig. 15).[110]

The family metaphor prevented the duchess's Good Wife persona
from including the stereotypically weak female image. She was far
more valuable as a symbol of Bourbon bravery. In the illustrations,
newspapers, and reports filed by the government, she was continually
praised for displaying such courage and spirit the night of the assassination. Newspaper readers were told how she never left Berry's side,
holding him throughout his ordeal. In virtually every crime scene illustration, the duchess was drawn sitting or standing in the carriage,
arms raised trying to warn Berry,[111] and in death scene illustrations,

she was invariably shown sitting in a chair or kneeling next to Berry, in terrible anguish.[112] Chateaubriand noted proudly that when Berry cried out for his wife during a moment of particular agony, she replied, "I am here; I will never leave you."[113] Chateaubriand was also impressed that she offered her belt to stop the blood flow from the wound. In strictly romantic terms, a less powerful persona would certainly have attracted more sympathy; however, the spring of 1820 was not a moment to publicize Bourbon weakness. Royalism and the Bourbon regime needed glory, and the duchess's Good Wife persona helped deliver it.

The principal contribution[114] of the visual media was to interpret the duchess's sorrow as an indication of the greatness of the Bourbon for whom she mourned, and by extension, for the Bourbon royal family and the Restoration. This interpretation was most apparent in illustrations of mourning scenes,[115] and the image of the duchess as grieving widow was featured in many of them. Significantly, this image had a longer shelf-life than any other illustration of the assassination or the miracle birth, and it continued to appear throughout the Restoration. Purchasers of illustrations clearly wanted to see the duchess in the guise of grieving widow, and moreover wanted to see her that way even ten years after the assassination.

A review of some illustrations that starred the eternally grieving princess will testify to the transcendence of the dynastic element. A useful starting point is an illustration called "The Duchess of Berry Cutting Off Her Hair."[116] The duchess is dressed in black, the widow's weeds that would become her official uniform in all pictures of her published during the Restoration,[117] and she is standing in front of a mirror. She had just cut off her long blonde hair. The shadowy form of Berry appears beside her, shrouded in a black veil and dressed in military uniform. The duchess offers him a lock of hair, but he is unable to accept. Below the illustration reads the following caption:

> Too soon she cuts her flowing hair,
> No shining tresses does she spare,
> By power of love alone descries,
> Her husband's shrouded form, and sighs. (fig. 16)

Why did Berry not take the Duchess's hair? What was preventing him? Certainly, to have pictured him doing so would have been a dramatic and romantic symbol of their undying love; he would have had a wonderful keepsake of his wife in heaven. It might be argued that Berry could not take the hair simply because he was dead, but that rather crude analysis is contradicted by two points. First, it must be remem-

Figure 16   The Duchess of Berry offers her husband a
lock of her hair. The personal – and dynastic – tragedy
of an unfulfilled destiny. Vinck, 10602

bered that Berry's premature death not only prevented him from accepting his wife's locks, but also kept him from fulfilling his destiny of
becoming king of France and producing the next heir. Second, he appears in uniform – hardly the costume of the lover – odd considering
the duchess is wearing a gown. Berry appears as a military man, in his
official capacity as a general in the French army, and his inability to
take the hair symbolizes his inability to fulfill his destiny as a great
warrior. Admittedly, an element of personal tragedy exists. The duchess
certainly looks pathetic enough, and the caption is a testimony to their
love. However, that element is overshadowed by the dynastic implications of Berry's death and France's loss.

Figure 17   The duchess cuts off her hair on her return from
the Opéra. Shown here in her persona as a grieving "good
wife." Vinck 10600, 28 April 1820

That interpretation is supported by the analysis of the illustration
"The Thirteenth of February," discussed on page 121, in which the
duke and the duchess were shown sitting on his death bed. Again, we
see what at first blush is a romantic vision of a couple separated tragically by death. However, on closer investigation, in light of the *Cordon
du Saint Esprit* draped across the bed, Berry's robust figure, the duchess's calm demeanour – and the reference to Berry's forgiveness of Louvel – we must see the illustration as a testament to the magnificence of
the Bourbon dynasty and to the extent of the tragedy suffered by the
nation on 13 February.

Dynastic symbolism was front and centre in two illustrations published together in the spring of 1820. The first depicts the duchess cutting her hair, surrounded by her weeping ladies-in-waiting, after
returning home from the Opera House the morning of Berry's death
(fig. 17). The second had the same structure, but the ladies-in-waiting
are replaced by a crowd of people around Berry as he lay on his death

Figure 18   "How cruel to die at the hand of a Frenchman."
The assembled members of the Bourbon family contemplate
the death of a dynasty. Vinck, 10597, 8 March 1820

bed.[118] Both are powerful images of a royal family in mourning. The assassination's dynastic ramifications are made quite clear in the Berry illustration. Louis XVIII is seated at the head of the bed, his eyes downcast, crushed by the loss; behind him is Artois, and to the side Angoulême. The duchess is embracing Berry. Once again, this is the family metaphor in picture form, and to look at this picture is to feel a connection to the royal family united in grief. The sorrow conveyed by the picture is clearly personal and familial; but at the same time, the people who appear in it represent the Bourbon regime (fig. 18).

Consider also "In Memory of Charles Ferdinand, Duke of Berry," a mourning illustration published in March, 1820. The Duchess, in her usual black dress, stands before a (fictitious) tombstone in a forest that overwhelms her tiny figure. The use of scale heightens our sympathy for her, as she stands before the grave, alone, surrounded by the immensity of nature. The epitaph was Berry's by then almost clichéd

Figure 19   "*O ma patrie ... malheureuse France.*" The duke's
famous dying words supported the view that his assassination
was the result of the Berry Conspiracy. Vinck, 10623,
13 March 1820

statement, supposedly uttered on his death bed: "*O ma patrie ... mal-heureuse France.*" As noted in our discussion of Berry's public persona,
the use of this phrase taps into the official interpretation of the assassi-
nation, which saw Berry's death in the context of the royalist struggle
against the evil forces of the Revolution. Even in a picture of the duchess mourning her husband, we see a direct reference to the Berry Conspiracy. In addition, a verse below the illustration expressed the sorrow
of the whole country: "O dark times, O grieving hearts, Say if there are
sorrows equal to my sorrows." The duchess mourns her husband; but
he was more than that – he was a Bourbon (fig. 19).[119]

An illustration called "The Marvellous Dream," published in September, 1820, has a similar perspective. The duchess is standing in
front of a crib, in which Bordeaux lies sleeping. She is not wearing her
customary black dress, however, but appears in white, wearing the
crown and fleur-de-lys cape that symbolize *la France*. Berry floats
above her in the clouds, accompanied by angels who are showering
flowers upon the crib. The duchess is now the nation, as she gazes up
to show Berry the newest heir to the throne. She is no longer grieving,
but proud and glorious, as a cheering throng in the background acknowledges its allegiance to the Bourbon regime (fig. 20).[120]

Figure 20   "The Marvellous Dream." The duchess, no longer
grieving but symbollically clothed as *la France*, proudly invites
the duke to gaze upon the new heir. Vinck, 10695

The grandiose nature of Berry's new public persona gave credence to
the duchess's persona as the eternally grieving widow. Moreover, from
a royalist perspective it was only natural for her grief to be fundamentally rooted in the dynastic implications of the assassination. Who
more than Berry's wife would appreciate the tragedy the French nation
suffered that fateful night. Louvel's crime had robbed France of a van-
guard against evil, a warrior to protect it from Jacobinism, Bonapar-
tism, and revolution. In addition, the duchess was well aware of her
reproductive responsibilities; she had been chosen to marry Berry to
provide an heir to the throne; and would be assumed to be devastated

by the prospect of not fulfilling that obligation. But the Duchess would indeed meet her dynastic obligations by giving birth to the Duke of Bordeaux seven months after Berry's death, which unleashed the second manifestation of the duchess' public persona as the Good Mother. When that element of her persona took life, it developed along the same lines as her Good Wife persona. The duchess's personal joy at giving birth to her child and her role as Bordeaux's biological mother were ignored. The media, the government – and this time the Catholic Church – chose to refer to her predominantly in dynastic terms.

By the middle of March, the press seemed to have lost interest in Pierre Louvel. The reason was simple: Louvel was not good copy. Uncommunicative, morose, relatively unintelligent, and – perhaps most significantly – unattractive, he provided little to write about. Louvel did excite some interest in regard to allegations of the Berry Conspiracy, however, and royalist pamphleteers intent on proving the existence of that conspiracy discussed his life at some length. But their purpose was to prove a connection between the assassination and the liberals rather than to shed light on why Louvel killed Berry. Louvel differs in this regard from an assassin like Charlotte Corday, who had killed Jean-Paul Marat on 13 July 1793; her physical and intellectual charms had titillated the public and turned her into a national celebrity. Louvel's fame was far more fleeting. He was locked away in prison until his execution on 7 June, and the public heard little about him. Even his trial was a banal affair; he denied having accomplices and reiterated his hatred of the Bourbon royal family, all in as few words as possible.

The visual media alone remained interested, and Louvel illustrations continued to be published. Significantly, these pictures created a persona that had virtually nothing to do with Louvel the man and everything to do with the fight for public opinion waged by royalists and liberals. In the months leading up to his execution and then for years thereafter, the visual media published Louvel portraits that depicted him as a revolutionary fanatic. This image[121] corresponds to the official interpretation of the assassination, so it is understandable that market-savvy editors used it. It also made for some very interesting pictures. One Louvel illustration, published in April as part of the Bulla-Charon series, showed the assassin as a slim, narrow-faced man, entering a prison cell to answer questions.[122] He was bound by a straightjacket and surrounded by three guards. The caption gives an excerpt of the interrogation; when asked what motivated the crime, Louvel responded, "My hate for the Bourbons." Louvel showed no signs of remorse, we are told; he was proud of his "savage act," and "in his face

Figure 21   Louvel, seen here as the anti-royalist fanatic, broods in his cell. Did he act alone? Vinck, 10638, 24 March 1820

one sees the coldness and hardness of heart of a profoundly evil man." Another illustration of Louvel in prison, published in March, made the final leap by connecting Louvel directly to the Revolution and Restoration liberalism (fig. 21).[123] A round-faced, stout Louvel is portrayed with the dark, brooding eyes and heavyset eyebrows that became his trademark in portraits depicting the fanatic image. On the wall of the cell are portraits of Napoleon and Abbé Grégoire. Louvel is seated behind a desk on which the liberal newspaper *La Minerve* is displayed. As if the picture were not sufficiently explicit – with a grindstone in the corner to boot – the following caption was added:

Scornful of goodness, craven to force,
Sophists, corrupters, your words are the source
    Of unbridled license and strife;
Your poisonous screeds to Louvel were a feast;
And your hatred transformed him into a beast,
    as your pens sharpened his knife.

Figure 22   Louvel approaching the scaffold.
A face befitting an assassin. Vinck, 10638,
12 June 1820

   These illustrations were entirely the product of imagination. Yet, royalists would repeat for years to come that even if Louvel had acted alone his mind was corrupted by liberal and revolutionary writers and journalists; those "thinkers" must therefore bear the principal responsibility for the assassination; their evil texts justified the exceptional laws and any other measures needed to destroy liberalism. The media's representation of Louvel provided royalists with the face they needed to legitimize the Berry Conspiracy. It also provided the public with a Louvel they wanted to see brought to the scaffold (fig. 22).

THE BERRY SUBSCRIPTION

In April the *magistrats de la ville de Paris* formally requested – and were immediately granted by Louis XVIII – the right to set up a national subscription to raise funds to build a monument to Berry at the site of the Opera House, which was then in the process of being torn down.[124] A commission was formed to administer the subscription, and mayors and lawyers throughout France – 114 in Paris alone – were appointed to collect the funds. Similar to the addresses, subscriptions were a common means of acknowledging an important event, so a subscription honouring Berry was not unexpected. Regardless, the Berry Subscription was still a special event because it had official status; that is, it was sanctioned by the government and organized by government personnel. There were only a few such subscriptions during the Restoration: an 1819 campaign to build a monument to Malesherbes, Louis XVI's trial lawyer; the Chambord Subscription, a subscription to purchase the Château de Chambord for Bordeaux; and in 1825, a subscription headed by the Duchess of Angoulême to erect a monument for the victims of Quibéron.[125] Far more numerous were the unofficial subscriptions, which tended for the most part to support anti-Bourbon causes. Some of the most popular subscriptions of this type were a subscription to pay the legal costs of those charged under the liberty law, another to build a monument to Lallemand, a student killed by the National Guard during demonstrations against the double vote law,[126] and one organized in Isère in 1819–20 to raise funds to pay a libel fine on behalf of the editors of L'Echo des Alpes, a radical liberal periodical.

What really set the Berry Subscription apart – as well as the Chambord Subscription – was its astounding success. The prefect, mayors and adjutants of Paris made the first contribution of 12,000 francs, to the Berry Subscription[127] and the money kept rolling in until it totalled 900,000 francs, far exceeding expectations. Costs for the monument had grown from 50,000 francs to 468,000; however, even with the increase a 432,000-franc surplus remained. Clearly, Berry's death had touched a sensitive nerve in the general population, and served the same function as the addresses by providing an outlet for the anger about the assassination. The opportunity for members of the general public to express an opinion upon a political issue was limited severely by the elite power structure, as exemplified by the voting provisions under the Charter. Nevertheless, the Berry Subscription and the addresses show that thousands of people were ready to make their opinions known when an opportunity arose. The government was remarkably sensitive to those feelings, and the Berry Subscription was evidence of its successful reading of the public temperament during the Royalist Reaction. It was also a further step in spreading the official interpretation of the assassination. Government officials worked diligently to ensure the Subscription made the intended impression on the public. In one instance, for example, Baron Haussez went as far as to formally chastise the Mayor of Grenoble for announcing the Berry Subscription in the Journal Libre de l'Isère, a liberal newspaper, rather than the royalist *Journal de Grenoble*.[128] However, the Berry Subscription was far more than an example of an effective propaganda campaign – although it was that. It provides concrete evidence of a popular Royalist Reaction. Subscribers had to part with their money – quite a different matter from simply signing an address and sending it to Paris. Yet, they did so in unprecedented numbers in the months following Berry's death, and would do so again after Bordeaux's birth. This immense show of support for the Bourbon regime provided much needed moral ammunition for Richelieu and his ministers during their fight to push the exceptional laws though the Chamber of Deputies. Although violent demonstrations against the laws took place throughout the spring and summer, the Berry Subscription, along with the Berry memorial services, the addresses, and the Chambord Subscription, gave a strong impetus to the Royalist Reaction.

A random sampling of Berry Subscription lists from Isère and Haute-Garonne reveals an interesting profile of the typical subscriber. Surprisingly, both departments contributed around 8,000 francs. There were clearly enough royalists in Isère to match the contributions made in an ultra-royalist department like Haute-Garonne. Less surprising is that most contributions were made in the first few months after the subscription was established, with the majority being given by September. At the same time, contributions continued in significant amounts throughout 1821. Group contributions complicate attempts to determine the precise number of subscribers and the average contribution per subscriber, but rough estimates are possible. It appears that the average contribution was a relatively modest seven or eight francs. In Haute-Garonne, twenty individuals gave twenty francs or more – a sum that represented more than two weeks' wages for a field labourer – even though, 1,394 men in that department met the 300-franc *cens* in the 1820 deputy election. Jean-Pierre Amilhau, a liberal, and a lawyer and *notaire* from Toulouse, was an extraordinarily wealthy landowner whose direct taxes in 1820 were 5,758.73, third highest in the department; yet, he felt that 20 francs was a sufficient contribution to honour Berry's memory. Baron Antoine de Lapasse of Muret and Jean-Joseph Roquefort of Ville-franche, two other subscribers from Haute-Garonne who donated twenty francs to Berry's Subscription, paid direct taxes in 1829 of 2,291 francs and 3,829 francs, respectively.[129] Almost 75 percent of all individual contributions were under ten francs, and only 12 percent were twenty francs or more. In all, only three contributions topped 100 francs; of those, Mathieu Hocquart's astonishing contribution of 1,600 francs stands out.[130] Despite these findings, nothing in the official correspondence suggests that contributions were disappointing – quite the opposite, in fact. It can only be assumed that 1,000 subscribers giving a total of around 8,000 francs in departments like Isère and Haute-Garonne signified a very successful subscription.

The individual subscribers were nearly all men; perhaps only one percent of the names on the lists were female. This male majority could simply mean that men controlled the money in the family; or, since women were excluded from participating in politics and subscribing to the Berry Subscription could be interpreted as expressing a political opinion, the political nature of the subscription may have been the reason. Far more women contributed to the Chambord Subscription; at the risk of reinforcing a stereotype, it is perhaps understandable that women would be more attracted to a subscription involving a baby than they would be to one related to violence and death.

Subscribers usually provided their occupations with their contributions. Note that any conclusions based upon such information must be tempered by the notorious unreliability of such information. Men often received income from more than one source, and so usually had more than one occupation. As Thomas Beck demonstrated in his study of French notables, men invariably reported the occupation that provided the highest status in any given circumstance; one might be a landowner for an electoral list and a mayor for a subscription list.[131] At the same time, it is statistically significant that almost 50 percent of the subscribers listed occupations related to the government – salaried government employees and those such as mayors, adjuncts, and members of municipal councils who occupied a government post but did not earn their living from it. Military occupations were cited by approximately 20 percent of the subscribers. All told, some 70 percent of all subscribers were connected to the government or the military. Church officials as a group did not show much interest, although that changed for the Chambord Subscription. Again, hard data are difficult to find, but it appears that subscribers claimed an occupation in the Church less than 3 percent of the time.

A geographic analysis suggests that contributions tended to be made in clusters; that is, in a few particular regions, towns, offices, or by specific industries in those places. Nineteen tobacconists from Villefranche gave thirty francs, for instance, while tobacconists from surrounding regions gave nothing. Contributions among government officials were similarly irregular. Some departments gave generously, others modestly, and some not at all.[132] Naturally, more work would be useful in this area, although it is doubtful that a detailed local study would reveal much more, apart from the potential finding that the most political regions contributed most often, and that the influence of a few prominent individuals, government officials, or families frequently explained the largesse of a specific region, industry, or office.

The caveat regarding the interpretation of the Berry addresses must also accompany the Berry Subscription: contributions were not made for purely altruistic reasons. Subscription lists were published, usually in newspapers, and as with the addresses, they were a convenient and often expected means of advertising one's royalism. The preponderance of government and military personnel among the Berry subscribers supports this conclusion. At the same time, the Berry Subscription was seen by contemporaries as a magnificent success story. Budgetary concerns were even ignored in light of the perceived importance of the cause: Claude Mounier gave Grenoble's municipal council permission to deduct their 1,200 franc contribution from the 1821 budget;[133] in a letter to Mounier, St-Chamans explained that he had allowed Toulouse's municipal council to donate 5,000 francs in 1820, even though the city had a budget deficit of 81,710 francs.[134] Moreover, the sheer volume of contributions and the overall success of the subscription suggests that self-interest was not at the heart of the matter. Nothing speaks sincerity like a financial contribution; the Berry Subscription was tantamount to thousands of sincere royalists announcing their commitment to the Bourbon regime, most obviously during the Royalist Reaction, but also after that, until contributions slowed down by the end of 1821.

Ironically, despite the importance the government and the royalists attached to the Subscription, and despite the amount of money raised, Berry's monument was never built, and the land where the Opera House once stood remained empty throughout the Restoration. By 1826 it was decided to build a *chapelle expiatoire* at the site rather than a formal monument.[135] Construction had only just begun when the July Revolution halted the work, and the project was ultimately abandoned. The land was turned into a small park with a large fountain in the middle. Today the only reminder of the assassination at the site is a plaque with an inscription noting the date of Berry's death.[136]

6 May–June:
The Law of the Double Vote

On 15 May 1820 the amended electoral bill was read to the deputies. From that moment until 12 June the deputies debated the merits of the bill to the exclusion of all other matters, as some 120 deputies and ministers took the podium. The double vote would operate as follows. The basic criteria for voting, as set out in the February 5th Law remained unchanged; men over thirty years old who paid at least 300 francs a year in direct taxes were eligible to vote for candidates to fill 258 seats in the Chamber of Deputies. The amendment proposed the creation of seats for an additional 172 deputies; however, only electors whose direct taxes put them in the top 25 percent of all electors in their department would be eligible to vote for those 172 additional deputies. Elections for the 172 deputies would take place in newly created departmental colleges, whereas elections for the original 258 deputies would take place in the arrondissement colleges.[1] The crux of the controversy over the proposed bill was that electors who qualified to vote for the 172 deputies in the departmental colleges were also eligible to vote for the original 258 deputies in the arrondissement colleges. As a result, the electoral law became known as the law of the double vote. The "double-voters" were roughly the same men who qualified to stand as candidates in a deputy election. The *cens* for candidates was 1,000 francs; the minimum *cens* to qualify for a double vote in the 1820 election in Haute-Garonne was 1,025 francs.[2]

The double vote inspired the fiercest and most eloquent parliamentary debate of the entire Restoration period, particularly in the

Chamber of Deputies. Led by Pasquier,[3] Siméon, Serre, Constant, Lafayette, Jordan, Royer-Collard, Manuel, Villèle, and Bonald – a virtual who's-who of Restoration politics – ministers and deputies debated the merits of the double vote as if their lives were at stake. The debate resembled a war between two sides that had skirmished for years and then decided to settle the matter in a single battle. The ministers and the ultras would fight with the liberals; the Chamber of Deputies would be the battlefield, and the prize would be the support of the moderate royalists, whose numbers would determine the eventual outcome of any vote. Liberals and royalists alike decried the internal divisions and petty squabbles that crippled the ability of the government and the two chambers to work together effectively, but to no avail. The debate soon involved issues of far greater magnitude than the workings of the electoral system – the structure of France's political institutions, the purpose of law, the appropriate balance of power in the government, the influence of the Revolution on French society, and even the nature and purpose of property ownership. In the end, the ministers and the deputies agreed on only one thing: the double vote gave royalists control of the Chamber of Deputies.

Why did the double vote turn into such a contentious affair? For one thing, the passage of the liberty and press laws emboldened those who supported the double vote. It also encouraged the opponents of the double vote to step up their resistance, knowing that the double vote meant their extinction as a political force in the Chamber. Their resistance was also stronger because the initial panic that followed the assassination had subsided and Berry's name had lost some of its emotional impact. The pro-law forces realized that the deputies would not be so easily convinced that radical action was necessary. Moreover, the double vote by definition could not be promoted as a temporary measure; the electoral law could not have a time limit as the liberty or press laws did. Perhaps an even more fundamental reason is that the double vote affected the deputies personally. With their own political futures at risk, they were less willing to accept defeat.

Royer-Collard stated that the double vote included enormous questions that embraced "all governments and all society ... and carried revolutions in their bosom."[4] Royalists agreed that a revolution was imminent, but in their minds, the double vote was the final legislative act needed to prevent it. There is no question the participants in the debate expected dramatic changes depending upon whether the double vote became law or not; and in that they proved prophetic. A month later, when the double vote finally did pass, the Age of the Moderates, one short chapter in the history of French politics, had closed and a new chapter was opened – the Age of the Ultras.

THE STORM BEFORE THE STORM

If the two weeks prior to the debate over the double vote were any indication, then the acrimony and violence that characterized the debate should not have surprised anyone. On 8 and 9 May, in Grenoble, rioting and protests directed at the Duke of Angoulême, during a rather ill-advised visit, turned into a national incident. The government had encouraged the visit as a conciliatory gesture after the liberty and press law debates. Royer-Deloche, the mayor of Grenoble, proclaimed: "The prince ... faithful to beliefs of Louis XVIII, has come to remind us of those sacred words, *union et oubli.*"[5] A number of Grenoble law students, however, saw the visit as the perfect moment to voice their displeasure with Baron Cuvier's efforts to silence them[6] and express their opposition to the exceptional laws. As the prince made his way to the *hôtel de la préfecture* where he would stay, the students followed his carriage chanting *Vive la charte, Vive la liberté*, drowning out attempts to chant *Vive le roi*. The next day, while Angoulême reviewed some troops, law students surrounded him and again chanted *Vive la charte*. Police and military personnel on horseback charged the students, and four arrests were made. Later that same day, at the *hôtel de la préfecture*, with Angoulême inside, law students gathered again to chant anti-Bourbon slogans; yet another student was arrested. Only a day before Angoulême had arrived in Grenoble, the *Commission de l'instruction publique* had issued an *ordre général* declaring that any university student found engaging in an illicit or seditious activity would be suspended. On 10 May, Grenoblois law students met at the Café des Aveugles to denounce the arrests and the *ordre général*. The *conseil académique* at the university responded promptly. Three students who had attended the meeting were suspended for one year.[7]

Any hopes that the suspensions would silence the student population were dashed almost immediately. Seemingly overnight, students published diatribes against the exceptional laws, the prohibitions against them, the arrests, and the suspensions. One such pamphlet, titled *Attention!*, described the Angoulême incident from the law students' perspective. University and government officials received equal doses of criticism for what were termed high-handed and oppressive actions. The pamphlet soon found its way onto a list of banned publications, and a number of copies were confiscated from reading rooms across the country and burned. A Grenoblois law student, François Ducros, wrote another pamphlet called "An Account of the Events at the Faculty of Law of Grenoble, 24 April 1820."[8] It commented on Baron Cuvier's letter forbidding any law student from expressing a political opinion in public. Ducros vowed to resist such an arbitrary breach of his liberty: "He is requiring twenty-year olds to show silent and base resignation to arbitrary rule, when men in their sixties are seething with indignation at the loss of our liberties; he underestimates the law students of Grenoble so much that he is beginning this hateful and degrading experiment with them." A first edition was printed in Grenoble and confiscated by the police. A second edition was printed outside of Grenoble and also banned. Despite those efforts, however, Ducros's pamphlet reached a national audience, prompting Baron Haussez to write to the *procureur général* that "everyone seemed to have read it."[9]

The Grenoblois students were still not finished. Another student published a pamphlet addressed to the 115 deputies who voted against the liberty law, in which he stated boldly: "We wish to assure you that whatever you may be forced to do to save the country, we will be ready to die with you, if necessary, to defend the pact which the King entrusted to the care of all citizens."[10] A law student from Rennes published a very popular pamphlet that further vilified the prohibitions against them. He condemned the liberty and press laws; praised the Angoulême protests, and offered solidarity with his fellow law students in Grenoble; and he called for solidarity among all law students. Grenoblois law students responded with their own pamphlet praising their counterparts in Rennes for demonstrating against the exceptional laws. They would ignore Cuvier's letter, the students declared: "We are menaced with losing our degrees; they can keep them if we have to buy them at the price of degradation ... We will always prefer tempestuous liberty to quiet servitude."[11]

The drama over Angoulême was repeated the next week in Besançon. The prince arrived 17 May, and students again surrounded him chanting *Vive la charte*. Three students were arrested, and a rumour circulated that the Mayor of Besançon had given Angoulême a list of political suspects. The Duke of Guiche, Angoulême's *aide-de-camp*, was also widely quoted as saying that the Bourbons would never forget that Besançon's prefect, Arnouville, "had once worn the *bonnet rouge*."[12]

The Angoulême visits, the student pamphlets, and the demonstrations against the exceptional laws all fostered rumours of a nationwide rebellion. In Haute-Garonne, St-Chamans reported a rumour to Mounier that the *tricolore* had been hung at Lyon and Dijon. The prefect of Basses-Pyrénées sent a letter to St-Chamans informing him that a traveller had entered his department and told people that Lyon, Grenoble, and Piedmont were in revolt. He requested information about the state of affairs in Haute-Garonne and asked if St-Chamans had heard anything about the revolts.[13]

All this was grist for the conspiracy mill. By the middle of May, the Berry Conspiracy was in full swing. Coussergues had not yet filed his accusation with the Chamber; he would not do so until 12 August. However, other works published and sold to the general public ensured that the conspiracy issue remained popular. The most notable was a report submitted to the Chamber of Peers on 15 May by Count Bastard. Bastard investigated the allegation that Louvel had accomplices. Significantly, despite a lengthy review of all available evidence, including interviews with virtually everyone connected to Louvel, Bastard concluded that no credible evidence existed to support the allegation. However, in his mind, that conclusion did not rule out the proposition that Louvel had not been solely responsible for Berry's death. Bastard brought forward the argument that while Louvel may have held the knife, his hand was directed by liberal writers and journalists. These men, he said, cultivated an *esprit fanatique* by criticizing government actions constantly, using the most inflammatory language, and accusing its agents of tyrannical and selfish actions. This "relentless propaganda" resulted in a dreadful loss of prestige for the Bourbon regime, and "exposed the most noble names and most sacred objects to public derision."[14] Liberal writers and journalists, Bastard charged, were responsible for planting the idea of the crime into Louvel's mind, and for that they were as guilty as Louvel.[15]

The prosecutor filed an indictment against Louvel when Bastard filed his report. He also addressed the conspiracy issue by posing four questions: Did Louvel have accomplices? If he had accomplices, who were they? If there were no accomplices, then what were Louvel's motives? and, finally, what contributed to Louvel's state of mind at the time of the murder?[16] The prosecutor reviewed a number of pieces of evidence to answer the first question. He noted that before the assassination there had been predictions of an attack on a member of the royal family throughout France and Europe. After Berry died, "the concert of fabricated and inflammatory lies that served to sully and outrage Berry's memory" suggested that a conspiracy may have been behind the assassination. He referred to a letter written in 1816, author and address unknown, that mentioned a plot to murder Berry. The prosecutor thought it significant that a glass of rum had been offered to Desbiez the night of the murder, he being the only armed guard near Berry at the time of the assassination. Finally, Louvel was overheard to have said he had heard a cannon just before the attack, a statement that implied that an accomplice signalled the appropriate time to strike.[17] In the end, however, the prosecutor concluded there was no positive proof of a conspiracy, although the evidence did not rule out the possibility.[18] The next two questions were dealt with summarily. In response to the second, the prosecutor reported that not a single suspected accomplice had been uncovered; and to the third, he found simply that Louvel was motivated by an intense hatred of the Bourbon royal family and had targeted Berry because he was the sole hope for a Bourbon heir.

The fourth question is really the same as the first: Why did Louvel kill Berry? The prosecutor noted that Louvel was barely literate: he could not read very well, he could not write or spell, and he did not really understand what he read. What, he asked, gave this man, whose talents designated him to be a lowly worker, such confidence in his own judgment that he felt justified in killing Berry? Echoing Bastard's report, he concluded that society was to blame: "Nature made a man. Society took a man and made him a monster."[19] Louvel may have committed the crime of murder; however, those who opposed the Restoration, be they revolutionaries, Bonapartists, liberals, or otherwise, committed two crimes: they inspired him, and they turned him into a criminal by directing his hate towards the royal family.[20]

THE DEBATE ON THE DOUBLE VOTE

Debate over the double vote in the Chamber of Deputies started formally on 15 May. For the next month, France's political community spoke to, wrote on, and demonstrated about nothing else. Extracts from the deputy debates filled newspaper columns, entire editions often being dedicated to the debate. The deputies' speeches were published separately and sold to the general public; ministerial speeches were also printed and sent to government personnel. Despite this flurry of words, the double vote debate can be boiled down to four main issues: the Charter, the character of the double-voter, loyalty to the Bourbon regime, and fear of a revolution.

Debate over the Charter focused on the constitutionality of the double vote. The character of the double-voter – that is, the type of person the double-voter was likely to be – became a hotly contested issue because the deputies returned by them would hold the balance of power in the Chamber. Since the *cens* was so heavily weighted towards the *foncière* (land tax), there was little doubt that the double-voters and the double-vote deputies would essentially be the *grands propriétaires*. That fact led to debate regarding the moral influence of land ownership, soil mysticism, and the necessity for those exercising the franchise to possess large amounts of land. The loyalty issue was promoted by the ministers. They appealed to the deputies' personal sense of loyalty to France, calling for unity in the face of a potential civil war. Note that this appeal was focused mainly on the king, but not entirely. Loyalty was defined both in terms of the monarchy and the nation-state.

"Fear of a revolution" has been listed at the end for two reasons. First, although no strict chronology determined when each issue was discussed, the first three tended to dominate in May, while the fourth came to the fore in June. Second, the prospect of another revolution overshadowed the entire debate, even as deputies delved into the complexities of constitutional interpretation. Moreover, in the end, it was the belief that France faced serious civil unrest that won the day for the double vote. Sophisticated legal arguments and philosophical arguments about property ownership ultimately took a back seat to the persuasiveness of emotion rooted in France's not-so-distant revolutionary past. Again, we see the pattern that was established in the Grégoire controversy and continued in the liberty and press law debates. The double-vote debate would be about how people felt, not about the wording of the Charter.

The Charter

The ambiguity of the Charter regarding deputy elections has been discussed at some length in Part One. To summarize, the ministerial position was that the Charter provided for age limits, the *cens*, and electoral colleges, but did not specify the exact number of electoral colleges or the *cens* for any specific college. The minimum *cens* was 300 francs, but nothing prohibited a higher one. The opponents of the double vote adopted a substantive approach; in their view, the double vote offended the Charter's guiding spirit, which required that all voters be treated equally. That meant two *cens* limits were unconstitutional.

Three groups took part in discussions on the constitutionality of the double vote: the doctrinaires, the ministerials, and the ultras. Constitutional interpretation was the doctrinaires' stock in trade, so naturally they approached the issue with great enthusiasm. Royer-Collard suggested that the deputies must first determine how the protection of individual rights related to the existence of an independent representative body, in this case, the Chamber of Deputies. In his mind, the double vote destroyed the delicate balance the Charter created among the monarchy, the peerage, and the deputies by reserving too many seats for electoral colleges dominated by royalist supporters.[21] If that balance was disrupted, the Chamber of Deputies would cease to be an independent body able to resist the despotic tendencies of the monarchy and the peers, and France would once again be ruled by an aristocracy. In Royer-Collard's words: "Aristocratic power will increase in proportion as democratic power is weakened, and social harmony, re-established by the Charter, guaranteed by the King and gratefully accepted by the nation, will be broken."[22] In order to protect individual rights and the liberty of all French people, the balance of powers consecrated by the Charter needed to be maintained at all costs, otherwise the government would forfeit its legitimacy: "Legitimate monarchy and liberty are the absolute conditions of our government because they are the absolute needs of France. If you take away liberty from legitimacy you are on the way to barbarism; if you take away legitimacy from liberty you bring back those dreadful struggles which destroyed them both."[23]

Camille Jordan, a doctrinaire with somewhat more radical views than Royer-Collard, provided an alternative construction. To him, individual rights existed apart from any institution, political or otherwise, with the Charter's age and tax requirements granting absolute, positive rights. If a man met the requirements, the right to vote in all electoral colleges could not be denied. In the case at hand, the double vote prevented all electors from voting directly for a deputy, thereby offending the right of equality under the law. Jordan concluded that individual rights were paramount to the interests of the government and the royalists. Since the double vote pandered to those interests, it breached a fundamental principle of French constitutional law. Jordan made that point early in the debate as follows: "The bill you are proposing would completely overturn the principles of the electoral system; the very nature of representative government is deeply affected by it; the wishes of the minority would prevail over those of the majority; it would transform our elections into periodic attacks on rights, honour and national character; royal prerogative is itself bound up with the rights and liberties of citizens."[24]

Supporters of the double vote responded to the doctrinaires' Charter arguments in two ways. The ultras, led by Bonald and Villèle as usual, challenged their view of the Charter and its relationship to legal rights. Villèle and Bonald spoke of a French society based on the monarchy, the Church, and landed property – a society where individual interests were relevant only in relation to society's interests as a whole.[25] Villèle accepted that elected assemblies were sometimes useful in curbing a king's despotic tendencies; however, democratic tendencies were far more dangerous, as the Revolution had proved. In his view, trust was more safely placed in a king's hands than in an elected body such as the National Convention. Royer-Collard's suggestion that three independent and equally powerful institutions could coexist was dismissed out-of-hand as absurd and naïve.[26] Such a system would inevitably disintegrate into chaos.

The ministers also dismissed Royer-Collard's definition of rights, but rather than ignore it completely, as the ultras recommended, they offered an alternative set of definitions – definitions that suggested the double vote did not offend the Charter. Baron Cuvier identified three categories of rights in society: natural, civil, and political. The goal of the social order was to protect natural rights. Civil rights were characterized by the rule of law or equality before the law and were enshrined in the Charter. Finally, political rights were created by the Charter to protect civil rights. Accordingly, political rights, such as the right to vote, could lawfully be denied to the vast majority of Frenchmen because no civil right required that all Frenchmen vote. On the other hand, the civil right to own private property could not be denied, unless some natural or more important civil right required it. The double vote fell into the category of political rights; therefore, as long as the law applied equally to all electors, no right was breached *per se*. Only an elector who qualified for the double vote but was denied the right to vote in a departmental college could argue that his rights were abrogated.[27] The political orientation of the double-voters was beside the point; they could just as easily be liberals.

Pasquier and Siméon provided a more technical Charter argument based on a strict reading of articles 35, 38, and 40. Although article 35 required that electors must vote in some form of electoral college, the number of colleges was not specified, and the organization of the colleges remained to be determined by law. Moreover, the constitutional principle of inequality was established by articles 38 and 40, because the Charter established one set of criteria for electors and another set for candidates; therefore, liberals were in error when they argued that the double vote introduced inequality to the electoral system. In fact, they stated, it had been there since the Charter was proclaimed in 1814. As Siméon noted, "The Charter neither commands nor forbids direct election."[28] Pasquier added that given the small number of voters in relation to France's total population, Royer-Collard's position that the electoral provisions in the Charter were merely exceptions to the general principle of equality upon which the Charter rested was untenable and misguided. In his view, the goal of the Charter's electoral provisions was to establish electoral capacity. The double vote introduced new qualifications for electors; however, all electors who met those qualifications would be treated equally.[29]

The Character of the Double-Voter

The *cens* under the February 5th law limited eligible voters to less than 0.3 percent of the total population; an even smaller percentage could stand as candidates. Since the double vote applied to the wealthiest 25 percent of that tiny minority, the proposed amendment was essentially a debate over whether the extremely wealthy and the extraordinarily wealthy should be treated differently. Put in another way, since the *cens* was in itself a symbol of substantial landed wealth, the double vote would be a symbol of even greater landed wealth. Clearly, the intention of the double vote was to give added weight to the electoral decisions made by the *grands propriétaires*.

All parties to the debate agreed that the franchise had to be limited by age and fortune to ensure that the electorate and the deputies had the necessary experience, education, and leisure time to exercise their political responsibilities effectively.[30] In fact, at no time did liberal deputies demand that the *cens* be lowered or eliminated. Instead, the deputies argued over whether the extraordinarily wealthy, that is, those who qualified for the double vote, had certain character traits or moral qualities that warranted their having such a profound influence over the composition of the Chamber of Deputies. The proponents of the law suggested they did; its detractors suggested instead that, rather than benefiting from that influence, the double vote would simply legislate a legal aristocracy into existence, and society would once again suffer from the corruption that crippled the Old Regime and made the Revolution necessary in the first place.

Ultra deputies extended the idea that political power was best exercised by the wealthy to its logical conclusion, and it is in their argument that we see the philosophical importance of soil mysticism. The ultras argued that if the *cens* provided a guarantee that the right type of men participated in the political process, then surely a higher *cens* provided an even stronger guarantee. More specifically, as the *foncière* was the most important component of the *cens*, then surely a direct relationship existed between land owership and political acumen. If that was not the case, then why was the *cens* for an elector lower than for a candidate? Clearly, candidates' responsibilities were far greater and more important than those of the voters. It followed that the double vote ensured that those heavier responsibilities were borne by the *grands propriétaires*, the men best able to handle them.[31] Even before the debate on the double vote, ultras had stated publicly that the *grands propriétaires*, France's greatest human resource, needed more representation in the Chamber: "The strongest supports of liberty are to be found in those various kinds of superiority of wealth, education, and intelligence, in the spirit of solidarity, in the firm principles that come from having an independent position ... they will not be gained from empty theories about the excessive use of absolute power."[32] That view became more pronounced during the debate. According to Villèle, mere land ownership was not enough. Landed property was timid and inert, and therefore it needed an environment to protect it from being dominated by the new forms of wealth typical of the petty bourgeoisie and small landowners.[33] To protect France against that domination, political power needed to be based upon the *grandes masses d'accumulation* owned only by the *grands propriétaires*.[34] Men whose fortunes lay in industry and securities did not have the resources or the strength of character to resist the corrupting influences of political power. The ultra deputy Puymaurin reduced the question to a simple equation: the bourgeois's love for money versus the *grands propriétaires'* love for the soil. In his mind only men whose fortunes were rooted in French soil possessed the necessary will power to overcome the evil influences of Paris intrigue. Only they were worthy of the honour of serving France in the Chamber of Deputies.[35] Labourdonnay, another ultra deputy, seconded Puymaurin's view, proclaiming that the Bourbon regime's very existence rested solely on the wealthy shoulders of the *grands propriétaires*.[36]

Liberal deputies agreed in principle that land ownership endowed its owner with character traits essential for direct participation in the electoral process, and that the *cens* ensured that the electors stood above the antisocial and selfish passions of the general population.[37] They did not agree, however, that the *grands propriétaires* represented France's greatest human resource. Quite to the contrary. The double vote would do nothing less than turn those men into aristocrats.[38] History proved, Laisné de Villevesque charged, that power in the monarchy aspired to absolute power, and that members of an oligarchy tried unceasingly to gain riches, honours, and influence.[39] Moreover, the double vote was a blatant attempt by former noblemen to regain their lost powers: "They want to ensure that their descendants will always have a pre-eminent place in the State."[40] Benjamin Constant questioned the loyalty of the *grands propriétaires*, noting that they had been all too willing to serve Napoleon with "a zeal, an ardour, and a devotion far greater than the lower class ever showed."[41]

Implicit in the charge that the double vote created a new aristocracy was a threat that its passage would lead to another revolution, the very thing it was supposed to prevent. As Général Foy put it: "If the plots of the aristocracy are flagrant, the resistance will also be terrible ... To put the throne on the back of the aristocracy is to begin a revolution; it is to provoke the people."[42] Constant warned the government to take note of recent history, when the French people had decided that they would no longer accept a tyrannical monarch: "This is a shameful theft, poorly disguised by unworthy subterfuges; no self-respecting citizen would lower himself to receive power or exercise authority at that price."[43] He also warned moderate deputies in even stronger terms of the dangers that faced them if the ultra royalists came to power. It was not liberals, Constant stated, who led the revolutionary forces in 1789, executed the king in 1793, ousted Louis XVIII in 1815, or conspired against the Bourbon regime in 1820. France's real enemies were those who since 1789 had fought against liberty under the guise of the

Counter-Revolution, had provided military assistance to foreigners invading France, and had flocked to serve Napoleon. The double vote, Constant concluded, took power away from France's greatest patriots and gave it to her greatest traitors.[44]

The law's supporters expressed shock at Constant's suggestion that the double vote would create a new aristocracy. They responded that his position was absurd given that the double vote was based on landed property and not birth. Moreover, to qualify one needed only to meet the age limit and pay the required sum in direct taxes. Equality was not an issue because all men who qualified for the departmental colleges would be able to vote, regardless of political affiliation. In the end, a majority of deputies accepted the principle that greater wealth was an indicator of greater political wisdom. They agreed that the best guarantee against the revolutionary threat, a threat that had most recently manifested itself in Berry's assassination, was to entrust the *grands propriétaires* with France's political future.

The Plea for Unity

Minister after minister took the podium and pleaded with the deputies to put aside their differences for the good of France. A vote for the double vote was represented as a vote for the monarchy, for Louis XVIII, and for peace.[45] The ministers drew a direct link between France's current state of political unrest and the February 5th law. According to Serre, the law permitted too many electors and would lead to factionalism and destructive violence. Pasquier added that if the amendment of the electoral law was left up to them, each liberal deputy would propose a separate plan.[46] Decisive action was needed immediately to counteract the revolutionary influence of excessively radical liberal deputies, whose very presence in the Chamber showed the danger inherent in the current electoral system. Siméon urged all deputies to "love the monarchy, the dynasty, the liberty it established, which is in their interests to preserve as the finest claim to glory, the greatest of its benefits, and the surest guarantee of the people's loyalty."[47] Baron Cuvier argued that the factionalism that dominated the Chamber was leading France perilously close to another revolution: "If today, more than at any other time, the public is restless, the government is uneasy, if a few misguided spirits have yielded to fanaticism and inspired more and more atrocious crimes, must not every sensible man see in this sad state of affairs the natural progress of an evil which emerged long ago?"[48] Pasquier reduced the debate to a simple question of loyalty: Louis XVIII's wisdom had led him to grant the Charter to France, and his experience now told him that the electoral law needed amending in order to protect the peace brought by the Restoration. Pasquier noted that while the liberal opposition argued that the amendments contravened the Charter, in fact, the intention of the double vote was to place the throne and the Charter above the reach of factions.[49] He then pleaded with the moderate deputies, both royalist and liberal, to join the forces of peace and order so that Frenchmen could finally enjoy the *repos* they so desperately needed. "This perpetual combat that plays itself out so vividly is not what France needs right now; it will take us too close to the abyss."[50] France's first need was peace, Pasquier held; without peace the rights and freedoms contained in the Charter could very well disappear: "I believe that although liberty may sometimes be born in the midst of storms, it can only be consolidated in quiet times."[51]

The ministers' arguments implicitly raised a contentious question: Why had the Bourbon regime been restored? Louis XVIII had not returned to France because its people hungered for their former king; even the ultra royalists knew that. Louis XVIII provided a practical solution to the political dilemma of replacing the Imperial regime. Yet, it was significant that Louis XVIII's rallying cry was not *Vive le roi*, but *union et oubli*. The Bourbon regime existed again because of the goal that *union et oubli* represented: peace and the end to all hostilities. So, as the ministers equated support for the double vote with support for Louis XVIII in the Chamber, what was most appealing to the deputies was the idea that the double vote represented peace.

Fear of a Revolution and the June Demonstrations

On 30 May, Camille Jordan proposed an amendment to article 1 of the double vote law, which established the two colleges. Jordan's amendment effectively reinstated the February 5th law. In response, Delaunay de l'Orne proposed his own amendment, which reinstated the indirect voting system. Both amendments were dismissed two days later: Jordan's by a vote of 133 to 123 and Delaunay's almost unanimously. In the interim, a violent debate erupted over which amendment would be voted on first. A vote on that question was held, and a deadlock was announced: each amendment had received 127 votes. At the last possible moment, Chauvelin, a liberal deputy and an extremely ill man who had missed most of the debate until then, entered the Chamber. Literally carried to the podium by his fellow liberal deputies, Chauvelin cast the deciding vote for Jordan. He was then carried out of the Chamber to a hero's welcome from the throngs of liberal demonstrators who had gathered outside the *Palais Législatif*.

Jordan's initial victory and the closeness of the vote over his amendment suggest that the Chamber was evenly divided over the double vote; yet, thirteen days later the law passed easily, 154 to 96. The relatively sudden shift in support can only be attributed to a single source: the spectre of the Revolution. From the outset, ministers and ultra royalists warned the deputies that France stood on the precipice of revolution, and that the double vote represented a vital step – in conjunction with the liberty and press laws – in preventing that from happening. Ministers were especially insistent on equating opposition to the double vote with conspiracy and factionalism, which they charged reduced the government's ability to act decisively in dangerous times.

Each deputy at the podium phrased the argument differently. Serre accused the independent deputies of purposely inciting the crowds: "There is a party, a faction, which in opposing all changes to the electoral law, calls on the people to rise up; it seeks to obtain by revolt what it has given up hope of getting by the free will of the legislative power." Pasquier blamed the exceptional-law debates in the Chamber for the current disorder in France. "I am convinced that these dangers can arise only from the storms that are brewing in this very Chamber."[52] Hyperbolic attacks on the government must stop, he continued, along with the use of grandiose words like *despotisme*, *arbitraire*, and *pouvoir absolu*. Despotism was to be feared, Pasquier warned, and France would know despotism again if the double vote was not passed.[53] Siméon in his turn reminded the deputies that less than thirty years had passed since the French had lost their king and their liberty.[54] Ultra deputies seconded this position, but in even stronger terms. Barthe-Labastide went as far as to announce that the demonstrations reminded him of the fateful day of 10 August, when commoners assaulted Louis XVI in the Tuileries.[55] Bonald declared the current electoral law fundamentally incompatible with the principles of law and order. In his mind the Chamber faced a clear choice: the double vote or the Terror.

At first, liberal deputies seemed to relish the prospect of a revolution. Camille Jordan stated that the implementation of the double vote would cause "a profound gulf," that the government would "find difficulties everywhere" and that "a very strong opposition was emerging."[56] General Foy, suggesting that revolutionary feelings would rise up against the new aristocracy created by the double vote, asked the deputies rhetorically, "Our history, is it not simply the story of the war waged by the third estate and the monarchy against the nobility?"[57] If revolution came, the liberals threatened, then responsibility for it rested on the shoulders of those supporting the exceptional laws – legislative measures that symbolized the aristocratic and tyrannical character of the Bourbon regime. Just as predicted, by the end of May crowds flocked daily to the *Palais Législatif* to protest against the double vote.

This seemingly uncanny foresight suggests strongly that liberal deputies organized the demonstrations. Ultra royalists believed the demonstrations signified a liberal conspiracy to intimidate the Chamber, leading Joseph de Villèle to speculate that Lafayette, Manuel, and Constant were behind it all.[58]

While the double vote debate inside the Chamber was coming to a boil, the street demonstrations were starting to seethe. On 2 June, the crowd became so unruly that the police and the National Guard were called in to restore order. The next day article 1 was passed by the slim margin of 130 to 125. That was followed by an even larger and more unruly demonstration at the *Palais Bourbon*. By 6:00 p.m., the crowd had turned violent. The military were called in to disperse the crowd, and in the confusion that ensued, a young student named Nicolas Lallemand was shot and killed by a royal guard. His death, publicized by liberal newspapers, catapulted him to national fame. On 5 June, a letter from Lallemand's father was read to the deputies, in response to suggestions that Lallemand was a revolutionary and that he had attacked a soldier. His father stated categorically that his son had been murdered: "Yesterday, my son was shot dead; today he is libelled by *Le Drapeau Blanc*, the *Quotidienne* and the *Journal des Débats*. I must reject the accusations made against him; he certainly did not try to disarm a soldier; he was walking, unarmed, and he was hit from behind; the investigation will prove that this was so."[59]

Lallemand's death stimulated demonstrations against the double vote all across France. In Paris student radicals tried to rouse the legendary revolutionary *faubourgs* of Saint-Antoine, Saint-Martin, and Saint-Denis, as the crowds outside the *Palais Législatif* and the *Palais Bourbon* grew larger daily. Similar demonstrations occurred in most large cities. In Grenoble, the demonstrations worried government officials so much that a 100-franc reward was offered to anyone providing information about the organizers. In Haute-Garonne, student-led demonstrations were suppressed by a ban on all meetings and assemblies of any kind, and the closure of all cafés by 10:00 p.m.

On 5 June, Louvel's trial began. It lasted only one day. Without any evidence to the contrary, the Peers had to accept Louvel's testimony that he had conceived and carried out the assassination on his own. After a mere two hours of deliberation, the Peers found him guilty of high treason and sentenced him to death; two days later, Louvel mounted the scaffold and was executed. For several months the media had ignored Louvel – he was not a personable individual. Extracts from his trial were published in royalist newspapers, and a few publications about his prosecution were offered for sale. Apart from that, Louvel drifted from the public eye almost as quickly as he entered it. Of course that mattered little; long before his execution, Louvel the individual had ceased to be a significant player in the Royalist Reaction. Once Berry had died, Louvel's historical significance was reduced to his symbolic representation as a revolutionary and a liberal, which continued to be promoted during the double-vote debate. Spurred by Louvel's approaching trial and then by his execution, a number of Louvel portraits with the fanatic face appeared on the market. One such portrait included the following extract from his trial:[60]

Question: What led you to commit such an act?
Louvel: My opinion.
Question: What are these opinions?
Louvel: That the Bourbons are the cruelest tyrants France has ever known.

That portrait, clearly an imaginary image, resembled Robespierre, complete with a handkerchief around his neck, a coat and vest, and curly hair. Perhaps the most famous Louvel portrait, published 12 June, drawn by a young engraver named Henriquel-Dupont, introduced the authoritative fanatic face that endured for years to come. His eyes burned with a stereotypic revolutionary fervour. His appearance made him seem cruel, vicious, and uncaring, more animal than human, the very face of the Revolution.

As the second week of June began, that face was emphasized more and more. Anti double-vote demonstrations reached a climax on 9 June in Paris, as some 20,000 people gathered to protest and mourn Lallemand. During that demonstration, one man was killed and 150 people were arrested. Further violence seemed inevitable as the huge crowd moved towards the Palais Bourbon. But suddenly a tremendous rainstorm broke out, lasting several hours; anger at the double vote and Lallemand's death were seemingly no match for the dampening effects of the storm, and the crowd slowly melted away.

The rain apparently did more than disperse the crowd; it also stopped the demonstrations. After 9 June the threat of insurrection subsided. On 12 June the double vote debate was closed, and the law passed by a comfortable margin. Clearly, the June demonstrations alarmed the deputies, causing the moderate royalists ultimately to support the double vote. The ministers' support was really a vote for law and order, rather than for a new electoral law. The timidity of the liberal deputies in the last few days of the debate is more puzzling, however. It seems that the demonstrations intimidated them even more than the royalists. At the least, we can conclude that neither the liberal deputies nor the liberal movement were prepared to lead a rebellion. For example, in the midst of the unrest, the previously tough-talking Jordan demanded that the government suspend the Chamber until order was restored. In a strange twist of historical perspective, Jordan remarked that the public disturbances reminded him of 18 Fructidor, and that even the Jacobins maintained order more effectively than the present government: "How can we maintain respect for the laws, if the freedom of the Assembly which makes them is so shamefully violated?"[61] Two days before the final vote, Jacques Lafitte, whom the ultras accused of leading the demonstrations, called on the *Conseil* to send in the National Guard to preserve order.[62] As the royalist press noted, these were strange words for revolutionaries.

Protest greeted news of the double vote's passage. A large crowd of men gathered in Toulouse to protest. The army was called to disperse them, but the demonstrators refused to move. As a result, the soldiers had to use force, and some "serious incidents" occurred.[63] No arrests were made and the demonstrators eventually dispersed; yet, Bellegarde, the mayor, and St-Chamans, the prefect, considered the demonstration to be a serious act of sedition. The next day, Bellegarde issued an ordinance denouncing "the dangerous individuals whose sinister intrigues endangered the public order." In the circumstances, it was felt that immediate measures were needed to prevent further demonstrations. The ordinance outlawed all meetings in the Commune of Toulouse. Anyone failing to obey an order to disperse would be arrested and charged with rebelling against the state. Finally, until further notice, all cafés, cabarets, and other public places had to close by 10:00 p.m.[64] St-Chamans issued a separate proclamation to the entire department the same day. The first part of the proclamation was taken from a letter written to him from Mounier.[65] It informed the population that the deputies had just passed the double vote, a law that would "increase the guarantees based on property, and make the law simpler to implement by the new method used to create departmental electoral colleges." St-Chamans praised the inhabitants of Toulouse for distinguishing themselves by refusing to join the malcontents who demonstrated against the double vote, thereby proving their loyalty to the king and the royal family. He advised them to be "on guard against those who seek to spread false alarms, and to lead you into actions that are both contrary to the public good and to your own personal interests." The proclamation ended with the prefect urging the people of Haute-Garonne to trust the government and refrain from acts that threatened to disrupt the peace France so desperately needed.[66]

Two days later, Toulouse law students defied the authorities and met at the university to protest the double vote. A few days after that, Étienne Pinac, a law student and an ex-artillery officer and *chevalier de la légion d'honneur*, led another demonstration against the double vote at the *Pont des Demoiselles* in Toulouse. Pinac, a student leader named Tarateau, and two others were then arrested and expelled from the law school. In a final act of defiance, the law students held a memorial service for Lallemand. Ferrand-Puginier, the rector of the law school, reported to the dean with some irritation that the service was very well attended, in contrast to the attendance at a Berry memorial service previously hosted by the *École de Droit*. Ferrand-Puginier added that the students were motivated by "the spirit of faction, and show a very pronounced tendency to take part in seditious movements, to which several troublemakers [had] already succumbed." The report was subsequently published in the *Journal de Toulouse*.

In Isère, the department's outspoken prefect Baron Haussez chose to publish his own proclamation on the double vote. He suggested that while an exchange of ideas was vital in a constitutional regime, France's newly established political institutions were still fragile and therefore needed zealous protection. As a result, all seditious actions would be dealt with severely. He expressed dismay at the continued acts of defiance and "expressions of hatred" against the government. In the climax to the article, he declared in bold letters: "THE KING WANTS THE CHARTER"; however, the legitimacy of the Charter, the "constitutional regime itself" rested on the monarch, "its noble author."[67] He concluded by imploring the inhabitants of Isère to support Louis XVIII and his government, and help the authorities weed out the subversive elements in society that were conspiring to bring about a second revolution.

In retrospect, the exceptional laws, and the double vote in particular, were a disaster for the Bourbon regime. They came to symbolize the regime's supposed corrupt and reactionary character, and for the liberals at least, justified any efforts to overthrow it. If the exceptional laws were ill-advised in symbolic terms, the government and royalists felt they were imperative politically, and clearly so too did a majority of the deputies. Was this really the case? The historical record suggests otherwise. The political conditions for a civil war simply did not exist prior to the assassination, and the protests that followed occurred only in reaction to the exceptional laws themselves. If the government had continued to focus on marginalizing extremists, starting with those who had called for Decazes's dismissal, rather than using the Berry assassination as an opportunity to gain ground in the Chamber of Deputies, then there is every reason to believe the crisis would have passed peacefully. Ironically, Richelieu's legislative measures ultimately failed in their primary objective of destroying the liberal opposition. They also failed in their secondary objective of unifying French royalists around the throne. As the same time, while hindsight suggests the exceptional laws were a political blunder, royalists saw them as essential and the ultras as a rather tepid response to a revolutionary situation. In the months following the passage of the double vote, an increasing number of royalists, ultra by temperament if not actively involved in the movement, felt that the current moderate royalist regime was not up to the job; and they began to turn to the ultra-royalist leadership for direction. The conditions were thereby set for the ultras' eventual takeover of the government and the subsequent end of the *union et oubli* policy. Royer-Collard was therefore correct when he declared that the exceptional laws "carried revolutions in their bosoms." He simply missed the date by a decade.

7 August–September: Conspiracy and Providence

The double vote heralded a new chapter in the history of modern French politics, as political power transferred almost completely to the royalists for the remainder of the Restoration period. The Royalist Reaction was not over, but its focus had shifted from the conflict between royalists and liberals to the question of what the royalists would do with their newfound political power. Unexpectedly, three events followed the double vote's passage that dealt a death blow to any hopes the liberals had of reversing their recent setbacks. The first was the publication of Coussergues's accusation against Decazes. Six months in the making, the accusation finally set out the Berry Conspiracy for all to read. The second was the discovery by government officials of the 20 August Plot. The third came to pass on 29 September, with Bordeaux's birth. In May, Villain de Sèvres published an illustration titled "The Mother's Vision."[1] The duchess was sleeping on a bed; above her floated St Louis, with two children, her daughter and a boy. This was a depiction of the duchess's famous St Louis dream, in which Bordeaux's birth was foretold. For months, the question of the sex of the child carried by the duchess had been overshadowed by the political convulsions that followed Berry's death. As the due date approached, royalist worries grew exponentially. A girl would spell the end of the Bourbon line. As we know, the St Louis dream proved prophetic. The Duke of Bordeaux's birth ensured that the Bourbon dynasty survived, and represented the apex of the Royalist Reaction, inaugurating a third French Restoration. Paradoxically, French royalists never realized that his birth actually was the beginning of the end.

COUSSERGUES'S ACCUSATION
AND THE 20 AUGUST PLOT

On 12 August 1820, almost six months to the day when he first rose in the Chamber of Deputies to accuse Decazes of complicity in Berry's death, Clausel de Coussergues finally submitted a written accusation to his fellow deputies. The accusation ran to over 150 pages, plus extensive documentary evidence. The first section catalogued ultra royalist grievances against Decazes and his alleged fellow liberal conspirators. Decazes was accused of negligence in his handling of the Didier affair; he had known Didier's intentions and also of his whereabouts, but had done nothing to stop him.[2] Absolving Louis XVIII of any wrongdoing, Coussergues accused Decazes of masterminding the dissolution of the *Chambre introuvable* and manipulating the subsequent elections in 1816 to ensure that ultra-royalist candidates were not re-elected.[3] Equally damning in his mind was Decazes's absence from the debate in the Chamber over Grégoire's eligibility: "[He] did not condescend to defend a cause so close to the honour of the crown … He had made a pact with the enemies of legitimacy, and would do nothing to interfere with the regicides."[4] Although the first section makes for entertaining reading, to all but the most gullible it amounts to little more than a series of vague allegations. The following charge of electoral fraud was typical: "Of having violated the liberty of elections, by writing circulars, by giving orders to prefects, by threatening public officials and policemen with dismissal, and by spreading the darkest rumours against the most respectable citizens, all with the sole object of excluding the King's most faithful servants, the deputies who had been freely elected the previous year for their deep attachment to the legitimate succession and to all the principles which could preserve France from new revolutions."[5]

The second section, far longer, dealt specifically with the assassination. Decazes was accused of failing to carry out his duties, rather than actively planning Berry's death. That failure had provided Louvel with the opportunity to assassinate Berry, and for Coussergues and the more radical ultras who supported him, that was a sufficient connection to justify accusing Decazes of murder. Coussergues asked why the streets were safe for a Bonaparte, but not for a prince of the blood, adding that security measures for members of the royal family had been lax since the passage of the February 5th law.[6] "The reason is clear," he answered. "You did not want the princes to be protected."[7] According to regulations, Coussergues wrote, on the day of the assassination there ought to have been a *commissaire de police*, an *officier de la paix*, and eight *inspecteurs de police* at the Opera, but not a single one was at the crime scene.[8] He added that Decazes had accepted Louvel's declarations that he had acted alone only to cover up his own involvement.[9]

Coussergues did not limit his accusation to specific allegations of wrongdoing; in fact, the most strongly worded parts dealt with Decazes's relationship with revolutionaries. That, Coussergues declared, was the most significant and ultimately the only evidence necessary to prove Decazes's duplicity in Berry's death. He accused Decazes of allowing seditious works to be published and sold throughout France, works that warped the minds of French people and, in the case of Louvel, led them to commit horrible crimes: "He did not cease to encourage over many years, among all classes of society, the most seditious writings, those designed to destroy authority and morality, and to encourage the most violent of actions against the monarchy ... These writings were filled with the most fanatical and revolutionary hatred against anything that obstructed the senseless passion for democracy and the leveling of classes, that is, the things most likely to inflame the imagination and put a dagger into the hands of monsters like Louvel!"[10]

Cousserges characterized Decazes's entire career as a conspiracy to undermine the Bourbon regime. His every action was intended to destroy the royalists, "the defenders of the old dynasty."[11] That characterization illustrated perfectly what a great many royalists and virtually all of the ultras believed about the liberals: they were revolutionaries or Bonapartists, or both. Direct proof of their involvement in Berry's assassination was not considered necessary because of the preponderance of circumstantial evidence. Incendiary attacks against the government and the royalists in liberal newspapers and in the Chamber of Deputies, seditious pamphlets that encouraged revolutionary acts of violence, the dissolution of the *Chambre introuvable*, the February 5th Law, Grégoire's election – and finally, Berry's assassination – all proved beyond a shadow of a doubt that liberals were conspiring actively to overthrow the government and declare a revolutionary republic.

Ultra-royalist pamphleteers rushed to publish their own accusations of Decazes. Their pamphlets all shared the theme that the assassination must be interpreted as further evidence of a permanent, and imminent, liberal conspiracy to overthrow the Bourbon regime. In an anonymous pamphlet, *L'Homme de Gibeaux*, Decazes was accused of having ignored written proof that Berry was the target of an assassin.[12] The mother of a M. Lefebvre D ... a captain of the *gendarmerie* in Metz, had supposedly been paid a three-hour visit, in May, 1816, by a certain Jew who supplied the army with horses and knew the family from Metz. Since the family had been ruined by the two Allied invasions, the Jew believed she hated the Bourbons. He allegedly told her that the Bourbon dynasty would soon fall and, more to the point, that Berry did not have long to live: "This family will not reign long; it is lost; it will be slaughtered, and the Duke of Berry will be the first to be assassinated because he is a soldier, younger than the others, and capable of giving heirs to the line."[13] The Jew showed the mother papers proving the conspiracy, and she recognized Decazes's handwriting. However, the Jew had mistakenly assumed that she was disloyal. She informed her son immediately, and he sent a letter to Decazes. Decazes invited him to Paris the next day to discuss the matter. According to the pamphlet, what followed next provided absolute proof of Decazes's complicity: "Now the most atrocious betrayal that ever appeared in the annals of crime is revealed!"[14] Decazes sent the captain to Orléans, and upon his arrival, the *commissaire de police* put him under house arrest. "What a terrible shock for that zealous servant!"[15] The matter was never investigated further. The Jew, of course, remained free.[16]

The writer of *L'homme de Gibeaux* felt that even more heinous than Decazes's complicity was the fact that the conspirators remained unpunished and continued to spread their revolutionary ideas freely: "In France, and throughout Europe, their writers are stirring up revolutionary agitation to strengthen the hatred of Legitimacy, until finally the great explosion arrives, the culmination of their hopes and their crimes."[17] Every day their influence spread, and drastic action was needed to stop it, "as impious and regicidal liberals multiplied their libels against that noble family; that family which is so worthy of attention for its enduring misfortunes, so worthy of respect for the benefits it has bestowed."[18] Dismissing Decazes was not enough; his followers still remained in their posts.[19] Nothing less than a complete purge of liberals from the administration would suffice: "only their expulsion can stop them, and expose these criminal maneuverings."[20] The writer added that the attacks launched by the liberal deputies against the exceptional laws, laws intended to "close the abyss of revolution," and the allegations of occult governments working in secret to destroy the people's liberty, were both irrational and scandalous, and could only be the work of revolutionaries, "la patrie sous Robespierre."[21]

In August, A-F-H Greenlow de Neuville filed a *plainte* against Decazes with the Chamber of Peers.[22] Greenlow claimed he had seen definitive proof of a liberal secret society named "The Association," whose declared goal was to overthrow the Bourbon regime. Decazes allegedly headed the society, but other high profile members included St-Cyr and General Despinois. Greenlow learned of The Association through his wife. She was having some shoes repaired when the cobbler told her that some officers *en demi-solde* wanted to meet her husband. At the meeting, which occurred in November, 1819, the conspirators expressed their hatred for the royal family. Greenlow was shown orders signed by Decazes, St-Cyr, General Despinois, and others to assassinate Angoulême, who was scheduled to visit Nantes later that month. He also witnessed another letter, signed by Decazes and St-Cyr, outlining a plan to kidnap Artois and Louis XVIII and exchange them for Napoleon and his son. The definitive proof of Decazes's complicity, Greenlow wrote, came when his attempts to warn government officials were rebuffed by Decazes, then minister of police. Decazes allegedly later conducted a secretive campaign to discredit him. The *plainte* ended with a reference to a *societé européenne* dedicated to the extermination of all royalists and the assassination of kings and princes.

In the fall, L Guyon, an ex-artillery officer, published *Histoire complète du procès de Louis-Pierre Louvel* in thirteen parts.[23] Interested readers could enjoy each edition for the low price of one franc, plus 1.25 francs for delivery. There were interested readers aplenty; Guyon's work was sold across France, even though it added little to what had already been written. Its popularity derived not from its content, but rather from the tone of indignation that pervaded virtually every page. Angry royalists were certain to find comfort in Guyon's version of the Berry Conspiracy. Above all, Louvel was dehumanized and demonized, described as "dead to every feeling but hatred," and reduced to a revolutionary stereotype. Guyon wrote that Louvel's sole purpose in life was to kill, which he did cold-bloodedly and with ferocious pleasure. Anecdotes about his behaviour in prison suggested he was more animal than human. He was said to stare straight ahead, rarely looking around, becoming animated only at meal times, caring about nothing but his stomach.

The Berry Conspiracy was also notable for its ability to extend beyond the confines of the assassination to coopt seemingly unrelated matters. For instance, Coussergues's accusation included virtually every incident between 1814 and 1820 that ultras found distasteful. Other pamphleteers also surveyed recent political events to justify their conspiratorial allegations. One of the clearest examples can be found in a national controversy over the Didier Affair that surfaced in September. On 3 May 1819 a *plainte* was filed with the *procureur du roi* against General Donnadieu by family members of those executed.[24] The complainants stated that Donnadieu had exaggerated the seriousness of the rebellion to justify the brutality of his men and the executions. More specifically, they alleged he had lied to Decazes about the size of the rebel force to justify declaring a state of siege, which was a necessary precondition to convening a military tribunal. The complainants reasoned that civil courts, beyond Donnadieu's influence, would never have acted so hastily or judged the rebels so harshly. Donnadieu was motivated, the *plainte* concluded, by a desire to impress his fellow ultra royalists by crushing the rebellion so brutally, despite the fact that it had no chance of success. Compensation was demanded for this act of self-aggrandizement.

The *procureur du roi* refused to hear the *plainte*, so the complainants petitioned the Chamber of Deputies that it be heard. Both the *plainte* and the petition were distributed widely. By the fall of 1820 a blistering polemic had erupted between Donnadieu's lawyer, Antoine Berryer, and Count Ste-Aulaire, Decazes's father-in-law and a deputy, each of whom published a lengthy pamphlet in September. Significantly, the Didier Affair faded very quickly into the background, eclipsed by the issues raised by the Berry Conspiracy. But royalists would forever include it in their catalogue of Decazes's misdemeanours, and interpret it as evidence of the conspiracy that had killed Berry. For their part, liberals considered the affair as yet another cynical attempt to cover up ultra-royalist wrongdoing.

Berryer started the polemic.[25] Donnadieu was blameless, he claimed, because Decazes had agreed to the declaration of martial law, the convening of the military tribunal, and the executions. In his view, the complainants were merely covering for the master conspirator, Elie Decazes, who was directing a libellous campaign against Donnadieu: "Now we must lift the veil of secrecy that still covers the iniquities of a long and disastrous ministry."[26] Berryer charged that over the previous four years, Decazes had assiduously slandered important royalists in order to discredit the Bourbon regime. Next, Berryer spelled out the principal charge in the Berry Conspiracy – that liberal writers and politicians were poisoning the minds and corrupting the morals of otherwise loyal citizens: "It was so important for Monsieur Decazes to persecute and slander the royalists, without being seen to do so, that he turned to the best writers of the liberal opposition."[27] Finally, Berryer raised the spectre of revolution to convince his readers of Decazes's guilt. The accusations against Donnadieu in his mind did little to besmirch his client's character, but on the other hand illustrated clearly the liberals' desperation and corruption. In their slanderous attacks, he saw mirrored the methodology and political beliefs of those regicidal members of the National Convention who twenty-seven years earlier had voted to murder Louis XVI. "Isolated, the throne will fall," Berryer thundered, "and that terrible lesson must never be forgotten in the future."[28]

Ste-Aulaire, one of the few deputies who had been willing to defend Decazes in the Chamber in February, was now the sole liberal voice prepared to challenge Berryer and Donnadieu. He published his own version of the Didier Affair.[29] Most of his pamphlet addressed specific evidentiary issues related to the affair, but the final third discussed the

Berry Conspiracy. Decazes would have needed to be ten people to commit all the crimes alleged by Berryer. It was unfair criticism, not criminal intent, that forced him to resign. "Between 1816 and 1820, Monsieur Decazes has been held responsible for every mistake that has been committed, including those that occurred without his approval or in spite of his opposition; every day that burden grew larger and larger, until he finally succumbed."[30] Ste-Aulaire agreed that Decazes certainly was an influential political figure, who had played an important role in French politics during those years; however, he wrote emphatically that it was patently untrue to say "[Decazes] alone dominated all the affairs of France."[31] Ste-Aulaire went on to describe Decazes as an *homme nouveau*, hated by former aristocrats and *émigrés* who were interested in regaining their old privileges. His son-in-law had in fact attempted to steer France gently away from the past, away from the Old Regime; yet, he had been undermined by ultra radicals who claimed to protect the throne while all the time working to destroy the Charter, weaken the rights of all Frenchmen, and continue the Counter-Revolution. Ste-Aulaire ended the pamphlet with his own warning. Since the end of 1819 the ultras had gained significant political power, a process begun when the February 5th Law was threatened and completed by the passage of the double vote. "If France is not careful," he predicted, "she will once again find herself dominated by a corrupt aristocracy."[32]

The re-emergence of the Didier Affair in the fall of 1820 was accompanied by another former national controversy: Grégoire's election to the Chamber of Deputies in 1819. It started when Choppin d'Arnouville, who had been prefect of Isère during the election,[33] published a pamphlet accusing ultra-royalist voters of casting ballots for Grégoire.[34] They purportedly did so because a Grégoire victory would embarrass the liberals in Isère and him personally. This cynical reaction, Arnouville charged, illustrated with brutal clarity the ultras' willingness to achieve political power at any cost, even if that meant trampling on the Charter. Ultra royalists were outraged, naturally, and vehemently denied the charges.[35] In this case, the historical record offers little clarity. Arnouville's reasoning is somewhat obscure, and it has never been proven beyond doubt that the ultras allowed Grégoire to win – although it seems clear that at least some ultras did vote for him. Moreover, Arnouville had recently been dismissed as prefect of Franche-Comté in July, and so his pamphlet may have been motivated by a desire to attack a government that had rejected him. In any event, as with so much that occurred during the Royalist Reaction, the ultimate effect of Arnouville's pamphlet was to further alienate the royalists and the liberals. The former dismissed the charges as a preposterous attempt to deflect attention from the fact that the February 5th Law was a dangerously flawed piece of legislation requiring immediate amendment. The liberals accepted Arnouville's allegations without question, as further proof of the royalists' fundamental refusal to abide by the Charter.

The credibility of liberal allegations of ultra-royalist wrongdoing – and support for their calls to repeal the exceptional laws – was dealt a critical blow when Claude Mounier announced in *Le Moniteur Universel* on 20 August that a liberal plot to overthrow the government had been uncovered. At first, liberals denied that a plot existed, suggesting it was concocted by the ultras and the police to hurt liberal candidates in the upcoming November deputy elections. However, when conspirators were actually arrested and confessions were obtained, the reality of the August 20 plot became undeniable. Undeterred, however, the liberals quickly changed their tune – albeit not without a healthy dose of rationalization and self-interest. They argued that the plot was justified because the exceptional laws proved conclusively that the Bourbon regime was an utterly corrupt and aristocratic institution. The alleged conspirators were merely trying to save the French people from a tyrannical regime; therefore, the *Conseil* and all the supporters of the exceptional laws bore the ultimate responsibility for the 20 August plot. This position was patently absurd. Throughout the Restoration, liberals were all too willing to turn to violence and conspiracy to further their political aspirations. After the July Revolution, the very men who had defended the 20 August conspirators, men like Guizot and Thiers, used censorship and police powers to suppress political opposition, often with more force than any Restoration government. Nevertheless, liberals were in no humour to question their own motives. The failure of the 20 August Plot merely hardened their conviction that the Bourbon regime must be ousted. The immediate result was the Carbonari movement of 1821–23; in the longer term, it permanently alienated liberals from the Bourbon regime.

In the short term, the 20 August Plot substantiated what ultra royalists had been saying about the liberals for years; more specifically, it legitimized the Berry Conspiracy. With the revelation that prominent liberal figures were involved in a conspiracy against the Bourbon regime, Coussergues's accusation suddenly had a ring of truth. Richelieu and Mounier may have made one mistake in their handling of the plot by being too lenient with the conspirators. Some thirty-five men were arrested; however, the prominent names were conspicuously absent. Victor Cousin's involvement was widely known, as was Bérenger de la Drôme's, both well-known liberals. It appears likely that Lafayette knew about the plot as well. Yet, the only prominent conspirator charged was Joseph Rey, and he was by no means a household name. Rey and two others named Nantil and Lavocat were sentenced to death, although the severity of their sentence was rendered moot as all three were out of the country at the time. Six others received light prison sentences, ranging from two to five years, and twenty-three were found not guilty. Richelieu certainly opted for leniency in order to avoid alienating the liberals. But instead it was the ultra royalists who turned against him and his ministry in subsequent months, in large measure because of this unwillingness to uncover the plot's leadership and his lenient treatment of the perpetrators. The 20 August Plot symbolized the inability of moderate royalists to deradicalize French politics. Ultra royalists and liberals alike felt betrayed by the government's handling of it, and the polemical reactions to it followed the predictable and formulaic responses of royalist and liberal extremism.[36]

THE MIRACLE BIRTH: 29 SEPTEMBER 1820

With the stakes riding high, the duchess's due date was the focus of great attention in royalist circles. Across France, women held weekly masses to pray for a safe delivery. In La-Tour-de-Pin, for example, the wives of the mayor and the *inspecteur de l'enregistrement* were joined by other women in a series of masses to pray for a healthy male child and to ask for the Virgin Mary's blessing on the duchess.[37] In the village of Tullins, the parish celebrated a mass for the unborn child each week beginning 31 July. Collections at the masses were donated to the Berry Subscription.[38] In Muret also, a group of women attended mass daily until Bordeaux was born "to ensure a safe and healthy delivery."[39] In a proclamation announcing Angoulême's visit to Grenoble in May, Royer-Deloche contrasted the sorrow felt at Berry's assassination with the possible joy that would follow the birth of a boy: "Although we cannot express these wishes without sorrow, may we see our dearest hopes realized in this child for whom France awaits! *Vive le Roi! Vivent les Bourbons! Vive la Charte!*"[40] Church leaders took a particular interest in the duchess's pregnancy. Bishop Simon's Berry *mandement* offered a prayer for a safe delivery. In their Berry *mandement* announcing the memorial services, the *vicaires-généraux* of Toulouse wrote: "In the blessed fruit of her womb, we will see the Son who shall revive the glorious qualities of the Prince whom we mourn, the Son destined to transmit the royal and religious virtues of his ancestors to a long line of princes, the pride and the love of France."

A few illustration editors capitalized on the interest generated by the duchess's pregnancy well before the birth. Imagery of hope was added to a picture of Berry being greeted in heaven by famous Bourbon figures from the past and martyred victims of the Revolution. In that illustration, *Espérance* sat gazing into a crib, holding an anchor, the symbol

Figure 23   "Sweet Hope! ... Will You Fulfill our Wishes?" The Duke of Berry's military accoutrements symbolize the need for a male child. Vinck, 10660bis

of hope.[41] In "Sweet Hope ... Will You Fulfill our Wishes?" the duchess was shown kneeling before a women representing *Espérance*. *Espérance* held the duchess's outstretched arm. The two women are before an altar next to the sea, with ships in the background. To the left stands a column with Berry's profile on the side and a statue of Louis XVIII on top. Berry's military accoutrements lie scattered at the foot of the column, complete with a shield bearing his coat of arms, presumably ready for its next owner. A crucifix, clearly symbolizing Berry's martyrdom, hangs behind the women and the empty crib, with an anchor resting against it. The duchess's embrace with *Espérance*, the empty crib, and the anchor symbolized hope for the birth of a male heir. Ships in the background referred to the city of Bordeaux, because Louis XVIII had declared in 1816, after the marriage of Berry and the duchess, that their first son would be named after that port city – it had been the first city to fly the *drapeau blanc* in 1814. The continuity of the Bourbon line was confirmed by Louis XVIII's statue, with Berry's profile suggesting what might have been (fig. 23).[42]

As the due date approached, royalists prepared to celebrate a miracle; while no one was willing to say it publicly, it seemed unthinkable that the duchess would not deliver a boy. In effect, the child was a miracle before it was born. At 2:35 a.m., on 29 September, the miracle occurred. God had truly blessed France, by giving her a new prince to replace his tragically murdered father.

News of Bordeaux's birth spread like wildfire. That morning Siméon sent a letter to every prefect, crediting God with preserving the Bourbon line and calling for "solemn thanksgivings to be offered to Him." Bordeaux was declared a gift as much as a child, and a recompense for the duchess's grief for her lost husband: "Heaven has granted her the greatest compensation she could receive for the loss which she is still mourning." The letter concluded by informing the prefects that the king had ordered that a *Te Deum* be sung for Bordeaux in every church in France.[43] The prefects passed the news on to their subordinates, and large proclamations were hung in village squares. The proclamations and newspaper coverage ensured that the general population found out within two or three days. Mounier then sent a *circulaire* to the prefects providing further details, extracts of which were published in local newspapers. Since the *circulaire* articulated the government's official interpretation of Bordeaux's birth, an interpretation that subsequently became authoritative for the Church and for all royalists, it merits closer attention.

The *circulaire* presented three conclusions: Bordeaux was a miracle, Providence had determined his sex, and the nation was overjoyed. Each conclusion related to a more general and long-term campaign to improve the Bourbons' public image and to imprint that image on the nation's collective consciousness. Bordeaux's birth provided the ideal opportunity to strengthen that campaign.

The *circulaire* began by praising the duchess for her courage throughout her ordeal; it proudly noted her refusal to allow the umbilical cord to be cut until witnesses arrived – which took almost five minutes. That refusal was well publicized because it protected Bordeaux against claims that he had been substituted for a girl. In fact, despite the witnesses' confirmation, allegations of a switch still circulated. The most scandalous was the publication of a *protestation* in the *Morning Chronicle*,[44] an English newspaper. It was an outright fabrication, presumably filed by the Duke of Orléans with the Chamber of Peers. The *protestation* accused the duchess of counterfeiting her entire pregnancy, suggesting that Orléans had been prevented from seeing the birth for that very reason. An illustration called "The Shell Game" showed Louis XVIII sitting at a table holding two lampshades, in the process of dropping one lampshade over a figure of a girl while lifting the other to reveal a boy.[45]

After reviewing the actual birth, the *circulaire* moved on to the symbolic and dynastic significance of the event. It noted that Louis XVIII arrived to anoint the infant's lips with a clove of garlic and some drops of *jurançon*, which had been done after Henri IV was born, "whom the DUKE OF BORDEAUX shall perpetuate in name and in memory." The royal line from St Louis to Louis XVIII would remain unbroken, "to keep the kingdom of the fleur-de-lys at the head of European civilization." At one o'clock, a mass was held, after which Louis XVIII named the infant, and a *Te Deum* was sung. By this time, the *circulaire* noted, joyous crowds had gathered at the Tuileries, and the royal family waved to the throngs from a balcony. Louis XVIII made a "heartwarming speech": "My friends, your joy increases mine a hundred fold; a child is born to us all ... This child will one day become your father: he will love you as I have loved you, as you love all my family." Crowds continued to flock to the Tuileries throughout the day, and the infant was occasionally held up to rapturous applause. The duchess was able to appear on the balcony to wave to the crowd.[46] By mid-afternoon, the *pavillon Marsan* was opened to the public, and some 15,000 people came by to view the baby.

A great deal was said about the hidden forces involved in Bordeaux's birth. The infant's sex and the fact that enormous crowds gathered at the Tuileries to offer their unconditional love and affection all were interpreted as the intervention of a higher power: those occurrences "provide continuing evidence of the visible protection of Providence, and its plans for the family of our kings." Anecdotes from the event added to the providential theme. The *circulaire* recounted the story of a woman, "a good royalist, although a bit superstitious," who thought it was unlucky that the baby was born on a Friday. A priest overheard her remark and replied: "Don't worry, my good woman ... Jesus Christ died on a Friday for the salvation of all, and my lord the Duke of Bordeaux was born on a Friday to save France." The editorial comment at the end of the *circulaire* left no doubt as to the Bourbons' relationship with God and Providence: "He will be just because he is a living witness to eternal justice; he will be merciful because he is himself a work of divine mercy; he will be strong because he is a miraculous sign of God's omnipotence."

Royalists fell in love with the miracle child instantly. Rochefoucauld could barely contain his enthusiasm when he heard about Bordeaux's birth. His rapturous words typify the cataclysmic impact of Bordeaux's birth on France's political community: "Finally, a drop of honey in the glass of absinthe so long held to our lips! A ray of sunshine breaking through the shades of death which enveloped us on the awful night of February 13th, a cry of joy after much wailing ... Resurrection! A child is born to us: the Duke of Bordeaux has been given to France."[47] More than any other single event, the birth of the miracle child legitimized the Restoration. The king and the royal family would never be so popular as during the months following the birth. The miracle child provided the royalists with an unstoppable moral advantage over the liberals that translated into a tremendous political victory in the November deputy election. However, Bordeaux had an even greater effect in the realm of popular politics. Napoleon had forced the Pope to crown him emperor to legitimize his rule. The royalists used the miracle birth for the same purpose, but they went a step further; rather than relying on God's representative on earth, they were able to claim that God, the Pope's supreme master, had ordained that the Bourbons were to rule over France for eternity.

8 October–November: Celebrating the Miracle

Now stares the world at thee, poor infant thing
Whose father sees thee not – My King!
These thoughts of piety profound
As homage to thee here I bring.

Thy mother's lasting sorrow,
The sorrow of all France,
Console, O thou in suffering brought to life.

O'er thee may God his mighty arm extend,
And may this Bourbon crown defend
Its bearer from all harm![1]

With this ode, the eighteen-year-old Victor Hugo paid homage to the miracle child. The ode caught the king's eye, and for his efforts the poet received a thousand-franc pension. Literary merits aside, the ode is significant because it dramatically illustrates how desperately French royalists desired a sense of closure to the Revolution. The euphoria of the First Restoration had been dashed by the Hundred Days, and political divisions seemed as rigid as ever, as Berry's assassination had testified. The birth of the miracle child did far more than secure the continuation of the lineage; it confirmed and validated what royalists considered to be an even more profound miracle: the Restoration itself. Bordeaux was God's recompense both for Berry's murder, and in historical terms, for the revolutionary and imperial eras: "Heaven, moved by our prayers, has made amends for the loss over which we wept so many tears."[2] That psychological need resulted in the word *espérance* being attached to Bordeaux's name, an adjunct to his persona as a miracle.

Grenoble's *vicaire-général*, Testou, published a *mandement* ordering the *curés* in his diocese to say a mass and sing a *Te Deum* in Bordeaux's honour. Bishop Simon issued his own *mandement*.[3] Testou wrote that Bordeaux's birth was a divine act of Providence, proof that prayers were indeed answered by God, and "a token of peace and happiness." Simon interpreted the miracle birth as proof of God's love for the French people, which had manifested itself in an alliance between Providence and the Bourbons: "Can we still be of two minds after the marvels of the King's return and restoration, after the birth of this young prince, which has astonished the most skeptical among us? Surely it is evident that he is the miraculous child, the token of peace, the sign of the covenant which God formerly gave to his people, and which is shining, before our eyes, like a rainbow in the sky."[4]

The visual media expressed those sentiments in even more dramatic fashion. In "The Prediction of the Prophet Isaiah," Isaiah, holding a wand in one hand and a scroll in the other, is standing before a seated woman, the personification of France.[5] Printed around the picture was the prophet Isaiah's prediction that foretold of a child that would be born with "the spirit of the Lord within him, the spirit of wisdom and intelligence ... the spirit of counsel and might ... of knowledge and piety."[6] That child, "a symbol for all Frenchmen,"[7] would unify people from the four corners of the world. Bordeaux fit the description of the child perfectly; a Bourbon born with God's blessing, he was destined to bring the French people back into the loving fold of the monarchy. In another illustration, published in October, a profile of a crowned Bordeaux floated in the clouds. Below was an anchor, the symbol of *espérance*, and a *bouquet d'immortelles*, the everlasting flower, the symbol of Bourbon rule over France.[8] Finally, a miracle-child illustration, published 26 December 1820, was titled *L'espoir Réalisé*,[9] a succinct declaration that Bordeaux had satisfied the collective hopes and dreams of French royalists since 1789.

THE BORDEAUX BIRTH *FÊTES*

The government decided that Bordeaux's birth called for a national *fête*; however, it determined that his baptism, planned for the spring of the following year, was the most appropriate occasion, rather than some arbitrary day after his birth or on his first birthday. The choice also offered the additional advantage of giving organizers time to put together a spectacular show. Unfortunately, by the time the baptism was held on 1 May 1821, much of the excitement that attended the news of his birth had subsided, and as a result the official Bordeaux *fête* failed to live up to expectations. However, that later waning of enthusiasm should not be taken as evidence of the general population's indifference to the miracle child. Bordeaux was an absolute sensation, and people across France took to the streets to express their happiness and good wishes for the Bourbon royal family, for Louis XVIII, and for the Restoration.

The central government sent word to local and Church officials to wait until the day of Bordeaux's baptism to officially celebrate his birth. They were to organize modest celebrations, limited mostly to the singing of a *Te Deum* in Bordeaux's honour. But most officials would have none of that. The celebrations that followed the birth are one instance where the central government failed to control national *fêtes*. Spontaneous celebrations erupted across France. Local officials also sponsored formal *fêtes*, directly contrary to *Conseil* orders. In virtually every village, town, and city, church bells rang on a given Sunday announcing the start of the *fête*. People then made their way to church for a mass of thanksgiving in Bordeaux's honour and a *Te Deum*. All the while the attendees chanted *vive le roi, vivent les Bourbons, vive la Duchesse de Berry,* and *vive le Duc de Bordeaux*. Church officials distributed the collection from the mass, along with bread and wine, to less fortunate members of the community. At night, homes were lit up, and local dignitaries gathered for dinner and dancing. A report from the mayor of Boulogne-sur-Gesse to St-Chamans typifies the spirit of the *fêtes*. Despite the poor crops that year, he wrote to the prefect, news of Bordeaux's birth "has dried our tears of grief and misery with the loudest shouts of joy and the merriest of songs." On 14 October, a *fête* to celebrate Bordeaux, was held, complete with parade, *Te Deum*, distribution of bread to the poor, and banquets at night.[10] In Beaurepaire, the mayor was so excited that he published two proclamations. The first announced the birth: "Our agricultural pursuits prevent us from celebrating immediately," he noted, "but a large *fête* will be held the following Sunday." The second proclamation set out the program for the *fête*. After mass and the *Te Deum*, the church bells rang twenty-four times. At the ensuing banquet, the mayor and the adjutant toasted Bordeaux, Louis XVIII, and the royal family. Later in the evening a candlelight dance – with orchestra – was held. "If the attack of 13 February plunged France into mourning," he enthused, "then the birth of a prince of the royal family, the Duke of Bordeaux, fills us with joy."[11]

Cities prepared even more extensive celebrations. In Toulouse, the mayor ordered a general illumination of the city, a free show at the *Place Royale*, to be followed by fireworks, the decoration of houses with the *drapeau blanc*, and a suspension of public works.[12] After one celebratory church ceremony, lieutenant-general Comte de Partouneaux, the commander of the 10ᵗʰ military division, made a speech. He began by referring to the cruel loss France had suffered with Berry's murder and then declared that the days of mourning and tears had finally been succeeded by joy and glory: "The auguste widow of the Duke of Berry, who had been the object of our eternal regrets, now has given France a new Henri ... this precious child." The "Descendant of kings" was born at a propitious time, he added. "While European monarchies are threatened from all sides, France's monarchy remains strong." He called on his fellow soldiers to rally around the throne, pledging to battle what he called "treasonous projects and criminal attacks."

Partouneaux's speech also alluded to a darker companion to *espérance*: the desire for revenge against the revolutionaries who had murdered Berry and were plotting to overthrow the regime. These two themes acted as bookends framing royalist sentiment on Berry and Bordeaux. In that light, the miracle birth aroused both a positive and negative reaction; positive in that it brought great hope for the future, and negative in that it incited intolerance, division, and hatred. Some Church officials were even more explicit than Partouneaux. The *vicaires-généraux* of Toulouse issued a *mandement* in Bordeaux's honour soon after the birth,[13] and a few days later, the newly appointed Archbishop of Toulouse, Clermont-Tonnerre, issued a *lettre-pastorale* to the *curés* under his authority, both of which included a number of references to Bordeaux.[14] The *mandement* and *lettre-pastorale* reveal how the themes of *espérance* and *revanche* became intertwined.

First, the *espérance* theme was sounded. Bordeaux was repeatedly referred to as "the heir to the throne of Saint Louis and the illustrious son of Saint Louis's line." He was "the providential son of Saint Louis ... whose noble dynasty would perpetuate the throne of Clovis." His birth answered the prayers of "the friends of religion, of legitimacy, and of the nation." The *vicaires-généraux* asked how anyone could doubt the authenticity of the miracle, for was it not "the most striking sign of the protection which Heaven deigns to accord us?" The archbishop called Bordeaux "that miraculous child whom divine Providence has granted us in accordance with our desires." He implored his *curés* to remember "the designs that Providence manifested to us by the birth of his Royal Highness the Duke of Bordeaux, for that happy event unites the people of France around the throne of Saint Louis, and reveals to us the help we may expect from Heaven."

How then could Bordeaux avenge his father's murder? According to the *vicaires-généraux*, the birth gave evidence of the efficacy of prayer, and further prayers would doubtless be answered. And what should one pray for? In short, to overthrow and destroy "the criminal hopes of the monarchy's enemies, and shelter us from the political storms that were menacing us." In his *lettre-pastorale*, the archbishop declared that Bordeaux's birth was a clear sign of God's will, of his "precious plans" for the "providential order." It was this providential order that ordained members of the clergy to fight against "the wretched agents" who spread "the most absurd rumours" in their effort to "plunge France once more into the abyss of revolution." In his view, the miracle birth represented a call for the clergy to "suppress the serpents of revolution, to give us back that public peace and happiness that has so long been disturbed by evil plots. Providence itself has exposed the authors of these plots, revealed the conspiracies, foiled their evil projects, and prevented all of their hateful attacks against the noble Bourbon dynasty." The time for revolution has ended, the Archbishop pronounced: "It is more than time to end the malevolence of these eternal plotters."

THE CHAMBORD SUBSCRIPTION

As contributions for the Berry Subscription continued to pour in, royalists were called upon to contribute to yet another national subscription. This time it was to purchase the Château de Chambord for Bordeaux,[15] a gift from the nation to commemorate the miracle birth. Like the Berry Subscription, it was also an astonishing success; by 1823, when it was closed, 1,412,687 francs had been contributed.[16] Even more astonishing was the symbolic significance that royalists attached to the Chambord Subscription and its success. The Marquis d'Herbouville, a member of the Chamber of Peers and president of the Chambord Subscription committee, stated in a pamphlet publicizing the campaign that this was not a mere collection to buy a *château*, but the embodiment of the struggle between royalism and goodness on the one hand, and evil and revolution on the other. The gift would prove to the world how the French nation felt about its future king, "the hope of the nation, the child of Bourbon blood, who will love the *château* of his ancestors, where everything evokes memories of power, valour, and goodness." To those who argued that the royal family already had too many royal houses, he responded that the king was the source of all goodness in society and the sole guarantor of future prosperity; as such, his presence could not be too widespread, nor his houses too numerous.[17] There are people, Herbouville noted, who want to turn Versailles into a hospital and Fontainebleau into a school. Those people want to weaken the monarchy: they are revolutionaries. On 23 February 1823, upon making the final payment on Chambord, Herbouville declared that the revolutionary forces had finally suffered the mortal blow: "This fine abode, this refuge of honour, this imposing witness to the magnificence of the Valois and the grandeur of the Bourbons, was about to fall under the revolutionaries' hammer; the subscription has preserved it."[18]

As with the Berry Subscription, most subscribers donated in the first six to eight months.[19] They did so, though, in much greater numbers. In Haute-Garonne, 25,000 francs were donated in total, in contrast to 8,000 for the Berry Subscription. The higher figure did not result from a higher average contribution but rather from a larger subscriber base. In most parts of France, the Chambord Subscription attracted two to three times more individual subscribers than did the Berry Subscription.

Occupational distributions also differed. The Chambord Subscription attracted a much higher percentage of low-income or low-status subscribers. Occupations such as butcher, labourer, innkeeper, or baker appeared far more frequently on Chambord Subscription lists. Clearly, Bordeaux appealed to a much wider spectrum of the population than his father, as even butchers were sufficiently moved by the miracle child to donate fifty *centîmes* so that Bordeaux could live in a *château*.

The pressure to do the right thing, that is, contribute something to get on a list, is of course a complicating factor, as it was with the Berry Subscription. Newspapers published the names of subscribers, both individuals and groups, along with the amount they contributed. Presumably, a subscriber's largesse illustrated the depth of his or her royalism. In addition, since subscriptions were a well-established tradition in France, a Bordeaux subscription of some type had been expected. Those caveats notwithstanding, the Chambord Subscription evidences a phenomenon that amounted to nothing less than a Third Restoration. The number of individual subscribers and the occupational distributions noted above testify to a powerful groundswell of popular support for the Bourbon regime that climaxed in the months after Bordeaux's birth. Chambord symbolized the Bourbons' return; in the splendour of their housing their former and legitimate position at the head of French society was affirmed.

Chambord's enduring symbolic significance was most clearly expressed by the visual media. In an 1822 illustration, "France Presents Chambord to the Duke of Bordeaux," a personification of France is shown giving the keys of Chambord to Bordeaux, while three cherubs display renovation plans (fig. 24).[20] In October, 1832, another Chambord illustration was re-released.[21] It was a reprint of a cover page to an illustrated series on Chambord originally published in 1821. An angelic Bordeaux is sitting on a throne, surrounded by angels, one of whom presents the renovation plans for Chambord. The picture is

Figure 24   "France presents the keys of the Château de Chambord to the young Duke of Bordeaux." Vinck, 10720, 10 June 1822

somewhat pathetic, given that by then an Orléans sat on the throne – not to mention that Bordeaux was twelve years old at the time. Nevertheless, it shows how strongly Chambord touched royalist hearts in France. Chambord remained dear to Bordeaux throughout his life, and he would refer to himself as the Count of Chambord until his death in 1883.

THE DUCHESS AND THE MIRACLE CHILD: THE GOOD MOTHER

The Duchess's Good Wife persona was characterized principally by dynastic tragedy. Her Good Mother persona had a corresponding and complementary theme as well: *espérance*. The theme of hope flowed from the circumstances of the birth itself which had led royalists to interpret Bordeaux as a providential symbol of God's desire that a Bourbon sit on the French throne. Significantly, the official interpretation of the miracle birth did not depict the duchess as a Good Mother in the biological sense, but rather as the maternal medium through which the power of Providence acted to perpetuate the Bourbon dynasty. In other words, the manner in which her status as Bordeaux's mother was depicted to the nation at large was determined principally by the government's official interpretation of the miracle birth.

From the dynastic perspective, it is interesting to ask why the Duchess's public persona took on such a domestic aspect as the Good Mother persona in the first place. In essence, the historical process that saw women excluded from participating in French public life, more specifically, in the political system, influenced the duchess's Good Wife and Good Mother personas, coloured as they were also by the dynastic and political elements already noted. Those two personas offered the government two advantages: they contributed to the overall national campaign to enhance the popularity of the Bourbon regime during the Royalist Reaction; and second, they corresponded to current sexual stereotypes and generally accepted gender roles, thereby harmonizing the duchess's public persona with attitudes of the general population.

We will start with the duchess's Good Mother persona in relation to the official interpretation of the miracle child. The linking of this persona and the *espérance* theme emerged well before the actual birth. Women held weekly prayer meetings for a safe and masculine delivery, and editors published *espérance* illustrations alluding to the potential miracle growing in the duchess's womb.[22] The *ésperance* theme also emerged in relation to a dream the duchess allegedly had before Bordeaux's birth. She reported that she had been visited by the ghost of St Louis as she slept, and that St Louis had told her she was carrying a boy.[23] Mounier made reference to the dream in his *circulaire*, stating that the duchess had actually felt the spirit of St Louis inside her throughout her pregnancy. This dream perhaps illustrates that the duchess played more than a passive role in the development of her public persona. In any event, it supports the miraculous and providential characterization of the birth, and reinforces the family metaphor that promoted the Bourbon royal family as the divinely appointed rulers of France. On 29 September *espérance* became a reality. Interestingly, the duchess would receive much of the credit for delivering a boy, as if she had played an active role in determining the child's sex. Again, that attitude suggests that her Good Mother persona was related to her participation in the miracle birth, and not to her maternal skills. Mounier's *circulaire* reflected this perspective. As noted, it spoke of the providential nature of the birth, the magnificence of the Bourbon dynasty, and the absolute joy Parisians expressed upon hearing news of the birth.[24] Any reference to the duchess in the *circulaire* should be viewed from this definitively dynastic interpretation of the miracle birth. Mounier's mention of the duchess's premonition of a male because she had felt the spirit of St Louis inside her suggests that Bourbon historical figures from the past had assisted Providence in determining the child's sex. Capitalizing on popular enthusiasm, Mounier reported that the duchess was hailed by an enraptured crowd when she appeared on the balcony of the Tuileries; and at the Place de la Fontaine des Innocents, soldiers, vendors, and market women chanted "*Vive la duchesse de Berry*," to accompany "*Vive le roi!*" "*Vive le duc de Bordeaux!*" and "*Vivent les Bourbons*!"

In the months following the birth, Church officials also made sure to refer to the duchess in any *mandements* regarding Bordeaux. The Archbishop of Toulouse, Clermont-Tonnerre, urged his *curés* to "Pray ardently with us for the noble monarch whose goodness will create a legacy for the Bourbon dynasty that can never be lost; pray for these virtuous princes, for these heroic princesses, who have given us such fine examples, for this young child who is born to all of us."[25] This reference was typical. The duchess was invariably linked to the family metaphor and the dynastic implications of the birth. In October, a bronze pendant was presented to the duchess, and newspapers published the inscription written on it: It summarized concisely the official interpretation of the birth: "All the wishes have been fulfilled, all the hopes based on love and religion are justified, the real or pretended alarms, the menacing clouds that obscured our horizon have lifted, we live in brighter, gentler days. France rejoices and is reassured to see that Providence is protecting the line of its kings. Hell had spoken through the mouthpiece of Louvel: I will strike down the last of the Bourbons, and I will put an end to the blood of Saint Louis and Henry IV."[26]

The illustration called "The Marvellous Dream,"[27] mentioned above in regard to the duchess's Good Wife persona, also provides a pictorial example of this dimension of her Good Mother persona. This was the illustration in which the duchess symbolized France, Bordeaux lies in a crib, and Berry is in the clouds, accompanied by four angels. The cheering crowd in the background is the key feature in regard to the Good Mother persona. The crowd symbolizes the entire nation, the millions of French citizens, filled with love for their new son, who have enthusiastically accepted him as their future king. The duchess may dominate the illustration in terms of size, but the most powerful impact belongs to Bordeaux and the miracle of his birth.

In 1830 an illustration entitled "You Live Again in Him" showed the duchess standing beside a pillar with sword and shield resting against its base and a bust of Berry on the top. Clouds above them have parted and a beam of light shines down upon a crib, where the infant Bordeaux lies – this despite the fact that he was ten years old at the time. The duchess, in mourning attire, motions toward the baby, as if to direct his gaze to the Berry bust. Again, we see the classic representation of the *espérance* theme and the dynastic component of the Good Mother persona, a decade after it first appeared (fig. 25).[28]

Figure 25   "You live again in him." By 1830 the Duke of
Bordeaux was ten years old, but the duchess's "good mother"
persona was still popular. Vinck, 10713, 17 December 1830

Even in less symbolic illustrations, in which the duchess was given a
more traditional motherly character, the *espérance* theme dominated.
Over the course of the decade, a number of birth scenes were published.[29] In virtually all of them, the duchess was shown in bed, in a
white bed dress and bonnet, while Bordeaux was presented to, or held
by, Louis XVIII under the gaze of a crowd of onlookers. The duchess
was invariably off to the side, and the focus of the illustration was the
king paying homage to the miracle child for the first time. The presence
of Louis XVIII, and the fact that he dominates the illustrations, is reminiscent of the images of the Berry death scene and is therefore highly
suggestive of the dynastic theme. Louis XVIII also dominates virtually
every death scene, despite the fact he arrived at the Opera House barely
an hour before Berry died.

The most dramatic presentation of a birth scene was painted by
Fragonard and shown in the 1824 Salon; it was later reproduced as an
illustration and hung in the 1827 Salon. A large crowd, including a few

Figure 26   "The birth of His Royal Highness the Duke of Bordeaux." The duchess's persona as the "good mother" does not entitle her to centre stage. Fragonard. Vinck, 10671, 26 April 1827

saluting and genuflecting soldiers, surrounds Louis XVIII, who is holding Bordeaux and raising a glass of *jurançon* to the child's lips. Everyone is looking down at the royal pair, seemingly breathless with anticipation. The duchess is in bed, in white gown and bonnet, Artois's hand on hers. The significance of her presence, however, is indicated by her position in the scene; she is off to the side, and along with the others, stares intently at the king and Bordeaux. In addition, note the distance between the duchess and her child, a distance further emphasized by the fact that everyone's gaze is on the royal pair. Clearly, the picture is about a royal event; the duchess's presence is both necessary and natural because she gave birth to the miracle child, but her maternal role does not entitle her to centre stage. A personal element is perhaps evident in the fact that Artois has his hand on hers. At the same time, that interpretation is ambiguous, considering that Artois is standing between the king and the duchess; in that sense, he is acting as a barrier between mother and child. By including the duchess, Artois, Louis XVIII, and Bordeaux all together, the artist may simply have intended to present the most important royal figures in France as a group (fig. 26).[30]

In what was perhaps the quintessential Good Mother illustration, published in 1821, the duchess, dressed in black, is shown embracing her children as she kneels next to an elaborate crib.[31] A bust of Berry

Figure 27   "My only hope this cradle holds, Thy joy and glory, France, may it enfold..." Dynastic symbolism overpowers the familial scene. Vinck, 10693, 11 January 1821

dominates the background and overshadows the little bust of Bordeaux (fig. 27). An engraved tablet on the crib expressed her hopes for Bordeaux and her love for Berry:

> My only hope this cradle holds,
> Thy joy and glory, France, may it enfold;
> My children's hearts will always grateful be,
> That the nation keeps loving watch with me.

Similar to the way in which images of the duchess mourning Berry had a fundamentally dynastic basis that overshadowed the personal dimension of the duchess's grief, here too the image of a mother embracing her children is superseded by the presence of dynastic symbolism. The key to the illustration is the *espérance* theme, not the fact that the duch-

Figure 28   The future king of France and his sister: children of the nation. This lithograph was hung in the Salon of 1824. Vinck, 10692

ess gave birth to Bordeaux.[32] That point is made clear in a lithograph of the duchess's two children in which her daughter stands beside Bordeaux, who is lying in a cradle. The same message is conveyed, but this time without the duchess: here is the future king of France and his sister, it says, and these two children belong to all French people (fig. 28).[33] Even more explicit was an illustration called "The New Jeanne d'Albret."[34] The duchess, in black, sits next to a crib where her son lies sleeping, a guard dog close by. Her daughter sits on her lap, as they gaze together at a bust of Berry. It too is accompanied by a verse that begins: "Protected by the faithful." Since Jeanne d'Albret was Henri IV's mother, the implication is clear that the duchess has given birth to the next Henri IV – worthy praise indeed. The dog and the verse add to this obviously dynastic image. The comparison between the duchess and Henri IV's mother appeared again at Bordeaux's baptism. A sign placed before a statue of Henri IV exhorted: "Frenchmen, love my grandchild as I loved your fathers, Jeanne d'Albret, 1533, Caroline, 1820." In another related example, a play called *Jeanne d'Albret* or *The Crib* was performed at the Théâtre Français.

Not all illustrations overrode the maternal theme with the dynastic theme quite so explicitly. One illustration that emphasized the duchess's personal grief and her maternal relationship to Bordeaux depicted an imaginary scene of the Duchess kneeling before a Berry bust, gazing at it reverentially, clutching the miracle child to her breast, as her daughter stands next to her, in tears. The text below the picture reads: "O Charles! Is it true that I must embrace these children without you?" Such scenes, however, were extremely rare. It bears repeating, though, that the personal or maternal elements of the duchess's public persona were not entirely set aside by the official interpretations of the assassination or the miracle birth, but were relegated to a lower status by the dynastic implications of Berry's death and Bordeaux's birth (fig. 29).[35]

The duchess's persona was also affected by an additional factor: gender. The topic of French women and their relationship to France's political system has spawned a growing historiography in recent years.[36] These works have collectively articulated an interesting paradigm that has relevance to the duchess: in essence, French women were systematically excluded from participating in public or political life during the Revolution, and from then on were prevented from exercising any significant political power. Women were expected to focus on domestic duties, in the "private sphere," circumstances deemed more suitable to their inherent character. Married women were to devote themselves to their husbands, children, and extended families; young and unmarried women were to prepare themselves for marriage and childbearing: and spinsters were encouraged to turn to religious and social works. This model continued until the second half of the nineteenth century, when women such as Flora Tristan and Julie-Victoire Daubié began agitating for better treatment.

The paradigm of the public sphere begs the question: were the duchess's Good Wife and Good Mother personas determined to any extent by gender? Quite obviously, domesticity itself is defined by those two roles; what, then, is the potential connection between the redefinition of the duchess's public persona and the historical process that saw women forced to accept the private sphere as their primary domain. It will be argued that the duchess's public persona potentially could have overcome the limits set upon it by the paradigm, that is, it could have adopted an explicitly political dimension similar to Berry's, Bordeaux's, and Louvel's; however, gender issues prevailed. The official interpretations of the assassination and the miracle birth determined the content of her Good Wife and Good Mother personas; the paradigm of the public sphere ensured that those personas dominated. The possible directions her public persona could take were thereby prescribed by the male political monopoly.

Figure 29   "Is it true that I must embrace these children without you?" In a rare portrayal of parental intimacy, the duchess is cast in the domestic role. Vinck, 10711, 28 March 1821

Historians generally go back to the Romantic period in the late eighteenth century in seeking the intellectual foundations of the historical process that culminated in the formal exclusion of women from the public sphere, although some have gone back as far as Ancient Egypt.[37] Setting aside this chronological debate and accepting the French Revolution as the most influential period, the thesis holds that as part of the *philosophes'* overall campaign to reform the Bourbon monarchy and the Catholic Church, some enlightened writers criticized what they considered the excessive influence of women at the royal court. The power exercised by such women of the court as Madame de Pompadour and the Comtesse du Barry made women a convenient symbol of aristocratic corruption. The central theme in these attacks was sexual worldliness. These politically minded women were depicted as sexual predators, whose almost magical powers to seduce men were said to have contributed to the state of moral degradation that the *philosophes* believed defined the Old Regime. The identification of sexual prowess as the key means by which women obtained power at the royal court reached its zenith in the 1780s with pornographic images of Marie-Antoinette. The queen was shown engaged in shocking sexual scenes, including lesbian relationships and threesomes. The most damaging to her reputation were pictures of her in bed with an impotent Louis XVI, suggesting the Queen had stolen the king's virility in order to satisfy her own lust for power. Combined with the infamous Diamond Necklace Affair[38] and her reputation for excessive spending, which earned her the nickname Madame Déficit, the pornographic images turned Marie Antoinette into the quintessential evil woman. In Louise de Keralio's 1791 publication, *Les crimes des reines de France*, she was described as "a political tarantula, that impure insect, which, in the darkness, weaves on the right and left fine threads where gnats without experience are caught and of whom she makes her prey."

As politically connected women were gaining notoriety, a parallel development occurred that conjured up a more sympathetic image. Instead of striving for political power and public life, women were encouraged to find fulfillment in domestic duties. Rousseau's works were foremost here. He wrote that women were constituted by nature for that express purpose; therefore, women would be happier if they contented themselves with the private sphere. It followed that society at large would also be healthier if women remained in the private sphere for which they were more suited by nature. In *Émile,* Rousseau described in detail the natural relations between husband and wife, man and woman. He spent four chapters on Émile's education, outlining how men should cultivate their questioning minds, and then allowed Émile to roam the country to spread his seed. In contrast, little is said about the education of Sophie, Émile's perfect wife. Her role is to please Émile and raise his children – at home, the only place for a virtuous woman. Tremendous value was placed on chastity to ensure the legitimacy of Émile's offspring. The glorification of female domesticity also directly counterbalances the image of the female sexual deviant, who had ostensibly acquired her deviance from her unnatural participation in public life.

The French Revolution held the promise of a golden age of political opportunity for women. The principle of *égalité* theoretically meant that women and men would participate equally in the running of the *patrie*. For the first few years, it appeared that this principle would indeed result in women joining France's political community. The October Days and the march on Versailles by Parisian women in 1789, the prominence in the revolutionary movement of such women as Mme Rolland, Olympe de Gouges, Théroigne de Méricourt, and Etta Palm d'Elders, and the establishment of the *Club des citoyennes républicaines révolutionnaires* in May 1793 all presaged this change in political culture. It seems, however, that the men who dominated revolutionary politics at the same time, particularly the Jacobins, believed as strongly as the *philosophes* in the notion of female sexual deviance and the glorification of domestic duties. The Jacobins were the first to act on these notions: women were banned from attending political clubs, a number of female revolutionaries were guillotined, and political protests led by women were crushed without remorse. An example was the Journée of 1 Prairial (20 May 1795), on which members of the National Guard publicly whipped and beat a number of women who tried to occupy the National Convention. This crackdown was rooted in gender, not politics. They were forbidden to enter the public sphere because their sexuality was said to distract men from important civic obligations, and because they would have to neglect their husbands and children to participate fully in political life. The beating of Théroigne de Méricourt on 15 May 1793 at the hands of some unruly Parisian market women was a tangible illustration of how French society, even women, treated those who dared transgress the paradigm.

The Code Napoléon drove the final nail into the proverbial coffin some years later. With few civil rights and absolutely no legal right to participate in public life, women had little choice but to accept their banishment to the private sphere. The Restoration has not received nearly the same attention from historians interested in this subject as the Revolutionary years, but there is little to suggest that the paradigm is not applicable. The strict prohibition against women's participation in the political system was maintained. Women were not allowed to vote in deputy elections, nor were they appointed as prefects, sub-prefects, mayors, or members of municipal councils. Even single or widowed women who met the *cens* because of inherited property or through their own endeavours were not allowed to cast a ballot in deputy elections. They were entitled to designate a male representative for that vote; however, that representative had complete freedom to vote as he wished.

As with any overarching thesis, some historians of late have nuanced the paradigm: they have extended the definition of public sphere, identifying a wide variety of ways that women influenced and participated in France's political milieu, even though the law prevented them from holding office or voting. Public protests were an important means for women to express their political views to the authorities. Historian Suzanne Desan has examined the Catholic lay religious revival in the late 1790s, in particular the right to worship in public. She discovered that women gained spiritual and political power at the local level by leading religious riots and female worship services. The battle with the government over the right to worship provided an arena for the collective activism of all women, and also a public voice for that activism.[39] Women continued to participate and lead public demonstrations during the Restoration and the July Monarchy, although their struggle was usually related to food prices rather than religious issues.[40] The social historian, Michelle Perrot noted perceptively that women were as mobile as men during the nineteenth century, usually looking for work as domestics. As a result, the constraints that applied to middle and upper class women did not pertain as much to the popular classes, where men and women mixed more freely. Also, the mobility of such women disrupted cohabitation and therefore granted women a degree of freedom difficult for wealthier women to match.

Since politics remained an elitist preoccupation for much of the first half of the nineteenth century, at least in terms of the formal expression of political power, it was in elite society that we see women participating most effectively in public life. The Bourbons' return to power in the Restoration allowed a revival of the Old Regime salon culture. The salons became venues for vital political information, contacts, and exchanging ideas. As hostesses, women often dictated the style of speech and the topics of conversation, and, perhaps most importantly, determined the principal guests.[41] Marriage was another means by which intelligent women could become involved politically. Villèle and his wife, for instance, carried on a prolific correspondence that showed her to be cognizant of the most serious political issues of the day. Similarly, the Marquise Céleste de Vaulchier exerted a tremendous influence over her husband, the Marquis Louis-Anne de Vaulchier du Deschaux, as a political adviser and assistant – and also as his conscience. Other such examples include Mme de Montcalm, Albertine de Broglie, and Mme de Rémusat, all of whom had a political life through their husbands' careers.[42] Charitable works provided yet another portal through which women could influence the public at large. Since the Old Regime, women had dominated the field of charitable works, which had become a significant source of power by the 1820s.[43] Women were the organizers of great charitable events such as large-scale theatrical performances and concerts. In fact, the duchess's public appearances prior to the assassination were principally related to good works and charity,[44] and she continued to take part in charitable events thereafter. Through such events women were able to exert pressure on men of influence to act on particular social issues. There were also public spaces that allowed women a forum for their political opinions. The *salons de thé, chambrettes provençales*, and churches were such spaces – four walls and a roof under which women could meet without the company of men.

These revisions to the public-sphere paradigm suggest that during the Restoration women did express themselves on matters of public interest, even if formal participation in the political process was prohibited. In the cases reviewed above, however, that political expression derived principally from practical considerations, rather than being a symbolic representation of political power. In other words, what the revisionists point out is that it was not practicable that half the population be entirely shut out of public life. Among the popular classes, the institutional and cultural measures needed for such a prohibition simply did not exist. Women had far too much freedom for the paradigm of the public sphere to have been strictly enforced. In the middle and upper classes, those measures indeed existed, and there we see women forced to abide more closely by the strictures of the paradigm. However, these women did play a vital social role, and who would argue that social and political society are not closely linked? It is therefore not in the least surprising that the wife of a prominent political figure would also exercise no small measure of political influence through her social status, by hosting a *salon*, a ball, or a charitable event. These are practical observations, however, and do not mean that society at large attached a symbolic significance to the influence of any woman in the public sphere. Although, as a practical matter, the wife of a political figure participated in French political society, her influence was not recognized as a legal or *de jure* power.

A historical evaluation of the duchess's public persona is made interesting both by the public-sphere paradigm and the revisions to it. Her Good Wife and Good Mother personas clearly fit the general pattern established by the paradigm – nothing is more domestic than marriage and children. Her public persona, as articulated through the official interpretations of the assassination and the miracle birth, could not therefore be more stark in this regard. She was Berry's perfect wife, the Sophie to his Émile, forever mourning his passing, forever chaste and loving. She was also a perfect mother, even though, as noted earlier, her Good Mother status was dynastic rather than maternal in theme. Under the paradigm, duty represents a woman's greatest character trait, and the duchess is ultimately glorified through the Good Mother persona for fulfilling her express duty to provide an heir to the throne. In short, her public persona represents the culmination of the paradigm. Any possible political qualities that might have attached to her public persona were suppressed, ignored, or simply not considered. The duchess was praised widely for her bravery during the assassination and then again when she delivered Bordeaux. The image of the brave princess could have easily been exploited by the government to reinforce the dynastic component of the official interpretations. She could have toured the country with Bordeaux, signed proclamations, and made speeches exhorting the general public to support the Bourbon regime. Instead, the duchess's participation in the public sphere was limited to actions that served

her Good Wife and Good Mother personas – playing the role of the
princess in mourning and the mother who lived solely for the glory of
France's future king. Even well after the Royalist Reaction the duchess's political influence followed avenues outlined by the revisionists,
namely, through her contact with powerful men at the royal court
and her role as the hostess of social and charitable events.

A striking parallel between the duchess's public persona and those of
Marie-Antoinette and Charlotte Corday further reinforces the relevance of the public-sphere paradigm. All three were used by their respective governments for a political end – in explicitly sexual terms.
Moreover, each woman was connected by marriage or conduct to a
man, and each man was dealt with by the same governmental authority
in political terms. Marie-Antoinette was condemned as a sexual deviant, while her husband, Louis XVI, was guillotined for political crimes
against the state. The entire pornographic attack against the queen
prior to the Revolution also shows the paradigm at work. Corday's
own assertion of a political motive for her crime was ignored. Instead,
prosecutors suggested that as a women she was unable to handle the
strain of dealing with political issues; she exemplified the inherent
weakness of women and their unsuitability for public life. In addition,
her fame rested largely on her beauty, as men were titillated by the
combination of her attractiveness and the violence of her actions.
Corday's victim, Marat, on the other hand, was eulogized in political
terms without reference to his sex.[45] Now let us turn to the duchess.
She too was useful politically to the current government – this time as a
sympathetic royal figure who helped attract support for the Bourbon
regime. She too was sexualized in that the exclusive focus on her domestic qualities made her public persona conform to the demands of
the public-sphere paradigm. Contrast also her public persona as the
Good Wife and Good Mother to Berry's invented public persona as the
revolutionary martyr and symbol of Bourbon dynastic greatness. His
persona belongs to the public sphere, while hers remains in the private.
In each case, we see a high-profile woman linked subordinately to a
male public figure, and a government that used both men and women
for political purposes according to the historical process that led to
women's exclusion from public life.

THE NOVEMBER DEPUTY ELECTION

At the beginning of November Alphonse Martainville published a
lengthy pamphlet called "La bombe royaliste." He maintained that
Richelieu and his ministers had systematically manipulated the royal-

ists into supporting them, while at the same time conspiring to perse-cute those same royalists. In his mind, the exceptional laws did not constitute an attack against the liberals, nor was France bracing against a royalist reaction of any sort. The reality was that the excep-tional laws simply enhanced the power of the ministerial party. Martainville criticized his fellow royalists for failing to take advan-tage of Decazes's fall in allowing Richelieu to return. He concluded that Richelieu and the passage of the exceptional laws meant that Berry had died in vain: "We have lost all advantage that may have come from the ruin of that hated minister, and in so doing have al-lowed his successors to exploit the blood of a Bourbon to enhance their power and ambition."[46]

Martainville hoped his "bomb" would convince the electorate to vote for ultra-royalist candidates. In the end, the electorate was con-vinced to vote for royalists, but not exclusively for the ultras. The arrondissement colleges opened on 4 November to fill the one-fifth annual renewal seats. The departmental colleges opened on 13 No-vember to fill the 172 double-vote seats. When the election was over, out of 430 deputies, 80 were liberal, 160 were ultra, and 190 were ministerial. The royalists now effectively overwhelmed the liberals, although Richelieu was concerned about the number of ultra deputies who remained in the Chamber. The ministerial candidates, however, tended to win their seats in more convincing fashion than did the lib-eral or ultra candidates. Almost 80 percent of the ministerial deputies received 50 percent of the votes cast in their respective colleges. Sig-nificantly, voter turnout was tremendous, the highest of any Restora-tion election. Ninety percent of the successful candidates, regardless of political orientation, were elected by three-quarters of the regis-tered voters.

Liberal deputies argued in May and June that the double vote would lead to their political extinction. The November deputy election sug-gests they were correct. The wealthiest 25 percent of the electorate was decidedly royalist. Only 10 percent of the renewal seats were filled by titled nobles, as compared to 43 percent of the double-vote seats. In terms of prior political experience, a striking 43 percent of the double-vote deputies had served the Empire in some capacity, while only 15 percent had held a post during the Revolution and only 6 percent had held one during the Hundred Days.[47]

The double vote ensured that the balance of power in the Chamber of Deputies was determined by the departmental colleges. In 1820 the double-voters chose to support Louis XVIII and Richelieu. The opposi-tion was by no means eliminated completely; liberals had around eighty seats, and the ultras twice that. However, given all that had preceded the election, the moderate royalists must have been very satisfied with the results. Government preparation contributed greatly. Richelieu faced the daunting task of moderating political opinion in order to prevent another *Chambre introuvable* while at the same time ending the run of liberal victories that had begun in 1817. His ministers may have managed to convince enough deputies to support the exceptional laws, but no united body of royalists supported the government's policies. Exceptional laws aside, political divisions continued to bubble away. With the 20 August Plot, the danger of a *coup d'état* had surfaced. Ultra royalists echoed Martainville's "Bombe royaliste," arguing that France stood on the edge of the precipice, and, therefore, extreme measures – and by extension extreme deputies – were needed to save the nation.

Richelieu and his ministers responded to the extremists by distancing the election from the chaotic events that preceded it. A rapidly improving economy certainly helped in that regard;[48] however, Bordeaux was the more significant factor. Ministers took advantage of the groundswell of public support for Louis XVIII and the royal family after the miracle birth. On the administrative side, Siméon sent no fewer than ten separate *circulaires* to the prefects outlining procedures for producing electoral lists and conducting the elections.[49] Electoral fraud was a matter of great concern, and it appears that the government worked diligently to make sure that the *cens* was adhered to strictly.[50] In addition, Siméon ordered the prefects to review electoral lists and estimate how each elector would vote. The surveys were sent to Paris, complete with the names of the most influential electors. Voting boundaries were also changed wherever possible to reduce the possibility of extremist pockets affecting election results. For instance, at the request of Baron Haussez, the arrondissements of Grenoble, Vienne, La-Tour-du-Pin, and St Marcellin were combined to reduce the influence of Grenoblois liberals.[51]

On 25 October Louis XVIII issued a proclamation pleading with voters to elect ministerial candidates. Failure to do so, he wrote, would destroy the peace, the glory, and the future of "*notre commune patrie.*" In short, electors had two choices: vote for Louis XVIII or vote for anarchy. "Choose amongst them; your deputies will help me to uphold that order without which no society can exist." Why did he believe that? Bordeaux's miracle birth had proved that Providence desired a Bourbon on the French throne, and further, that it supported the *union et oubli* policy: "You have shared the consolation Providence has sent to me and my family; may this sign of perpetuity, which Heaven has given to France, be also the token of reunion. Let it unite all those who sincerely want the institutions I have given you, and with them, the order, peace and happiness of our homeland."

In the electoral colleges of Isère and Haute-Garonne, college presidents reiterated Louis XVIII's belief that the miracle child had determined the ministerial candidates' success in the upcoming election. In Isère's departmental college, Planelli de la Valette[52] called on the electors to display their "devotion to the King's person, and to add their congratulations to those of the authorities on the birth of the Prince, which Providence has just bestowed on France, and which, by perpetuating the noble line of our kings, the descendants of Saint Louis, Henri IV, and of Louis XIV, is a source of rejoicing to all the people of France..."[53] Joseph de Villèle, president of the departmental college of Haute-Garonne, made a similar reference to the hand of Providence as he opened that college: "We will not go back to revolution; Providence has seen to that by the birth of the miracle child. That birth led to unanimous rejoicing among the people, disproving the ominous words of the slanderers; Providence did not do this in order to abandon the King." Villèle added that he hoped the electors would put aside their differences for the good of France: "The political rights given to citizens to preserve the established order should not be used to provoke revolutions."[54]

A number of bishops and archbishops issued *mandements* concerning the upcoming election. Since it was the first time they had published their opinion about an election – something they would do only once again during the Restoration in 1824 – it seems more than likely they were acting on direct orders from the *Conseil*. Bishop Simon advised his followers to "choose deputies who will ensure the tranquillity, peace and happiness of our *patrie*." France needed deputies who were "honest men, virtuous men, men who are attached equally to God and to their King." Those deputies were the ministerial candidates, not the king's enemies, "who stir up trouble, sow discord, propagate injustice, and defy their government ... men who are too blind to see the divine light, perverse men who lead new intrigues and new plots, and who work against the king and his people."[55]

The Bordeaux illustrations, the October *fêtes*, the *mandements*, the Chambord Subscription, the duchess's Good Mother persona, and the November deputy elections provide cumulative evidence of a nation captivated by the very idea of the miracle child, *l'espoir réalisé*.[56] This chapter began with Victor Hugo's "Ode to Bordeaux." Another of France's premier literary figures was not to be outdone by this young upstart. Alphonse de Lamartine, then thirty years old, penned his own

tribute to the miracle child. His words declared Bordeaux the actualiza-
tion of God's will that France be ruled by the Bourbon dynasty:

> Heir to a martyr's blood!
> The miracle child is born,
> Born as it was foretold,
> Born of a dying sigh! ...
>
> Blessed cradle, fragile promise,
> Sheltered in his mother's arms,
> All the nation now is witness;
> A miracle is shown to us![57]

Bordeaux's actual life did not measure up to this lofty standard: How
could it? But future events and hindsight should not cloud the very real
and profound impact his birth had on French history. In the minds of
royalists, he represented all that was good in the world: his characterization as the miracle child was well earned.

Postscript:
Leap into the Abyss

The spirit of cooperation between moderate and ultra royalists that powered the Royalist Reaction retreated almost immediately after the November deputy election. Ultra royalists demanded a presence on the *Conseil*. Richelieu tried to placate them by appointing Corbière and Villèle as ministers without portfolio. Anti-Bourbon demonstrations continued, but for the most part France's political community was calm. The most notable exception occurred in Grenoble. On 20 March 1821 rumours that Louis XVIII had abdicated led to a small riot. A crowd gathered in front of the *Hôtel de la Préfecture* to chant slogans. Half-hearted attempts were made to take over the building, after which the crowd dispersed. Local authorities took the incident seriously enough to declare martial law, but Baron Haussez cancelled it the next day.

The riot had dramatic consequences for the Grenoble law school. Corbière referred both to the riot and the demonstrations against the Duke of Angoulême on 8 and 9 May, in a report to Louis XVIII: "Several students of the Faculty of Law have been seen taking part in the riots, enthusiastically proclaiming principles which are contrary to order, and showing a lack of the respect due to the presence of a Prince, the worthy object of the people's love, who brought only words of peace and union."[1] Ultra royalists had long considered Grenoble law students to be a disloyal and seditious group, and on 4 April the school was suspended indefinitely. In his report, Corbière added harsh words for those who had protected Grenoble's law school from disciplinary action in the past: "If these men had devoted themselves to setting a good example to the young men entrusted to their charge, if they had not constantly sought to cover up their faults instead of repressing them with just severity, it is probable that the Government would not today, regretfully, have to take such strict measures." Seven men were arrested. One law student named Marc Colombat was sentenced to a year in prison and fined 1,000 francs for raising the *tricolore* at the Citadelle in Grenoble and for wearing the *cocarde tricolore*. Three non-students were also sentenced to prison and fined,[2] and four others were released, much to the displeasure of the *procureur général*.

The suspension of Grenoble's law school illustrates how dramatically the Royalist Reaction altered France's political landscape. A changing of the guard had taken place. Without sympathetic ministers to protect them from the wrath of the ultras, the law students continued, perhaps foolishly, to protest against a government that would no longer tolerate such criticism. The suspension came as a stunning blow to the university and represented a significant loss of revenue to the city as well.[3] The suspension was lifted in 1824, but students generally were silent on political matters until 1830, when the opportunity arose again to demonstrate their anti-Bourbon feelings.

On 1 May 1821 inhabitants in every city, town, and village turned out to celebrate the baptism of the Duke of Bordeaux at the official national *fête* ordered by the central government. On the day of Bordeaux's birth, Mounier had sent a letter to the prefects containing detailed instructions for the baptism *fête*. He envisioned the *fête* as a "holy ceremony [that] will give the nation another opportunity to show its feelings for its noble family to whom it owes the liberty and tranquillity which Providence has bestowed on France after so many years of licentiousness and despotism."[4] By all accounts the *fêtes* were a success, particularly the Parisian *fête* that was described as "magnificently celebrated."[5] Seven months in the making, the affair was elegant and refined; decorations were spectacular, in a gothic style à la mode at the time, described as emotional and poetic.[6]

The enthusiasm of the central government was not matched by local officials, however. The spontaneity that had marked the Bordeaux birth *fêtes* in October was conspicuously absent. Mayoral reports suggest that financial concerns took precedence over Bordeaux's baptism. The Mayor of St Symphorien-d'Ozon reported that the church wall had recently fallen, and also that his town had a deficit of 1,821 francs from 1820. A mass was held, but it was voluntary and no celebrations followed.[7] The mayor of the Commune of Vaux sent a letter to the sub-prefect of Vienne apologizing for the simplicity of their *fête*, citing the commune's poverty as the reason: "The Municipal Council only has one regret, that it lacks adequate resources to display the joy it feels on the birth of His Royal Highness, the Duke of Bordeaux."[8]

Pecuniary considerations aside, the Bordeaux baptism *fêtes* did provide a final opportunity to propagate the royalist creed in connection with the assassination and the miracle birth. As with the Berry memorial services and the October Bordeaux birth *fêtes*, the baptism celebrations of 1 May united the nation on a single day to commemorate an event that honoured the royal family. At the same time, the lacklustre enthusiasm on the part of local officials suggests that the assassination and the miracle birth were beginning to lose their tenure in the public's imagination. And future *fêtes* were never able to capture the magic that the Berry and Bordeaux *fêtes* of 1820 had inspired. By the end of the decade, the national *fêtes* had a stale, mechanical feel commonly seen in government-sponsored events.

In October 1821, deputy elections were again held, to renew eighty-eight seats. Ultra candidates captured twenty of those seats. As the renewal elections included the entire electorate, that number represented a significant achievement, particularly when compared to the fourteen seats won by liberal candidates.[9] Buoyed by that success, Villèle and Corbière threatened to resign if more cabinet posts were not given to ultra royalists. Richelieu refused, and when Villèle and Corbière withdrew their support in December, his ministry fell. Richelieu resigned on 13 December and Villèle took over as president of the *Conseil* two days later, a post he held until 3 January 1828. In the immediate wake of Berry's assassination and Decazes's resignation, Richelieu was seen as the only man capable of preventing a civil war. A year later, no longer indispensable, he was forced to leave by the very people who had previously begged him to return to politics. On 9 May 1822, at only fifty-five years of age, Richelieu died. No one from the royal court or the peerage attended his funeral. The man who had directed the Royalist Reaction became its last political casualty. On 16 September 1824, an extremely ill Louis XVIII finally passed away. He was replaced on the throne by his brother Artois, who took the name Charles X. The ultra-royalist *Conseil* now had an ultra-royalist king. The coronation of Charles X in 1825 finalized the ultras' rise to power. The Restoration belonged to them.

French political history turned a page after the Royalist Reaction. The Age of the Ultras had arrived, and any analysis of the Restoration must from that point focus more exclusively on the causes of the July Revolution. However, the Royalist Reaction still made itself felt after 1830. On 14 February 1831, a group of prominent legitimists gathered at the Church of Saint Germain de l'Auxerrois in Paris to hold a mass in Berry's honour to commemorate the assassination. White flags, fleurs-de-lys, and rows of aristocratic carriages with armorials completed the scene. Outside the church, a crowd also gathered. The crowd allowed the legitimists to leave, but a detachment of the National Guard was needed to escort the priests from the church. The crowd then sacked the church and the Archbishop's palace, which was next to Notre Dame. The next day, a group of people, and it is not known if they were the same individuals, returned to raze the palace to the ground and to take part in mock religious rites in the ruins. Similar scenes occurred in other towns. On 17 February rioters in Lille destroyed a statue of Berry that had been erected at the Place du Concert on 25 August 1829; the statue had been placed on the site of a statue of Napoleon that had been destroyed in 1815 after the Hundred Days.[10] The government and the police may have been behind the riots, and the spontaneous outbursts ended almost as soon as they broke out.[11] After that, however, memorials to the departed prince were held in secret, if at all.

On the night of 29 July 1830, the royal family fled St Cloud to Rambouillet where they stayed until 3 August. On 2 August, Charles X and Angoulême abdicated in favour of Bordeaux, duly named Henri V. The child was taken before the few loyal troops that accompanied them, and presented as their new king. For one day, at least, Bordeaux was King of France. The Duchess of Berry, in a combative mood, tried to convince Charles X to return to Paris and fight for her son's throne. In fact, she had left St Cloud with two pistols in her belt. However, Charles X was not that kind of man. He had no intention of risking anyone's life, least of all his own. By 16 August the royal family was safely ensconced in Scotland. No Bourbon would ever return to France in any official royal capacity.

The duchess was not quite ready to give up. In 1832 she attempted to foment a rebellion to overthrow the July Monarchy and restore the Bourbon regime, with her son as king. She travelled in disguise across France from Marseilles, but found little support until she reached the Vendée. On 15 May she issued a call to arms to the people of the Vendée and Breton: "Henri V is calling on you; his mother, the Regent of France, is devoted to your happiness. Let us take up together the old cry and the new. Long live the King! Long live Henri V!" Twenty thousand copies of her proclamation were distributed. Remarkably, the duchess actually managed to begin a rebellion of sorts in June, but it was crushed in a matter of days. She escaped and went into hiding, only to be captured in November. On 19 November she was placed in a prison cell in Blaye, while the government tried to decide its course of action. There was little to gain by punishing her. The duchess was still a very popular figure in France, and her daring escapade and willingness to risk her life for her son only enhanced her reputation as the "brave little princess." Her imprisonment became a cause of sorts for royalists, who flooded Paris with petitions for her release. Berryer, the lawyer who had defended Donnadieu back in 1820 in regard to the Didier Affair, led the fight for her release, and he was joined by a number of deputies in the Chamber of Deputies. Some two thousand students flocked to Chateaubriand's house every night to demonstrate their outrage.[12] By mid-December, just as the controversy over what should happen to her was becoming a national crisis, the duchess suddenly became ill. She refused to cooperate with the doctors. Their inability to discover the cause of her illness must certainly be one of the most incredible cases of medical incompetence ever recorded. On 22 February, Dr. Gintrac examined the duchess and discovered the real reason: she was pregnant. That diagnosis ended the protests over her imprisonment instantly. The obvious question was put to her: Who was the father? In what remains a murky and suspicious matter, the duchess revealed that she had secretly married an obscure Italian count named Hector Lucchesi-Palli when she was in Italy before arriving in France to start the rebellion.[13] On 10 May 1833, the duchess gave birth to a girl, nicknamed sarcastically, *l'enfant de la Vendée*. Charles X refused to see her until he received an authentic copy of the marriage certificate, and though one was duly procured, dated 14 December 1831, relations between him and the duchess remained strained until his death.

The protest over the duchess's imprisonment speaks volumes as to the popularity and longevity of her public persona. The only possible reason for the protests was her public persona as the Good Wife and Good Mother.[14] Royalists did not gather at Chateaubriand's house because of the duchess's standing as the former darling of the Parisian social scene. The abrupt end to the protests also suggests that her popular public persona was at the root of it all. Once her Good Wife persona was shattered by news of her pregnancy, a fact that could not have augured well for the Good Mother persona either, the entire campaign to free her ended. In short, the duchess they believed was incarcerated simply ceased to exist. She was no longer a Good Wife, for she had betrayed Berry's memory. The question of whether she was a Good Mother is more complex, for, after all, the "brave little princess" had risked her life and freedom for her son. Unfortunately, the persona of the miracle child was tarnished by the July Revolution – nor was it helped by the abject failure of the Vendée Rebellion. In other words, the duchess may have been Bordeaux's mother, but most royalists would have to question whether he truly was the miracle child.[15] Interestingly, after the Vendée Rebellion, the duchess's Good Mother public persona took on a more maternal character; she was promoted by the legitimists "as a royal mother of exemplary zeal."[16]

She would no longer be a symbolic Good Mother, but a real one. In this way, it can be argued that the duchess's public persona became more authentically political. She provided an image of the royal family in keeping with current middle-class values, which after the Vendée Rebellion were the values reflected by "the cultural mainstream of national political life."[17]

After the Vendée fiasco, the Bourbon royal family settled into their life outside of France. As the years ticked by, the elder members slowly died off, reducing the ranks of the Bourbon dynasty. On 16 August 1832, Charles X died; Angoulême on 2 June 1844. The duchess went on to have four children between 1836 and 1840: three girls – Clémentine, Francesca, and Isabelle – and one son, Adinolphe. She and Hector lived well until his death in 1864. Hector was always attentive to his wife, but he was profligate with money, enjoying the good life and collecting art. He left the duchess with an enormous debt, which was covered by the Duke of Luynes and Bordeaux. The duchess had grown fat and somewhat bad-tempered by that time, but she kept busy visiting her children, especially Bordeaux, and her thirty-two grandchildren. In 1870, she became ill and died of typhoid at the age of seventy-two.

Bordeaux turned out to be a good-looking fellow with blue eyes, blond hair and a solid build. A riding accident in 1842, in which he broke his left thigh, left him lame for the rest of his life. The accident contributed to his gaining weight, and he fought a losing battle against it until he died. Bordeaux travelled Europe extensively during the July Monarchy years. He married Marie-Thérèse, daughter of Francis IV of Modena, a gloomy, timid, and depressed woman who was never able to have a child. His political life suggests that he inherited that lack of shrewdness characteristic of both Louis XVI and Charles X. The 1848 Revolution came and went without Bordeaux making the slightest effort to put himself forward as a candidate to head up a new government. Life had not prepared him to take advantage of opportunities, and he would continue to miss every subsequent opportunity to restore the House of Bourbon.[18] Yet, there were opportunities aplenty. The Legitimist movement remained a powerful political force in France during the July Monarchy, the Second Empire, and the first decade of the Third Republic. His best chance came with the fall of Louis-Napoleon's government in 1870–71, after France's defeat at the hands of the Prussians. On 2 July 1871, Bordeaux arrived in Paris incognito, invited by the leaders of the legitimists and a number of other political figures who believed he offered the best means of re-establishing order. The stage was set for the Third Restoration. Incredibly, in what can only be described as snatching defeat from the jaws of victory, Bordeaux broke ranks with his fellow legitimists by insisting that

France accept the traditional Bourbon white flag over the tricolor. On 5 July, he went to Chambord, and issued the White Flag Manifesto. In it he stated, "Henri V cannot abandon the flag of Henri IV. I have received it [the white flag] as a sacred bequest from the old King, my ancestor, dying in exile; it has always been for me an inseparable souvenir of my country; it floated over my cradle, and I want it draped over my tomb." The manifesto was published on 7 July. Victor Hugo called it "a noble suicide."[19] Noble or not, his gesture splintered the monarchical movement, destroyed any hope he had of restoring the Bourbon throne, and allowed the republicans to establish the Third Republic. If Bordeaux wanted the white flag draped over his tomb, then he would not be king of France. His attachment to principle is praiseworthy to be sure; beyond that it is difficult to assess Bordeaux's involvement in French politics as anything other than an abject failure. On 24 August 1883, at 7:27 a.m., after a two-month illness, the last of the Bourbon kings died. Louvel's dream was finally a reality. The House of Bourbon was extinct.

The Restoration is generally considered to be a transitional stage in French history. The political, economic, and social structures that characterized France in the eighteenth century had not yet lost their hold on society, while the institutions that shaped modern France were still in the initial stages of development. There is much in the Royalist Reaction to suggest that France was already a relatively modern state in 1820. The attention paid to the Charter, the importance of deputy elections, the existence of a national media network that actively covered political issues, and the emergence of party-style politics all point to the emergence of modern democratic thinking, and a steady retreat from the old style, personal forms of politics that dominated pre-Revolutionary France. At the same time, there is much to suggest that Restoration France was still strongly rooted in the eighteenth century. The family metaphor that manifested itself through the Royalist Reaction's popular elements illustrates that point. The Bourbons were reconfirmed as the "magic family," destined by Providence to rule over France.

The accomplishments of the last Bourbon regime should not be underestimated. During Louis XVIII's reign, he and his ministers showed a remarkable ability to reconcile a wide range of disparate political groups, from republicans to ultra royalists. Moreover, the roots of democracy were maintained and in some ways even strengthened, censorship and the double vote notwithstanding. The Charter became entrenched in French political thought, as did the idea of an elected national body. Overriding the self-evident inequality of the *cens* system, France's political community itself often acted in democratic fashion, debating the issues in public, participating in elections, and keeping abreast of important political developments. Moreover, while France's political community was very small, it was still more substantial than the group of courtiers that had dominated French politics in the previous century. It was also more representative of French society than were the elites that controlled France during the Napoleonic Empire, for it included royalists and liberals across the political spectrum. In overall terms, the political system in place during the Royalist Reaction may well have been anti-democratic, and ministers and members of the political community were more than willing to manipulate the system to suit their personal goals; at the same time, a constitution existed and political decision-making was carried out, for the most part, without the use of violence. That point must be stressed. It seems clear that the fundamental concepts of constitutional democracy were in the process of becoming accepted by a majority of the members of France's political community, even if that acceptance was perhaps, at times, less than wholehearted.

Naturally, the unconstitutional aspects of the Restoration's political system are all too evident. It bears repeating that the franchise was limited to approximately 0.3 percent of the total population, and women were expressly excluded from officially participating in any way. In fact, the elites acted in truly aristocratic fashion, feeling quite justified in deciding all significant political, social, and economic questions without consulting the vast majority of the population. It is somewhat ironic that independent deputies accused the government of creating an aristocracy with the double vote when in many ways the men sitting in the Chamber of Deputies were an aristocracy unto themselves, the principal difference between them and their earlier counterparts being that their membership was based solely on wealth, rather than wealth and birth.

The unconstitutional aspects of the Royalist Reaction also suggest that France had far to go before democratic ideals became mainstream. The tendency of liberals and royalists to join conspiratorial movements – and the growing support they gave to radical violent acts – evidences the incompleteness of the process. At the same time, this radicalization had a modern element in that it was clearly a precursor to the dominant radical political movements of the nineteenth and twentieth centuries: socialism (communism), anarchism, and fascism. The Restoration's conspiracy mentality had much in common with the emergence of the classical nineteenth-century conspiracy to which those three movements are so closely allied. Finally, the process whereby politically active citizens joined together to promote a common cause, evidenced by the tumultuous debates on exceptional laws, certainly contributed to the growth of modern political parties.

By 1820 newspapers were the most important conduit of political information for the literate community and the dominant forum for expressing political opinion. That the Restoration government had difficulty constructing a precise definition of freedom of the press is self-evident; yet, it would be unfair to dismiss the Restoration government in 1820 as absolutist or anti-democratic for that reason alone, since governments to this day continue to struggle with the question. What is important is that the issue of freedom of the press was discussed earnestly in open society, and that for a brief period in 1819 and early 1820, the press was genuinely free. France had to wait until the 1870s for the end to censorship, but any account of the growth of a free press in France must undoubtedly make reference to the role the French press played in political matters in the months before and after Berry's assassination.

The ability of the French government to control and disseminate, on a nationwide scale, an official interpretation of the assassination and the miracle birth evidences the existence of a modern state. Interestingly, the symbolism used in the Berry and Bordeaux *fêtes* was decidedly Old Regime in character. Moreover, the *fêtes* had an eighteenth-century orientation. The king was portrayed as father to the nation, and the royal family as an ideal for the general population to emulate. How, then, to interpret the *fêtes*? Ultimately, they suggest a political system in transition. A modern-styled centralized state organized the *fêtes* for their own political ends, but that same government used old-fashioned methods to achieve them.

The role of public opinion deserves some mention. Before the French Revolution, it played a limited role in politics, beyond the occasional bread riots that necessitated an official response, usually in the form of a bayonet. The Revolution taught those in power that the millions of disenfranchised French citizens could cause problems if their needs were ignored. Napoleon certainly understood the importance of public opinion, even if he generally dismissed it; and the governments under Louis XVIII were also well aware that public opinion had to be taken into account. Moreover, that awareness extended throughout France's political community, particularly among the deputies who used the podium in the Chamber to speak to an audience that extended well beyond parliamentary walls. It was not so much that these wealthy men were at all interested in consulting the general population about a particular political issue, but rather that they at least had to take the general population's response to their actions into account. During the Royalist Reaction members of France's political community took explicit steps to sway public opinion in their favour. That occurred not only in the Chamber of Deputies, but also in newspapers, brochures, *mandements*, illustrations, and judicial pronouncements. The finding that public opinion played an increasingly important role in French society in the nineteenth century is pedestrian; however, what is less understood is at what time and in what manner public opinion significantly affected political or social events. The Royalist Reaction represents an event where the influence of public opinion can be measured with some precision.

Economic issues were expressly excluded in this study for the simple reason that Berry's death had no identifiable impact in that area. The French political community was deeply divided in political terms, but it had less trouble reaching a consensus on economic issues. They were generally content with the protectionist and high tariff policies then in effect. The years between the Royalist Reaction and the July Revolution probably were the last decade before the influences of the Industrial Revolution forever changed the functioning of France's society and economy. The Restoration therefore was the last time political issues could be discussed without dealing at length with questions related to the working and industrial classes. Not to say that industrial issues did not surface at all. France's political community was already beginning to distinguish between wealth based on land and wealth generated by industry, an issue that came to the fore during the debate on the double vote. Ultra royalism was characterized by a determined rejection of modernity and bourgeois industry. France's political community was just beginning to be transformed by industrialization when Berry was killed, and that transformation expressed itself politically in 1820.

Royalists were certain that a vast liberal conspiracy was ultimately responsible for Berry's death. How could a man like Louvel, the reasoning went, conceive of and then carry out such a terrible crime? The advantage of hindsight has shown that even a Louvel is capable of single-handedly affecting history. He killed Berry with the intention of ending the Bourbon line and set in motion the series of events that we now call the Royalist Reaction of 1820. It is a remarkable story, this tale of assassination and miracle birth – a story that left an indelible mark upon modern French history.

Appendix One:
The Political Background
of Isère and Haute-Garonne

The famous Journée des Tuiles of 1788 in Grenoble earned Isère a radical, anti-monarchical reputation that continued into the nineteenth century. A meeting held soon after the Journée at the Château de Vizille, where those assembled called for the convening of the Dauphiné Estates and the Estates-General, became an important symbol of resistance during the revolutionary period, and liberal radicals from Grenoble made frequent reference to it during the Restoration.

After 1789 inhabitants of Isère supported the revolutionaries and the republicans, and then transferred their allegiance to Napoleon. The Grenoblois illustrated their Bonapartist sentiments when, on 6 March 1815, their former emperor approached the city after his escape from Elba. Escorted by some 2,000 peasants, Napoleon was welcomed with open arms. Members of the National Guard pillaged at least four châteaux, and the mayor of La Sône was murdered because he tried to prevent the raising of the *tricolore*. Napoleon spent an evening in Grenoble before proceeding to Lyon.

The emperor's defeat at Waterloo and Louis XVIII's return did not change loyalties in Isère. Troops from Austria and Piedmont entered Grenoble on 9 July 1815, effectively ending the Hundred Days in Isère, but not before three days of fierce fighting.[1] The Count of Montlivault,[2] the prefect of Isère after the Hundred Days, noted in his report to Paris in 1815 that the general population remained uneasy with the Bourbons; they were a population characterized by "a spirit of opposition and defiance towards the government."

Two events occurred in Grenoble after the Hundred Days and before Berry's assassination which propelled that city and Isère into the royalist-liberal political fray and cemented its anti-Bourbon reputation: the Didier Affair of 4–5 May 1816, and Abbé Grégoire's successful candidacy during the September, 1819 deputy election.

Grenoble was also a centre for liberal conspiracies. During the Restoration, a secret society, L'Union, headed by Joseph Rey, actively conspired against the Bourbon regime. Rey was one of the leaders of the 20 August Plot of 1820, which aimed to overthrow the Bourbon regime, and he was one of three men sentenced to death in absentia for his efforts. One of the most popular liberal newspapers, the *Journal Libre de l'Isère*, was based in Grenoble; and it was a vocal critic of the Bourbon regime until the censor commission, established in 1820 after the passage of the press law in March of that year, put an end to its verbal barrage. More radical liberals published a journal called *L'Echo des Alpes*, a vitriolic publication that was shut down when its owners were successfully sued for libel. Finally, in 1821, Grenoble's law school was shut down after a student-led riot. This was on the heels of an earlier national incident, when law students and others shouted insults at the Duke of Angoulême during his visit in 1820.

TOULOUSE AND HAUTE-GARONNE

Haute-Garonne and its capital Toulouse were to royalists what Isère and Grenoble were to liberals. This south-western department remained loyal to the Bourbons throughout the revolutionary and imperial eras, and its inhabitants welcomed Louis XVIII back enthusiastically. As a result, the department became an important spiritual symbol of the Counter-Revolution and of the nation's devotion to the Bourbon regime.

Resistance to the Revolution began almost immediately. The May Edicts of 1788[3] were resented bitterly because the Toulouse *parlement* was both the political and legal centre for the entire region and a considerable source of income.[4] Without the *parlement*, Toulouse ceased to be an important city. The Civil Constitution of the Clergy was even more controversial. The Archbishop of Toulouse, François de Fontagnes, formed a secret organization called *l'Aa* to counteract the measure.[5] Some clergymen emigrated, but most remained in hiding in the area to administer to their congregations and to lend a spiritual legitimacy to the Counter-Revolution.

The failed federalist movement of 1793, in which inhabitants of Haute-Garonne played a prominent role, and the local clergy's continued refusal to swear an oath to the Civil Constitution of the Clergy contributed to the severity of the Terror in the South-West. As many as 1,000 suspects in and around Toulouse were arrested.[6] Relative calm returned after 9 Thermidor,[7] until August 6, 1799, when royalist rebels, commanded by General Rougé,[8] attacked Toulouse.[9] News of the rebellion sparked similar insurrections throughout the south. On August 20, however, the royalist forces were routed by the French army at Montréjeau. Similar to the effect the Didier Affair had on Isère and Grenoble, the First Battle of Toulouse, as the rebellion became known, provided Haute-Garonne and its capital with an enduring ultra-royalist reputation.

Napoleon's defeat in Russia and the Empire's subsequent disintegration provided Toulousians with their next opportunity to live up to their royalist reputation. In April 1814, General Soult met General Wellington in the field of battle in what was called the Second Battle of Toulouse. During Soult's stay in Toulouse, the inhabitants refused almost to a person to help the imperial troops. When Wellington entered Toulouse on 12 April, he was welcomed as a liberator.

Predictably, Napoleon's escape from Elba was not welcome news. Royalists and Bonapartists battled in the streets for a week before the Empire was proclaimed in Toulouse. The counter-revolutionary spirit returned immediately, again led by the clergy, as royalists organized secret military companies. After Waterloo, Angoulême chose Toulouse as the headquarters for the royalist army in southern France.

The White Terror that followed the inauguration of the Second Restoration was particularly severe in Haute-Garonne. Charles de Rémusat wrote in his memoirs, "I doubt very much that Paris, in the days that followed 24 February 1848, was more deprived of guarantees of order than Toulouse from the end of June to the beginning of September, 1815."[10] The most notable terrorist act was the assassination of General Ramel in August. Ramel's murder was planned by ultra-royalist members of the *Chevaliers de la foi*; they resented Ramel's appointment as commander of the National Guard and the regular army troops in Toulouse, over their candidate, General Rougé, leader of the 1799 royalist rebellion.

All those who supported Napoleon during the Hundred Days soon lost any government post they may have held, and were replaced by ultra royalists. Content with their new-found authority and positions, ultra royalists in Haute-Garonne kept the peace for the most part, until the assassination ended this period of relative moderation. Ultra royalists in the department supported the exceptional laws unconditionally and were vocal participants in the acrimonious political discourse between liberals and royalists that swept France during the Royalist Reaction. Ultra royalists won all the seats in the November deputy election, and the department remained firmly under their control for the remainder of the Restoration.

Notes

PROLOGUE

1 The Duke of Angoulême was born on 6 August 1775 and the Duke of Berry on 24 January 1778.

2 Both sons died young. The first son died of natural causes in 1789. In 1795 the second son, the unfortunate Louis XVII, died in prison from neglect.

3 Definitive proof of the marriage has never been found. Castelot, 335–44; Brown, 4–5.

4 Provence became Louis XVIII after Louis XVII died in 1795, and Artois became Charles X upon Louis XVIII's death on 16 September 1824.

5 Dupland, 50–1.

6 Dupland, 73.

7 Oreille delivered their second son, named Ferdinand, on 10 October 1820. Before he died, Berry had already made her a wealthy woman. In 1843 she married a rich landowner, and she died at the age of eighty in 1875.

8 Chateaubriand, *Mémoires, lettres et pièces*, 222.

9 Roullet, 22–3.

10 The dagger penetrated his left lung between his fifth and sixth ribs.

11 Bastard, 11–13.

12 Lucas-Debreton, 64. The Municipal Council of Toulouse sent Paulmier and Desbiez five hundred francs each for catching Louvel. ADHG, 4 M 45. Letter from Mayor of Toulouse to Prefect, 7 March 1820. Some people felt Paulmier deserved sole credit for catching Louvel. Roullet, 82.

13 Louvel was detained in the office waiting-room. He was first interrogated by Ferté, the *commissaire de police de la section et du théâtre*. The Duke of

Fitz-James, a member of the Chamber of Peers, asked a few questions, as did Elie Decazes, the first minister. The next day, Louvel was interrogated by Séguier (the *Procureur général*), Bellard (the *Premier président*), Decazes, and the Prefect of Police.

14 On 9 June 1820 Louvel was executed by hanging.

15 Sauvigny, 165.

16 Ten doctors attended Berry. Dupuytrin, who took charge after they moved Berry from the guard room to an adjacent office, tried to stop the flow of blood with his finger. He then tried to use a bandage, but had nothing to hold it in place. The duchess and the Countess of Béthizy offered their garters, and a shopkeeper gave his tie, but neither worked. Eventually, the duchess's belt was used. Roullet, 29.

17 Roullet, 29–30.

18 Joseph de Villèle wrote to his wife that the duchess jumped into Artois's arms when she saw Decazes and shouted, "Papa, Papa! Take that man away! I cannot bear the sight of him; he terrifies me. O heavens! He is going to poison my child!" Villèle, II, 351.

19 Louis XVIII knew of the attack by two in the morning.

20 It is not entirely clear when Berry said the Duchess was pregnant. Modern and contemporary sources contradict each other. Lucas-Dubreton wrote that after Berry was moved and Dupuytrin began to probe the wound, Berry was unable to control himself and started to cry out in pain. Distressed to see her husband in such pain, the duchess began to cry, and her laments led Berry to beg her to "control herself for the sake of our child." Lucas-Dubreton, 64–5. Evelyne Lever provided a completely different time-scenario. She suggests that Berry was just about to die when Louis XVIII arrived. Before he passed away, though, he begged for Louvel's life to be spared, pleaded for *bonté* for his legitimate and illegitimate children, and also asked the duchess to take care of their unborn child. Lever, 518–20. Contemporary versions were more consistent. Newspapers reported that the announcement followed shortly after the move to the second room; however, Berry was not screaming in pain but rather imploring his wife to take care of their unborn child. François-René Chateaubriand, in his popular account of Berry's life and the assassination published in the spring of 1820, concurred, quoting Berry as saying, "My dear, do not allow yourself to be overcome with grief; calm yourself for the sake of the child in your womb." Chateaubriand, *Mémoires, lettres et pièces*, 240.

21 Roullet, 42–5.

22 Ironically, Berry hated the bishop to whom he gave his final confession. Brown, 6.

23 Roullet's description of events differed from others' on a number of accounts. According to his version, a priest arrived shortly after Dupuytrin tried using his finger to stop the blood. Berry confessed soon after moving

to the second room, and he asked for Louvel's pardon only when he was in the upstairs office. Roullet, 28, 35.

24 When told of the duchess's decision to adopt Amy Brown's children, Louis XVIII immediately gave them noble titles: the Countess of Vierzon and the Countess of Issoudun.

25 Chateaubriand, *Mémoires, lettres et pièces*, 252–5. We will never know, of course, exactly what Berry said to Louis XVIII. A number of different versions were published. For example, the Bishop of Grenoble wrote that Berry said, "Pardon, Sire! Pardon for the man who struck me! At least spare his life! And let me commend to your care those who are dependent on me." BMG, T.5719–85. Roullet did not record a single word passing between Louis XVIII and Berry. In his version, Berry was no longer conscious by the time the king arrived. Roullet, 47–9.

26 Lucas-Dubreton, 65.

27 Roullet, 47.

28 After Berry's marriage, Louis XVIII had declared that the couple's first son would be named Bordeaux, because that city was the first to fly the *drapeau blanc* upon his return to France in 1814. Brown, 5.

29 Gontaut-Biron, II, 42.

30 Luz, 2.

INTRODUCTION

1 Charles X and his rather incompetent first minister, Jules Polignac, had grown tired of an uncooperative Chamber of Deputies and an unruly and highly critical media. Issued on 25 July 1830, the Four Ordinances dissolved the Chamber, amended the electoral law to assist their candidates in future elections, called for a new deputy election, and imposed strict censorship.

2 See Pilbeam, *The 1830 Revolution in France*.

3 Kroen, 294.

4 *Oubli* means "forgetting"; however, historical context suggests that "forgiveness" is more appropriate. This point is discussed in more detail in chapter three.

5 A virtual avalanche of political pamphlets flooded France during the Royalist Reaction. Parliamentary speeches were followed closely by the press as well, and lengthy extracts were included in most editions.

6 These provisions were established by the Charter.

7 Double-voters met at their respective department capitals to vote in the departmental colleges. Each department would have more than one arrondissment college, but only one departmental college.

8 See Thomas D. Beck, *French Legislators*, and Thomas D. and Martha Beck, *French Notables*, where it is shown that this assumption was not entirely true.

9 Mansel, *Louis XVIII*, 374.

CHAPTER ONE

1 Other important powers included the right to appoint *conseillers généraux, conseillers d'arrondissement*, and mayors.

2 Joseph de Villèle was appointed mayor of Toulouse after the Hundred Days. He won a seat in the Chamber of Deputies soon afterwards, and quickly became one of the most influential ultra royalists in the period leading up to the Royalist Reaction. He was appointed to the *Conseil* after the Royalist Reaction, and in December 1821, was made first minister, a post he retained until 1828.

3 Chateaubriand, *De la monarchie*, 1–2.

4 Waquet, 134.

5 Rosanvallon, 57–64.

6 Provence became Louis XVIII upon the death of Louis XVII in 1795.

7 Mansel, *Louis XVIII*, 182.

8 Bonald, *Législation primitive*, 153.

9 Bonald, *Législation primitive*, 156–7.

10 Chateaubriand, *De la monarchie*, c. XV.

11 Rémond, 32–3.

12 See Beck, *French Legislators* and Thomas and Martha Beck, *French Notables*, for a complete statistical analysis of the *cens* community.

13 Direct taxes included two other minor taxes that further increased the property component of the cens: the *contribution des portes et fenêtres*, a tax essentially based on the size of one's home; and the *contribution personnelle et mobilère*, a poll tax, plus a percentage of rent (usually 5 percent). In a few cases those two taxes were substantial. In 1820 Guillame Bois, a lawyer in Isère, paid a *portes et fenêtres* tax of 179 francs, and François de Rigaud de Seresin paid 481 francs in *personnelle* taxes and 407 francs in *portes et fenêtres*. BMG, *Liste des électeurs du collège de département*, 1820; ADHG, 2 M 23. *Liste des électeurs du collège de département, 1820.*

14 Beck, *French Legislators*, 138.

15 ADHG, 2 M 23. *Listes des électeurs des collèges d'arrondissement et de département, 1820.*

16 Beck and Beck, *French Notables*, 73.

17 The Chamber of Representatives was similar to the Chamber of Deputies. Men who met a property and age qualification voted in electoral colleges. The elections were held in May, 1815.

18 The most serious problem with the indirect system was that the 600 wealthiest men in one department could be far wealthier than the 600 of another. As a result, men who did not qualify in their own departments often went forum shopping to find a less affluent department where they could vote.

19 Lucas-Dubreton, 16–18; Resnick, 117–8.

20 Sauvigny, 130.

21 Mansel, 328.

22 Kroen, 43–60.

23 Mansel, 328; Sauvigny, 137; Stewart, 40.

24 Chateaubriand, *Mémoires d'outre-tombe*, III, 16. See also Chateaubriand, *De la monarchie*, 250–7.

25 An 1806 Imperial decree granted the right to pass such a law.

26 BMG, R 9676. Letter from Pison du Galland, 18 August 1816.

27 The deputies passed the law by 132 votes to 100, and the peers by 95 votes to 77.

28 Molé, IV, 469.

29 AP, 18:286, 25 January 1817, Molé (Peers). Unless otherwise indicated, all *archives parlementaires* cites are from the Chamber of Deputies.

30 AP, 28:74, 24 May 1820, Royer-Collard.

31 Of those thirty-five liberal deputies, half had accepted a government post during the Revolution, twenty-two had held a government post during the Empire, and seven had begun their legislative careers during the Hundred Days. A further thirteen had also been elected in May, 1815, the only election held during the Hundred Days, and another fourteen took a government post during the Hundred Days. Only five had held a post before the Revolution. Sauvigny, 163; Beck, *French Legislators*, Table 6.

32 In his memoirs, Elie Decazes estimated that one third of eligible voters turned out; therefore, the government had to rely on urban notables for votes, rather than royalist landowners who did not live in the cities. Atrocious road conditions also made long-distance travel time-consuming, uncomfortable, and expensive. Price, 7–8; Dunham, 4, 10, 14–26.

CHAPTER TWO

1 Waresquiel, *Richelieu*, 304.

2 Caron, 16.

3 *La Minerve*, 27 November 1819.

4 All three were born in Isère. Louis-Charles Sapey first joined the Chamber of Deputies during the Hundred Days. In 1820 he sat with the independents, or radical liberals. Baron Jacques-Fortunat Savoie-Rollin was a moderate liberal. Savoie-Rollin was elected deputy in 1815 and remained in the Chamber until his death. Antoine Français (better known as Français de Nantes) was an avid revolutionary, heading *La société des amis de la constitution* in Nantes. He was elected deputy to the Legislative Assembly for Loire-Inférieure, and gained fame for his fiery speeches. He did not accept an office during the Hundred Days. He returned to the legislature in 1819 and sat with Sapey and the radical liberals. He left public life in 1824.

5 Ironically, ultra voters in Isère may have conspired to elect Grégoire once it became clear that their candidate had no chance of winning. The ultras

hoped to embarrass the liberals by electing such a radical candidate. See 200–1.

6 *Le Conservateur*, 24 November 1819.

7 Molé, 332.

8 *La Minerve*, No. 95, February, 1820.

9 Rémusat, *Mémoires*, 416–17.

10 Cited by Cabanis, 237–8.

11 Her husband was Charles-François Armard, duc de Maillé de la Tour-Landry. In 1828 he became the *premier gentilhomme* of the King's Chamber.

12 The Count of Bastard headed the investigation. He filed a report to the Chamber of Peers on 15 May 1820. The conspiracy question was a central component of that report.

13 Maillé, 59.

14 Rochefoucauld, VI, 287.

15 Frénilly, 308.

16 *Le Masque Tombé*, 1818.

17 *La Minerve*, 21 February 1820.

18 JLI, 26 February 1820.

19 Ste-Aulaire, 20, 22, 40–6.

20 Jay, *Pétition adressée à la Chambre des Députés*; Spitzer, *Old Hatreds*, 31–2. The petition was discussed by the deputies on 25 April. The Parisian press followed the story closely: *La Renommée* devoted four pages to it, *Le Constitutionnel* five, and *Le Censeur Européen* six. Pamphleteers also published essays on the subject. In reality, liberals never appreciated the power and influence of real ultra-royalist secret societies such as the *Chevaliers de la Foi* and *l'Aa*. See Sevrin, II, 382–3; Spitzer, *Old Hatreds*, 31–2; Genevray, 363–4.

21 Bastard, 46–7.

22 Bastard, 73.

23 Sand was a devoted follower of Friedrich Ludwig Jahn, a leader of the *Burschenschaften*, a student association that rejected the modern world, preferring the values of the Middle Ages. Sand hated Kotzebue for his criticisms of the student movement. Jahn instructed his followers to carry with them a small dagger to signify their affinity with the huntsman and the forest dweller of the past. Sand used such a dagger to assassinate Kotzebue.

24 Spitzer, *Old Hatreds*, 24–5, 31.

25 Rey, *Mémoires sur la restauration*, 176.

26 Claude Mounier (1784–1843) was the son of Jean-Joseph Mounier, drafter of the Tennis Court Oath and President of the National Assembly. Claude Mounier was named a peer in 1819. He lost his seat in the *Conseil* after Richelieu's second ministry fell. After the July Revolution, he swore allegiance to Louis-Philippe and continued to sit in the Chamber of Peers.

27 AN, AB xix 3064.
28 That belief persisted into the twentieth century as well. See Artz, "The Electoral System," 213. Alan Spitzer dismisses the *comité* as a figment of the ultra royalists' overactive imagination. Spitzer, *Old Hatreds*, 34.
29 Vaulabelle, IV, 547, 550.
30 Rey, *Mémoires Politique*, 35. Questions exist regarding the accuracy of Rey's memoirs. Spitzer wrote that while Rey's manuscripts were "certainly self-justifying ... they have the ring of truth." He added: "Like the other leaders of contemporary secret societies Rey chiefly errs in exaggerating his own importance." Spitzer, *Old Hatreds*, 213. Georges Weill corroborated a number of Rey's contentions by cross-referencing them with other sources. Weill, "Les Mémoires de Joseph Rey," 291–307.
31 Rey, *Mémoires Politique*, 28–9, 67–8.
32 Vidalenc, *Les Demi-Solde*.
33 Spitzer, *Old Hatreds*, 23–4.
34 Spitzer, *Old Hatreds*, 18–39.
35 Maillé, 59.
36 At the time of the rebellion, Didier was a *maître des requêtes au conseil d'état*. Didier's initial plan was to take over Lyon, but he changed his mind and decided to attack Grenoble. At his trial, Didier revealed that he had left Paris seven months before the rebellion with 3,600 francs, journeyed through eighteen departments spending only thirty sous a day on himself, trying to organize a rebellion. Dreyfus, 131; Jardin, 288.
37 For example, on 6 March, a prominent radical liberal from Grenoble, a former notary named Proby, was arrested and exiled to Montbrison. He was prohibited from receiving any visitors or corresponding with his family for eight months, during which time he was not charged with any crime. BMG, R. 9676. Letter from Proby, 11 March 1816. In 1819, along with some fellow radicals, Proby wrote a series of virulently anti-Bourbon tracts, published as a semi-periodical under the name *L'Echo des Alpes*.
38 Cubitt, *The Jesuit Myth* and "Denouncing Conspiracy," 144–58.
39 Tackett, 691–713.
40 The following comments rely upon Geoffrey Cubitt, along with Hofman, "The Origins of the Theory of the Philosophe Conspiracy," and Kley, *Religious Origins of the French Revolution*.
41 Kley, 216.
42 Kley, 216.
43 The chronology is interesting. Tackett found that this was true well before the coming of war and threats of invasion, a finding that challenges much of what has been written to date about the conspiracy theories of the French Revolution. Tackett, 711–13.
44 Tackett, 707, 711–13.
45 Antoine de Barruel, *Les Helviennes*.

46 Riquet, 84–8.

47 Antoine de Barruel, *Histoire du Jacobinisme*, I, xiii.

48 The role of the family metaphor in Restoration royalism was noted briefly in the introduction and is discussed on pages 76–8.

49 Kroen, 109–60.

CHAPTER THREE

1 Kroen has argued that this is precisely what *union et oubli* meant. Kroen, 39–43.

2 See also Margadant, "Political Imaginary," 1464.

3 AN F 1CIII (Garonne-Haute) 6; ADHG, 2 M 24.

4 Mansel, *Louis XVIII*.

5 Resnick, 29.

6 Along with Richelieu, these three men dominated the *Conseil* during the Royalist Reaction. Siméon had the most important portfolio as minister of the interior.

7 Discours de … Pasquier, 4–5.

8 Kantorowicz, *The King's Two Bodies*.

9 Kantorowicz focused on the English monarchy, but he referred to the French monarchy as well. Kley has demonstrated the applicability of the thesis of the king's two bodies to the French monarchy. Kley, 18.

10 Kley, 19.

11 Merrick, *The Desacralization of the French Monarchy*, and Kley.

12 Kantorowicz, 22–3.

13 Mansel, *Court of France*, 90–116.

14 Mansel, *Court of France*, 134.

15 Waquet, 129, 137.

16 The law proclaiming the memorials was issued 19 January 1816. Louis XVI was executed on 21 January and Marie-Antoinette on 16 October. In 1825, by royal ordinance, the two ceremonies were combined and held on 21 January. ADI, 54 M 4. The joint memorials were held throughout France until the July Revolution.

17 Cobban, II, 71.

18 Waquet, 133.

19 Waquet, 129–30. Louis XVIII appointed Marquis de Dreux-Brézé to organize the national *fêtes*, a post he had held prior to 1789.

20 Waquet, 130.

21 AN, F1C I 106; cited by Waquet, 135.

22 Henri IV was the Restoration's most popular historical figure. For one thing, his life neatly corresponded to Louis XVIII's in that both returned to Paris promising to forget all past wrongs in the name of national unity. His diplomatic skills represented hope for those who desired a government ded-

icated to tolerance, liberty, and the rights of the people. Finally, as a great figure from the Bourbon past, all male Bourbons were eager to associate their names with his. Reinhard, 113–15, 133–4, 143–5, 147–53; Waquet, 136–7.

23 Waquet, 129–31.

24 AAT, 1 E. *Mandement de Monseigneur L'Archevêque de Toulouse, Qui ordonne les Prières de Quarante Heures, dans toutes les églises de son Diocèse, pour réparer les outrages faits à Dieu pendant la Révolution*, 14 September 1815; *Mandement de Monseigneur L'Archevêque de Toulouse, Qui ordonne des Prières publiques en action de grâces de l'heureux retour de Sa Majesté LOUIS XVIII, dans ses états*, 21 July 1815; BMT, T.5719–68, *Mandement de M.gr L'Évêque de Grenoble, pour ordonner un Te Deum en actions de grâces de l'heureux retour de S.M. Louis XVIII dans la Capitale de son royaume*, 21 July 1815.

25 ADI, 51 M 18; 54 M 4; BMG, T 5719:59–62.

26 ADI, 54 M 18.

27 ADI, 54 M 4.

28 BMG, T 5719–65, 7 January 1815.

29 BMG, T 5719–65, 7 January 1815.

30 ADI, M 54. M 4. Letter from Bishop Simon to Haussez, 3 March 1816.

31 Kroen, 43–59. Kroen noted that these "*fêtes of destruction*" were generally "stiff, formulaic and ineffective," except in regions where the White Terror was strongest. In addition, while most physical reminders of the Revolution and the Empire were removed from public places, the campaign was a complete failure with regard to private possessions. Kroen, 60.

32 Kroen, 58.

33 As 1815 came to a close, Vaublanc seemed particularly intent on those instructions being followed, and to that end he sent two reminders to the prefects before the ceremony. ADI, 54 M 4. *Circulaire*, No 47. Vaublanc to Prefect of Isère, 20 December 1815; ADI, 54 M 4, Letter from Vaublanc to Prefect of Isère, 9 January 1816.

34 The letter focused on Marie-Antoinette's role as a martyred Christian, rather than as a victim of the Revolution: "Marie-Antoinette expressed all the sentiments which Religion could inspire in a truly Christian Queen and a most loving mother." BMT, T 5719:74.

35 ADI, 54 M 4. Letter from Minister of Interior to Prefects, 7 January 1824.

36 BMG, T 5719–74. *Lettre de MGr L'Évêque de Grenoble, A MM. les Archiprêtres et à tous les Curés de son Diocèse, Pour ordonner le service anniversaire de MARIE-ANTOINETTE, Reine de France*, 17 January 1816.

37 BMT, uncatalogued. Proclamation of Rémusat, 23 December 1815.

38 "Such a dreadful catastrophe only serves to confirm the timeless truth that in a revolutionary crisis the extreme goodness of kings is a sure guarantee of their ruin and of the loss of their states." BMT, uncatalogued.

Proclamation of Demouis, interim Mayor of Toulouse, to his Fellow Citizens, 10 January 1816.

39 BMT, uncatalogued. Ordinance of Thoron, interim Mayor of Toulouse, *Concernant la célébration de l'Anniversaire du 21 Janvier*, 18 January 1817.

40 The following phrase was added in 1827: "for the loyal people of Toulouse who have given so many proofs of their devotion to the august Bourbon family." BMT, uncatalogued. Ordinance of Baron de Montbel, Mayor of Toulouse, *Concernant la Célébration de l'Anniversaire de 21 Janvier*, 18 January 1827.

41 According to a report from the mayor of St Jean de Bornay to the prefect, the curé became particularly exercised over the issue of married priests. ADI, 54 M 4, 31 November 1818.

42 Bishop Simon, the sub-prefect of the arrondissement of Vienne, the minister of the *police générale*, and the mayor of St Jean-de-Bournay all sent reports of the incident to the prefect. ADI, 54 M 4.

43 For example, Angoulême visited Grenoble for three days in November, 1815, but he did little more than meet public officials and review troops. The purpose of the visit was probably to reconcile Isère to the Second Restoration. In a poster displayed throughout the department, the Count of Montlivault, prefect of Isère, published a statement from Angoulême stating that neither he nor the royal family resented the people of Isère: "I believe that the inhabitants of Grenoble took no part in the events of March ... They were suffering, but not unfaithful. I will say this to the King, who knows it already." ADI, 51 M 20. Proclamation of ... Montlivaut ... to the Inhabitants of Isère, 24 November 1815. During Angoulême's next visit in May, 1820, only some one thousand francs were spent. ADI, 51 M 20. That visit became a national incident after students hurled insults at the duke to protest against the exceptional laws. See page 177.

44 The passing of time naturally affected the ceremonies. For example, in an 1817 memorial service for Louis XVI in Toulouse, four men who had served in the royal army prior to the Revolution joined the procession and were honoured after the service. By 1824, they had died. BMT, uncatalogued.

45 Waquet, 132.

46 Cholvy, 33–56.

47 Klinck, 200.

48 Neely, 132.

49 Rémond, 43.

50 Pilbeam, *1830 Revolution*, 149.

51 Oechslin, 56, 62.

52 Chateaubriand, *Mémoires, lettres et pièces*, 286.

53 Villèle, II, 347.

54 Rémond, 28–9; Mansel, 341–2.

55 Bonald, *Législation primitive*, 150–1.

56 Maistre, *Considérations*, 132–3.

57 Maistre, *Considérations*, 166.

58 Maistre, *Considérations*, 153.

59 Bonald, *Législation primitive*, 145.

60 Initially, some ultras proposed a lower *cens* to take advantage of a perceived liberal backlash. However, by 1817 the ultras argued for the double-vote model or an indirect system.

61 Gibson, "The French nobility," *Elites in France*; Higgs, *Nobility*; Higgs, "Politics and Landownership," 105–21; Tudesq, *Les Grand Notables*.

62 Broglie, II, 209.

63 Bagge, 99–100.

64 Gibson, 272; Langlois, "*Le catholicisme au féminin*," 29–53.

65 Rémusat, *Correspondance*, III, 92.

66 Pilbeam, *Middle Classes*, 242.

67 Thureau-Dangin, 121.

68 Constant, *Principe de politique*. Cited in Bagge, 58.

69 Rey, *Mémoires Politique*, 9–10.

70 Cobb, 170–1.

71 Rémusat, "*Le Gouvernement représentatif.*"

72 Cobban, II, 94.

73 Chateaubriand, *Mémoires d'outre-tombe*, t. IV.

CHAPTER FOUR

1 Lever, 520; Nabour, 103.

2 Étienne, a liberal writer, proposed that those paying a 600-franc *cens* or more vote for one-third of the Chamber, and the 300–600 franc voters cast ballots for the remaining two-thirds. Harpaz, 131–33.

3 AP, 26:220, 15 February 1820, Decazes.

4 Villèle, II, *Mémoires*, 351. In reality, Artois embraced Decazes and told him to tell Louis XVIII about the attack.

5 JLI, 30 March 1820.

6 Molé, 329.

7 Villèle, II, *Mémoires*, 20 February 1820, 343–4.

8 Polignac, 71.

9 The Marquis de la Maisonfort was a writer and *émigré* who published several important counter-revolutionary pamphlets. On 19 July 1820, he was made France's ambassador to Tuscany. Maisonfort, 327.

10 Waresquiel, 389.

11 Weiss, 281.

12 BMG, R 9676. Letter from Josephine Badon, 7 March 1817.

13 Baron Charles Lemercher de Longpré d'Haussez was born to a family of magistrats in 1778. During the Revolution, Haussez joined the royalist

army in Normandy, and he remained a committed royalist for the rest of his life. Nevertheless, Haussez did well under the Empire and was rewarded with the title of baron in 1805. He almost destroyed his career by running for deputy during the Hundred Days, but fortunately for him he lost. Napoleon's defeat at Waterloo marked the beginning of Haussez's rise to national prominence. He won a seat in the *Chambre introuvable*, sitting with the ministerial minority. Haussez ran unsuccessfully for re-election in 1816, but was appointed prefect of Landes in 1817. In 1819, he became prefect of Gard. In February 1820, Louis XVIII appointed him prefect of Isère, where he remained until 1824. He became minister of the marine in 1829 during the Polignac ministry, and was a signator to the Four Ordinances in 1830. Haussez's career ended with the July Revolution, after which he went into exile.

14 Louis Marie Joseph de St-Chamans was appointed an *auditeur au conseil* by Napoleon in 1810. After the Hundred Days, he was named prefect of Isère and then Vaucluse, before settling in as prefect of Haute-Garonne in 1817. He remained there until November 1823, at which time he had to step down because of ill-health. St-Chamans died shortly thereafter.

15 ADI, 51 M 21.

16 ADI, 51 M 21.

17 ADI, 52 M 24, folder 12.36. The men were found not-guilty at trial.

18 ADI, 52 M 24, folder 12.19.

19 ADI, 52 M 24, folder 12.37. In his journal, Weiss noted that a soldier in Chamars had the impudence to "express his revolutionary or Bonapartist beliefs." He added that two members of the bourgeoisie denounced him to the *lieutenant du roi*, and he was arrested.

20 ADHG, 4 M 45. Letter from Sub-Prefect of Villefranche to Mayor of Villefranche, 18 February 1820; ADHG, 4 M 45. Letter from Sub-Prefect of Villefranche to St-Chamans, 19 February 1820.

21 ADHG, 4 M 45. Letters from Sub-Prefect of St Gaudens to St-Chamans, 18 February 1820 and 21 February 1820.

22 ADHG, 4 M 45. Confidential letter from Sub-Prefect of St Gaudens to St-Chamans, 1 March 1820.

23 ADHG, 4 M 45. Report from Police Commissioner to St-Chamans, 19 February 1820.

24 ADHG, 4 M 45. St-Chamans to Minister of Police, 21 February 1819. The individual reportedly said, "Oh! The royalists are showing their faces because of the changes to the electoral laws, but before a week is out they will be forced to hide them again."

25 ADHG, 4 M 45. Letters from Sub-Prefect of Muret to St-Chamans, 18 February 1820, 19 February 1820, 21 February 1820. Letter from St-Chamans to Sub-Prefect of Muret, 22 February 1820.

26 ADHG, 4 M 45. Letter from Mayor of Blagnac to St-Chamans, 25 February 1820.

27 ADHG, 4 M 45. Letter from *Procureur général* to Mayor of St Sulpice (Tarn), 22 February 1820; Letter from *Procureur général* to Mayor of Buzet-sur-Tarn, 23 February 1820.

28 This contravened art. 475 of the *Code Pénal*.

29 ADHG, 6 T 1, 6 T 2; Rémond, 50–1; Parent-Lardeur, 113, 167–8.

30 The *Journal de Grenoble* and the *Journal de Toulouse* were moderate royalist newspapers. As noted above, the *Journal Libre de l'Isère* was a liberal publication.

31 JDT, 21 February 1820, 1–2.

32 It was reported that after examining Berry's corpse doctors expressed shock that he had lived for over six hours after being stabbed. Religious leaders used the doctors' report as proof that the Bourbons enjoyed a magical relationship with God. JDG, 22 February 1820, 1. Bishop Simon wrote that surgeons and doctors declared unanimously that the fact he lived so long after the attack was a true miracle and must be attributed to supernatural causes. In his mind, the reason for the miracle was "that truly Christian charity which distinguishes our royal princes and was so marked in the Duke of Berry." BMG, T.5719–85. *Mandement de Mgr, l'Évêque de Grenoble ...*, 20 March 1820. Chateaubriand was not so sure that Providence shone brightly on Berry. He felt a dark cloud followed the Berry name. "Almost all of the Dukes of Berry (including Louis XIV who once bore that name) met an unhappy end." Chateaubriand, *Mémoires, lettres et pièces*, 216.

33 Bishop Simon wrote that Louis XVIII closed Berry's eyes "with a feeling or sentiment that seemed to transcend humanity." BMG, T.5719–85.

34 JDT, 21 February 1820.

35 JLI, 29 February 1820.

36 JDT, 21 February 1820.

37 JDT, 21 February 1820, Supplement.

38 Baron Gary described Louvel as "another Ravaillac who, with a parricide's hand, has shed the blood of Henri IV." JDT, 21 February 1820, Supplement, 2–3.

39 *La Minerve*, 21 February 1820.

40 JLI, 22 February 1820.

41 JLI, 26 February 1820. In the subsequent issue, the editors included the following short verse from a fable called *La pierre à fusil*. The verse suggested that the royalists' false accusations against the liberals would ultimately force the liberals to turn against the Bourbon regime: "Oh, dangerous stone, with fire in the vein, have you come to scatter the evil you contain? Oh, fool, the fault is yours. If a spark should break free, the blame is not mine, but his who strikes me." JLI, 29 February 1820.

42 JDT, 21 February 1820.

43 JDT, 21 February 1820. In the *Journal Libre de l'Isère*, Louvel was quoted as stating that a weeping Decazes asked only one question: Was the knife poisoned? JLI, 26 February 1820.

44 JDT, 21 February 1820.

45 JLI, 24 February 1820.

46 JLI, 22 February 1820.

47 Bastard, 37–40.

48 JLI, 29 February 1820.

49 "That unspeakable lie is more than a calumny when one recalls that three days ago the same publication was calling the royalists to arms. Was it a signal?" JLI, 24 February 1820.

50 JLI, 4 March 1820.

51 Bastard, 71.

52 In Chateaubriand's version, Berry cried out for his wife from time to time, and the duchess replied, "I am here: I will never leave you." Chateaubriand noted proudly that the duchess offered her belt as a bandage. Chateaubriand, *Mémoires, lettres et pièces*, 229. In fact, she first offered her garters, but their elasticity made them ineffective. Roullet, 29.

53 JDT, 21 February 1820.

54 Vinck, 10650, 11 February 1836.

55 Adhémar, 195–7.

56 The editors (*éditeurs*) financed the publication of an illustration. They either sold the illustrations themselves or distributed them to retailers. The engravers (*graveurs)* did the actual drawing and printing. A third person sometimes designed the illustration.

57 Palmer, 38.

58 Henin, 14,015, 25 February 1820.

59 Adhémar, 142.

60 Illustrations had to be deposited with the *Bureau de l'imprimerie et de la librairie* before being sold. The *bureau* was created by ordinance on 24 November 1814 and revised by the press law of 1820.

61 Johnson, *Art History*, 12, 16–17. According to Johnson, lithography reduced the cost of reproducing a particular scene from tens or even hundreds of thousands of francs to merely hundreds.

62 Johnson, *French Lithography*, 17.

63 Thiers, "*De la lithographie*." Cited in Johnson, *French Lithography*, document VII, 46–8.

64 By the middle of the century, lithography was the dominant technique.

65 Vinck, 10547, February, 1820.

66 Although most crime and death scenes contained factual errors, few assassination illustrations were outright fabrications, apart from allegorical or symbolic images. The exception was a picture of an alleged visit by the

duchess and Bordeaux to the Château of Chambord in 1821. Vinck, 10721, 23 July 1821.

67 Vinck, 10579, 26 February 1820.

68 See Vinck, 10580; 10584, 23 February 1820. The caption reads: while the nation was overcome by the horror of the crime, he alone did not despair; and with magnanimous heart begged for the pardon of his cowardly assassin. Thus a Bourbon seeks revenge and thus he dies.

69 See Vinck, 10580; 10584, 23 February 1820.

70 Vinck, 10643, 25 February 1820.

71 ADHG, 4 M 45. Letter from Bellegarde to St-Chamans, 9 March 1820; Letter from Mayor of Caraman to St-Chamans, 2 March 1820; JDT, 8 March 1820.

72 ADI, 51 M 21; ADHG, 4 M 45.

73 ADHG, 4 M 45, 24 February 1820.

74 The Municipal Council of Pamier (Ariège) called upon Louis XVIII to "put an end to the misfortunes which have so long afflicted the descendants of our good king Henry." JDT, 6 March 1820.

75 JDT, 24 February 1820. The editors added that some 500 signatures from private citizens were attached to the address, and that the signatures were from all classes and professions.

76 ADHG, 6 T 2. *Circulaire* from Richelieu to Prefects.

77 Weiss, 21 February 1820, 281.

78 ADHM, 4 M 45, 5 April 1820.

79 JDT, 6 March 1820.

80 Henin, 14,036.

81 Waquet, 85–6.

CHAPTER FIVE

1 Not all radical liberals supported Grégoire. Benjamin Constant and liberal publications, such as, *La renommée* and *La Minerve*, campaigned against Grégoire.

2 Sylvia Neely suggested that the inabilty of Constant and others to prevent Grégoire's election was clear proof that no single *comité directeur* controlled liberals in the provinces. In her view, while yielding considerable power, deputies had to depend on journalists and local politicians to take the initiative, and such people were often more radical than the liberal leaders. Neely, 118. In his memoirs, Baron de Barante wrote that many leading liberals, especially Constant, were against Grégoire's candidacy. However, the need for popularity, a fear of newspapers, an intimacy with journalists, and a condescension to young people and zealous partisans precluded a formal protest. Barante, II, 383.

3 BMG, O 6969.

4 BMG, O 6969.

5 BMG, O 7907. *Dernier Mot, à MM Électeurs du département de l'Isère, sur l'abbé Grégoire*, 1819.

6 BMG, O 7907.

7 BMG, O 7903. *Duchesne, avocat et électeur. Aux Électeurs de l'Isère. Réponse au Libelle intitulé. Notice historique tirée des Moniteurs du temps*, 10 September 1819. Most pamphlets were anonymous. Duchesne was one of the few willing to include his name. Duchesne charged that pamphleteers who attacked Grégoire anonymously were cowards; however, most pro-Grégoire pamphlets were anonymous as well. Pro-Grégoire pamphleteers loved to quote Louis XVIII's famous phrases, "Keep your word: *oubli et union*" and "Forget all political crimes; the revolution is over." See BMG, O 7906 and BMG, U 2997. *Aux Électeurs Libéraux du Département de l'Isère*, 1819.

8 Duchesne added that it was unfair to label Grégoire a regicide without considering the conditions that existed in France during the Revolution: "At that period, to speak in an intemperate manner of the king and royalty was to give way to the flood of depraved public opinion, to fall into the common error; to make a judgement on men involved in politics in those disastrous times it is necessary to choose the moment when the blindfold of general illusion had fallen, the moment when each citizen could become himself again, and act according to his own heart." O 7903.

9 Grégoire used the same argument in his own electoral pamphlet. BMG, O 7923. *Lettre de M. Grégoire.*

10 BMG, O 7903.

11 BMG, O 7911. *Deuxième Tour de Scrutin*, September 1819.

12 BMG, O 7906 By R**. *Aux Électeurs Libéraux du département de L'Isère*, 1819.

13 BMG, U 2997. *Aux Électeurs Libéraux du Département de L'Isère*, 1819; BMG, O 7891. By A. Duchand (*Electeur, non éligible*) *Pensées d'un Électeur*, 9 September 1819.

14 BMG, O 7891. Duchand advised the voters to elect only those men of independent spirit and mind, sincerely devoted to constitutional principles, who unlike the ministerials did not want power for themselves, nor for their "*créatures*," men like Lafayette, Voyer-d'Argenson, and Dupont (de l'Eure). An anonymous pamphleteer seconded Duchand, suggesting that one should only vote for those "who keep their eyes firmly on the constitution; they are strangers to deception and ambition." BMG, O 7894.

15 BMG, O 7894.

16 Villèle made the same argument during the debate over the double vote, arguing that France's newly formed institutions needed legislative protection against the revolutionary forces that threatened to topple the government: "We should replace the present system with a combination of methods: it

must include mechanisms that would inhibit reckless actions; and it must be based on a fundamental principle that would ensure the conservation and stability of the representative government which we wish to establish." BMT, LmC6624. *Discours de M. De Villèle, Extrait du Moniteur,* 20 July 1820.

17 BMG, O 7891.

18 BMG, U 2997.

19 The final results were as follows. In the first round, 1019 votes were cast; 997 in the second. Savoie-Rollin (801 votes), François de Nantes (718 votes), and Sapey (707 votes) were elected after the first round. Grégoire received 512 votes in the second. M. Rogniat, the ministerial candidate, came behind Grégoire with 353 votes. AN, F 1 cIII Isere 4. *Procès-verbal du collège électoral de l'Isère,* 1819.

20 The reading of the names of newly elected deputies began on 2 December 1819. At that time, the question of Grégoire's admission was adjourned to a later date. A full debate regarding Grégoire occurred on December 6. AP, 25:712–715, 2 December 1819.

21 AP, 25:727, 6 December 1819, Laisné.

22 AP, 25:730, 6 December 1819, Bourdonnaye.

23 AP, 25:741, 6 December 1819, Salaberry.

24 AP, 25:731, 6 December 1819, Manuel. Several deputies pointed out that in the first days of the Restoration Louis XVIII had accepted another regicide into his cabinet, Fouché. Mellon, 54.

25 AP, 25:731, 6 December 1819, Manuel. In *De la doctrine,* Benjamin Constant noted that revolutionaries and Bonapartists were just as French as counter-revolutionaries and royalists. "It is not necessary to pronounce political excommunication against all those who served either Bonaparte or the Republic, to declare them born enemies of our present institutions ... without reflecting that these men are France itself." Constant, *De la doctrine,* 10.

26 Schermerhorn, 328.

27 Benjamin Constant drafted the *Acte Additionel* for Napoleon during the Hundred Days. Cobban, II, 68.

28 Haussez, I, 322–7. The election results were helped along by Haussez's decision to move the electoral college from the liberal-dominated Grenoble to the town of Vienne. Haussez claimed the move infuriated the liberals, but helped rally royalist voters.

29 ADHG, 6 T 2.

30 ADHG, 6 T 2.

31 Waresquiel, 302.

32 AP 26:368, 7 March 1820, Siméon.

33 AP 26:227, 15 February 1820, Pasquier; 26:248, 26 February 1820, Broglie (Peers); 26:277, 28 February 1820, Pasquier; 26:296, 1 March 1820, Siméon; 26:475, 21 March 1820, Labourdonnaye.

34 The law was passed on 16 January 1817. It allowed the government to arrest individuals suspected of "plots and conspiracies against the king, state security, or the royal family." Within twenty-four hours after the arrest, the accused had to be shown a copy of the *procès-verbal*. AP, 18:192–3. The law expired 12 January 1818.

35 Article 11 of the Declaration of the Rights of Man defined freedom of the press as follows: "The free communication of thoughts and opinions is one of the most precious rights of man; every citizen may speak, write, and print freely, except for being held responsible for the abuse of this liberty in the cases specified by the law." Fernand Terrou suggests that we must measure liberty of the press against this standard until the Charter of 1881, which finally ended censorship. For the most part, France's press struggled for independence, despite occasional moments of freedom. Terrou, "De 1815 à 1871," *Histoire générale de la presse française*, II, 3–12.

36 Censorship never really disappeared. In his Declaration of Ouen of 2 May 1814, Louis XVIII promised that the liberty of the press would be respected, except for "the precautions necessary for public tranquility." By the law of 21 October 1814, all writings over twenty pages were subject to government censorship.

37 The act was passed on 22 April 1815.

38 The press law was passed on 8 August 1815, and it came complete with a system of authorization and prohibition. Subsequent legislation not directly related to censorship also increased the government's power over the press. The law of 9 November 1815 provided for prison terms of three to five years for those charged with attacking the government and the established order. The laws of 20 and 27 December 1815 conferred special jurisdiction to the *Cour prévôtale* over all plots or conspiracies, both direct and indirect, intended to overthrow or weaken the government.

39 The law was passed 17 May 1819, and survived the July Revolution.

40 Caron, 16–17.

41 ADHG, 6 T 2.

42 AP, 26:370, 7 March 1820, Siméon.

43 AP, 26:630, 23 March 1820, Pasquier. Duke de Lévis told the Peers that firm action was needed to protect the Church and the Monarchy, France's two most beloved institutions, to preserve order and liberty, and to forever end the possibility of another revolution. AP, 26:256, 26 February 1820, Lévis.

44 AP, 26:386, 8 March 1820.

45 AP, 26:223, 23 February 1820, Rochefoucauld (Peers). See also, AP 26:256, 26 February 1820, Lévis; 26:598, 22 March 1820, Josse-Beauvoir.

46 AP, 26:357, 6 March 1820, Courvoisier. See also, AP 26:598, 22 March 1820, Josse-Beauvoir.

47 AP, 26:381, 8 March 1820, Bonald.

48 AP, 26:381, 8 March 1820, Bonald.

49 As the ultras grew more powerful after Berry's assassination, Bonald became bolder in his defense of the Monarchy and the Church. See Klinck, 197–204.

50 AP, 26:598, 22 March 1820, Josse-Beauvoir.

51 JLI, 14 March 1820.

52 The *Journal Libre de l'Isère* equated the press law with censorship under Napoleon: "The more the ministry expresses aversion to the person of Bonaparte, the more it turns to the system of that despot. What is the new tribunal of censorship proposed in this last bill, but the imperial and senatorial censorship tribunal?" JLI, 24 February 1820.

53 AP, 26:572, 16 March 1820, Laisné.

54 AP, 26:384, 8 March 1820, Laisné; 26:274, 28 February 1820, Lanjuinais (Peers); 26:475, 13 March 1820, Manuel; 26:577, 21 March 1820, Chauvelin; 26:629, 23 March 1820, Lafayette. Neely, 136.

55 AP, 26:645, 23 March 1820, Constant. Never one to restrict himself to a single view, Lafayette also supported Constant's position. Referring to his own colourful past, Lafayette accused the government of reimposing certain aspects of the Old Regime: "Sirs, thirty-three years ago at the Assembly of Notables of 1787, I was the first to call for the abolition of the *lettres de cachet*: I vote today against their re-establishment." From a speech on 8 March 1820. Cited in Neely, 136.

56 AP, 26:476, 13 March 1820, Constant. *Le Censeur Européen* referred sarcastically to the seemingly endless need for French governments to impose censorship. After the press and liberty laws were passed, *Le Censeur Européen* proclaimed "Freedom is no more! The Chamber of Deputies has voted for slavery! Does any authority have the power to make us free men or slaves? No, freedom is still alive; it lives deep in our hearts, and will only die when we do."

57 In the Chamber of Peers, the Duke of Broglie, a leading doctrinaire, argued that the press law would re-establish the rights of the old aristocracy. "It gives the principle of heredity a special status for those who rule over us." AP, 26:249, 26 February 1820, Broglie.

58 Two days before the press law was passed, the *Journal Libre de l'Isère* wrote that the new law "leaves citizens' liberties to the discretion of dictators, and dispenses these all-powerful arbiters of our destiny from any feelings of humanity toward those on whom the ministerial party are impatient to take revenge." JLI, 28 March 1820. Two inhabitants of Grenoble, Joseph Rey and François Régnier, sent a petition to the Chamber of Deputies urging the liberals to reject the laws and accusing the royalists of pretending to mourn Berry's memory in order to further their own private agendas: "You will comfort Justice as it mourns … You will not be the accomplices of those dreadful hypocritical men who only pretend horror at civil strife in order to have more freedom to foment it."

59 JLI, 22 February 1820.

60 The editors added that the press law was merely the first step in a campaign to destroy the liberals: "It is particularly odious that the government wishes to silence everyone, at the same time as it is proposing major changes to the electoral laws." JLI, 24 February 1820.

61 JLI, 24 February 1820.

62 JLI, 21 March 1820.

63 JLI, 23 March 1820 and 25 March 1820.

64 JLI, 24 March 1820.

65 Weiss, 28 March 1820, 286–7.

66 Thirty-four cities applied to have a law faculty. Nine were established, a substantial drop from the pre-1789 total of nineteen. The nine schools were stationed in Paris, Aix-en-Provence, Caen, Dijon, Grenoble, Poitiers, Rennes, Strasbourg and Toulouse. Until 1864, only those nine offered law degrees in France. Weisbuch, 84–95, 292.

67 AN, F17 1977 339. Letter from Gremane and Montivaut to Minister of Interior, 06/04/1820.

68 AN, F17 1977 163, 21 June 1817.

69 AN, F17 1977 65. Letter from Bertier to Minister of Interior, 17 July 1817.

70 AN, F17 1917 90, 1 July 1817.

71 ADI, 26 T 17. Letter from Cuvier to Rector, 15 April 1820.

72 ADHG, 6 T 1. *Direction générale* from Mounier to Prefects, 22 April 1820.

73 BMG, O 7934. Martainville, 34–5.

74 BMG, 6956. *Les choses comme elles vont*, 17 May 1820.

75 In cases where the order arrived too late, the memorial services were held on 31 March.

76 BMG, T 5719–85.

77 ADI, 51 M 21.

78 JDG, 7 March 1820.

79 JDT, 28 February 1820.

80 Vinck, 10560, 8 April 1820.

81 Vinck, 10568, 3 April 1820; 10570, 30 March 1820; 10571, 3 April 1820. The caption reads: "When the Duke of Berry felt his strength weakening and he knew the end was near, he asked to see his daughter. When she was presented to him, he embraced her tenderly, then lifted his arms over this sad token of his marriage and gave the following benediction: Dear child, I hope you have more happiness than your tragic family. At these words, everyone present burst into tears, but the Prince, after carrying out this pious duty, maintained until the end a constant and grand spirit. A Christian and Frenchman, he died a hero, having forgiven his assassin, and having dedicated his final breath to his country."

82 Vinck, 10562, 15 March 1820; 10563, 20 March 1820; 10566, 4 April 1820; 10567, 20 April 1820. Delpech published the first recorded assassination illustration. Vinck, 10584, 23 February 1820.

83 JDT, 4 July 1820. The article also informed readers that the duchess had decided to maintain Berry's tradition of giving all his servants sixty francs at Easter.

84 All three anecdotes were printed in the JDT, 24 March 1820.

85 JDT , 17 April 1820.

86 Vinck, 10626. The text below each illustration explained the heroic deed. The illustrations were taken from the works of other artists, such as Fragonard and Desenne. The booklet was sold through the mail, and divided into two parts. Delivery cost nine francs. The advertisement for the booklet boldly stated that "this work already has a great number of very distinguished subscribers."

87 Vinck, 10626 (7).

88 Vinck, 1026 (13). The caption reads: "Among the demonstrations of the Duke of Berry's zeal to serve the public good, one can cite his conduct at the freight company's workshop. He is seen in the midst of the flames, directing the firemen, encouraging their efforts, and offering aid and comfort to the injured."

89 The *Régiments de chasseurs*, in which Berry was *colonel-général*, mourned for one month, and other army corps mourned for twenty-one days. Bishop Simon called Berry "the idol of warriors." BMG, T 5719–85.

90 JLI, 25 March 1820.

91 JDT, 3 March 1820.

92 JDT, 21 February 1820.

93 Chateaubriand, *Mémoires, lettres et pièces*, 283–4.

94 Chateaubriand, *Mémoires, lettres et pièces*, 105–6.

95 JDT, 21 February 1820.

96 Roullet, 42–7.

97 Vinck, 10572. Some illustrations more realistically conveyed Berry's physical condition. See Vinck, 10578, 23 March 1820; 10545, 26 February 1820; 10581.

98 "Act of Goodness" told the story of Berry, dressed in military gear and escorted by a soldier, hunting in the forest of Rambouillet. He came across two deserters, who threw themselves at his feet begging for mercy. Berry presented the pair to Louis XVIII and successfully obtained a pardon. Vinck, 10626 (6). In "Greatness of Spirit," Berry is shown leading 4,000 soldiers into Bethune in 1814. Seditious cries were heard from 300 rebel troops. When his efforts to convince them to change their cries to *Vive le roi!* failed, Berry let the rebels go, leaving them "astonished at such greatness of spirit." 10626 (11)

99 Vinck, 10626 (12). The caption reads: " 'In the midst of a pitched battle during a campaign of Condé's army, the Duke of Berry, leading his troops forward, is waiting to charge. A foreign general suggested he move back to avoid danger, to which the Duke replied: Those at the back must ride

quickly if they want to keep pace with me. A son of France does not wait for glory, he rides forth to meet it.' "

100 Chateaubriand, *Mémoires, lettres et pièces*, 242.

101 Chateaubriand, *Mémoires, lettres et pièces*, 250–1.

102 Chateaubriand, *Mémoires, lettres et pièces*, 250–1.

103 Bastard, 26.

104 Vinck, 10617, 12 February 1823. The sculpture was finished in 1825 and placed in the Chapelle de St Charles in the Eglise St Louis at Versailles. It was moved after 1830, but then put back in 1852.

105 Vinck, 10609, 26 September 1822. The illustration was a lithograph made of a painting by an artist named Monsiau. He presented the painting to Louis XVIII in August of 1820. *Le Moniteur* reported that the king and the duchess enjoyed the painting immensely. *Le Moniteur*, 17 August 1820.

106 Vinck, 10610. Below the illustration, Espérance, symbolized by her anchor, gazes upon the miracle child. The shields of France and the Two Siciles lean against the crib.

107 Vinck, 10608, 13 March 1820.

108 See Margadant, "Duchess de Berry."

109 Mansel, *The Court of France*. The annual expenditure of the Restoration's royal court paled in comparison with its Old Regime predecessor; however, finances were extremely tight in the first five years after Napoleon's final defeat, and so in that context the money spent on the royal court was not insignificant. Moreover, the establishment of the royal court occupied an essential philosophical place in the royalists' collective psyche that belies the amount spent. Interestingly, Mansel criticized Louis XVIII for worrying too much about balanced budgets. He suggested lavish spending on the royal court would have yielded political benefits that far outweighed the economic costs. Mansel, *Louis XVIII*, 189–91.

110 JDT, 21 February 1820. This portrait of the duchess in mourning (Vinck, 10604) was a fragment of a larger painting by François-Joseph Kinson, who in 1819 was named official painter for the royal courts of Louis XVIII and the Duke of Angoulême. Kinson's painting was displayed at the Salon of 1822.

111 Vinck, 10547, February 1820; 10549, 22 March 1820; 10554.

112 Vinck, 10593, 2 May 1820; 10566, 4 April 1820; 10563, 20 March 1820.

113 Chateaubriand, *Mémoires, lettres et pièces*, 229.

114 Note that chronology will not be strictly adhered to. Illustrations related to the duchess's Good Wife persona were published throughout the Restoration. For the purposes of clarity, it seems helpful to include all these materials in the following discussion, even if they were not all published in March or April. At the same time, her Good Wife persona was most clearly defined during those months and its treatment belongs, chronologically speaking, in this chapter.

115 The Berry mourning illustrations constituted approximately 20 to 25 percent of the total number of assassination illustrations, and they were published throughout the Restoration. By comparison, almost half of all assassination illustrations were crime and death scenes, and the great majority were published in the three months following Berry's death.

116 Vinck, 10602. There is no known publication date for this illustration. However, two other similar illustrations of the duchess cutting her hair were published in April and May, 1820. Presumably, this one appeared on the market at the same time. See Vinck, 10600, 28 April 1820; 10601, 13 May 1820.

117 See Vinck, 10713, 17 December 1830.

118 Vinck, 10600, 28 April 1820;10597, 8 March 1820.

119 Vinck, 10623, 13 March 1820.

120 Vinck, 10695, October 1820.

121 Louvel's non-descript image was discussed earlier. See pages 124–5.

122 Vinck, 10630, 7 April 1820. See also, Vinck, 10638.

123 Vinck, 10627, 24 March 1820.

124 Louis XVIII ordered the Opera House demolished after the assassination.

125 The Lallemand Subscription was organized by two Parisians: M. Rouen, a lawyer at the *Cour royale* and M. Mary, a café owner. Contributions were fixed at one franc.

126 AN, F 1 cI 107 2.

127 JLI, 05/23/1820. ADI, 51 M 21. Haussez to Royer-Deloche, 30 May 1821.

128 ADHG, 2 M 23 and 2 M 24. *Liste des électeurs formant le collège électoral du département*, 11 July 1820.

129 Hocquart was the *Premier président de la cour royale de Toulouse*. He was elected deputy for Haute-Garonne by a wide margin in the 1820 November deputy election. Comte de Péré, a member of the Chamber of Peers, and the Marquis de Faumels each gave one hundred francs, the second highest individual contributions.

130 Beck, *French Notables*, 39–72, 155. Viscounte Marie de Marin and Baron François de Papus listed their occupations for the Berry Subscription as members of the Municipal Council of Muret. In electoral lists, their occupations were posted as *colonel de cavalerie* and *propriétaire*, respectively.

131 The *Division d'administration département, 1er Bureau* gave forty francs, the *Secrétariat général et division du personnel* seventy-nine francs, the *Bureau d'administration communale*, 126 francs (the department head gave ten francs), and the *Bureau des journaux (Administration département et de la police)* thirty-four francs. AN F 1 cI 107 2.

132 ADI, 51 M 21. *Direction générale* from Mounier to Haussez, 2 October 1820. Earlier that year in a *circulaire*, Mounier detailed how the municipal

councils were to deduct their contributions. ADHG, 4 M 47. Circulaire No. 15. Mounier, *Direction générale*, 14 April 1821.

133 AN, F 1 cI 77. Letter from St-Chamans to Mounier, 18 January 1821. In some cases, prefects reduced what they considered overly generous contributions.

134 Government reports suggest the duchess was very interested in the chapel. AN, F 21581. Letter *from Directeur des travaux* de *Paris* to Minister of Interior, 13 April 1826.

135 Information regarding the whereabouts of the money collected for the Berry monument was not found. Presumably, it was either used by the government after the July Revolution to build the fountain, or it was returned to the subscribers.

CHAPTER SIX

1 Double-voters met at their respective department capitals to vote in the departmental colleges. Each department would have more than one arrondissement college, but only one departmental college.

2 ADHG, 2 M 23. *Liste des électeurs formant le collège électoral de département*, 11 July 1820.

3 A twenty-four page reprint of an 18 May speech given by Pasquier regarding the double vote was sent to every prefect. Cited as Pasquier, *Discours*.

4 AP, 27:654, 17 May 1820, Royer-Collard.

5 AMG, 6 Fi 1084. Proclamation from Royer-Deloche, 6 May 1820.

6 See chapter 5.

7 ADI, T 45. Deliberation of 20 May 1820.

8 BMG, T 266.

9 ADI, Série U liasse 7. Letter from Haussez to the *Procureur général*, 4 June 1820.

10 BMG, T 266. *Aux cent quinze députés, fidèles mandataires du peuple*, 1820. The *Journal Libre de l'Isère* printed the names of the 115 deputies. JLI, 25 March 1820.

11 BMG, T 266.

12 Weiss, 16 May 1820; 18 May 1820; 20 May 1820, 292–5. Arnouville had been Isère's prefect during the Grégoire election.

13 ADHG, 4 M 46.

14 Bastard, 74.

15 Bastard, 73.

16 *Réquisitoire définitif*, 392–406.

17 Bastard's report discussed the cannon shot. Bastard concluded that there was no proof that the cannon shot was even fired, let alone that it was a signal for Louvel. Moveover, Louvel denied he ever admitted to hearing a cannon. Bastard, 69.

18 *Réquisitoire définitif*, 392, 395.

19 *Réquisitoire définitif*, 406. Louvel's mental health never became an issue. Certainly, an understanding of Louvel's actions would be enhanced by a psychiatric evaluation, similar to Elisabeth Roudinesco's treatment of that famous figure of the Revolution, Théroigne de Méricourt. See Roudinesco, *Théroigne de Méricourt*.

20 *Réquisitoire définitif*, 406.

21 Camille Jordan stated that the double vote would "change the nature of one of the three powers created by [the Charter]" because "the strength of the three powers will no longer be exactly equal." *Journal de Paris*, 31 May 1820, Supplement, Camille Jordan.

22 AP, 27:702, 19 May 1820, Royer-Collard.

23 Barante, 16. Royer-Collard's position suggests that individual rights, representative government, and the Charter were not separate entities, but rather merged to form an unalterable institution that history had woven into France's political life. "The Chamber of Deputies acquired, in the Charter, a real legitimacy, that is to say, a distinctive and unalterable nature which appears unequivocally." Barante, 18.

24 Cited in Vaulabelle, 514.

25 Rémond, 35–6.

26 Villèle made a similar argument in 1816. See AP, 20:700, 26 December 1816, Villèle.

27 AP, 28:74, 24 May 1820, Cuvier.

28 AP, 27:652–3, 17 May 1820, Siméon.

29 Pasquier, *Discours*, 9–11.

30 After the July Revolution, the *cens* was retained, although it was lowered to 200 francs. The *cens* also had a practical element. Elections involved travel and often took several days. That required a certain degree of wealth.

31 Deputies had to live in Paris for much of the year; however, they did not receive a salary, so a certain level of financial independence was necessary. Also, without that wealth, it was feared that the high cost of living in Paris would force some deputies to accept bribes. In that way, the *cens* would limit corruption.

32 AP, 23:125, 2 March 1819, Fontanes (Peers).

33 The reference to the fortunes of small landowners was undoubtedly an allusion to purchasers of *biens nationaux*.

34 AP, 27:689, 19 May 1820, Villèle.

35 *Journal de Paris*, 30 May 1820, Supplement, Puymaurin.

36 Vaulabelle, IV, 507.

37 Barante, 36.

38 See AP, 27:601, 15 May 1820, Foy; 27:674–8, 18 May 1820, Rodet; 27:702, 19 May 1820, Ternaux; 28:57, 23 May 1820, Constant; 28:244, 1 June 1820, Foy. Siméon denied that most of the double voters would be

Old Regime nobles. He stated that purchasers of *bien nationaux* enabled a great number of non-nobles to qualify. AP 27:653, 17 May 1820, Siméon.

39 AP, 27:691, 19 May 1820, Laisné.

40 AP, 27:691, 19 May 1820, Laisné. See also, AP 27:691, 18 May 1820, Laisné; 28:59, 23 May 1820, Constant.

41 Vaulabelle, IV, 511. Richelieu ridiculed Constant's accusations. He pointed to fundamental changes in the legal and social spheres. All property was guaranteed, defended, and protected by the law. Justice was common to all. Religious liberty "was not an empty word." Suggestions of the return of the tithe and feudal rights were unfounded and ludicrous, the "eternal phantoms" of the revolutionaries. Moreover, a citizen's rights were guaranteed by the Charter. Finally, Richelieu denied most vigorously that the double vote created a new aristocracy: "Everyone bears the costs of society, everyone benefits from its advantages, all careers are open, and no one is restricted except by his own abilities." ADHG, 6 T 2.

42 AP, 27:601, 15 May 1820, Foy.

43 AP, 28:57, 23 May 1820, Constant.

44 AP, 28:56–9, 23 May 1820, Constant.

45 Waresquiel, 306. St-Chamans published a proclamation announcing the passage of the double vote. In it, he quoted a section from a *Direction générale* from Mounier praising the deputies for ignoring partisan interests and voting for a law that benefited all French citizens: "This impressive majority is made up of the votes of many members of the Chamber, who, on other occasions and in various circumstances, have voted on opposite sides. This union of so many enlightened men, who have previously differed in their views, but not in their feelings, must have been a sweet recompense to his Majesty for his constant efforts to rally all legitimate interests and all honest opinions around the throne." ADHG, 4 M 45. *Proclamation de la Préfecture de la Haute-Garonne aux habitants du département*, 13 June 1820; ADHG, 4 M 45. *Direction générale* from Mounier to St-Chamans, 10 June 1820.

46 AP, 27:690, 19 May 1820, Pasquier.

47 AP, 27:651, 17 May 1820.

48 AP, 28:72, 24 May 1820, Cuvier.

49 ADI, 7 M 1. *Direction générale* from Mounier to Prefects, 29 May 1820. Cover letter to Pasquier, *Discours*.

50 AP, 27:679, 18 May 1820, Pasquier.

51 Pasquier, *Discours*, 3–5. In Pasquier's view, the annual renewals contributed greatly to the Chamber's divisiveness.

52 AP, 27:670, 18 May 1820, Pasquier. Serre stated that the violence within the Chamber was mirrored in the streets. "The crisis will be even more violent and oppressive outside of the Chamber, than what has occurred to date inside the Chamber." *Journal de Paris*, 31 March 1820, Supplement, Serre.

53 Pasquier, *Discours*, 17. Pasquier believed that students, whom he called "the reckless youth!" thought that revolution was a romantic adventure because they had not lived through one. Older men, those who sat in the Chamber of Deputies, with actual experience of the Revolution and who remembered "the tears and … the blood," had a responsibility to protect the students from a new revolution. Pasquier, *Discours*, 17–18.

54 AP, 27:651, 17 May 1820, Siméon. The phrase "thirty years of unrest" was popular among royalist deputies who wanted to equate liberalism with revolution. See AP 27:654, 17 May 1820, Villefranche; 27:698, 19 May 1820, Villèle; *Journal de Paris*, 31 May 1820, Serre.

55 AP, 27:672, 18 May 1820, Barthe-Labastide.

56 *Journal de Paris*, 31 May 1820.

57 AP, 27:601, 15 May 1820, Foy.

58 Villèle claimed to have seen Manuel, dressed as a deputy, walking among the demonstrators. Villèle, II, *Mémoires*. Letter from Villèle to Mme de Villèle, 06/04/1820, 384; Mansel, 376; Newman, 38.

59 The letter was read by Jacques Laffitte, a liberal deputy. AP 28:275, 5 June 1820. Laffitte added that Lallemand was killed because he dared shout, *Vive la Charte*. An editorial in the *Journal de Grenoble* stated that the liberal deputies' pretended sorrow over Lallemand's death would not prevent the passage of the double-vote law. JDG, 22 June 1820.

60 Vinck, 10640.

61 AP, 28:273, 5 June 1820, Jordan.

62 AP, 28:354–6, 10 June 1820, Laffite.

63 ADHG, 4 M 45. Proclamation by Prefect of Haute-Garonne, 13 June 1820.

64 ADHG, 4 M 45. Ordinance of the Mayor of Toulouse, 13 June 1820.

65 ADHG, 4 M 45. Letter from Mounier to Prefects, 10 June 1820. Every prefect in France was informed by letter that the double vote had passed.

66 ADHG, 4 M 45. Proclamation of Prefect of Haute-Garonne, 13 June 1820. The *Journal de Toulouse* printed a statement from St-Chamans three days later in which he dismissed the demonstrators as "foolish people who fail to see the ineffectiveness of their efforts." He continued that the inhabitants of Haute-Garonne were solidly behind the government: "The bulk of the population has rejected them with indignation, and the gendarmes and the guards, as well as the regimental soldiers, have been outdoing each other in devotion and zeal." JDT, 16 June 1820.

67 JDT, 29 June 1820.

CHAPTER SEVEN

1 Vinck, 10664, 24 May 1820.

2 Coussergues, 24–9.

3 Coussergues, 30–40, 89–93.

4 Coussergues, 93.

5 Coussergues, 39–40.

6 Coussergues, 117–18.

7 Coussergues, 125. In his memoirs, Baron Haussez wrote that he had a short audience with Berry the day of the assassination. At that meeting, Berry stated that he was tired of the constant surveillance by government agents. Haussez noted that at the time he believed Berry neglected his personal safety. Haussez, 313–15.

8 Bastard did not blame security for the assassination. He reported that there were nineteen royal guards and thirty-two policemen at the Opera that night. Stating the obvious, he added that perhaps Berry was not sufficiently well protected when he escorted the duchess to her carriage. Bastard, 7–12.

9 Coussergues, 129–31.

10 Coussergues, 127. In *Le Conservateur*, Salaberry blamed both Decazes and radical liberal writers for Louvel's actions: "All-powerful minister, it was under your rule that a French prince fell … The frightful doctrines, the inflammatory and sacrilegious writings that you protected, forged and sharpened the dagger and impelled the assassin's hand." *Le Conservateur*, т VI, 379. In the same paper, Chateaubriand wrote that "The hand that dealt the blow was not the most guilty party." *Le Conservateur*, т VI, 382.

11 Coussergues, 114–15.

12 Decazes was accused of leading virtually every liberal conspiracy. The dissolution of the *Chambre introuvable* was characterized as a Decazes plot to enhance his influence over Louis XVIII. See *L'homme de gibeaux*, 37–18. Decazes and Charles Sapey, a leading liberal deputy from Isère, were accused of organizing the Didier rebellion. *L'homme de gibeaux*, 4–7, 21, 37–8. Grégoire's election was offered as further proof of Decazes's guilt. It was termed "a sinister and seditious event," that occurred in the "city where M. Decazes tried to plan a conspiracy, where his associates, *le comité directeur*, fraudulently manufactured ballots to put Grégoire into the Chamber." *L'homme de gibeaux*, 21.

13 *L'homme de Gibeaux*, 14.

14 *L'homme de Gibeaux*, 15–16.

15 *L'homme de Gibeaux*, 16.

16 The writer added that the Jew knew a certain *sieur* Worrhaye, a saddler in Metz where Louvel worked. He also noted that while Louvel was not Jewish, his name was Jewish in origin. *L'homme des gibeaux*, 16–17. In his indictment of Louvel, the prosecutor mentioned another Jew named Samuel. Apparently, Samuel had made statements to a certain dame Bonet that made her suspect he knew of the crime before it happened. Samuel was interrogated and cleared of any suspicion; however, he was the only suspect whose religious origins were mentioned. *Réquisitoire définitif*, 211–12.

17 *L'homme de Gibeaux*, 20.

18 *L'homme de Gibeaux*, 11.

19 Many ultra royalists believed Decazes had agents hidden throughout France even after his resignation. BMG, O 2504. Anonymous, *Mercuriale A M Le Comte de Sainte-Aulaire*, 24–5.

20 *L'homme de Gibeaux*, 19.

21 *L'homme de Gibeaux*, 22, 30–6.

22 Greenlow de Neuville, *Plainte à la Chambre des Pairs, Contre M. Le Duc Decazes*.

23 Guyon, *Histoire complète du procès de Louis-Pierre Louvel*.

24 See Chapter 2.

25 BMG, O 2490. *Affaire de Grenoble. Mémoire pour le Vicompte Donnadieu sur la plainte en calomnie par lui portée contre Les Srs Rey, Cazenave et Regnier, Auteurs et signataires d'une pétition pour quelques habitants de Grenoble*, 16 September 1820. The pamphlet was 102 pages, along with twenty-seven pages of documentary evidence.

26 Berryer, *Affaire de Grenoble*, 35.

27 Berryer, *Affaire de Grenoble*, 76.

28 BMG, O 2491. Berryer. *Affaire de Grenoble, No. II*, 11 October 1820.

29 BMG, O 2506. Ste-Aulaire, *Réponse Au mémoire de M. Berryer*.

30 Ste-Aulaire, *Réponse Au mémoire de M. Berryer*, 20.

31 Ste-Aulaire, *Réponse Au mémoire de M. Berryer*, 22.

32 Ste-Aulaire, *Réponse Au mémoire de M. Berryer*, 46.

33 He had also recently been dismissed as prefect of Franche-Comte in July.

34 BMG, O 7913. Choppin-d'Arnouville, *Quelques faits historiques relatifs à l'élection de M. Grégoire, en 1819*, 1820.

35 BMG, O 7914. Journal des Débats, 14 September 1820. In his memoirs, Baron Haussez wrote that the ultras voted for Grégoire to force the government to amend the electoral law and to destroy Arnouville's credibility.

36 Spitzer, *Old Hatreds*, 50.

37 ADI, 54 M 5. Letter from Mayor of Tour-du-Pin to Prefect, Summer, 1820.

38 ADI, 54 M 5. Letter from Mayor of Tullins to Prefect.

39 JDT, 28 August 1820.

40 AMG, 6 Fi 1084. Proclamation from Royer-Deloche, 6 May 1820.

41 Vinck, 10610.

42 Vinck, 10660. The original caption read: Frenchmen, an heir to the Bourbon throne has been promised to you; and after so much hardship, that promise may soon be kept. This most blessed of unions is destined to do so.

43 ADI, 54 M 5. Letter from Siméon to Prefects, 29 September 1820.

44 Vinck, 10675.

45 Henin, 14,057.

46 A large portion of the *circulaire* was devoted to describing how Parisians celebrated the news. It stated that the enthusiasm was such that "the deep

feeling of joy produced in Paris by the birth of the Duke of Bordeaux is impossible to describe to those who did not see it."

47 Rochefoucauld, 312.

CHAPTER EIGHT

1 Victor Hugo, *Ode sur la naissance du duc de Bordeaux*, October, 1820.

2 ADHG, 4 M 43.

3 BMG, T 5719–86. *Lettre de MGr. L'Évêque de Grenoble, A MM. les Archiprêtres et à tous les Curés de son Diocèse, Pour ordonner un Te Deum solennel en actions de grâces de la naissance du Prince dont Madame la duchesse de Berry est heureusement accouchée*, 10/02/1820; BMG, T 5719–87. *Mandement de Monseigneur l'Évêque de Grenoble sur les élections*, 3 November 1820.

4 The last line contains a reference to Genesis 9.10. Simon's *mandements* generally included a sprinkling of biblical references, which he dutifully footnoted.

5 Henin, 14,064.

6 Isaiah, 11:1–11, 11:2, and 12:1–5; Henin, 14,064.

7 Isaiah, 11:10.

8 Vinck, 10691, 10/21/1820.

9 Vinck, 10705, 26 December 1820.

10 ADHG, 4 M 45. Report from Mayor of Boulonge-sur-Gesse to Prefect, 19 October 1820.

11 ADI, 54 M 5. Letter from Mayor of Beaurepaire to Prefect, 9 October 1820.

12 Proclamation from Bellegarde to inhabitants of Toulouse, 2 October 1820.

13 AAHG, 1 (E) 2. *Mandement de Messieurs les Vicaires-généraux de Monseigneur l'Archevêque de Toulouse. Pour rendre grâces à Dieu de la naissance du Prince auquel Son Altesse Royale Madame la Duchesse de Berri a donné le jour*, 2 October 1820.

14 AAHG, 1 (E) 2. *Lettre pastorale de Monseigneur l'Archevêque de Toulouse, Paris de France à l'occasion de la retraite ecclésiastique qui vient de se donner aux curés de ce diocèse*, 20 October 1820.

15 Located in the Loire Valley, the *Château* had been confiscated during the Revolution and no longer belonged to the royal family. Chambord had a long and spectacular history. Francis I started construction in 1519. Two princes supervised 1800 workers for 30 years, but the château was only completed by Louis XIV. There were some 400 rooms when it was all done. In one of the rooms, Molière first showed his comedy *Le Bourgeois Gentilhomme* before Louis XIV. Only after the construction of Versailles did Chambord cease to welcome France's kings. Chambord became part of the *domaine nationale* in 1791. In 1820, Chambord was owned by the Prince

of Wagram, who had spent some 600,000 francs renovating it. He came into possession during the Empire.

16 The cost to purchase and renovate Chambord was higher than at first estimated, and an additional 390,157 francs had to be found.

17 Herbouville added that eleven royal houses existed at present, but they were either in Paris or close by, or in the far corners of the realm. A royal house was needed, therefore, in the interior.

18 AN, F I cI 78; ADHG, 4 M 43. *Souscription de Chambord, Quatrième Rapport*, 15 April 1823.

19 AN, F I cI 77.

20 Vinck, 10720, 10 June 1822. In February 1841, in an attempt to appeal to legitimist sentiments, the picture was released with a new title: Justice proclaims the incontestable ownership of Chambord.

21 Vinck, 10702, 9 October 1832.

22 See Vinck, 10660, discussed in chapter 7.

23 Vinck, 10664, 24 May 1820; Vinck, 10663.

24 Prefects published proclamations announcing Bordeaux's birth, and most archbishops and bishops issued a *mandement* as well.

25 AAT, I (E) 2. *Lettre Pastorale de Monseigneur L'Archevêque de Toulouse, Paris de France à l'Occasion de la retraite ecclésiastique qui vient de se donner aux curés de ce diocèse*, 20 October 1820.

26 JDT, 9 October 1820.

27 Vinck, 10695, October 1820.

28 Vinck, 10713, 17 December 1830. An illustration with the same title and layout was published in 1843, after the death of the Duke of Orléans and in honour of the Duchess of Orléans and the Count of Paris.

29 See Vinck, 10667; 10669, 31 October 1820; 10690.

30 Vinck, 10671, 26 April 1827.

31 Vinck, 10693, 11 January 1821.

32 See also Vinck, 10720, 10 June 1820. In that illustration, France, personified by a woman, is about to put a crown on the infant Bordeaux, who is sitting on the duchess's lap. Her daughter is standing by her side as well. The Château of Chambord appears in the background, as three angels sit next to them holding the deed to the Château.

33 Vinck, 10692, 21 February 1821. The lithograph was displayed at the Salon of 1824; a painting of it was hung at the Musée de Versailles.

34 Vinck, 10710, 9 November 1820.

35 Vinck, 10711, 28 March 1821.

36 Bakos, ed., *Politics, Ideology and the Law*; Barry, *Women and Political Insurgency*; Darrow, "French Noblewomen and the New Domesticity," *Feminist Studies*: 41–65; Gutwirth, *Twilight of the Goddess*; Hunt, *The Family Romance*; Hunt, ed., *Eroticism and the Body Politic*; Landes, *Women and*

the Public Sphere; Orr, *Wollstonecraft's Daughters*; Outram, *The Body and the French Revolution*; Tallet and Atkin, eds., *Religion, Society and Politics*.

37 Barbara Garlick, Suzanne Dixon, Pauline Allen (eds.), *Stereotypes of Women in Power*.

38 The Diamond Necklace Affair of 1785–86 involved two swindlers, the Comtesse de la Motte-Valois and Count Cagliostro (both pseudonyms), who pretended that Marie-Antoinette wanted to buy a necklace from Augnst Bohmer, a renowned jeweler. The two swindlers convinced the ambitious Cardinal de Rohan to purchase the necklace for the queen, who would then promote him at court. Marie-Antoinette knew nothing about the deal, and when Rohan began missing payments, the entire scam was discovered. Remarkably, Marie-Antoinette received most of the blame, as people assumed she had indeed purchased the necklace in secret, and that Rohan was covering up for her avarice.

39 Lack of clerical leadership provided the opportunity and the necessity for women to take a leadership role in the battle for the right to worship in public. Desan, *Reclaiming the Sacred*.

40 Béliveau, "Le droit à la rébellion", *Femmes dans la cité*: 41–55.

41 Noelle Dauphin, "Les Salons de la Restauration," *Femmes dans la cité*: 251–60.

42 Brelot, "De la tutelle à la collaboration," *Femmes dans la cité*: 237–50.

43 Duprat, "Le silence des femmes," *Femmes dans la cité*: 79–100.

44 Dupland, 61–77.

45 In addition to the works cited above, see Kindleberger, "Charlotte Corday," *French Historical Studies*: 969–999; Lecanuet and Damien (eds.), *Charlotte Corday*; Thomas, *La reine scélérate*.

46 Martainville, 15.

47 Only 9 percent of liberal deputies elected in 1820 had Imperial titles, and just 4 percent had seats in the *Corps législatif*. Beck, *French Legislators*, 74–5.

48 Waresquiel and Yvert, *Histoire de la Restauration*, 315.

49 Most of the *circulaires* discussed the implementation of the double-vote law, with less than gentle reminders of deadlines for posting electoral lists and other administrative matters.

50 Haussez suspended two *percepteurs* for not sending electoral lists on time. ADI, 7 M 1. Liberal electors in Isère complained bitterly about mistakes on electoral lists and accused Haussez of purposefully excluding liberal electors who rightfully belonged on the lists, and including royalists who did not meet the *cens*. A group of influential liberals from Grenoble sent three very lengthy and complex petitions to Haussez complaining about the lists. The petitions were sent to the *Conseillers d'état et maîtres des requêtes*, and the petitioners were successful in six cases. In September, Grenoblois liberals published a list of some 261 electors who voted in the 1819 elections, but were left off the 1820 lists. ADI, 4 M 16.

51 AN, F IC III (Isère) 4. Letter from Haussez to Minister of Interior, 11 August 1820; *Extrait du rapport sur la circonscription électorale*, 27 August 1820.

52 Marquis de Charles-Laurent-Joseph-Marie Planelli was born in Grenoble (1763–1854). He was elected deputy in 1815 and sat in the *Chambre introuvable* as a moderate. Planelli was re-elected in 1816, 1820, and 1824. Planelli lost his seat in the 1827 election, but was re-elected in 1829 by Isère's departmental college to replace a deputy who had died. Planelli retired from active politics in the spring of 1830.

53 AN, F IC III Isere 4. *Procès verbal du collège électoral du département de l'Isère*, November 1820. Prior to the election to replace Grégoire, the president of Isère's electoral college pleaded with electors to choose an appropriate candidate. He warned that failure to do so would cause further unrest, and as wealthy landowners, they would suffer the consequences: "Who among us does not risk losing everything if new quarrels bring new troubles and open new wounds?" Avezou, 27.

54 JDT, 15 November 1820.

55 BMG, T 5719–87. *Mandement de Monseigneur L'Évêque de Grenoble sur les Élections*, 3 November 1820. Fear of civil unrest also played a part in the 1824 election. Bishop Simon and Archbishop Clermont-Tonnerre of Toulouse both issued *mandements* during that election. The two *mandements* urged their *fidèles* followers to support the ministerial candidates. Simon wrote that the elections were important to ensure "the peace and stability of the State" and the future prosperity of the Church. Clermont-Tonnerre's *mandement* added that only the ministerial candidates had the courage and fortitude to resist the revolutionaries, and he implored God to provide them with "the courage and strength to destroy evil doctrines and to protect religious institutions, without which nothing can be solid or durable." In his mind, the future was bright since the troubles stemming from the Revolution were now over: "Now nothing hides the brightness from us, the future has no more worries; God's plans are no longer a mystery, the spirit of evil is foiled and stays silent." BMG, T 5719–99. *Mandement de ... l'Évêque de Grenoble, Pour ordonner des prières relatives aux élections des nouveaux députés de la France*, 27 January 1824; AHG, I E 3. *Mandement de ... Clermont-Tonnerre, Archevêque de Toulouse et Narbonne*, 16 March 1824. The Archbishop of Albi also published a *mandement* prior to the 1824 election. In it, he described the Revolution and Empire as "a state of anarchy, violence and oppression under which France has so long suffered; it exasperated spirits, bred hatred, fomented division, inspired prejudice, created parties." He also informed his clergymen that their mission prior to the election was to "warn against the insidious speeches, seditious writings, and evil insinuations of these so-called friends of the people, who on the pretext of an imaginary liberty, would lead them into revolt." AHG, I E 3. *Lettre pastorale et mandement de Monseigneur l'Archevêque d'Albi, pour les élections de 1824*, 27 January 1824.

56 Vinck, 10705, 26 January 26 December 1820.

57 Alphonse de Lamartine, *Ode sur la naissance du duc de Bordeaux*, 20 November 1820.

POSTSCRIPT

1 AN, F17, 1977, 344. Report to Louis XVIII, 2 April 1821.

2 Antoine Dussert received a one-year sentence and was fined 500 francs. Joseph Foulquier received a two-year sentence and a 200-franc fine. Auguste Domas got two years and a 500-franc fine.

3 Grenoble's Municipal Council bemoaned the pecuniary loss that resulted from the suspension: "We think it unnecessary to mention the monetary losses we have suffered because the Faculty of Law was closed ... it is easy to understand that in a town where there is very little commerce, the money spent by two hundred young men is very important to the less wealthy class, and it undoubtedly suffers from this measure." AMG, Deliberation of 23 May 1822, register No. 33.

4 ADI, 54 M 5. Letter from Mounier to Prefects, 29 September 1820.

5 Waquet, 78.

6 The *fêtes* organizers, Lecointe and Hittorff, defined the principle that guided their work as follows: "We have tried to adapt the richness and beauty of the fabrics, the choice of ornaments and emblems, to the building and to the ceremony, but we have respected the style of the architecture, and tried to enrich but not overload it, to embellish but not alter it." Hittorff and Lecointe, *Description des cérémonies*, II; cited in Waquet, 72.

7 ADI, 54 M 5. Letter from Mayor of St. Symphorien-d'Ozon to Prefect, 7 May 1821. Contrary to instructions in Mounier's *circulaire*, Haussez did not advance funds to cover the cost of the *fête*.

8 ADI, 54 M 5. Letter from Mayor of Commune of Vaux, 5 May 1821.

9 Twenty seats went to ministerial candidates and twenty-four to moderate royalists.

10 A lithograph of the Berry statue was published to commemorate the erection of the statue. Vinck, 10615, 22 September 1829.

11 Cobban, II, 100–1.

12 Dupland, 233–4, 342–7, 431–2.

13 Larignon and Proust, *Edouard de Monti de Rezé*.

14 During the July Revolution, rampaging crowds left stores displaying the duchess's name or insignia untouched. Margadant, 37.

15 Significantly, the miracle child idea disappeared over the years, even as the legitimist movement gained strength. In 1871, when Bordeaux had his final opportunity to return to France as king, his supporters made little mention of it. Brown, 82–90.

16 Margadant, 45.

17 Margadant, 45.
18 Brown, 58.
19 Brown, 89.

APPENDIX ONE

1 Grenoble's resistance against foreign troops at the end of the Hundred Days was celebrated in the area for the next 15 years. Avezou, 15. On 5 July 1818, some two hundred people attended a banquet to commemorate the occasion. BMG, R 9676.

2 A known liberal sympathizer, Montlivault was prefect of Isère from 1815 to 1816. In 1819 he was named prefect of Calvados. Montlivault joined the Carbonari movement in the early 1820s, and became somewhat famous during the July Monarchy as a minister of the interior.

3 The Edicts of 8 May restricted the jurisdiction of the *parlements* to cases concerning the nobility and civil actions over 20,000 livres. Provincial courts were raised to the status of high courts and given jurisdiction over the vast majority of criminal and civil cases. The *parlements* were also stripped of their power to register royal edicts before they became enforceable, a power given to a plenary court appointed by the government. Those changes effectively ended the *parlements'* political influence.

4 Toulouse was also hurt by the abolition of provinces and the formation of departments. Industry was not well developed in the area; without the *parlement*, Toulouse lost the principal reason for its being the capital of Languedoc. All *parlements* were officially surpressed by the law of 24 August 1790. On 25 September 1790 a protest was signed by a number of men from Haute-Garonne against the law. The signatories became known as the parlementaires, and many emerged as leaders of the Counter-Revolution in Haute-Garonne.

5 Very little is known about this group. Some speculate that it established ties with the *Chevaliers de la foi*, the secret association of Ferdinand de Bertier de Sauvigny, founded in 1810 in the last few years of the Empire. A number of Toulouse's *noblesse* belonged to or were affiliated with *l'Aa*, including Joseph de Villère. Both organizations participated in the *congrégation*, a royalist conspiracy to overthrow Napoleon. Godechot, 428.

6 The *parlementaires* were a favourite target for arrest. Excluding Paris, only Bordeaux had more arrests than Toulouse. Thirty-one people were executed in Toulouse, with another fifty-four parlementaires guillotined in Paris. Godechot, 416–18. In terms of overall executions, the thirty-one executed in Toulouse placed it in the middle ranks among department capitals.

7 Thermidor began a difficult period for Toulousians. The end of the wage and price controls imposed during the Terror, known as the *maximum*, stimulated rapid inflation and a subsequent rise in food prices. The harsh

winter of 1795 devastated crops. By the end of 1795, Toulouse was all but abandoned, a shadow of its former self. Godechot, 418–22.

8 Maréchal de Camp Adrien de Rougé was a former republican general turned royalist. He joined Angoulême in April, 1815 to fight Napoleon, and then followed the prince to Spain during the Hundred Days. Resnick, 31–8.

9 Toulouse was the primary target, but similar attacks were planned for Bordeaux and Nantes. Events prior to the rebellion made Toulouse a logical choice. In 1798 liberty trees were systematically cut down in the city. In January 1799, near the anniversary of Louis XVI's death, royalist placards were posted on city walls. Finally, the law of 5 September 1798, which established conscription, led to increased desertions and added to the agitation. Ramet, 805–6. Haute-Garonne was also very poorly defended in the summer of 1799, with only thirty line troops in the entire department and a mere 539 National Guardsmen in nearby Ariège. Sutherland, 328.

10 Rémusat, *Mémoires de ma vie*, I, 220. Rémusat's father became prefect of Haute-Garonne after the Hundred Days on 21 July, much to the displeasure of Toulousian ultra royalists. The ultras campaigned more effectively for mayor, and Joseph de Villèle was appointed by Angoulême in July 1815.

Bibliography

KEY TO ACRONYMS

AAT   Archives de l'archevêque de Toulouse
AP   Archives parlementaires
ADHG   Archives départementales de la Haute-Garonne
ADI   Archives départementales de l'Isère
AN   Archives nationales
BMG   Bibliothèque municipale de Grenoble
BMT   Bibliothèque municipale de Toulouse
JDG   Journal de Grenoble
JDT   Journal de Toulouse
JLI   Journal de l'Isère, Libre, Politique et Littéraire

MANUSCRIPTS

A Archives de l'Archevêque de Toulouse
i. Mandements
  1 (E) 2
  1 (E) 3
ii. Correspondance
  Registre 12: between 22 March 1820 and 21 October 1820
  Ministère des cultes 27: between 19 November 1808 and 8 October 1820

B Archives parlementaires. 2nd Series.
Vols. 17–20, 23–28

C Archives départementales de l'Isère
Series M: Personnel et administration générale
Series T: Archives de l'inspection académique, fonds de l'académie, fonds des facultés, et fonds de la préfecture, instruction publique, sciences et arts depuis 1800

D Archives départementales de la Haute-Garonne
Series M: Personnel et administration générale
Series T: Divers

Fonds Villèle

E Archives municipales de Grenoble

F Archives municipales de Toulouse
5 s 76: deliberations of the Faculté de Droit

G Archives Nationales
AB xix 3064
Personnel administratif: série départementale
F 1bII (Garonne, Haute-) 8
F 1bII (Isère) 5
Esprit public
F 1cI 77
F 1cI 78
F 1cI 107 2 (4)
F 1cI 77
F 1cI 106
F 1cI 1072
Esprit public et élections
F 1cIII (Isère) 4
F 1cIII (Garonne, Haute-) 6
Instruction publique
F 17 1977 65, 90, 163, 226, 334, 338, 339, 344
F 17 2072
F 17 2105
F 17 6809
F 21 581

H Bibliothèque municipale de Grenoble
Series N: Lettres et autographes du Fonds Dauphinois
Series R: Manuscrits du Fonds Dauphinois

I Bibliothèque municipale de Toulouse

J Bibliothèque nationale
Lb 48 1663

K Bibliothèque Université Stendhal, Grenoble

L Université des Sciences Sociales de Toulouse

PRINTED SOURCES AND BOOKS

Anonymous. *Apologie de Louis XVIII*. Malte-Brun, 1815.

Barante, Amable Guillaume Prosper Brugière, baron de. *La vie politique de M. Royer-Collard: ses discours et ses écrits*. 2 vols. Paris: Didier et Co., 1863.

Barruel-Saint-Point, Antoine de, le père d'Augustin. *Mémoires Pour Servir à l'Histoire du Jacobinisme*. 4 vols. London, 1797–1798.

– *Les Helviennes, ou Lettres provinciales philosophiques*. Amsterdam, 1781.

Bastard, Comte de. *Rapport Fait à la Cour des Pairs le 15 Mai 1820 et jours suivans, par M. Le Comte de Bastard, du procès suivi contre Louis-Pierre Louvel*. Lyon: September, 1820.

Bonald, Vicomte Louis Gabriel Ambroise. *Législation primitive. Considérée dans les derniers temps par les seules lumières de la raison. Suivie de divers traités et discours politiques*. 5ᵗʰ ed Paris: Librairie Adrien Le Clere et Cie, 1857.

– *Oeuvres. Mélanges littéraires, politiques et philosophiques*. 3rd ed Paris: Librairie Adrien Le Clere et Cie, 1852.

– *Pensées sur divers sujets et discours politiques*.

Broglie, duc de. *Souvenirs*.

Burke, Edmund. *Reflections on the Revolution in France*. London: Penguin Books Ltd., 1969.

Chateaubriand, François-René, vicomte de. *De la monarchie selon la charte*. Paris: Normant, 1816.

– *Mémoires d'outre-tombe*. Ed Maurice Lavaillant. 9 vols. Paris: Tallandier, 1982.

– *Mémoires, lettres et pièces authentiques touchant la vie et la mort de S.A.R. Monseigneur Charles-Ferdinand-D'Artois, fils de France, Duc de Berry*. Paris: Chez Le Normant, Imprimeur-Libraire, 1820.

Constant, Benjamin. *Fragments d'un ouvrage abandonné sur la possibilité d'une constitution républicaine dans un grand pays*. Paris: Aubier, 1991.

Coussergues, Clausel de. *Projet de la proposition d'accusation contre M. le duc Decazes*. 2ᵉ ed. 1820.

Foy, Maximilien Sébastien, comte. *Discours du Général Foy*. Paris: Gaultier-Laguionie, 1826.

Frénilly, Baron de. *Recollections of Baron de Frénilly*, trans. by Frederic Less. London: William Heinemann, 1909.

Greenlow de Neuville, A.-F.-H. *Plainte à la Chambre des Pairs, Contre M. Le Duc Decazes, Pair de France*. Paris, 1820.

Guyon, L. *Histoire complète du procès de Louis-Pierre Louvel*. 2 vols Paris: P. Plancher, 1820.

Haussez, Baron d'. *Mémoires du Baron d'Haussez, dernier ministre de la Marine sous la Restauration*. 2 vols. Paris: Calmann Lévy, 1896–97.

Hugo, Victor. *Ode sur la naissance du duc de Bordeaux*. October, 1820.

Lamartine, Alphonse de. *Ode sur la naissance du duc de Bordeaux*. 20 November 1820.

Maillé, Duchesse de. *Souvenirs des deux restaurations*. Paris: Librairie académique Perrin, 1984.

Maisonfort, Marquis de la. *Mémoires d'un agent royaliste, sous la Révolution, l'Empire, et la Restauration*. Paris: Mercure de France, 1998.

Maistre, Joseph de. *Du Pape*. 2ᵉ edition. Genève: Librairie Droz, 1966.

– *Considérations sur la France*. Paris: Vrin, 1936.

Martainville, Alphonse. *La bombe royaliste*. Paris, 1820.

Mme de Gontaut-Biron, Duchesse de. Memoirs of the Duchesse de Gontaut, Governess to the Children of France during the Restoration, 1773–1836, trans. Mrs J.W. Davis. New York, 1894.

Molé, Louis Mathieu, comte. *Le Comte Molé, 1871–1855. Sa vie – ses mémoires*. 6 vols. Paris: Édouard Champion, 1925.

Pasquier, Étienne Denis, Duc. *Histoire de mon temps, mémoires*. 6 vols. Paris: Plon, 1893–95.

Polignac, Jules de. *Souvenirs d'un vieux critique*. 10ᵉ série. Calmann-Lévy, 1889.

Rémusat, Charles de. *Correspondance de M. de Rémusat pendant les premières années de la Restauration*. 6 vols. Paris, 1884.

– *Mémoires de ma vie: Enfance et Jeunesse. La Restauration Libérale (1797–1820)*. 2 vols. Paris: Plon, 1958–59.

– *"Le Gouvernement représentatif." Revue des Deux Mondes*. 1 September 1857.

Réquisitoire définitif de M. Le Procureur-Général près la Cour des Pairs, dans l'affaire Louvel. Paris: Imprimerie de J.G. Dentu, 1820.

Rey, Joseph. *Mémoires politique*.

– *Mémoires sur la Restauration*.

Rochefoucauld, Duc de Doudeauville. *Mémoires de M. de la Rochefoucauld, Duc de Doudeauville*. Paris, 1862.

Roullet. *Récit historique des événements qui se sont passés dans l'administration de l'Opéra la nuit du 13 Février 1820 (Assassinat du Duc de Berry)*. Paris: Librairie Poulet-Malassis, 1826.

Thiers, Adolphe. *"De la lithographie et de ses progrès," La Pondore*, no 259. March 30, 1824, n.263, April 3, 1824.

Vaulabelle, Achille Tenaille de. *Chute de l'empire. Histoire des deux Restaurations jusqu'à la chute de Charles X.* 7 vols. Paris: Perrotin, 1847–54.

Villèle, Comte de. *Mémoires et correspondance du Comte de Villèle.* 5 vols. Paris: Perrin et Cie, Libraires-éditeurs, 1888–90.

Weiss, Charles. *Journal 1815–1822.* Paris: Annales littéraires de l'université de Besançon, 1972.

PAMPHLETS, ELECTORAL LISTS, ORDINANCES, AND PROCLAMATIONS

Anonymous. *Mercuriale à M. le Comte de Saint-Aulaire, sur son pamphlet apologétique de M. le Duc Decazes,* 1820.

ATTENTION!, 17 May 1820.

Aux cent quinze députés, fidèles mandataires du peuple, 1820.

Aux électeurs de l'Isère. Notice historique tirée des moniteurs du temps, August-September 1819.

Aux électeurs libéraux du département de l'Isère, 1819.

Avis aux électeurs du département de l'Isère, 1819.

Berryer, Antoine. *Affaire de Grenoble. Mémoire pour le Vicomte Donnadieu sur la plainte en calomnie par lui portée contre les Srs. Rey, Cazenave et Regnier, auteurs et signataires d'une pétition pour quelques habitants de Grenoble,* 16 September 1820.

Berryer, Antoine. *Affaire de Grenoble, No. II: Lettre à M. le Comte de Saint-Aulaire,* 11 October 1820.

Choppin-d'Arnouville, A. *Quelques faits historiques relatifs à l'élection de M. Grégoire, en 1819,* 1820.

Conseil d'État. Extrait du registre de délibération du comité, 1 August 1823.

Dernier Mot à MM. Électeurs du département de l'Isère, sur l'abbé Grégoire, 1819.

Deuxième tour de scrutin, September 1819.

Discours de … Pasquier … sur le projet de loi relatif aux élections; prononcé dans la séance du 18 mai 1820. Extrait du *Moniteur,* 19 May 1820.

Duchand, A. *Pensées d'un électeur,* 9 September 1819.

Duchesne. *Aux électeurs de l'Isère. Réponse au libelle intitulé: Notice historique tirée des moniteurs du temps,* 10 September 1819.

Extraits du registre des délibérations du Conseil Municipal de Toulouse, 25 November 1820.

Grégoire, Abbé. *À MM. Les électeurs du département de l'Isère.*

– *Lettre de M. Grégoire, Ancien évêque de Blois, Aux électeurs de l'Isère,* 28 September 1819.

Guyon, L. *L'Histoire complète du procès de Louis-Pierre Louvel.* Paris: P. Plancher, 1820.

Jay, M.-A. *Pétition adressée à la Chambre des Députés par Madier de Montjau suivie de considérations constitutionnelles.* Paris, 1820.

"L'éloge historique de Son Altesse Royale Charles-Ferdinand d'Artois, duc de Berry," 1820.

L'homme de Gibeaux, 1820.

Le Masque Tombé, Dialogue entre un ministériel et un ultra. Paris, 1818.

"Les choses comme elles vont," 17 May 1820.

Les étudiants en droit de Grenoble à leurs frères de Rennes, 1820.

Listes des électeurs des collèges d'arrondissement et des collèges de département de la Haute-Garonne.

Liste des électeurs du collège de département de l'Isère, 1820.

Liste des électeurs du collège de département de la Haute-Garonne, 1820.

Liste des électeurs formant le collège électoral de département de la Haute-Garonne, 18 September 1820.

Liste des électeurs formant le collège électoral de département de la Haute-Garonne, 7 November 1820.

Liste des électeurs formant le collège électoral de département de la Haute-Garonne, 16 October 1829.

Liste des éligibles du département de l'Isère, Grenoble, 12 November 1820.

Notice sur l'origine, la composition, et la contenance du Domaine de Chambord, 5 March 1821.

Ordonnance of Bellegarde, Mayor of Toulouse, 13 June 1820.

Ordonnance of Baron de Montbel, Mayor of Toulouse, concernant la célébration de l'anniversaire de 21 Janvier, 18 January 1827.

Ordonnance of Thoron, interim Mayor of Toulouse, concernant la célébration de l'anniversaire du 21 Janvier, 18 January 1817.

"Précis de ce qui s'est passé à la Faculté de Droit de Grenoble, le 24 avril 1820, Grenoble," 1820.

Proclamation of Baron d'Haussez ... to the inhabitants of Isère, 21 March 1821.

Proclamation of Bellegarde, Mayor of Toulouse, to the Inhabitants of Toulouse, 2 October 1820.

Proclamation of Demouis, interim Mayor of Toulouse, to his Fellow Citizens, 10 January 1816.

Proclamation of ... Montlivaut ... to the Inhabitants of Isère, 24 November 1815.

Proclamation of Royer-Deloche, Mayor of Grenoble, 6 May 1820.

Proclamation of St-Chamans, 13 June 1820.

Proclamation of St-Chamans to his Administrators and Inhabitants of Haute-Garonne, 1 October 1820.

R**. *Aux électeurs libéraux du département de L'Isère*, 1819.

Souscription de Chambord, quatrième rapport, 15 April 1823.

Souscription pour le monument en l'honneur de Mgr. le Duc de Berri, 1820.

Ste-Aulaire, Comte de. *Réponse au mémoire de M. Berryer pour M. le Général Donnadieu, par M. le Comte de Ste-Aulaire.* 3rd ed. Paris: A la librairie Française de L'advocat, 1820.

CHURCH "MANDEMENTS," "CIRCULAIRES," AND "LETTRES PASTORALES"

Association de Charité entre MM. les ecclésiastiques du diocèse de Toulouse, en faveur de leurs confrères qui sont dans le besoin, 29 December 1820.

Circulaires de Mgr. l'Évêque de Grenoble, à MM. les curés des paroisses & curés-desservans des succursales de son diocèse, 5 June 1813.

Lettre de Mgr. l'Évêque de Grenoble, à MM. les archiprêtres et à tous les curés de son diocèse, pour ordonner le service anniversaire de MARIE-ANTOINETTE, Reine de France, 17 January 1816.

Lettre de Mgr. l'Évêque de Grenoble, à MM. les archiprêtres et à tous les curés de son diocèse, pour ordonner un Te Deum solennel en actions de grâces de la naissance du Prince dont Madame la duchesse de Berry est heureusement accouchée, 2 October 1820.

Lettre pastorale de Monseigneur l'Archevêque de Toulouse, pair de France à l'occasion de la retraite ecclésiastique qui vient de se donner aux curés de ce diocèse, 20 October 1820.

Lettre pastorale et mandement de Monseigneur l'Archevêque d'Albi, pour les élections de 1824, 27 January 1824.

Mandement de Mgr. l'Évêque de Grenoble, pour ordonner un Te Deum en actions de grâces dans la capitale de ses états, 20 May 1814.

Mandement de Mgr. l'Évêque de Grenoble, pour ordonner un Te Deum en actions de grâces de l'heureux retour de S.M. Louis XVIII dans la capitale de son royaume, 21 July 1815.

Mandement de Mgr. l'Évêque de Grenoble, qui ordonne un Service solennel pour le repos de l'âme de S.A.R. Mgr. le duc Berry, 20 March 1820.

Mandement de Messieurs les Vicaires-Généraux de Monseigneur l'Archevêque de Toulouse. Pour rendre grâces à Dieu de la naissance du Prince auquel son Altesse Royale Madame la Duchesse de Berri a donné le jour, 2 October 1820.

Mandement de Monseigneur l'Archevêque de Toulouse, qui ordonne des prières publiques en actions de grâces de l'heureux retour de Sa Majesté LOUIS XVIII, dans ses états, 21 July 1815.

Mandement de Monseigneur l'Archevêque de Toulouse, qui ordonne les prières de quarante heures, dans toutes les églises de son diocèse, pour réparer les outrages faits à Dieu pendant la Révolution, 14 September 1815.

Mandement de Monseigneur l'Évêque de Grenoble, pour ordonner des prières relatives aux élections des nouveaux députés de la France, 27 January 1824.

Mandement de Monseigneur l'Évêque de Grenoble sur les élections, 3 November 1820.

Mandement de son Éminence Mgr. Le Cardinal de Clermont-Tonnerre, Archevêque de Toulouse et Narbonne, Primat des Gaules, Docteur de Sorbonne, Abbé commendataire de la basilique de Saint-Sébastien à Rome, Duc et Pair de France, etc., etc.; Qui ordonne des prières d'actions de grâces pour le succès général des députations à la Chambre de 1824, 16 March 1824.

COLLECTIONS OF ILLUSTRATIONS

Collection de Vinck. Bibliothèque Nationale, département des estampes. Inventaire analytique. Paris, 1938.

Duplessis, Georges. Catalogue de la collection des portraits Français et étrangers conservée au département des estampes de la Bibliothèque Nationale. Paris, 1896.

Henin, Michel and George Duplessis. Inventaire de la collection d'estampes relatives à l'histoire de France léguée en 1863 à la Bibliothèque Nationale. Paris, 1882.

NEWSPAPERS

Le Conservateur
Le Drapeau Blanc
Journal de Gard
Journal de Grenoble
Journal Libre de l'Isère
Journal de Paris
Journal des Débats
Journal Politique et Littéraire de Toulouse et de la Haute-Garonne
L'Echo des Alpes
La presse de la Haute-Garonne. Inventaire Manuscrit. 1815–1865.

SECONDARY SOURCES

Aaron, Raymond. "Societé industrielle, idéologies, philosophies," *Preuves* (1965).

Adhémar, Jean. *Imagerie populaire française.* Milan: Electa Instituto Editoriale, 1968.

Agulhon, Maurice. *Marianne into Battle: Republican Imagery and Symbolism in France, 1789–1880.* Cambridge: Cambridge University Press, 1981.

Artz, Frederick. "The Electoral System in France during the Bourbon Restoration: 1815–30." *Journal of Modern History* 1 (June 1929): 205–218.

- *France Under the Bourbon Restoration: 1814–1830.* New York, Russell & Russell, Inc., 1963.

Avezou, Robert. "L'opinion dans l'Isère sous la Restauration." *Procès-Verbaux mensuels de la Société Dauphinoise d'Ethnologie et d'Archéologie.* Oct.– Dec., 1954: 14–35.

Bagge, Dominique. *Le conflit des idées politiques en France sous la Restauration.* Paris: Presses Universitaires de France, 1952.

Balteau, J., M. Barroux, and M. Prévost, eds. *Dictionnaire de biographie française.* Paris: Librairie Letouzey et Ané, 1929.

Bargeton, Réné, Pierre Bougard, Bernard Le Clère, and Pierre-François Pinaud. *Les Préfets du 11 Ventôse an VIII au 4 Septembre 1870.* Paris: Archives Nationales, 1981.

Barry, David. *Women and Political Insurgency. France in the Mid-Nineteenth Century.* New York: St Martin's Press, Inc., 1996.

Beck, Thomas D. *French Legislators.* Berkeley and Los Angeles: University of California Press, 1974.

Beck, Thomas D. and Martha Beck. *French Notables: Reflections of Industrialization and Regionalism.* New York: Peter Lang Publishing, Inc., 1987.

Bellanger, Claude, Jacques Godechot, Pierre Guiral, and Fernand Terrou. *Histoire générale de la presse française.* Paris: Presses Universitaires de France, 1969.

Berenson, Edward. "Politics and the French Peasantry: the debate continues." *Social History* 12 (May, 1987): 213–29.

Blache, Jacques Vidal de la. *Marie-Caroline Duchesse de Berry.* Paris: Éditions France-Empire, 1980.

Blanc, Louis. *Histoire de dix ans.* 12ème édition. T 1. Paris: Librairie Germer Baillière et Cie, 1877.

Bligny, Bernard, V. Comel, J. Emery, J. Godel, A. Jobert, and J. Solé, eds. *Histoire du Diocèse de Grenoble.* Paris: Éditions Beauchesne, 1979.

Boime, Albert. *Hollow Icons: The Politics of Sculpture in Nineteenth-Century France.* Kent, Ohio and London, England: Kent State University Press, 1987.

Bourset, Madeleine. *Casimir Perier: un prince financier au temps du romanticisme.* Paris: Publications de la Sorbonne, 1994.

Boutry, Philippe and Jacques Nassif. *Martin l'Archange.* Gallimard, 1985.

Boyer, George. *La Faculté de Droit de l'Université de Toulouse.* 2 vols. Paris: Sirey, 1962.

Brown, Marvin L. Jr. *The Comte de Chambord. The Third Republic's Uncompromising King.* North Carolina: Duke University Press, 1967.

Buzon, Christine de. *Henri V, comte de Chambord ou le "fier suicide" de la royauté.* Paris: Albin Michel, 1987.

Cabanis, José. *Charles X, roi ultra.* Paris: Gallimard, 1972.

Carlisle, Robert B. *The Proffered Crown: Saint-Simonianism and the Doctrine of Hope.* Baltimore: Johns Hopkins University Press, 1987.

Caron, Jean-Claude. *La France de 1815 à 1848.* Paris: Armand Colin, 1993.

Carter, Edward C. II, Robert Forster, and Joseph N. Moody, eds. *Enterprise and Entrepreneurs in Nineteenth- and Twentieth-century France*. Baltimore and London: Johns Hopkins University Press, 1976.

Casanova, R. *Montlosier et le parti prêtre: Étude, suivie d'un choix de textes*. Paris: R. Laffont, 1970.

Castelot, André. *La Duchesse de Berry*. Paris: Librairie Académique Perrin, 1964.

Castries, Duc de. *La Fin des rois, 1815–1848*. 2 vols. Paris: Jules Tallandier, 1972.

Catalogue de l'histoire de France. Paris, 1856.

Cau, Christian. "Joseph Villèle." *Petite Bibliothèque*. N.29. Toulouse, Archives Départementales de la Haute-Garonne, 1991.

Charléty, S. "*Histoire de France contemporaine depuis la Révolution jusqu'à la paix de 1919*," *La Restauration (1815–1830)*, ed Ernest Lavisse. Paris: Librairie Hachette, 1921.

Chevallier, Pierre. *Histoire de la franc-maçonnerie française*. Paris: Librairie Arthème Fayard, 1974.

Chiappe, Jean-François. *Le Comte de Chambord et son mystère*. Paris: Perrin, 1990.

Cholvy, Gérard and Hilaire, Y.-M. *Histoire Religieuse de la France Contemporaine, 1800–1880*. Toulouse: Bibliothèque Historique Privat, 1985.

– "Du dieu terrible au dieu d'amour" ... 109ᵉ Congrès National de Société Savantes, Dijon, 1984: *Transmettre la foi: XVIᵉ–XXᵉ siècles*, I, *Pastorale et prédication en France, Section d'Histoire Moderne et Contemporaine*. Paris: CTHS, 1984: 141–54

Chomel, Vital. *Histoire de Grenoble*. Toulouse: Bibliothèque Historique Privat, 1976.

Clinchamps, Philippe du Puy de. "Le Royalisme." *Que sais-je?* n.1259, 1967.

Clough, Shepard Bancroft. France: *A History of National Economics, 1789–1939*. New York: Octagon Books, Inc., 1964.

Cobb, R.C. *The Police and the People. French Popular Protest, 1789–1820*. Oxford: Clarendon Press, 1970.

Cobban, Alfred. *A History of Modern France*. 3 vols. London: Penguin Books, 1961, 1965.

Contamine, Henri. *Diplomatie et diplomates à l'époque de la Restauration*. Paris: Hachette, 1970.

Corbin, Alain, Jacqueline Lalouette, Michèle Riot-Sarcey, eds. *Femmes dans la cité*. Grâne: Créaphis, 1997.

Crémieux, Albet. *La censure en 1820 et 1821: étude sur la presse politique et la résistance libérale*. Paris: Edouard Cronely, 1912.

Cubitt, Geoffrey. *The Jesuit Myth. Conspiracy Theory and Politics in Nineteenth-Century France*. Oxford: Clarendon Press, 1993.

– "Denouncing Conspiracy in the French Revolution." *Renaissance and Modern Studies* 33 (1989): 144–58.

Cuno, James. "The Business and Politics of Caricature: Charles Philipon and La Maison Aubert." *Gazette des Beaux-Arts* 106 (October 1985): 95–112.

Daigle, Jean-Guy. *La culture en partage. Grenoble et son élite au milieu du 19ᵉ siècle.* Ottawa: Éditions de l'Université d'Ottawa, 1977.

Dansette, Adrien. *Religious History of Modern France*, trans. John Dingle. New York: Herder and Herder, 1961.

Darrow, Margaret. "French Noblewomen and the New Domesticity, 1750–1850." *Feminist Studies* 5 (Spring 1979).

Desan, Suzanne. *Reclaiming the Sacred: Lay Religion and Popular Politics in Revolutionary France.* Ithaca and London: Cornell University Press, 1990.

Devaux, Olivier. *L'enseignement à Toulouse sous la Restauration.* Toulouse: Presses de l'Université des Sciences Sociales de Toulouse, 1974.

Devlin, Judith. *The Superstitious Mind: French Peasants of the Supernatural in the Nineteenth Century.* New Haven and London: Yale University Press, 1987.

Dictionnaire biographique et album de l'Isère. 2 vols. Paris: Flammarion, 1907.

Doyle, William. *The Origins of the French Revolution.* Oxford: Oxford University Press, 1988.

Dreyfus, Pierre. *De César à l'Olympe.* Grenoble, 1980.

– *Histoire du Dauphiné.* Paris: Hachette, 1976.

Ducoin, A. *Paul Didier, Histoire de la conspiration de 1816.* Paris, 1844.

Dumolard, H. *La terreur blanche dans l'Isère. Jean-Paul Didier et la conspiration de Grenoble.* Grenoble, 1928.

Dunham, Arthur Louis. *The Industrial Revolution in France.* New York: Exposition Press, 1955.

Dupland, Edmond. *Marie-Caroline, Duchesse de Berry.* Paris: France-Empire, 1996.

Fauchon, Pierre. *L'abbé Grégoire, le prêtre-citoyen.* Tours: Ed. de la Nouvelle-République, 1989.

Ford, Caroline. "Religion and Popular Culture in Modern European Thought." *Journal of Modern History* 65(March 1993): 152–75.

Fourcassié, Jean. *Une ville à l'époque romantique, Toulouse.* Paris, 1953.

Forrest, Alan. *Conscripts and Deserters: The Army and French Society During the Revolution and Empire.* New York: Oxford University Press, 1989.

Fridenson, Patrick and André Straus (eds). *Le capitalisme français, XIXᵉ–XXᵉ siècle: blocages et dynamismes d'une croissance.* Paris: Librairie Arthème Fayard, 1987.

Gadille, Jacques. "On French Anticlericalism: Some Reflections." *European Studies Review* 13 (1983): 127–44.

Garnier, Adrien. *Frayssinous, son rôle dans l'Université sous la Restauration (1822–1828).* Paris: Picard, 1925.

Gaudriault, Raymond. *La Gravure de mode féminine en France.* Paris: Éditions de l'Amateur, 1983.

Geertz, Clifford. "Ideology as a Cultural System," ed David E. Apter, *Ideology and Discontent*. New York: Free Press, 1964, 47–76.

Genevray, Pierre. *L'administration et la vie ecclésiastiques dans le grand diocèse de Toulouse pendant les dernières années de l'Empire et sous la Restauration.* 2nd ed Toulouse: Édouard Privat, 1941.

Gibson, Ralph. *A Social History of French Catholicism, 1789–1914*. London and New York: Routledge, 1989.

– "Hellfire and damnation in nineteenth-century France." *Catholic Historical Review* 74, 3(July 1988): 383–402.

– "The French nobility in the nineteenth century – particularly in the Dordogne," *Elites in France: Origins, Reproduction, and Power*, eds J. Howorth and P.G. Cerny. London: Frances Printer Publishers, 1981.

Girard, Louis. *Le libéralisme en France de 1815 à 1875*. Paris, 1967.

Godel, Jean. *La reconstruction concordataire dans le diocèse de Grenoble après la Révolution 1802–1809*. Grenoble: Impr. Eymond, 1968.

Godechot, Jacques. "*La ville rose devient une ville Rose*" and "*le Grand Village* (1815–1914)," *Histoire de Toulouse*, ed Philippe Wolf. Toulouse: Éditions Édouard Privat, 1974.

Goguel, François. *La politique des partis sous la IIIe République*. Paris: Éditions du Seuil, 1948.

Griset, Pascal and Alain Beltran. *Croissance économique de la France*. Paris: Armand Colin, 1988.

Guillon, Edouard. *Les complots militaires sous la Restauration*. Paris, 1895.

Gutwirth, Madelyn. *The Twilight of the Goddesses: women and representation in the French Revolutionary Era*. New Jersey: Rutgers University Press, 1992.

Hanley, Sarah. "The Monarchic State in Early Modern France: Marital Regime Government and Male Right." *Politics, Ideology and the Law in Early Modern Europe: Essays in Honor of J.H.M. Salmon*. Ed Adrianna E. Bakos. Rochester, N.Y., 1994.

– "Social Sites of Political Practice in France: Lawsuits, Civil Rights, and the Separation of Powers in Domestic and State Government, 1500–1800." *American Historical Review* 102(February 1997): 27–52.

Harpaz, Ephaim. *L'école libérale sous la Restauration: le Mercure et la Minerve, 1817–1820*. Geneva: Droz, 1968.

Higgs, David. "Social Mobility and Hereditary Titles in France, 1814–1830: The *Majorats-sur-demande*." *Social History*. 15, 27(May 1981): 29–46.

– *Ultraroyalism in Toulouse: From its Origins to the Revolution of 1830*. Baltimore and London: The Johns Hopkins University Press, 1973.

– *Nobles in Nineteenth-Century France: the practice of inegalitarianism*. Baltimore: Johns Hopkins University Press, 1987.

– "Politics and Landownership among the French Nobility after the Revolution," *European Studies Review*, 1, 2(April 1971): 105–121.

Hofman, Amos. "The Origins of the Theory of the Philosophe Conspiracy." *French History* 2, 2(June, 1988): 152–72.

Hoffman, Robert L. *More Than a Trial*. New York: The Free Press, 1980.

Hunt, Lynn, ed. *Eroticism and the Body Politic*. Baltimore and London: The Johns Hopkins University Press, 1991.

Hunt, Lynn. *The Family Romance of the French Revolution*. Berkeley: University of California Press, 1992.

Jardin, André and Andre-Jean Tudesq. *Restoration and Reaction, 1815–1848*, trans. Elborg Forster. Cambridge: Cambridge University Press, 1983.

– *Les Grands Notables en France (1840–1849) Étude historique d'une psychologie sociale*. 2 vols. Paris: Presses Universitaires de France, 1964.

Johnson, W. McAllister. *Art History: Its Use and Abuse*. Toronto: University of Toronto Press, 1988.

– *French Lithography: The Restoration Salons 1817–1824*. Kingston: Agnes Etherington Art Centre, 1977.

Kantorowicz, Ernst. *The King's Two Bodies: A Study in Medieval Political Theology*. Princeton: Princeton University Press, 1957.

Kelly, George A. "Liberalism and Aristocracy in the French Restoration." *Journal of the History of Ideas* 26(October–December 1965): 509–30.

Kent, Sherman. *The Election of 1827 in France*. London: Harvard University Press, 1975.

– *Electoral Procedure under Louis Philippe*. New Haven: Yale University Press, 1973.

Kindleberger, Elizabeth R. "Charlotte Corday in Text and Image: A Case Study in the French Revolution and Women's History." *French Historical Studies* 18, 4(Fall 1994): 969–99.

Kley, Dale K. Van, *The Religious Origins of the French Revolution. From Calvin to the Civil Constitution, 1560–1791*. New Haven and London: Yale University Press, 1996.

Klinck, David. *The French Counterrevolutionary Theorist, Louis de Bonald (1754–1840)*. New York: Peter Lang Publishing, 1996.

Kroen, Sheryl. *Politics and Theatre. The Crisis of Legitimacy in Restoration France, 1815–1830*. Berkeley: University of California Press, 2000.

Kselman, Thomas A. *Death and the Afterlife in Modern France*. Princeton: Princeton University Press, 1993.

Lagoueyte, Patrick. *La vie politique en France au XIXe siècle*. Paris: Ophrys, 1990.

Lambert, Pierre. *Charbonnerie Française*. Paris, 1995.

Landes, Joan. *Women and the Public Sphere in the Age of the French Revolution*. Ithaca and London: Cornell University Press, 1988.

Langlois, C. "Le catholicisme au féminin." *Archives de Sciences Sociales des Religions*. 57 (1) (Jan.– March 1984): 29–53.

Larignon, Gilberte and Héliette Proust. *Édouard de Monti de Rezé: L'inébranlable certitude: Le mouvement légitimiste dans l'Ouest*. Laval: Silo, 1992.

Larousse, Pierre. *Grand dictionnaire universel du XIXe siècle*. Paris: Administration du Grand Dictionnaire Universel, 1867.

Laurent, Jeanne. *Arts et pouvoirs*. Université de Saint-Étienne: Centre Interdisciplinaire d'Études et de Recherches sur l'Expression Contemporaine, 1983.

Lecanuet, J. and M. Damien, eds. *Charlotte Corday: Une Normande dans la Révolution*. Maison des Champs de Pierre Corneille, 1989.

Ledré, Charles. *La presse à l'assaut de la monarchie, 1815–1848*. Paris, Armand Colin, 1960.

Lemaître, H. *Histoire du dépôt légal en France*. Paris, 1910.

Lerch, Dominique. *Imagerie et société. L'Imagerie Wentzel de Wissembourg au XIXᵉ siècle*. Librairie Istra, 1982.

Lever, Evelyne. *Louis XVIII*. Librairie Arthème Fayard, 1988.

Levin, Miriam R. *Republican Art and Ideology in Late Nineteenth-Century France*. Ann Arbor: UMI Research Press, 1986.

Levy-Leboyer, Maurice and François Bourguignon. *L'Economie Française au XIXᵉ siècle*. Paris: Éd. Economica, 1985.

Lucas-Dubreton, J. *The Restoration and the July Monarchy*, trans. E.F. Buckley. London: William Heinemann Ltd., 1929.

Luz, Pierre de (Pierre Henry de la Blanchetai). *Henri V*. Paris, 1931.

Magraw, Roger. "The Conflict in the Villages: Popular Anticlericalism in the Isère (1852–70)." *Conflicts in French Society: anticlericalism, education and morals in the nineteenth century*, ed. Theodore Zeldin. London: Allen & Unwin, 1970: 169–229.

Maignien, Edmond. *Catalogue des livres et manuscrits du Fonds Dauphinois de la* Bibliothèque municipale de Grenoble. Grenoble, Allier, 1912–14.

– *Dictionnaire des ouvrages anonymes et pseudonymes du Dauphiné*. Marseille: Laffitte Reprints, 1976. Reprint of 1st edition, Grenoble: Xavier Drevet, 1892.

Mansel, Philip. *Louis XVIII*. London: Blond & Briggs Limited, 1981.

– *The Court of France, 1789–1830*. Cambridge: Cambridge University Press, 1988.

– "How Forgotten were the Bourbons in France between 1812 and 1814?" *European Studies Review* 13(1983): 13–37.

Margadant, Jo Burr. "The Duchesse de Berry and Royalist Political Culture in Postrevolutionary France." *History Workshop Journal* 43(spring, 1997): 23–52.

– "Gender, Vice, and the Political Imaginary in Postrevolutionary France: Reinterpreting the Failure of the July Monarchy, 1830–1848." *American Historical Review* 104(December, 1999): 1461–96.

Marjoli, Robert, *"Troubles provoqués en France par la disette de 1816–1817," Revue d'histoire moderne*, 8(November–December, 1933): 423–60.

Marrinan, Michael. *Painting Politics for Louis-Philippe*. New Haven and London: Yale University Press, 1988.

Masson, F. *Revue d'ombres. L'envers d'une conspiration*. Paris, 1921.

McPhee, Peter. *A Social History of France, 1780–1880*. London; New York: Routledge, 1992.

Mellon, Stanley. *The Politics of History.* Princeton University: Dissertation in Partial Fulfillment for Degree of Doctor of Philosophy, 1954.

Ménager, Bernard. *Les Napoléon du peuple.* Aubier, 1988.

Merrick, Jeffrey. *The Desacralization of the French Monarchy in the Eighteenth Century.* Baton Rouge: Louisiana State, 1990.

Michaud, J. F.R. *Biographie universelle.* Graz, Austria: Akademische Druck- u. Verlagsanstalt, 1966.

Michel, Albin and Berger-Lavrault. *Dictionnaire national des communes de France.* Éditions: Albin Michel, 1992.

Morel. E. *Le dépôt légal, étude et projet de loi.* Paris, 1917.

Nabour, Eric le. *Les deux restaurations.* Librairie Jules Tallandier, 1992.

Necheles, Ruth F. *The Abbé Grégoire, 1787–1831: The Odyssey of an Egalitarian.* Westport, Conn.: Greenwood Pub. Corp., 1971.

Neely, Sylvia. *Lafayette and the Liberal Ideal 1814–1824: Politics and Conspiracy in an Age of Reaction.* Illinois: Southern Illinois University, 1991.

Newman, Edgar Leon (ed). *Historical Dictionary of France from the 1815 Restoration to the Second Empire.* New York: Greenwood Press, 1987.

– "The Blouse and the Frock Coat: The Alliance of the Common People of Paris with the Liberal Leadership and the Middle Class during the last years of the Bourbon Restoration." *Journal of Modern History* 46(March 1984): 26–58.

Nouvelle biographie générale depuis les temps les plus reculés jusqu'à 1850–60. Paris: Firmin Didot Frères, 1963–69.

Oechslin, J.-J. *Le mouvement ultra-royaliste sous la Restauration: Son idéologie et son action politique (1814–1830).* Paris: R. Pichon & R. Durand-Auzias, 1960.

Outram, Dorinda. *The Body and the French Revolution: Sex, Class and Political Culture.* New Haven and London: Yale University Press, 1989.

Palmer, R.R. *Twelve Who Ruled. The Year of the Terror in the French Revolution.* Princeton: Princeton University Press, 1941.

Parent-Lardeur, Françoise. *Lire à Paris au temps de Balzac. Les cabinets de lecture à Paris, 1815–1830.* Paris: *Éditions de l'École des Hautes Études en Sciences Sociales*, 1978.

Pierrard, Pierre. *L'Église et la Révolution, 1789–1889.* Paris: *Nouvelle Cité*, 1988.

Pilbeam, Pamela M. *The Middle Classes in Europe: 1789–1914.* London: Macmillan Education Ltd., 1990.

– *The 1830 Revolution in France.* Basingstoke: Macmillan, 1991.

Plongeron, Bernard. *L'abbé Grégoire (1750–1831): ou l'arche de la fraternité.* Paris: Letouzey et Ané, 1989.

Ponteil, Félix. *La monarchie parlementaire: 1815–1848.* Paris: Armand Colin, 1958.

– *Histoire de l'enseignement en France, les grandes étapes (1789–1964).* Paris, 1966.

Price, Roger. *The Economic Modernisation of France*. London: Croom Helm London, 1975.

Quinlan, Mary Hall. *The Historical Thought of Vicomte de Bonald*. Dissertation for the Degree of Doctor of Philosophy. Washington D.C.: The Catholic University of America Press, 1953.

Ramet, Henri. *Histoire de Toulouse*. Toulouse, 1935.

Reinhard, Marcel. *La légende de Henri IV*. Paris: Hachette, 1936.

Rémond, Réné. *La droite en France: de la première Restauration à la Ve République*. Paris: Editions Montaigne, 1968.

Resnick, Daniel P. *The White Terror and the Political Reaction after Waterloo*. Cambridge: Harvard University Press, 1966.

Rey, J. *Histoire de la conspiration de Grenoble en 1816*. Grenoble, 1847.

Riquet, Michel. *Augustin de Barruel: un jésuite face aux jacobins francs-maçons, 1741–1820*. Paris: Beauchesne, 1989.

Robert, Adolphe et Gaston Cougny, eds. *Dictionnaire des parlementaires français*. Paris: Bourloton, 1889.

Rosanvallon, Pierre. *La monarchie impossible: Les chartes de 1814 et de 1830*. Paris: Fayard, 1994.

Rosenbaum-Dondaine, Catherine and Jean-Pierre Seguin (eds). *L'image de la piété en France, 1814–1914*. Paris: Musée-galerie de la Seita, 1984.

Roudinesco, Elisabeth. *Théroigne de Méricourt. Une femme mélancolique sous la Révolution*. Paris: Éditions du Seuil, 1989.

Rousset, Henri. *La presse à Grenoble: histoire & physionomie, 1700–1900*. Grenoble: Alexandre Gratier & Co., 1900.

Roussilhe, Jean-Paul. *La Duchesse de Berry ou la mère persécutée*. Éditions Rencontre, 1966.

Saint-Amand, Imbert de. *The Duchesse de Berry and the Court of Charles X*. New York: Charles Scribner's Sons, 1892.

Sauvigny, Guillaume de Bertier. *The Bourbon Restoration*, trans. Lynn M. Case. Philadelphia: University of Pennsylvania Press, 1966.

Schama, Simon. *Citizens. A Chronicle of the French Revolution*. Toronto: Vintage Books, 1989.

Schermerhorn, Elizabeth W. *Benjamin Constant, His Private Life and his Contribution to the Cause of Liberal Government in France 1767–1830*. Boston and New York: Houghton Mifflin Company, 1924.

Sevrin, Abbé Ernest. *Les missions religieuses en France sous la Restauration, 1815–1830*. 2 vols. Paris: J. Vrin, 1948–1959.

Singer, Barnett. *Village Notables in Nineteenth-Century France: Priests, Mayors, Schoolmasters*. Albany: SUNY Press, 1983.

Smith, Bonnie E. *Ladies of the Leisure Class: The Bourgeoisie of Northern France in the Nineteenth Century*. Princeton: Princeton University Press, 1981.

Spencer, Philip. *Politics of Belief in Nineteenth Century France*. London: Faber and Faber Limited, 1954.

Spitzer, Alan B. *Old Hatreds and Young Hopes.* Cambridge: Harvard University Press, 1971.

– "Restoration Political Theory and the Debate of the Law of the Double Vote." *Journal of Modern History* 55 (March 1983): 54–70.

– *The Generation of 1820.* Princeton: Princeton University Press, 1987.

Stewart, John Hall. *The Restoration Era in France: 1814–1830.* New Jersey: D. Van Nostrand Company, Inc., 1968.

Sutherland, D.M.G. *France 1789–1815. Revolution and Counterrevolution.* London: Fontana Press, 1985.

Tackett, Timothy. "Conspiracy Obsession in a Time of Revolution: French Elites and the Origins of the Terror, 1789–1792." *American Historical Review* 105, 3(June 2000): 691–713.

Tallet, Frank and Nicholas Atkin, eds. *Religion, Society and Politics in France since 1789.* London and Rio Grande: The Hambledon Press, 1991.

Taulier, Jules. *Histoire du Dauphiné depuis les temps les plus reculés jusqu'à nos jours.* Grenoble, 1855.

Thomas, Chantal. *La Reine scélérate. Marie-Antoinette dans les pamphlets.* Paris: Éditions du Seuil, 1989.

Thureau-Dangin, Paul. *Le parti libéral sous la Restauration.* Paris: Librarie Plon, 1888.

Tournier, Mgr Clément. *Le Cardinal de Clermont Tonnerre, Archevêque de Toulouse (1820–1830) et le drame de la petite église.* Toulouse: Éditions de la Basilique, 1935.

Tudesq, André-Jean. *Les grands notables en France (1840–1849): Étude historique d'une psychologie sociale.* 2 vols. Paris: Presses Universitaires de France, 1964.

Vermale, F. and Y. Du Parc. *Un conspirateur stendhalien, Paul Didier, 1758–1816.* Paris, 1951.

Vidalenc, Jean. *Les demi-solde.* Paris, 1955.

Waquet, Françoise. *Les fêtes royales sous la Restauration ou l'Ancien Régime retrouvé.* Paris: Droz, Genève, and Arts et Métiers Graphiques, 1981.

Waresquiel, Emmanuel de. *Le duc de Richelieu, 1766–1822: Un sentimental en politique.* Paris: Perrin, 1990.

Waresquiel, Emmanuel de and Benoît Yvert. *Histoire de la Restauration, 1814–1830. Naissance de la France moderne.* Paris: Perrin, 1996.

Warner, Marina. *Monuments & Maidens. The Allegory of the Female Form.* London: Weidenfeld and Nicolson, 1985.

Weber, Eugen. "*Comment la politique Vint aux Paysans*: A second look at Peasant Politicization," *American Historical Review* 87 (Paris, 1982): 357–89.

– *France: Fin de Siècle.* Cambridge: Harvard University Press, 1986.

Wechsler, Judith. *A Human Comedy: physiognomy and caricature in 19th century Paris.* Chicago: University of Chicago Press, 1982.

Weill, Georges. "Les Mémoires de Joseph Rey," *Revue Historique* 158(Jan.–Apr. 1828): 291–307.

Weisbuch, Paul. *La Faculté de droit de Grenoble. Thèse.* Bibliothèque Université de Stendhal, Grenoble (1974).

Wilson, Stephen. *Ideology and Experience: Antisemitism in France at the time
of the Dreyfus Affair.* London and Toronto: Associated University Press,
1982.

Wood, G. S. "Conspiracy and the Paranoid Style: Causality and Deceit in
the Eighteenth Century." *William and Mary Quarterly.* 3rd ser. 39 (1982):
411–29.

Index